Equality, Responsibi

This book examines responsibility and luck as these issues arise in tort law, criminal law, and distributive justice. The central question is: Whose bad luck is a particular piece of misfortune? Arthur Ripstein argues that there is a general set of principles to be found that clarifies responsibility in those cases where luck is most obviously an issue: accidents, mistakes, emergencies, and failed attempts at crime. In revealing how the problems that arise in tort and criminal law as well as distributive justice invite structurally parallel solutions, the author also shows the deep connection between individual responsibility and social equality.

This is a challenging and provocative book that will be of special interest to moral and political philosophers, legal theorists, and political scientists.

Arthur Ripstein is Professor of Philosophy and Law at the University of Toronto.

Cambridge Studies in Philosophy and Law

Equality, Responsibility, and the Law

ARTHUR RIPSTEIN

CAMBRIDGE
UNIVERSITY PRESS

PUBLISHED BY THE PRESS SYNDICATE OF THE UNIVERSITY OF CAMBRIDGE
The Pitt Building, Trumpington Street, Cambridge, United Kingdom

CAMBRIDGE UNIVERSITY PRESS
The Edinburgh Building, Cambridge CB2 2RU, UK
40 West 20th Street, New York, NY 10011-4211, USA
10 Stamford Road, Oakleigh, Melbourne 3166, Australia
Ruiz de Alarcón 13, 28014 Madrid, Spain
Dock House, The Waterfront, Cape Town 8001, South Africa

http://www.cambridge.org

First published 1999
First paperback edition 2001

Printed in the United States of America

Typeset in Palatino 10/12 pt, in Quark XPress™ [AG]

A catalog record for this book is available from the British Library

Library of Congress Cataloging in Publication data is available

ISBN 0 521 58452 3 hardback
ISBN 0 521 00307 5 paperback

For Karen

Contents

Contents

Acknowledgments

In the course of writing a book about luck, I have been exceedingly lucky in the help I have received. The book's central idea first came into focus some years ago in a telephone conversation with Ernest Weinrib. Since then, he has continued to be a source of both inspiration and criticism. As my thoughts became more determinate, I had the good fortune to spend a year at Yale Law School, where I spent many hours discussing some of the book's central themes with Jules Coleman. A joint paper came out of those conversations and many of its ideas have been reworked here. Jules has been a constant help since then, often knowing better than I did what I was trying to say. Ben Zipursky, with whom I have been talking philosophy since I was eleven years old, discussed all of the book's ideas with me, and commented on many versions of it, starting with some too rough to dignify with the word "draft." The first draft of the book was written while I was a Laurance S. Rockefeller visiting fellow at the Center for Human Values at Princeton University. I benefited from the comments and discussions of the other fellows, Arthur Applbaum, Chris Korsgaard, Avishai Margalit, Jeff Spinner-Halev, and Michael Thompson. While at Princeton, I also had many useful conversations with Christopher Morris and Helen Nissenbaum. Other friends and colleagues have also been extremely generous with their time and comments. Donald Ainslie, Peter Benson, Alan Brudner, Bruce Chapman, Kevin Davis, Govert den Hartog, David Dyzenhaus, Gillian Hadfield, Joe Heath, Doug Husak, Nicola Lacey, Andrew Latus, Dennis Klimchuk, Cheryl Misak, Philippe Mongin, Mayo Moran, David Morris, Dan Ortiz, Stephen Perry, Anthony Sebok, Tim Scanlon, Scott Shapiro, Hamish Stewart, Mark Thornton, and Peter Vallentyne all commented on parts of the manuscript (some on all of its parts). I also benefited from conversations with Jean Baillargeon, the late Jean Hampton, Mahmud Jamal, Andrew Kernohan, and Brian Langille.

Gita Cale, Andrew Cunningham, and Vicki Igneski provided excellent research assistance.

The writing of this book was made easier by several institutions. My colleagues in the Philosophy Department at the University of Toronto enabled me to do most of my teaching over the last several years on topics related to the book. The Law and Philosophy discussion group at the Faculty of Law spent a term of weekly lunch meetings discussing the manuscript in detail. I am also grateful to the Princeton University Center for Human Values, and its former director, Amy Gutmann, for awarding me a year's fellowship, and to the University of Toronto for providing me with favorable leave arrangements. The Social Sciences and Humanities Research Council of Canada provided me a grant to defray research expenses.

I have been lucky in other ways as well. My parents, Ellen and Reg Ripstein, taught me both to care about justice and to believe that reasoned argument is the best way to approach difficult questions.

My greatest debt of all is to my wife, Karen Weisman. At every stage in the writing of this book, Karen has provided constant moral and intellectual support, as she does with all aspects of my life. I dedicate this book to her.

The book reworks material from several previously published pieces:

"Equality, Luck, and Responsibility," 23 *Philosophy and Public Affairs* 3 (1994).
"Mischief and Misfortune" (with Jules Coleman), 41 *McGill Law Journal* 91 (1995).
"Self-Defense and Equal Protection," 57 *University of Pittsburgh Law Review* 685 (1996).

Chapter 1

Equality, Luck, and Responsibility

Someone following political debates about crime control or welfare reform might come away with the impression that she was faced with a choice between two incompatible positions. One position, put forward by people usually described as conservatives, claims to make individual responsibility central to political morality. A commitment to a culture of responsibility is said to underwrite advocacy of harsh punishments and reduced social services, not only because such changes will lead to safer streets and more productive lives, but also because people are responsible for their own deeds. Another position in these debates, put forward by people usually described as liberals, advocates building schools instead of prisons, hoping to get at the root causes of crime and to provide adequate opportunities for those who are badly off. The same debates can be seen as revolving around the idea of luck. Liberals are said to be committed to the amelioration of the effects of luck, whereas conservatives resign themselves to the impossibility of doing so. So understood, the debates pit social equality against individual responsibility, and make any compromise between them seem inherently unstable.

One of the central claims of this book is that, far from being opposed ideals, individual responsibility and social equality need to be understood together. A society of equals – a just society, if you like – is also a society that supposes people are responsible for their choices. Though liberals and their conservative critics differ on some fundamental questions of political morality, those differences are not rooted in a liberal rejection of ideas of responsibility. Properly understood, liberalism has a distinctive conception of responsibility, one that is inseparable from an abstract understanding of equality.

This book is also about law.[1] The classical tradition of liberal

---

[1] My discussion focuses exclusively on legal systems descended from the English common law. The common law has made the idea of the reasonable person

1

thought, from Hobbes and Locke through Kant and Hegel, supposed that an adequate account of political philosophy must also include accounts of both private law and crime. Those accounts were not merely incidental to a larger project of studying the basis and limits of state power. Instead, they were integral to the project, for those philosophers took the fundamental question of political philosophy to concern how people interact *with each other*. This liberal outlook contrasts in important ways with the Aristotelian-Thomist view of political life, which views the state as a sort of organism, with a good of its own, and also with the utilitarian view that supposes the state exists because force is sometimes required in order to make people happy. On the view I will develop, the exercise of state power is necessary to sustain conditions of fair interaction, but the first question of justice concerns the limits on people's treatment of each other. Coercion is important, but its justification rests on the ideas of freedom and equality that underwrite fair terms of interaction. Much of this book is devoted to articulating those ideas of freedom and equality, and interpreting their application in tort and criminal law. The root idea, fundamental to both fair terms of interaction and the idea of responsibility, is one of reciprocity, the idea that one person may not unilaterally set the terms of his interactions with others. Since tort and criminal law are no more (and no less) coercive than are distributive institutions, I articulate a conception of responsibility for all three.

By looking at issues of responsibility in terms of fair terms of interaction, I also aim to highlight the relations between corrective justice and criminal law, and the questions of distribution that have animated recent political philosophy. The two sets of issues are connected because they both express the underlying idea that the justice of an outcome depends on how it came about. Tort law serves both to specify the boundaries of acceptable behavior and to transfer the costs of wrongful injuries back to injurers. Criminal law specifies the boundaries of acceptable behavior and serves to vindicate those boundaries in the face of conscious denials of them. Institutions of distributive justice serve to guarantee the conditions of free interaction, so that the results of voluntary interaction reflect choices rather than arbitrary starting points. Corrective justice, criminal law, and tort law together set out the conditions of respon-

explicit in a way that aids the exposition of the ideas that I will develop. I believe similar ideas animate the civil law tradition, but are less explicit.

sibility, the conditions under which agents appropriately bear the costs of their choices.

1.1   THE PROBLEM: WHOSE BAD LUCK IS IT?

Questions about responsibility become pressing for political philosophy in those cases in which things do not work out quite as planned. Luck is sometimes thought to be morally arbitrary, and it is sometimes supposed that justice requires that its effects be removed, insofar as it is possible to do so. But the effects of luck cannot be removed entirely; at most, they can be shifted from one person to others. The cases in which luck is most clearly an issue – accidents, mistakes, emergencies, and failed attempts at crimes – are cases in which the effects of luck will simply not go away. The task is to articulate a principled account of where the results of luck properly lie.

When one person injures another unintentionally, social institutions must find some principled way of determining whose problem it is. Sometimes, losses appropriately lie where they fall, but other times, justice requires that the misfortune be shifted back to the person who was responsible for it. When someone makes a mistake about the rights of others, similar questions arise. Often, the mistake can be corrected and an apology made, at no expense to anyone. Other times, things are more complicated, and some way must be found of determining which mistakes are acceptable and which ones not. Again, the boundaries of acceptable behavior shift in emergencies, but once the emergency is over, some way must be found of determining whose problem any resulting losses are. And a system of criminal law must find a way of determining the appropriate treatment of those who mean to do wrong, but don't manage to do so.

Equality and responsibility come together in these cases. They are also cases that all modern legal systems need to confront. Legal conceptions of responsibility are a fruitful starting point for political philosophy for two reasons. First, they are cases in which judgments about responsibility are coercively enforced. People who are legally responsible for injuries must pay damages, and people who commit crimes must be punished. The role of coercive enforcement links legal philosophy with the rest of political philosophy. The conceptions of responsibility, social cooperation, and fairness that I identify in legal practice are independently attractive, and so are worth extending to other areas of social life, especially to questions of distributive justice. The interpretive and constructive tasks are analytically distinct but still related. Were the law's conception of responsibility less attractive, it would be interesting to develop it, simply in order to further understanding of the law, but it would not be an aid to reflection within political philosophy. Because the law's conception of responsibility can also be understood as giving expression to attractive ideas of freedom and equality, it is worth developing as a way of clarifying those ideas. Thus, abstract considerations of political philosophy are an aid to understanding law, and law helps to clarify issues in political philosophy. Both law and political philosophy seek to justify coercion on grounds of justice. It is hardly surprising that they should be mutually illuminating. Still, they are sufficiently distinct that my account leaves room for criticism of existing doctrine. By situating my account of the law in a broader understanding of political morality, I offer what is recognizably an account of its practices while avoiding the charge of attaching moral priority to something simply because it is enforced in fact.

Legal responsibility is also a fruitful starting point for reflection about political morality because its reach is limited. There are many things for which people might rightly hold themselves responsible, or blame others, where the law is silent. There are cases in which legal responsibility is appropriate even though blame is not. In this way, legal responsibility is related to moral responsibility, but distinct from it. The role of law and of a conception of fairness are, as Kant put it, to make freedom possible, rather than to make morality actual. Their primary concern is not with the quality of a person's will or character, but with the external aspects of action. Analytic philosophy of action is sometimes criticized for being too behavioristic and abstract; Kantian moral philosophy is sometimes criticized for being too legalistic. Whatever the force of those criticisms in other contexts, both of these putative flaws are arguably virtues in an account of law as a kind of public order. Law is behavioristic in the sense that the acts that it seeks to regulate are all out in the open. It is legalistic in the sense that fairness requires that it abstract away from detail and context that might be important from other perspectives.

If legal conceptions of responsibility are a fruitful starting point for political philosophy, so too is political philosophy a fruitful starting point for understanding legal practice.[2] The areas of law that make

---

[2] Ernest Weinrib's important work in tort theory seeks to understand tort law in its own terms rather than in terms of extrinsic purposes. Since I draw on some of Weinrib's insights about tort law, I should explain why I reject his method-

responsibility central are best understood in light of more general issues of political philosophy, especially questions about fair terms of interaction and the legitimate use of coercion. Understood as addressing questions within political philosophy, tort and criminal law provide concrete expressions of important conceptions of freedom and equality in the context of coercion. Explicating the conception of responsibility implicit in these legal practices in terms of social cooperation helps us to understand why their results so often seem fair in concrete cases, despite the ease with which they can be made to seem morally troubling when considered in the abstract. It also helps us to understand some of the characteristic distinctions drawn by the law, why, for example, the criminal law distinguishes between two levels of defenses, treating some acts as justified and others as excused, and why some mistakes must simply be sincere in order to excuse wrongdoing, whereas others are subject to reasonableness tests. Looking at responsibility in terms of social cooperation also sheds light on the familiar, though morally puzzling, absence of a tort duty to rescue, and such areas of doctrine as the rules governing intervening causes in tort law, and the role of consequences throughout the law, including the reduced punishment given to unsuccessful attempts.

I hope, of course, to cast the practices I consider in a morally attractive light. The point of avoiding familiar debates within moral philosophy is that moral responsibility may well be either broader or narrower than legal responsibility (morally) ought to be. That is, I hope to show that political morality, the morality governing the exercise of force, has its own standards of responsibility that may well be out of place in other moral contexts. Those standards reflect both an idea of reciprocity and a concern with remedies. By looking at the

ological strictures. Weinrib is right to reject instrumental accounts that suppose that law can only be justified in terms of its consequences. But he draws two further conclusions from this rejection, neither of which is compelling. First, he is wrong to conclude that from the failures of instrumentalism legal norms must bear no relation to anything else. Second, he goes wrong in supposing that legal ordering can be grounded in the capacity for choice. See *The Idea of Private Law* (Cambridge, MA: Harvard University Press, 1995). On the role of the will in Weinrib's account, see Martin Stone, "On the Idea of Private Law," 9 *Canadian Journal of Law and Jurisprudence* 235 (1996).

The insight that law is a distinctive and irreducible way of ordering social relations gives rise to two further questions: First, what sort of ordering is it? Second, is it appropriate to order other areas of social life in the same way? I answer the first in terms of an understanding of responsibility based on reciprocity. As for the second, I think it is the appropriate way of ordering those relations of which coercion is inevitably a part.

relation between responsibility and the remedies the law typically employs – damages for tortious injury, and punishment for crimes – many of the otherwise puzzling contours of legal doctrine come into focus. Looking at remedies also lets us understand why the law's concern with treating like cases alike leads it to distinguish between persons who might be thought to be morally indistinguishable. A recurrent temptation in thinking about responsibility is to suppose that the only relevant grounds for differential treatment rests on a person's thoughts about his or her own actions. This temptation to look inward in assessing responsibility is at odds with fundamental distinctions that legal systems have drawn, and, I will argue, must draw if they are to treat persons as equal and responsible beings. Those distinctions are particularly germane in cases where luck has a role to play – accidents, mistakes, emergencies and attempts – and so legal practice contains important insights into luck.

1.2 REASONABLE PERSONS IN PHILOSOPHY AND POLITICS

Both tort law and criminal law raise issues of justice, because both set the limits of acceptable behavior in contexts in which some balance needs to be struck between one person's liberty and another's security. Fair terms of interaction must allow people freedom to do as they please, but also make sure that they are secure from the activities of others. A world in which liberty alone is protected is one in which nobody is secure from the acts of others; a world in which security alone is protected is a world in which nobody is free to act for fear of injuring others. Instead of either of these extremes, legal institutions protect people equally from each other when they require each to sacrifice some liberty for the sake of the security of others.

Fair terms of interaction must balance liberty and security. There are two basic strategies available for striking such a balance. One, familiar from the utilitarian tradition in moral and political thought, supposes that liberty and security (and whatever else) should be aggregated across persons, so that one person's liberty might have to give way to another's security. Another approach, which will be developed here, balances liberty and security by constructing an ideal of a representative person, who is supposed to have interests in both liberty and security. By striking the balance between liberty and security within a representative person, this approach expresses an idea of equality, for it aims to protect people equally from each other, by supposing all to have the same interests in both liberty and security.

The familiar common-law idea of the reasonable person gives expression to this idea of a fair balance between liberty and security. The reasonable man has long been a central character in the common law, taking appropriate precautions against accidentally injuring others, making only allowable mistakes, and maintaining an appropriate level of self-control when provoked. The reasonable person is neither the typical nor the average person. Nor is the reasonable person to be confused with the rational person, who acts effectively in pursuit of his or her ends. Instead, the reasonable person needs to be understood as the expression of an idea of fair terms of social cooperation.[3]

To talk about reasonableness in this sense is not to talk from the agent's subjective point of view. John Rawls's distinction between the rational and the reasonable elucidates this point: I behave rationally when I act effectively to promote my own system of ends. I behave reasonably when I interact with others on terms of equality. As Rawls puts it, "Reasonable persons [are moved by a desire for] a social world in which they, as free and equal, can cooperate with others on terms all can accept. They insist that reciprocity should hold within that world so that each benefits along with others."[4] Thus, we can distinguish the rational person, who does what seems best from her situation given her ends, from the reasonable person, who takes appropriate regard for the interests of others.

On this view, reasonableness is tied to the idea of equality. The root idea is that reasonable terms of interaction provide a like liberty for all compatible with protecting a fundamental interest in security. There is no blanket protection of either liberty or security; which specific liberty and security interests are at the forefront will in turn inevitably reflect substantive views about what is most important to leading an acceptable life. The concept of the reasonable person makes it possible to take account of competing interests without aggregating them across persons. Rather than balancing one person's liberty against another's security, the reasonable person standard supposes that all have the same interest in both liberty and security.

---

3   This idea has been developed in a number of places by T. M. Scanlon. See his "Contractualism and Utilitarianism," in Amartya Sen and Bernard Williams, eds., *Utilitarianism and Beyond* (Cambridge: Cambridge University Press, 1982), pp. 103–28.

4   John Rawls, *Political Liberalism* (New York: Columbia University Press, 1993), p. 50.

Thus, the importance of liberty and security interests is weighed within a representative person. The fact that particular people might not care about certain protected interests is not relevant, for the point of the reasonable person standard is to specify the respects in which people can be required to take account of the interests of others.

Because they suppose persons to have the same interests in both liberty and security, reasonableness tests in the law abstract away from various details that might be thought relevant to a more complete assessment of responsibility. This is sometimes thought of as a pragmatic compromise between some independent conception of responsibility and the limited ability of various institutions to discover the full range of facts that might be relevant to it. Thus, employment of the reasonable person standard is sometimes thought of as an operational test of whether someone was trying his or her best to avoid injury to others, or of whether he or she actually believed what he or she claimed to believe. I will argue, to the contrary, that the law's abstraction from detail reflects the ideal of equality at its core. Reasonableness tests are not a proxy for some other measure of responsibility; they are constitutive of responsibility, understood in terms of equality.

The idea of reasonable persons expresses a distinctive conception of normative justification. Although a long and distinguished tradition in political philosophy supposes that coercion can be justified only on grounds of consent, the most pressing questions about the use of force arise when people are *unwilling* to accept the claims of others against them. If one person injures another and is unwilling to pay damages, the question is not whether the injurer is really willing to pay after all, but under what conditions it is legitimate to require payment. Again, the fundamental question of punishment is not whether the criminal already accepts the punishment, but whether it is justified anyway. In the same way, the general question of justification is not whether everyone against whom coercion is exercised is somehow committed to acknowledging its legitimacy. Whether or not such a question makes sense as part of a more general account of morality, it is out of place in political philosophy. Political philosophy must ask whether there is some way to justify the use of coercion in cases in which it is unwelcome. To suppose that coercion is illegitimate unless the wrongdoer accepts the standard by which he or she is judged is to give up on the idea of fair terms of interaction, for it is to allow wrongdoers to unilaterally set the terms of their interactions

8

with others.[5] If one person is free to refuse responsibility, he is thereby allowed to set the boundaries of his own behavior.

1.3 THE BASIC STRUCTURE

The idea that fair terms of social cooperation set the limits of allowable behavior is familiar from discussions of distributive justice and public law. Rawls's influential formulation of liberal equality makes this idea central. Provided that what Rawls calls "the basic structure" of society is just, nobody has grounds for complaint if the outcomes of particular interactions are not as they might have hoped. In Rawls's own account, a just basic structure must guarantee equality of opportunity, equal liberty, and contain redistributive mechanisms to ensure that any inequalities in income and wealth are to the advantage of all in real terms. A just society does not allow those with more bargaining power to renegotiate the basic terms of interactions, but once those terms are set, people are free to pursue their own advantage as they see fit. So, for example, people with unusual and highly valued abilities may not renegotiate the tax system to their own advantage. Once a just system of taxation is in place, however, they are free to negotiate their own terms of employment as they see fit. Fair terms of interaction set limits within which people must moderate their behavior in light of the claims of others. Within those limits, people are free to do as they choose.

Exactly which terms of interaction are fair is controversial, and those who are dissatisfied with the results of their interactions with

---

[5] I also avoid another, more abstract way of appealing to consent. A familiar style of philosophical argument proceeds by seeking to show that all persons are implicitly committed to whatever normative standards it defends. If successful, such an argument would show that those who reject its conclusions fail to live up to *their own* commitments. I have never found such arguments compelling, since they typically employ an ambiguous sense of "commitment," thin enough so that it is presupposed by all action, yet thick enough that it is incompatible with particular actions. Nothing can fill both roles at once. I argue this point in detail in "Foundationalism in Political Theory" 17 *Philosophy and Public Affairs* 115 (1986). A more attractive variant of this approach represents fair terms cooperation as the outcome of a hypothetical social contract. Although I do not employ it because it is potentially misleading, I have no real objection to this way of proceeding. It uses hypothetical consent merely as an expository device for bringing out other normative arguments. The *locus classicus* of this approach is, of course, John Rawls's *A Theory of Justice* (Cambridge, MA: Harvard University Press, 1971).

others might conclude that the terms were unfair. That those complaints are typically voiced in the language of fairness itself reveals the power of the basic idea of fair interaction. The boundary between fair terms of interaction and particular interactions is also not always clear; family structure, for example, is both pivotal in determining where benefits and burdens fall, yet in practice it is often open to renegotiation on an ongoing basis.[6] The basic distinction between fair terms of interaction and particular interaction is nonetheless important to political philosophy.

Without endorsing all of the details of Rawls's account, I adopt his basic strategy of drawing a distinction between fair terms of interaction and particular interactions. Rawls limits his account of the basic structure to what he calls "constitutional essentials." My account takes as its focus core areas of tort and criminal law. These are not areas that have been articulated within a constitution. Nor should they be. But they are the natural home of the idea of reasonableness. Both employ standards of reasonableness to mark the line between responsibility and luck.

Reasonableness standards enter tort law by dividing risks that accompany many ordinary and acceptable human activities. Those who fail to exercise reasonable care are responsible for the injuries caused by that lack of care. That is, whether or not someone has taken a risk with the safety of others depends on whether or not he was behaving unreasonably. Those who take risks with the safety of others must bear the costs that arise if those risks result in injuries. By contrast, any injuries that result from the acts of those who exercise appropriate care are simply the bad luck of those they befall. Further, whether the intervening acts of others serve to relieve a tort-feasor of responsibility depends on whether those acts are reasonable.

The idea of reasonable terms of cooperation enters the criminal law in two ways. First, core areas of the criminal law can be understood as protecting reasonable terms of cooperation against people choosing to wrong others or expose them to risks. Crime consists in the pursuit of private rationality in the face of the rights of others, of the wrongdoer's substitution of his private rationality for public terms of reasonableness. Punishment responds to crime by upholding those standards of reasonableness. It does so by denying the wrongdoer's putative claim to rationality. Second, reasonableness

---

[6] G. A. Cohen, "Where the Action Is: On the Site of Distributive Justice," 26 *Philosophy and Public Affairs* 3 (1997).

standards shape the boundaries of the rights protected by the criminal law: For purposes of the criminal law, what someone is doing is given by what a reasonable person would take them to be doing. The use of defensive force is not licensed by the fact that the defender fears for his or her safety unless the fear is reasonable. In crimes for which consent is a defense, sincere but unreasonable mistakes about consent are not a defense. In each case, the rights of one person are not set by the beliefs of others. Criminal acts, rather than guilty thoughts, are prerequisite for criminal liability, because only criminal acts can be recognized as such by reasonable persons. The idea of reasonableness enters distributive justice by setting the background against which people can be held responsible for the consequences of their actions.[7] Where tort law uses reasonableness tests to specify what counts as taking a risk with the safety of others, and criminal law uses them to specify what counts as choosing to injure others or put them at risk, distributive justice uses the same conception of reasonableness to set the conditions against which it is appropriate to hold people responsible for the risks they take, both with their own security and that of others.

Reasonableness standards set the limits of acceptable behavior. A second set of issues of justice comes up when people fail to behave reasonably. Tort and criminal law are both concerned with remedies. Although the basic terms of interaction are the primary subject of justice, results become an issue of justice in just those cases in which people violate the limits of acceptable behavior. A central claim of this book is that, properly understood, fair terms of interaction also make sense of the characteristic responses to violations of those limits, including both tort damages and punishment. Those remedies uphold fair terms of interaction in two ways. First, they uphold those standards by undoing the effects of violations, insofar as it is possible to do so. Second, and derivatively, they serve as incentives to acceptable behavior, by raising the prospective costs of wrongdoing. The prospect of damages or punishment will deter those who consider pursuing their ends at

---

[7]   The requirement that one person's rights should not be measured by the will of another does not mean that how a person's life goes should not depend on the choices of others. In conditions of scarcity, it is appropriate that each person's bundle of scarce goods should depend in part on how badly others want those things. If they are too scarce, one must give up other things in order to have them; if others are willing to give up more to induce someone to do something, the person with more to give should be free to do so. The results of such decisions only make sense provided that the circumstances are such that the consequences of choices are fairly imputable to the choosers.

the cost of the protected interests of others. Deterrence is a secondary concern though, inasmuch as the magnitude of both damage awards and punishment is set retrospectively in terms of the wrong done, rather than prospectively in light of their likely effects.

This idea of the reasonable person applies only to responsible agents, because it is at bottom the idea that people should moderate their claims in light of the legitimate interests of others. At one level, the idea of responsibility is just the idea that people can in large measure be expected to respect each other's limits. When people fail to behave responsibly, they can rightly be held responsible for the results.

1.4 RESPONSIBILITY AS POLITICAL MORALITY

Philosophers frequently suppose that questions about the limits of the criminal law are best understood as questions in liberal political theory. For example, laws regulating abortion or pornography are seen as falling within the purview of political theory. I carry this general approach further in two ways. First, I argue that the core areas of tort and criminal law are best understood in terms of general considerations of political theory, and that they express important conceptions of freedom and equality. Second, I argue that the concept of individual responsibility found in tort and criminal law is itself the basis for an attractive conception of individual responsibility in matters of distributive justice.

My approach seeks to stay on the level of political and legal philosophy in that the conception of the person and responsibility I develop is meant to be specific to coercive institutions. The strategy is to make responsibility a question that is – to borrow another phrase from Rawls – political,[8] not metaphysical.[9] To say that it is political is not to say that it is always best decided by democratic assemblies, nor that it is inevitably the result of partisan struggles for power. It is to say instead that the account is specific to political morality, rather than dependent on a more comprehensive moral or metaphysical account.

To talk about responsibility as political in this sense is an applica-

---

[8] By "political" here, I really just mean "for the purposes of public standards," as opposed to either private or ultimate. Unfortunately, there seems to be no political use of this term in contemporary debate – only various private ones claiming to be ultimate.

[9] John Rawls, "Justice as Fairness: Political Not Metaphysical," 14 *Philosophy and Public Affairs* 223 (1985).

tion of the familiar liberal strategy of separation. The strategy has its origins in Locke's *Letter Concerning Toleration*, which seeks to show how we can regard toleration as a special duty imposed by the office of magistrate, and so in no way incompatible with taking one's own religious views seriously. Subsequent liberals have both sought to generalize this strategy and found its application in everyday life – as a professor, I can coherently both care very much how my students vote, while at the same time not allow it to influence my grading.[10]

Liberalism's great insight about responsibility is that one can be responsible for different things depending on what is normatively at stake. Thus, antidiscrimination laws typically include the categories of religion or creed as well as those of race and color. Race and color are plainly not things over which anyone can exercise control, and indeed it seems to be the very heart of racism to hold people responsible for such things by deeming it appropriate that their fate in life should reflect them. Religion and creed, in contrast, seem like things that are very much within an individual's control, and indeed it is central to most religions and creeds that they are a matter of individual responsibility. Antidiscrimination laws recognize that, although for religious purposes, religion can be viewed as a matter of responsibility, for political purposes, it need not be.[11] As a result, certain kinds of "costs" imposed by religious beliefs – those imposed on offended bigots, for example – are not the responsibility of members of the despised religious group. It goes without saying that this separation rests on controversial claims about political morality and the relations between state and religion, claims that holders of some religious (or political) views might reject. Those who think that state power should be used to promote one religion, or suppress all religion, will not be happy with such a solution. But it is important to recognize that their disagreement is not about the nature of responsibility, but about its occasion. Again, most broadly democratic political views suppose the benefits of citizenship should not be distributed on the basis of party allegiance,[12] despite the fact that each

<hr />

10   The most helpful commentary on Locke is Don Herzog, "Liberal Neutrality," in his *Happy Slaves* (Chicago: University of Chicago Press, 1989); a contemporary statement of the view can be found in Michael Walzer, "Liberalism and the Art of Separation" 12 *Political Theory* 315 (1984).

11   Recent controversies about whether sexual orientation is innate turn in part on overlooking the idea of separation. Discrimination on the basis of sexual orientation is objectionable even if it is a matter of choice.

12   This leaves aside the question of patronage appointments, which have their advocates, if not their explicit defenders. It is difficult to imagine anyone using

citizen is in another sense fully responsible for his or her own political views.

Understanding responsibility as a problem in political philosophy enables my account to avoid certain other philosophical disputes. For example, I rely only on commonplaces about action, and do not wade into disputes that have been central in philosophical treatments of the subject. The only features of human action that are of interest to the law are the uncontroversial ones that accounts of action theory take as their starting point. Most philosophical discussions of action are driven by issues that legal theory need not resolve. Such questions as how acts are individuated, whether or how act descriptions are compatible with descriptive vocabulary of the natural sciences, and whether acts are distinct from bodily movements are of some interest in their own right, but make no difference to the issues considered here. Competing accounts of action divide on whether, for example, turning on a light, flicking a switch, lifting one's finger, and surprising an intruder are different descriptions of a single act, or a number of distinct acts. But all competing accounts start from the shared belief that it makes perfectly good sense to say that someone did all of them. The choice of the appropriate description of an act depends on the perspective from which the question is asked. In the context of legal and political morality, the appropriate description of what someone has done will always depend in part on its relation to the protected interests of others. Although I do not know how to establish such a claim in the abstract, the rest of the book can be thought of as attempting to establish it concretely, by accounting for and justifying familiar and important structural features of the law of torts and the criminal law without appeal to a developed theory of action.[13]

In the same way, my account of responsibility does not depend on a robust account of the capacity for choice. Philosophers have sought to explicate that capacity in terms of such things as reflective self-consciousness, the ability of the self to distance itself from its ends, and such higher-order mental states as desires to act on one desire

ideas of responsibility to argue that those who voted for the party in power are thereby entitled to special favors.

[13] Legal philosophy is independent of the theory of action in another way as well. The criteria of adequacy for an acceptable action theory are at odds with those for an acceptable legal theory. A theory of action needs to account for the uncontroversial cases of action, and it is a virtue in such a theory to be compatible with all actions. The law, by contrast, is regulative, and seeks a unique characterization of various outcomes.

rather than another. I begin instead with the familiar fact that, apart from such notable exceptions as children and the mentally ill, people are by and large capable of moderating their behavior in light of the interests of others. The basis of that capacity, be it empirical or metaphysical, is of no concern. That persons can choose makes them appropriate subjects of responsibility in a way that machines and (most?) animals are not. But the capacity for choice does not dictate either the standards to which people are appropriately held or the appropriate remedies when someone fails to meet those standards.

Just as I do not turn to metaphysics to resolve questions of political morality, so I do not presume to solve metaphysical problems by looking at political morality. It is sometimes tempting to find a metaphysical message implicit in an account of agency and liability, and to trace the absence of responsibility in such circumstances to the absence of agency. Some philosophers who have reflected on legal liability have concluded that agency is always "ascriptive," and that there is nothing to be said about human action except from some normative perspective.[14] Although such proposals are not without appeal, it is important that the account developed here depends on no such claim. There is a perfectly straightforward sense in which the person who is free of legal responsibility still acts. The question of liability, though, does not depend on having solved the more general issues of the metaphysics of agency. Like those who suppose that assignments of liability are beholden to the results of more general philosophical accounts of action, those who suppose that there are no further metaphysical questions about responsibility once we have solved problems of liability presume that all questions about action must have a single answer. The claim defended here is that there is an account of agency and responsibility appropriate to public personae, which does not require vindication from other conceptions of responsibility. The account is agnostic both on questions about responsibility and agency more generally, and also on the question of its own implications for a more general account of responsibility or agency.

1.5   THREE CONCEPTIONS OF RESPONSIBILITY

The questions about responsibility in which the law properly takes an interest only have answers against the background of fair terms of

---

[14]   Hart, "The Ascription of Responsibility and Rights," 49 *Proceedings of the Aristotelian Society* 171 (1948).

interaction. There is, I will argue, no point in asking about whether someone is responsible for some outcome except in relation to questions of appropriate standards of conduct. In deciding whether someone is responsible for some deed, we need to consider both fairness to that person and fairness to others. In cases of accidental injury, for example, questions of responsibility get their point from the fact that if the injurer is not held responsible for the injury, the injured party will be left to bear its cost. In the criminal law, the interests of others are implicated in questions of responsibility in a slightly different way. If a criminal goes unpunished, his victim is not punished instead. But the victim's rights against intentional aggression mean nothing if the criminal's assessment of them is the only determinant of his responsibility. The criminal law's unwillingness to recognize a defense of mistake of law reflects the idea that the limits of criminal responsibility are not given by the wrongdoer's own assessment of his responsibility.[15]

That normative standards should be implicated in questions of responsibility may seem surprising. People often judge themselves and others to be responsible apart from any questions of what they owe to others. Outside of legal contexts, responsibility is sometimes tied to causation, apart from questions of duty. Other times, its reach is limited, based on what a person can control. Both of these conceptions of responsibility are familiar aspects of ordinary moral thought.

People sometimes acknowledge responsibility for what they have caused, even if they exercised appropriate care for the interests of others. We can understand what it means to say that Oedipus is responsible for parricide and incest, despite the fact that he did not, and could not, know the identity of his parents. The story is tragic because Oedipus cannot disown his action, and cannot make things right, even though he could not have known. He holds himself responsible because the consequences of his deed make him the person he is, even though there is nothing he can do to make amends. This conception of responsibility also comes up in more prosaic cases: The careful driver who runs down a child rightly feels terrible about what she has done; others feel relief that they didn't bring about such a terrible outcome. Again, the gift shop sign warning that those who break things must pay for them expresses the same idea of responsibility.

People sometimes also deny responsibility, insisting that they

---

[15] At the same time, some mistakes of law do excuse minor public policy infractions, precisely because no individual rights are at issue.

meant no wrong or that they did not mean for things to turn out the way that they did. On this view, actual control is essential to responsibility, and any element of luck is irrelevant to attributions of responsibility. This idea first surfaces in Stoic thought, finds its medieval expression in Abelard, and is an important element of Kant's moral (but not legal) philosophy.

I will call the conception of responsibility that emphasizes causation "causalist" since it ties questions of responsibility to questions of what happens. I will call the conception on which a person is only responsible for the aspects of his conduct which he controlled "voluntarist." Causalist and voluntarist accounts of responsibility divide on the relative importance of a person's thoughts and events in the world; the causalist emphasizes what happens. The voluntarist regards consequences as arbitrary, and the person's intentions as central.

Both causalist and voluntarist views can be thought of as general views of responsibility. Both sever questions of responsibility from questions of what people owe each other, for both suppose that questions about whether a person is responsible for some outcome are prior to, and independent of, questions about the moral status of the person's act. Both might, for example, separate the questions of whether A is responsible for B's injury from questions about the appropriate response should A be responsible. On either conception, responsibility makes further responses appropriate. A person's responsibility for some event might lead that person to regret the event, or feel proud of it, to explain it to others (or some select group of others), to atone for it, or to seek to repair it. It might lead others to question, praise, blame, reward, or punish the person, or to force the person to clean up the mess he or she has made. It might also lead others to let the person keep something or make him give it back.[16]

---

[16] Agents can only be held responsible for their actions provided their behavior can be evaluated in light of some standard. In order for behavior to be so evaluated, it must, at the very least, manifest adequate complexity in relation to that standard. This requirement constrains attributions of responsibility in two ways. If what appears to be an agent always fails to behave appropriately, the vocabulary of responsibility has no purchase. Those who are generally incompetent with respect to some standard cannot be responsible in light of it. To take a familiar example, those who cannot know right from wrong cannot be responsible for what would otherwise be criminal acts. At the other extreme, the vocabulary of responsibility also has no purchase when the agent in question vacuously satisfies the standard. We might praise a thermos for its remarkable ability to keep hot things hot and cold ones cold. It is not, however, a candidate for responsible agency because it cannot fail to meet the supposed standard. It is only when something – a person – falls within a range of capacities that

Their very different attitude toward questions of control mark out extremes on a continuum, but causalist and voluntarist views are alike in supposing that questions of responsibility are at bottom questions of fact, whether about the impact some event had on the world or the way in which an agent thought prospectively about his own act. Thus, both seem to promise a way of getting behind questions of liability and culpability, to deeper questions of whether someone really is responsible for their act. The two perspectives can also be combined in a variety of ways, each setting limits on the apparent excesses of the other.

Not surprisingly, both causalist and voluntarist views have frequently found their way into discussions of legal and political morality. Both are sometimes put forward as appropriate bases for coercion. The idea is that coercion is not arbitrary if it is occasioned by acts for which the person being coerced already has independent grounds for acknowledging responsibility. If someone really is responsible for something, there seems to be no further question about whether it is appropriate to hold her responsible.

I will engage both views at various points in succeeding chapters. Here I will only advertise the problem that causalist, voluntarist, and views that seek to combine the two all face as accounts of legal responsibility. Because they make questions of responsibility independent of questions of what people owe each other, they cannot be reconciled with the idea that holding people responsible is itself required by fair terms of interaction. Nor can they explain why particular coercive responses are appropriate in some contexts but not others. These points will, I hope, become clearer as we proceed.

1.6 POSITIVE LAW AND POLITICAL MORALITY

In the rest of the book, the idea of a reasonable person carries a lot of weight. Some readers may wonder whether it is up to the task. The reasonable person standard is sometimes thought to be little more

makes it capable of meeting the standard in most cases, but does not guarantee meeting it in every case, that it can be held responsible.

Although the requirement that a person sometimes meet a standard is a necessary condition on ascriptions of responsibility, the concept of responsible agency does not, by itself, have sufficient conditions. Those are specific to particular conceptions of responsibility. That is, what the standards are depends on the norms in light of which responsibility is an issue.

than a facade behind which those with the power to decide cases pick the side they favor. On some views, such choices are governed by arbitrary factors, on others they rest on a range of shifting and incompatible grounds.[17] For example, tort law is sometimes said to rest on an irresolvable tension between liberty and community; criminal law on an irresolvable tension between a conception of individual responsibility and concern for public safety.[18] Understood in terms of equality, however, the reasonable person standard expresses a unified ideal of fair cooperation. I will show that it is more than a facade in the only way I can, by revealing the structure behind it. That structure provides the resources for a deeper understanding of the cases in which reasonableness standards have failed in practice. For example, the reasonable man was too often male in nature as well as name, and the law was correspondingly insensitive to important security interests. The possibility of describing that insensitivity in terms of liberty and security interests suggests that the underlying conception of responsibility can be redeemed when given a more adequate content.

1.7 IDEAL INTERPRETATION AND ACTUAL PRACTICE

One final clarification. Some may think that the positive law in general, and the tort system in particular, is a particularly unpromising place to begin an account of responsibility, because it is at best haphazard in its implementation of any conception of justice. Procedure is very expensive, which means that which cases make it to court may have little to do with their merits. Many of the leading cases of nineteenth-century tort law would probably not be litigated today. Fact finding is sometimes enormously difficult.[19] Expensive legal fees lead to inflated damage awards, which often means that defendants pay far more than the damage they do.[20] In cases involving smaller

---

17 See, for example, Mark Kelman, *A Guide to Critical Legal Studies* (Cambridge, MA: Harvard University Press, 1987).

18 On both tort and criminal law, see Kelman, *A Guide to Critical Legal Studies;* for a more focused consideration of criminal law, see Alan Norrie, *Crime, Reason and History: A Critical Introduction to Criminal Law* (London: Weidenfield and Nicholson, 1993).

19 An interesting, and often troubling, narrative of all of these problems can be found in Peter Shuck, *Agent Orange On Trial: Mass Toxic Disasters in the Courts* (Cambridge, MA: Harvard University Press, 1987).

20 See the discussion in Geoffrey Palmer, "The Design of Compensation Systems: Tort Principles Rule, O.K.?," 29 *Valparaiso University Law Review* 1115 (1995).

amounts where procedure is less costly, many small-claims judgments are never collected.[21]

These problems of implementation are real. I suspect, though, that they reflect less on the nature of corrective justice than on structural features of the system of private litigation as a way of implementing it. The law does not grant an injured party a right to redress as such. Instead, it grants a right to sue.[22] The difference is important. Those who are wrongfully injured do not simply apply to have the state coercively take damages from their injurers. Instead, they must make their case, often at considerable expense, and may need to take further steps to actually collect a judgment. We can imagine a different system that nonetheless aimed to protect the same rights recognized on the basis of corrective justice. Suppose that, rather than suing the person who injured me, I could report him or her to the authorities. The appropriate authorities might impose a fine on a minor charge, and threaten some further sanction, such as the loss of a license to do business, unless damages are paid.[23] We can imagine a large-scale version of this practice – unless the manufacturer of some hazardous product pays damages to those injured by the product, the manufacturer's other products cannot be sold. Although such a system would have problems of its own, particularly because of the amount of discretion its officials would have, it would solve some of the problems about access and collection that the current tort system faces. The choice between these problems is an interesting and difficult one, but beyond the scope of the present inquiry. A society of responsible agents faces costs that a society that minimizes the role of individuals does not. Among those are the costs of procedures for determining responsibility in contested cases.[24]

Palmer advocates abolishing the tort system, leaving all losses to lie where they fall, in the hopes that some better system will spring up to replace it. See also P. S. Atiyah, *The Damages Lottery* (Oxford: Hart Publishing, 1997).

[21] Another problem sometimes bruited is that the widespread availability of liability insurance means that people do not end up bearing the costs of their activities after all. I will discuss the role of insurance in Chapter 3. The basic argument I will offer goes as follows: To say a tort-feasor is liable for some injury is just to say that the injury is the tort-feasor's problem, not the plaintiff's. Just as one may insure against a wide variety of problems, including accidental losses, so one may insure against one's accidentally injuring another. In each case, one can make arrangements in anticipation of unwanted consequences that may come up.

[22] See Benjamin Zipursky, "Rights and Recourse," 51 *Vanderbilt Law Review* 2 (1998).

[23] A system something like this is used by some municipal licensing commissions to regulate contractors who do shoddy work.

[24] It is well worth wondering – though I shall not do so here – whether a system

1.8 PLAN OF THE BOOK

The central theme of the book is that equality and responsibility need to be understood together, in light of the idea of reciprocity. Chapters 2 through 4 fill out these ideas in an examination of tort law. Chapter 2 sets the stage for subsequent discussion, by locating corrective justice in relation to the idea that, provided starting points are fair and people respect each other, the outcomes of free interaction cannot be objected to on grounds of justice. That idea has been appropriated by libertarians in recent decades, but they cannot make sense of it, because they have a deficient view of both fair starting points and fair terms of interaction. I show that the idea of voluntary interaction is importantly indeterminate until some way of delineating which risks lie with which people is specified, and that doing so requires addressing substantive questions about the importance of liberty and security interests that all can be supposed to have.

Chapter 3 examines negligence liability as an expression of the idea that people should bear the costs of their activities. The root idea of the fault system is that whether a consequence of someone's activity is a cost to others depends on whether that person exercised reasonable care. If I am sufficiently careful and injure you, it is simply your misfortune – the situation is no different than if you had been struck by lightning. If, on the other hand, I was careless, then the injury is my problem, and I must pay damages so as to properly bear its costs. Chapter 3 also shows how this understanding of risk explains familiar features of tort doctrine.

Chapter 4 relates the idea that particular risks belong to particular people to more general ideas of responsibility for outcomes, and illustrates it by looking at examples of intervening agency. By viewing the distinction between what someone does and what merely happens in terms of the standard of care, I explain why responsibility

of private litigation is an appropriate second-best solution to problems of accidental injury. Even if the ideal of corrective justice is the appropriate response to accidents, it may be that a system that tries to implement it does worse than one that simply abandons it in favor of other strategies for dealing with accidental loss. Compare: Hawaii may be one's ideal vacation spot, yet if one is unable to afford to get there, going in its general direction and only getting to the Mojave Desert is a less sensible strategy than going in another direction entirely to a more suitable second-best. It may be that a widespread social insurance scheme would actually approximate corrective justice better at a micro level than does the current tort system. Regulatory regimes may do more to make sure that people internalize the costs of their choices.

sometimes flows through the intervening voluntary agency of others, and other times does not.

Chapters 5 through 7 extend the ideas of agency and responsibility developed so far to selected problems in the criminal law. Chapter 5 explores the differences between tort and criminal law, and offers an account of punishment as a response to intentional or reckless wrongdoing, that is, as a response to choosing to injure or risk injury to the rights of others. That account of punishment is then deployed to explain the role of excusing conditions in the criminal law.

Chapter 6 uses the ideas of reasonableness and equality to explain the distinction between mistakes of fact and mistakes of law. Mistake of fact provides a complete defense to a criminal charge, whereas mistake of law is normally no defense. I illustrate that distinction by looking at the two places in which reasonableness tests are central to the criminal law, namely, self-defense and consent. If someone makes a mistake about the danger posed by another and claims self-defense, or makes a mistake about someone else's consent, his or her beliefs only serve to exculpate if they are reasonable, that is, compatible with showing appropriate respect for the interests of others.

Chapter 7 uses the idea of reasonableness to solve several puzzles in the law of attempts: The distinction between attempting a crime, which is culpable, and merely preparing for one, which is not; the requirement of intention to attempt a crime where the same crime could be completed recklessly; and the reduced punishment that failed attempts receive.

Tort law and criminal law are regimes of individual responsibility. Chapter 8 concludes my discussion of them with an examination of critiques that hope to show that the ideas of agency and responsibility are themselves a reflection of a particular, and corrupt, form of social organization. In this context, I look to the arguments of Marx and Pashukanis. I show that those critiques are right about something – in particular, the idea that people should bear the costs of their own activities is only intelligible in light of a particular way of organizing scarcity. I then look to the alternative ideal put forward by Marx and articulated by Pashukanis, a world in which responsibility is abolished and all misfortunes are held in common. I argue that such a world is an attractive ideal only if scarcity can be overcome. As long as scarcity remains, individual responsibility must have a central place.

Chapter 9 looks at distributive justice from the point of view of reciprocity and responsibility. It defends the idea that certain risks must be held in common as a precondition for people being responsible for the costs their activities impose on others. The solution is the same as in tort and criminal law: To look to the importance of various activities and security interests, weighing them with the device of representative, reasonable persons.

Chapter 2

Corrective Justice
and Spontaneous Order

In this chapter, I lay out the place of corrective justice by relating it to two ideas. The first is the idea of fair terms of interaction; the second the idea that whether a particular outcome is justified depends in part on how it came about. Together, these ideas lead to a conception of justice in holdings: If starting points are fair, and everyone moderates his or her behavior appropriately, the resulting holdings are also fair. Unfortunately, these two conditions are not always satisfied. I postpone the question of what counts as a fair starting point until the final chapter. In this chapter, I focus only on the issues that arise when people fail to behave reasonably. Corrective justice is a remedial virtue, the purpose of which is to undo certain effects of unreasonable behavior.

To bring this structure into relief, I take as my starting point a world without any idea of enforceable responsibility, the "natural condition of mankind" described in Chapter Thirteen of Hobbes's *Leviathan*. I then explore what is missing in such a world by considering the libertarian view that responsibility can be demarcated in terms of causation. Libertarians find causation an attractive basis for liability because they suppose that changes in holdings that result from voluntary actions are, in general, legitimate. Only when one person causes an injury to another should the effects of voluntary actions be undone. I show why libertarianism lacks the resources to distinguish between changes that should be and those that should not be undone. To draw that distinction, we need the idea of reasonableness, which, in a world of uncertainty, requires a fair division of risks. The discussion of libertarianism may at first seem to be a digression, but it isn't. Despite the fact that it fails on its own terms, the libertarian approach reveals the relationship between corrective justice and the idea that outcomes are justified by the way they come about. Only some changes in holdings need to be undone; the need to undo them follows directly from the idea that outcomes are (sometimes) justified by the ways in which they come about.

2.1   HOBBES'S "NATURAL CONDITION OF MANKIND"

Imagine a world in which the idea of responsibility has no normative significance. In such a world, there might be various ways of distinguishing which people did which things. We might employ any of the ways in which we could answer a question of the form "who did that?" by picking out some person or persons. So we might, for example, look to all bodily motions, or all choices, as things that people did. In order to attach normative significance to the idea of responsibility, however, we need more. In particular, we need some way of attaching persons to outcomes so that how something came about makes a difference to the normative status of parties with respect to it. The connection between persons and outcomes might be abandoned in favor of the idea that all losses should lie where they fall. This is the world that Hobbes describes in Chapter Thirteen of *Leviathan* as "the natural condition of mankind," a situation in which life is, as he so memorably puts it, "solitary, poor, nasty, brutish and short."[1] In the Hobbesian state of nature, injuries lie where they fall regardless of how they come about.[2]

In the state of nature, fortune is allowed full sway at every level. All losses lie where they fall. Holmes recommends this as a default position for tort law, remarking that the cumbersome machinery of the law should only be used to move a loss from one person to another when there is a compelling reason to do so.[3] In the Hobbesian state of nature, there is no state, law, or other cumbersome machinery. As a result, there is no body authorized to shift losses. Of course, people might displace various misfortunes from themselves onto

---

[1]   Thomas Hobbes, *Leviathan*, edited by C. B. MacPherson (Harmondsworth: Penguin, 1968; originally 1651), p. 186.

[2]   Conversely, the distinction between what people do and what merely happens might also be effaced by holding all losses in common. Probably nobody has pursued this idea with the resolute consistency with which Hobbes describes the state of nature. Still, the Soviet jurist Evgeny Pashukanis comes close to advocating it when he argues that the very idea of individual responsibility is an expression of a specific and deformed set of social relations. See Evgeny Pashukanis, *Law and Marxism: A General Theory*, translated by Barbara Einhorn (London: Ink Links, 1978). We will return to Pashukanis's arguments in Chapter 8.

[3]   Oliver Wendell Holmes, *The Common Law* (Boston: Little, Brown, 1881), p. 94.

others – displacing their hunger by taking someone else's food, or injuring another while attending to their own wants. When such endeavors succeed, the misfortunes now lie where they most recently fell. As Hobbes puts it, "The notions of Right and Wrong, Justice and Injustice have there no place." Even deliberate shifting can be thought of as the full reign of fortune, because whether someone is in a position to shift their losses to another is itself a matter of fortune, at least from the perspective of the person who finds himself with a new misfortune. He just happened to be in the wrong place at the wrong time. As a result, there is "no *Mine* and *Thine* distinct; but only that to be every man that he can get; and for so long, as he can keep it."[4]

Hobbes himself offers the state of nature in a sort of cautionary tale, an explanation of why there must be limits on the misfortunes people are allowed to cause each other. His description of the state of nature makes the lack of security its most salient and troubling feature. It appears as a world of pure agency, in which each acts in pursuit of their perceived ends, with no room for ideas of concern or respect for others, let alone for even the thinnest idea of community or of a common fate. The lack of security means that "there is no place for industry; because the fruit thereof is uncertain."[5]

Although Hobbes does not describe it in these terms, the state of nature would also be terribly unfair. If I injure you in the Hobbesian state of nature, it is your problem, not mine. Whether through malice or indifference, people could take advantage of the efforts of others, and displace the costs of their activities onto them. Although the lack of incentives to industry can be traced to the absence of security, it can also be traced to the absence of any distinction between mine and thine, that is, between what someone does and what merely happens. Without such a distinction, there can be no connection between industry and outcomes, because there is no connection between anything and outcomes. Without such a connection, a way of understanding misfortune becomes a way of understanding all of life.

The state of nature can be thought of as a world of perfect agency, since each person can do whatever he is able to in pursuit of his ends. In another way, though, it fails to protect agency at all, because it doesn't leave only *mere* misfortunes where they lie. It does the same for misfortunes that one person creates for another, whether willfully or carelessly. That is, which problems belong to which persons bears

---

[4] Hobbes, *Leviathan*, p. 188.
[5] Ibid., *Leviathan*, p. 186.

an entirely contingent relation to anything they've ever done. Each person's agency is left entirely at the mercy of the agency of others.

In spite of its emphasis on agency, then, the problem with the Hobbesian state of nature lies in its inability to distinguish between misfortunes one person creates for another and those that are merely bad luck. If this is the problem, the solution should be apparent. Some line must be drawn between those misfortunes that lie where they fall and those that properly belong to some other person. Hobbes characterizes the problem of the state of nature of "no mine and thine"; the libertarian solution is to introduce coercively enforceable property rights. Once they are introduced, and enforced, libertarians suppose that no further basis for coercion is justified.

Property rights provide the starting point for the libertarian analysis. On their own, they seem to provide a way of drawing a line between misfortunes that must fall where they lie and those that must be shifted to others. The situation is complicated, however, because any account of enforceable property rights must also specify the incursions against which those rights are to be protected.

2.2   HISTORICAL ACCOUNTS OF JUSTICE

The libertarian emphasis on property rights is often presented as expressing a distinctive understanding of justice. I pause here to consider that conception, both because it has considerable appeal, and because its appeal is not something to which libertarians have an exclusive, or indeed even a coherent, claim. In *Anarchy, State and Utopia*,[6] Robert Nozick distinguished between what he calls "patterned" and "historical" theories of justice. A patterned theory evaluates the justice of a set of holdings by looking at the features of the overall pattern of holdings at a particular time. If they conform to the specified pattern – for example, exactly equal shares, measured on some dimension, or distribution in accordance with some measure of merit or virtue – the holdings are said to be just. An historical theory, by contrast, looks not at the current pattern of holdings, but at how it came about. Provided that the starting point was not itself unjust, and no injustice occurred in subsequent transfers of holdings, the resulting pattern of holdings is also just.

Nozick maintains that historical theories of justice are friendlier to liberty than are patterned theories. Since any pattern may be upset

---

[6]   Robert Nozick, *Anarchy State and Utopia* (New York: Basic Books, 1974), pp. 161–2.

by voluntary transfers, including gifts, maintaining a distributive pattern is sure to require constant interference, and either undoing of voluntary transfers or further forced transfers. Nozick illustrates his point with the example of Wilt Chamberlain, the basketball star who demands a premium of twenty-five cents from every fan who watches his games. No matter what pattern is chosen, if people choose to spend their fair shares on paying to see Chamberlain play, the original pattern of holdings will be substantially upset. From this example, Nozick concludes that in order to give liberty its proper place, people must be free to do as they wish with their legitimate holdings. The example gets its force from the intuitively plausible idea that the point of getting one's fair share is to be able to dispose of it as one sees fit. Since most patterned theories take it for granted that distributive shares are important because they enable people to act, any theory that requires readjustment whenever anyone uses his or her share will require constant intervention.

Nozick presents the virtues of historical theories as though they amount to a positive argument for libertarianism. In fact, the contrast between patterned and historical theories is at least partly overblown. No serious theory of justice advocates a totally patterned distribution.[7] Instead, from Bentham through Rawls, those who have discussed justice in distribution have advocated institutional structures within which individuals can pursue their private purposes. Rawls, for example, requires redistribution only to maintain the basic structure, so as to ensure that voluntary transactions do not end up aggregating in a way that limits the worth of anyone's liberty.

To provide an argument against economic redistribution, the libertarian needs something more, namely, an independently attractive

---

[7] Aristotle's discussion of distributive justice in the *Nichomachean Ethics* may fit Nozick's model. Aristotle's central example is the distribution of the power to rule on the basis of some conception of merit, though. Because the power to rule is presumably not exchangeable, it is not clear that Nozick's objection applies to it. As a more general matter, Aristotle's account of the distinction between corrective and distributive justice may well be out of place in the modern world, because of the conception of legal authority in which it is embedded. I discuss this issue briefly in Chapter 9.

I suggested that no serious conception of distributive justice is patterned in Nozick's sense. Less serious examples are easier to find. Kurt Vonnegutt's egalitarian dystopia, "Harrison Bergeron," provides an example of both patterning and constant interference in Nozick's sense. In pursuit of perfect equality, graceful people are made to wear heavy weights, and those with long attention spans have buzzers implanted in their heads to distract them every thirty seconds. See "Harrison Bergeron," in his *Welcome to the Monkey House* (New York: Dell, 1970).

account of the justice both of starting positions and of the boundaries between persons. Depending on the initial shares, and what counts as an illicit transfer, a wide variety of distributions are historical in the requisite sense. For, as many critics have pointed out, "libertarianism" is a misleading name. Any regime of individual rights prevents people from doing things that they otherwise might. Protecting private property stops people from camping in other people's yards, traffic rules stop people from going the wrong way down one-way streets,[8] and nuisance laws prevent people from operating feed-lots in residential neighborhoods. Something more is needed to show that the liberties that libertarians would protect are more important than those they would deny. What is needed is some way of specifying which changes in distribution need to be undone.

The same point might be made in terms of another favorite libertarian theme, Hayek's idea of spontaneous order. Hayek draws a contrast between social planning and the sort of order that emerges spontaneously through free individual choices. He advocates the latter on the grounds that individuals are in the best position to satisfy their own aspirations. Like Nozick's account, though, Hayek's account cannot mean quite what it says. The only truly spontaneous order is the Hobbesian state of nature. More attractive social orders are only spontaneous against the background of some guarantee that certain kinds of individual choices are either proscribed or their consequences undone. The hard questions all revolve around the questions of which various voluntary acts fall into those categories. Not all changes in holdings raise questions of justice; the idea of spontaneous order is only attractive once we have identified the changes that need to be undone.

Historical theories of justice nonetheless tap into a very powerful intuition, which suggests that a distribution of material holdings might change in various ways without raising any questions of injustice. If I give away my legitimately acquired possessions, no questions of the justice of the resulting holdings need arise. Likewise, if I exchange them. And, most salient for present purposes, if I lose my possessions, or damage them entirely on my own, the loss may be my misfortune and raise no issues of justice. Fairness may mandate dividing a cake into equal pieces; it does not mandate equalizing shares again if I give away or consume my share. The same point applies,

---

8   G. A. Cohen, *Self-Ownership, Freedom and Equality* (Cambridge: Cambridge University Press, 1995), p. 67.

though more controversially, in at least some cases of self-injury. The injured bungee-jumper has no automatic claim to indemnification from others. A defensible historical account of justice will be far more complicated than these intuitive examples suggest. But the intuitive idea is at the core not only of libertarian political theory, but of central aspects of tort doctrine and of egalitarian accounts of economic justice. All are process-oriented, and as such need to specify the conditions under which changes in the results of interaction are to be undone. Some cases are easy: Changes that result from force or fraud are prohibited. The other kinds of voluntary interactions are more controversial, and, as we shall see, some account of them is needed. Although libertarians are mistaken to suppose they have a monopoly on the underlying idea, their development of it is instructive.

2.3 A VOLUNTARIST MINIMAL STATE

If property rights are to provide a solution to the problems of the Hobbesian state of nature, we need some specification of what counts as an incursion against them. The specification of what counts as an incursion gives content to the idea of protecting property rights. Once the nature of incursions is specified, the effects of those incursions can be undone. An important theme in libertarian thought is that once property rights are protected, liberty is secure, because no *further* enforceable norms are required.

There are two ways in which a libertarian might seek to articulate the idea of property rights so as to determine what counts as an incursion against them. One way is broadly speaking voluntarist, the other causalist. The voluntarist solution is to leave losses to lie where they fall unless they are the result of intentional force or fraud. These are, on Hobbes's telling, the "cardinal virtues" of the state of nature. The causalist solution emphasizes agency in another way and appeals to the intuitive difference between the sufferings that one person *causes* another, and those that come about in some other way, whether as a result of the injured person's own choice or by chance. The former must be compensated, but the latter may be left where they fall. The resulting position is a regime of generalized strict liability for injuries, which allows no further nonvoluntary wealth transfers. This is the more standard libertarian solution. If one person injures another, it does not matter if the injury is intentional, careless, or entirely faultless. The injurer must compensate the victim.

Both of these formulations of libertarianism turn out to be unstable, but their failures are instructive. Both are unable to solve the normative problem of the Hobbesian state of nature: Because both allow one person to unilaterally set the terms of his interactions with others.

The voluntarist version of libertarianism has probably never been advanced as a serious position in political philosophy. Nonetheless, it is worth exploring for two reasons. First, examining its shortcomings will point the way to a more adequate account. Second, it has a certain amount of intuitive appeal. The idea that the only appropriate basis for responsibility is intentional or knowing wrongdoing is familiar. One of the standard ways in which children respond to criticism is by saying, "but I didn't mean to." Applied to a libertarian regime of property rights, the same approach would leave all misfortunes to lie where they fall, unless they were the result of intentional or knowing boundary crossings. In legal terms, such a regime would protect property rights by means of the criminal law and liability for intentional torts. All accidental (i.e., nonintentional) losses would lie where they fell. Thus, losses that were the result of carelessness would not be shifted.

The difficulty with such a proposal is that it fails to solve the normative problem of the Hobbesian state of nature. The normative problem, it will be recalled, was that each person was vulnerable to the acts of others because the "right of nature" allowed each person to unilaterally set the terms of interaction with others. That is the sense in which the Hobbesian state of nature is terribly unfair.[9] In the voluntarist minimal state, that unfairness survives. The libertarian's point in introducing property rights is to ensure that people bear the costs their choices impose on others. If property rights are only protected against intentional invasions, that idea is lost. The voluntarist minimal state effectively allows each person to decide what will and won't count as a cost of her activity. If I mean to hit you on the shoulder, and instead I hit you in the head, I escape liability, and you are left to bear the costs of my clumsiness, because I did not mean to be clumsy. If you mean to burn down one building, and burn down another, you escape liability. Where no injury is intended, costs simply lie where they fall. Each person determines the intended consequences of his or her conduct: After all, they are the consequences intended.

[9]   Hobbes's concern is with its level of insecurity; property rights protected only against intentional incursions may or may not solve that problem. They probably do not, because the total absence of liability for accidental losses would leave security as the overriding concern of life.

Rather than being justified on the grounds that it expresses the idea that one should bear the costs of one's activities, this suggestion is instead a way of determining what those costs are, and a normatively unattractive way at that. The intuitive idea is that people should bear the costs that their activities impose on others. It is not the idea that they are free to determine what those costs are. There can be no measurement of such costs unless we have some way of measuring them apart from the beliefs of those who impose them.[10]

2.4 A CAUSALIST MINIMAL STATE

2.4.1 Strict Liability and Boundary Crossings

The alternative way of protecting property rights is more familiar in libertarian writings. It is to leave losses where they fall unless one person has caused another's injury. I will refer to this as "the libertarian position" since it is the one to which prominent libertarian writers subscribe. This position is interesting both because of its initial intuitive appeal, and, more importantly, because a consistent development of it leads to the conclusions that the idea of a historical theory of justice needs to employ a conception of a fair division of risks. Even to describe responsibility in a world of interacting persons requires appeal to ideas of what people owe each other, ideas that go beyond simple ideas of property and causation.

The libertarian position seeks to capture the essential importance of agency in a way that is consistent with a conception of fairness, something the state of nature cannot do. It is broadly speaking causalist, for it supposes each person is free to make his or her own way in the world, yet is responsible for the impact of his or her actions on others. In the libertarian picture, the Hobbesian position serves as a default rule. Misfortunes do not simply lie where they fall. Instead, they lie where they fall *unless* they result from the causal agency of some other individual – in which case they are shifted to that person.

Libertarian writings often focus on the particular misfortunes that are the standard province of tort law – the person who wanders onto another's property, the cricket ball that goes astray, and so on. That focus is of a piece with the libertarian opposition to redistribution. A minimal state charged solely with protecting property rights and a

---

[10] I pursue this point further in the next chapter, where I consider several voluntarist variants on the fault standard.

regime of generalized strict liability in tort law come as a package. The underlying view is that agents must take back the costs their conduct imposes on others, *not* so much to rectify the other's loss as to take back what is one's own. As a result, libertarians tend to welcome economic metaphors of displacing costs, or of one person shifting her problems to another. Those who shift their problems must take them back. In contrast, if the costs that have befallen someone are not the result of another's agency, they lie where they fall. If the misfortune that befalls you is my doing, I own it; if it is your doing, you own it. And if it is no one's doing, it belongs to no one. It is the result of chance, not agency.

For this picture of shifting losses to make sense, a default rule is required. If a loss is no one's doing, just the result of chance, it must lie where it has fallen. The default rule is itself justified by a further appeal to agency: If by chance misfortune befalls you, it is yours, not because you deserve it, but because nobody else does. Shifting a loss to someone who didn't cause it is no different from causing a loss to someone else: In each case, one person imposes a cost on another. The same line of argument thus lends its support to an antiredistributive political theory. No human agent is typically responsible for such misfortunes of birth as poverty or disability. If these are genuine misfortunes, that just means that they are no one's doing. If they are no one's doing, though, there can be no grounds for coercively imposing them on anyone. Again, the default rule comes into play, and the losses must lie where they fall – on those disadvantaged by birth and chance. Chance plays an important role in both directions: Whether my activity injures you may well depend on factors outside anyone's control, as will all of those natural facts not attributable to any human agency. For the libertarian, this way of dividing agency and chance is essential to the idea that people should bear the costs of their activities.

The libertarian taste for strict liability can be understood as an attempt to provide an attractive conception of both boundaries and initial holdings, and in so doing to cordon off a sphere of prohibited acts without interfering with individual liberty. At the same time, it can be thought of as explaining the role of damages. Strict liability is supposed to do that job. When boundaries are crossed, the injurer must pay damages so as to take back the injury. Damages serve to make injuries that result from boundary crossings no different from injuries to oneself. Once a loss is shifted back to the person to whom it properly belongs, the fact that the responsible person has less than before the entire transaction is normatively equivalent to a situation in which the injurer had simply injured himself.

For the libertarian, boundaries are understood primarily in spatial terms. Direct assaults are boundary crossings, but so too are accidental bumps. If – but only if – a boundary is crossed, the boundary crosser must compensate the person whose boundary it is. Parallel reasoning generates the libertarian theory of property: The person who first takes possession of some unowned thing thereby expands his spatial boundary to include that thing.[11] The only way others can take or use it is with the initial owner's consent. Anyone who takes or damages the thing without the owner's consent crosses the first person's boundary. Negligence is irrelevant, because the person who exercises care has nonetheless crossed the boundary. If the wind blows me onto your lawn, I have to leave, even though I am not at fault in finding myself there. The only exception is if one person has put himself or his property in the way of others, in which case the person who bumps into it has already had *his* boundary crossed.

Agency and ownership are thus the key elements of the libertarian approach. Agency provides a way to express one's personality by making a mark on the world. One presumably owns one's own body and whatever one does with it. If I injure myself, I own my injury; if I injure someone else, it is as though I injured myself. In acting, I create things, and own my own creations.[12] In short, causation links

---

[11] I leave out the qualification that Nozick introduces, namely, that the acquisition of an unowned thing is only just if the Lockean proviso that there is "enough and as good" left for others to acquire holds. Nozick inconsistently construes the proviso in welfarist terms, emphasizing the way in which a system of private property leads to the creation of increased opportunities and thus benefits those who lose the ability to use unowned objects. As a result, he seems to abandon the core idea of libertarianism, namely, that each person has a purely subjective veto on how others may limit their freedom. The rustic who prefers a difficult life to increased opportunities may be made better off in many ways by the privatization of property, but he is not made better off by the libertarian standard of consent.

[12] This seems to be the reasoning underlying Epstein's discussion of *Vincent v. Lake Erie Transport*, 124 N.W. 221 (Minnesota 1910). In *Vincent*, a shipowner was held liable for damages to a dock that his boat had been tied to in a storm, despite the court's concession that it was reasonable for the shipowner to stay at the dock over the dockowner's protests. Epstein suggests that liability can be explained by recognizing that if both ship and dock had been owned by the shipowner, the shipowner would have decided whether to risk the ship or the dock, and been liable for the entire loss, whichever decision had been reached. Because the shipowner acted, he is liable for losses, wherever they fall. See Richard Epstein, "A Theory of Strict Liability," 2 *Journal of Legal Studies* 151 (1973). I discuss *Vincent* at length in Chapter 4.

agency with misfortune. If my body figures in a valid causal explanation of what happened, I am responsible. Putting this point in terms of ownership is perhaps misleading; the advantage of doing so is that the underlying issue is clear: Questions about misfortunes are always questions about whose problem some particular misfortune is. Whether problems can be owned in any robust sense, it certainly does make sense to suppose that a problem is someone in particular's problem. When someone refuses a request for sympathy or aid by saying, "that's not my problem," they are appealing to this minimal sense of ownership.

Libertarians find causation an attractive basis for liability for another reason: Questions about who caused what do not require any inquiries into such questions as whether various people behaved reasonably or had a fair chance to avoid liability. Libertarians are right to be wary of such questions, for inquiries about the basic conditions of agency may well lead to redistribution in order to protect those conditions. As long as causation is sufficient for liability, those difficult (and potentially embarrassing) questions need not be asked.

2.4.2   Causation and Indeterminacy

Although causation is plainly part of the story on responsibility, it is not the whole story. It is part of the story, because causation links actions to their effects; and the effects of actions are the only candidates for corrective justice to undo. But causation is a far broader notion than responsibility. Ronald Coase and Guido Calabresi independently invented the economic analysis of law when they realized that every injury is a joint product. Both injurer and victim cause any injury.[13] And of course the basic idea is much older than that; in the seventeenth century, Blaise Pascal made essentially the same point: "I have often commented that the sole cause of man's unhappiness is that he does not know how to sit quietly in his room."[14] The injurer's role is obvious, for the reasons on which libertarian advocates of generalized strict liability focus. But the victim's role is no less real. In all but the most bizarre cases,[15] the accident could have been prevented

---

[13]   Ronald Coase, "The Problem of Social Cost," 3 *Journal of Law and Economics* 1 (1960), Guido Calabresi, "Some Thoughts on Risk Distribution in Torts," 70 *Yale Law Journal* 499 (1961).

[14]   Blaise Pascal, *Pensées*, translated by A. J. Krailsheimer (Harmondsworth: Penguin, 1976), p. 67.

[15]   See, for example, *Tomaki Juda v. United States*, 6 Cl. Ct. 441 (1984). (The plaintiff

had the victim stayed home, taken a different route, or whatever. Thus, any injury is always a joint product, which must somehow be divided between the parties. If causation is made the basis for shifting losses, two questions can be asked in every case of injury. First, was the defendant the cause of the injury? Second, was the plaintiff? Trouble is, the answer to both questions seems to always be "yes." If we understand the causal question in terms of what would have happened but for the act of the defendant (plaintiff), we are likely to get the same result for every accident, both the injurer and the plaintiff cause the injury. Thus, we seem to find everyone liable for everything.

Consider a simple example. You are walking down a quiet residential street, minding your own business. I, meanwhile, am repairing my roof. As I reach for a new box of nails, I inadvertently kick my hammer, which falls and hits you on the head. Who is responsible? Looked at only in narrowly causal terms, it looks as though we both are. Had you not ignored Pascal's wise advice, my hammer would have fallen harmlessly to the ground. Had I secured my hammer, you would have walked uninterrupted down the street. Still, you would likely be (rightly) inclined to say that I was responsible for your injury, and you would probably add that I was responsible for it because I caused it. But, in naturalistic terms, it would seem you caused it as much as I did. In the case of accidents, focusing on causation does not exactly eliminate responsibility. Instead, it places it everywhere. When something goes wrong, there seem to be too many causes, including too many voluntary human acts, which need to come together in order for the accident to happen.

One response to the problem of too many causes is to draw a distinction between causes and conditions. Thus, the libertarian might hope to claim that my dropping the hammer is the cause of the injury, but your presence on the street is merely a condition. Both are necessary conditions, that is, "but-for" causes. Only one is *the* cause, though, because only one seems to have crucially made a difference. We ordinarily have no difficulty distinguishing between, for example, the striking of a match as a cause of a fire and the presence of oxygen as a mere condition. In the same way, the libertarian might hope to keep strict liability general by assigning losses to those who

was forcibly removed from his home in Bikini Atoll to allow nuclear weapons testing, and then returned when radiation levels were dangerously high. In this case, presumably nothing the plaintiff could have done would have prevented the injury.)

cause them, rather than to the victims who are the mere conditions of them. On this analysis, my dropping the hammer is the cause of your injury, whereas your decision to walk down my street is merely a condition. Although there are indefinitely many human actions that are "but-for" causal antecedents of any injury, it is worth remembering that not all injuries are the result of human action. If I hadn't planted the tree where I did, a storm would not have uprooted it, destroying my fence. Although the damaged fence is presumably my problem, it isn't because I am responsible. It's rather that nobody is, and so the problem belongs to the person it befalls – in this case, me. Again, if Lisbon is destroyed by an earthquake, Voltaire's Dr. Pangloss is wrong to attribute its destruction to the fact that it was built at all – though he is no doubt right that if it hadn't been built, or if it had been built differently, the earthquake would have done little or no damage. Intuitively speaking, the building of the fence, or of Lisbon, is merely a condition of the accident.

Although the distinction between causes and conditions is difficult to resist, it isn't sharp enough to underwrite the libertarian position. Any account of causation that will be adequate to account for the distinction between causes and mere conditions in scientific and commonsense explanations will, in virtue of that very adequacy, fail to identify causes with the specificity the libertarian needs. The legal account of causation requires uniqueness, but ordinary causal explanations do not. Merely being part of the broader causal story is not sufficient to establish one person's responsibility, because the problem of too many causes remains. Though we may be tempted to say that action is at least a necessary condition for responsibility, there are indefinitely many actions that led up to the harm in question. Why isolate one as "the" cause?

Any account of causation appropriate to nonlegal contexts needs to accommodate the fact that in ordinary discourse, the distinction between causes and conditions is contextual and malleable. For example, in some circumstances, we might say that a match was caused to ignite by being struck, taking the presence of oxygen to be merely a background condition. In other, less familiar, circumstances, such as a research laboratory that was supposed to be oxygen-proof, we might say that the presence of oxygen was the cause. Unusual circumstances might likewise lead to the conclusion that your injury was caused by your wandering onto a construction site, rather than by my dropped hammer. Again, while Candide might have been wrong about Lisbon, if an earthquake strikes Los Angeles, and the only buildings that collapse are ones that were poorly designed, an insurance adjuster might sensibly identify the way the buildings were built as the cause. And, for that matter, we can give different answers to causal questions about the same event, depending on our interests. The malleability of the distinction reflects the deeper fact that the two causal explanations are not incompatible. The person who claims that striking caused the match to ignite and the one who claims it was the presence of oxygen do not disagree about causation. The various factors they cite are not competing candidates, but complementary parts of a complete explanation. At most, they disagree about what is interesting about the situation of which both seek to make sense. And neither would declare the other's purported explanation irrelevant – the very fact that enables Pascal and Coase to claim that causation is reciprocal.

Now if our concern is with responsibility, we might use a responsibility-specific conception of causation, as Hart and Honoré developed in their *Causation in the Law*. Their analysis[16] is of little help to the libertarian, though, as it focuses on tracing the causal consequences of independently identified wrongdoing. Since the libertarian hoped to explicate the notion of wrongdoing in terms of causation, Hart and Honoré are no help. Causation provides no leverage in distinguishing plaintiff from defendant, unless we already have some other way to distinguish them.[17]

2.4.3 Commonsense Causal Claims

Alternatively, the libertarian might insist that liability be assigned on the basis of what would seem like the most natural causal explana-

---

[16] H. L. A. Hart and Tony Honoré, *Causation in the Law*, 2d ed. (Oxford: Oxford University Press, 1985).

[17] This approach poses further embarrassments for the libertarian position. If we tie liability to causation, and causation to what is atypical, the boundaries of a person's activity turn out to depend largely on how many other people engage in it. When white students at the University of Georgia rioted to protest integration, a number of white students screamed insults at the lone black student in a dormitory: "Does she realize she's causing all this trouble?" See Calvin Trillin, "An Education in Georgia," *New Yorker*, July 16, 1963, quoted in Joel Feinberg, "Action and Responsibility" in *The Philosophy of Action*, p. 115. Although many libertarians oppose antidiscrimination laws, presumably few would want to rest any judgments of liability on the claim that the black student caused the riot. More generally, tying causation, and thus liability, to statistical infrequency not only does badly as an interpretation of the idea that people should bear the costs of their choices. It also betrays another idea that libertarians claim to embrace, namely, that of attaching priority to individual liberty to do novel and interesting things.

tion independently of concerns about liability. This is Richard Epstein's strategy in his influential work on strict liability. Epstein suggests that we must narrow our notion of causation to include something less than all cases of "but-for" causation. Instead, Epstein insists, we can look to the clear commonsense paradigms of causation that the law recognizes. He focuses on force, fright, compulsion, and the setting of dangerous conditions as the paradigms of causal connection.[18] These cases of causation are easy to recognize, and appear to be non-reciprocal: If A hits or frightens B, or forces B to hit C, A is active but B is passive. If A sets dangerous conditions, either by leaving a roller skate on a walkway or building an exploding blender, and B stumbles onto them, both are active, but the injury is A's doing, not B's. There are obvious cases in which each of these paradigms operate, in which we can say decisively that A caused B's injury.

Epstein's paradigms are not the only apparent cases of nonreciprocal causation. Why not use Bob Dylan's more comprehensive list? I might compete with you, beat or cheat or mistreat you, simplify you, classify you, deny, defy or crucify you.[19] All of these things I might do are ways in which I could cause harm to you. Some of these are plausible grounds of liability, others not. Without an account of the obviousness of Epstein's paradigms, we are in danger of losing sight of what makes them obvious. The point isn't that causation's reach can't be appropriately narrowed, but that the paradigms are not themselves self-interpreting. There are clear and uncontroversial instances of legal causation, but they are clear precisely because of the role of uncontroversial cases of inappropriate boundary crossings by one party and not the other.

The problem for Epstein's analysis is that whether or not causation is reciprocal, interaction surely is. Epstein's paradigms have the right grammatical form, but nothing more. Interaction is always reciprocal in the way that his account needs to avoid. "A injured B" requires both A and B. If we cast causal claims in the form "A changed B," rather than "A interacted with B," we have already sorted A and B into active and passive. What we need, however, is some principled basis for doing so. An analysis of their interaction might lead to the conclusion that one was active and the other passive, but we need to

---

[18]   Epstein, "A Theory of Strict Liability."
[19]   Bob Dylan, "All I Really Want to Do." Dylan also mentions other possibilities: "fight with you, frighten you or uptighten you" and "select you, dissect you, inspect you or reject you."

determine what each contributed to the interaction before we can reach any such conclusion. That is, the inquiry Epstein's appeal to causation was supposed to avoid comes up again in the distinction between activity and passivity.

The core of the problem is that Epstein's analysis requires that an injury must have only one cause. Otherwise we are back in the world of Coasean indeterminacy. The problem is most evident in his paradigm of fright. Epstein insists that a *prima facie* case requires only that A frightened B, and does not depend on how sensitive B was. Thus, there is no occasion for asking about the reasonableness of B's response. All we need to know is whether A caused B's fright. Yet careful examination of the distinction reveals that this is anything but straightforward. Suppose you are frightened by my smile. To say that you are frightened by my smile is to say that my smile is at least a but-for cause of your fright. Since Epstein's concern is with a non-reciprocal concept of causation, the question of whether I frightened you or you frightened yourself depends on further inquiries. To answer such a question, a court needs to know such things as whether my smile would have frightened others, whether you are unusually sensitive, and so on. In other words, we must ask something that looks very much like a question about the reasonableness of your reaction.

Epstein concedes that inquiries about both parties to an injury will often be unavoidable, but maintains that such inquiries are purely evidential. Yet it is difficult to know what that claim could mean. In order for them to be evidential, there would need to be some independent matter of fact for which they are evidence. The evidence seems more to constitute the fact than uncover it, though.[20] A commonsense causal explanation would allow that *both* my smile and your sensitivity among the causes of your fright, and would reach that conclusion no matter how menacing my smile or fragile your disposition. Both are required, and they must interact in the right way. Having abandoned ordinary causal explanations, though, Epstein needs something more robust. Further inquiries about my smile or your sensibility might establish that my smile was a but-for

---

[20] In Chapter 5, I consider the parallel claim made in the context of the criminal law, according to which reasonableness tests merely provide evidence of whether someone believed what they said they did. That claim has problems of its own, but at least the question of whether someone believed something appears to be independent of the behavior of others. By contrast, whether someone caused something or reacted to an external cause does not even seem to be determinate.

cause of your injury. Finding out that my smile was a but-for cause is not trivial; we might, for example, conclude instead that you would have reacted in the same way without my smile, that my smile coincided with a peculiar metabolic or allergic reaction on your part. Short of that, though, it would not show that it was or was not "the" cause. Even if we know that you would not have been scared at that very second, we still do not know whether my smile was enough to frighten you, or whether instead it was merely the occasion for your inner fears to express themselves. Epstein's analysis precludes us from saying that it was both, but the only way to decide seems to be to consider whether you *should* have been more resistant – precisely the inquiry that Epstein's analysis was supposed to avoid.

The same point applies to the paradigm of force. If I bump into you on the street, and you drop your valuable parcel, in order to establish liability, we need to know whether my bump or your clumsiness was the cause of the dropped parcel. We can only establish that through inquiries parallel to those in the case of fright: Are you unusually clumsy? How hard did I bump you? How were you holding your parcel? If your parcel was balanced on your head as I brushed against you in a crowded subway car, I did knock over your parcel, but further questions need to be asked. Again, these inquiries seem not to identify a single cause; instead, they either simply determine whether I was the but-for cause (would you have dropped it anyway?) or else serve to show who is behaving unreasonably. Force and fright are paradigmatically causal in just those cases in which they are unambiguously wrongful.[21]

These difficulties come to a head in Epstein's fourth paradigm, the setting of dangerous conditions. The line between dangerous and safe conditions cannot depend on whether the defendant could have made them safer, on pain of falling back into Pascal's world. *All* conditions impose risk, and all conditions could be made safer if people are willing to try hard enough. What needs to be done to make conditions safer depends in part on what those who find themselves in the conditions can be expected to do. The defendant always could have done something, and the plaintiff virtually always could have avoided them. In any case in which two parties are involved, the one who was not "active" in Epstein's sense can be thought of as having

---

[21] Epstein's third paradigm, compulsion, combines force and fright, and so needs no independent analysis: We need to determine whether the person acting under compulsion was compelled or simply acted out of his own fears.

contributed to creating the conditions in which the active party acted. As you walk past my house, you create the conditions within which my dropping the hammer is dangerous. But of course not all conditions in which injuries occur in fact are dangerous in the requisite sense. The line can only be drawn in terms of some idea of how dangerous conditions are allowed to become.

It is important that the difficulty for generalized strict liability is not that there are no principled ways of deciding which but-for causes are grounds for liability. I will develop one such way in the chapters that follow. The point is that any principled distinctions will involve the very sorts of inquiries the libertarian had hoped to avoid, inquiries into the conditions under which someone is responsible for their actions, and the degree of care we owe each other.

Most of these criticisms of generalized strict liability are by now familiar.[22] One might wonder why its appeal persists despite what strike many as obvious problems. One answer is that the libertarian's root concern is with the idea of self-ownership. The idea of self-ownership is the product of interpreting a causalist conception of responsibility in terms of the idea of property. Since (it is supposed) we own ourselves, any harm that one person does another must be thought of on the model of a person (or piece of property) straying onto another person's property. If I trespass on your land, it does not matter whether I was being careful – I still need to leave. The libertarian wants to generalize this idea to cover all of tort law – I'm liable if I harm you, regardless of how careful I was being. If I cross your boundaries, I'm liable, regardless. But the very thing that makes the project initially appealing is also its fatal flaw. Even if we stick to metaphors of borders and boundary crossing, we need some independent account of where the boundaries between persons are to be drawn. Causation cannot provide the basis for such a distinction, since it requires that the distinction already be drawn.

2.5 RISKS

The difficulties posed by the reciprocity of interaction reflect the fact that almost anything anyone might do makes some types of injury

---

[22] In particular, Stephen Perry has underscored the pervasive problems of indeterminacy that plague Epstein's defense of strict liability. Stephen Perry, "The Impossibility of Generalized Strict Liability," 1 *Canadian Journal of Law and Jurisprudence* 235 (1988). See also Richard Wright, "Causation in Tort Law," 73 *California Law Review* 1752 (1985).

more likely, and other types less likely. That is why both parties make causal contributions to injuries. In the face of risk, everything anyone does can be seen as active in Epstein's sense. The problem of risk cannot be addressed without an account of reasonable behavior.

Nozick's defense of libertarianism seems to be attuned to the problem of defining boundaries in the face of risk. Nozick acknowledges that "no natural law theory has yet specified a precise line delimiting people's natural rights in risky situations,"[23] and goes on to give a qualified endorsement to Charles Fried's suggestion that people would allow each other to impose "normal" risks on each other. Unfortunately, the specification of such risks runs into one of two difficulties. On the one hand, it may require substantive judgments about the importance of various liberty and security interests, and so abandon the libertarian quest to clearly demarcate the sphere of boundary crossings. This requires abandoning the language of "liberty" in favor of talk about specific liberties. Specific liberties are not alone in their importance, though. They also need to be weighed against competing interests that others have in security, which cannot itself be defined in purely spatial terms. Alternatively, the libertarian could adopt Fried's declared approach, and regard "normal" as meaning "typical." Putting aside the difficulties any such account has in making sense of such banal claims as "evaporation causes cooling" or "eating causes weight gain," it is of no use to the libertarian. What counts as unusual will often depend on the circumstances and the purposes of the inquiry. If you are hopping on one foot or doing cartwheels when I drop the hammer on you, your eccentric behavior is unusual, but that does not relieve me of liability. If you live in a dangerous neighborhood where few people venture out after dark, your assailant is responsible for your injury, even though your behavior was ill-advised. Thus, any account that ties liability to infrequency will lose contact with both the idea of liberty and the intuitive idea that people should bear the costs of their activities. Those whose behavior is eccentric will count as creators of injuries; those who run with the crowd will not. As a result, the idea that people should bear the costs of their activities will also give way to the less attractive idea that only those who are innovative should bear the costs they create. Either way, the two routes out of indeterminacy both give up on the idea of a system of natural liberty in favor of either judgments about the importance of

---

[23]   Nozick, *Anarchy, State and Utopia*, p. 75.

various activities or a conventionalism about existing ways of doing things.

These difficulties of formulation do not simply undermine the libertarian emphasis on strict liability. They also show a deeper and more significant feature of historical theories of justice. The idea of a historical theory of justice is that given starting conditions that are not themselves unjust, and interactions that do not involve boundary crossings, the resulting outcomes are themselves just (or at least not unjust). A historical theory of justice requires more than a specification of property rights; it requires a way of protecting them in a world of risks. Not just any way will do, however. If people are to bear the costs of their choices in a world with risks, the boundary between what is and is not a cost must be defined in terms of those risks. Both the starting point and the boundaries must be defined in terms of those risks. So too must the "steps" between holdings. In order for transactions in such a world to be justice-preserving, we need some prior understanding of a fair distribution of risks. Some of the risks, as I will show in the next section, are risks of injury that attend many ordinary activities. In the chapters on criminal law, I will argue that risks of mistakes about the boundaries of rights against intentional wrongdoing require a parallel treatment. And in the final chapter, I will argue that such an account calls for holding certain risks and misfortunes in common.

A world of risks requires some conception of fair starting points *other* than that given by the idea that people own themselves. The fairness of the starting point, in turn, may need to be readjusted for cases in which actions that are not themselves otherwise unjust may aggregate to produce injustice.[24] An historical account of justice is not an account of a game with only one round, but of fair terms of interaction across generations. The idea that people should bear the costs of their activities is not the same as the idea that the sins (or bad judgment) of the parent (or grandparent) should shape the child's fortunes. Nor is an historical account of justice one in which those who lose in the first "round" must accept whatever terms others offer them. I will argue in the last chapter that unless people are left with adequate resources and opportunities, their actions do not bear a sufficiently close relation to their consequences. The point for now is that the idea that the justice of outcomes depends on how they come about need not be welcoming to the libertarian's more general political agenda.

---

[24] Cohen, *Self-ownership, Freedom, and Equality*, pp. 42 ff.

Deciding which risks belong to whom requires facing questions of substantive political morality. The core libertarian idea of self-ownership spreading itself onto unowned objects only makes sense if we abstract away from the existence of risks. Perhaps some find it helpful to talk about some Robinson Crusoe in a state of nature appropriating a previously unowned *thing*. Although there are substantive issues of political morality surrounding the question of which sorts of use are normatively significant, we can coherently suppose that a piece of land or natural object enters the stream of human interaction only when persons make use of it. If nobody does anything in relation to a plant or a piece of land, nobody's interests are affected in relation to it. Hence, whatever the problems of conceiving appropriation in this way, supposing that unused things are unowned is at least a candidate for a default position. By contrast, the idea of appropriating previously unowned *risks* does not even appear to make sense. If nobody does anything in relation to some risk – say, the risk of a flood or fire, to keep the examples suitably Lockean and agrarian – the risk to others is still there. The risks must already lie somewhere if we are to go on to talk about how various intentional actions create or shift those risks.

Now it might be thought that the impetus for the libertarian position is precisely in a default position of this sort, with the idea all risks lie with those injured by them, unless they are created by someone else. But that default position is precisely what is unavailable because of the problems of indeterminacy. Until we know where the background risks lie, we cannot say who has done what. As we've seen, virtually all injuries involve a variety of antecedent human actions without which they would not have happened.

And although I have so far spoken of risks of bad luck, the same considerations apply to questions of where chances of good fortune lie. For example, it is a question of substantive morality, rather than natural fact, whether owning a piece of land must also include owning the mineral rights underneath. More generally, the concept of self-ownership on its own cannot fix which good and bad fortune belongs to whom. One thing is clear. There is no way of drawing boundaries around risks in terms of natural causation, because the risks of causing things are even more indeterminate than the fact of causing things. There are too many chances involved in any outcome to simply assign those chances on the basis of some natural feature. Of course we might *pick* some natural feature to mark which chances belong to whom, just as we use natural features such as rivers or mountains to draw boundaries between states. The point is that natural features will not select themselves for us. We need some rationale for picking the particular features we do.

2.6 HISTORICAL JUSTICE WITHOUT LIBERTARIANISM

The idea of historical distributions is too powerful an idea to be left to libertarians. So too is the idea that liberty is important, and that people should be left to make their own arrangements insofar as possible. Libertarians go wrong in supposing that these ideas can be applied in a vacuum, that they can be made sense of apart from an inquiry into the conditions under which it is fair to hold people responsible for their choices. They also go wrong in moving from the plausible claim that the justice of a distribution depends on how it comes about to the conclusion that the justice of a distribution depends only on that. Once we get beyond those ideas, there is much that is appealing in the libertarian focus on liberty and agency. There is also much that is appealing in the idea that holdings are of interest to a theory of distribution because of the ways in which people can use them. Not all sources of dissatisfaction count as injuries in need of compensation. But we can only do justice to these ideas by spelling out the context of equality within which liberty gets its claim.

The idea that people come to own misfortunes they wrongfully create is also worth developing in a nonlibertarian way. In the next chapter, I will offer an interpretation of the fault system in light of the idea of owning risks and losses. Rather than analyzing boundary crossings into causation, the fault system explains the importance of causation by defining the boundaries that are relevant to attributions of responsibility. Causation turns my failure to exercise appropriate care into a wrongful crossing of your boundary. Without fault, causation does not signify a wrongful boundary crossing; without causation, crossing my boundary does not mean I have crossed yours.[25] That account begins with the idea of a fair division of risks, and explains tort liability in terms of the imposition of additional risks. Those who impose additional risks can be thought of as owning the risks. If those risks

---

[25] Boundaries between persons can be specified without supposing that all crossings are wrongful. The advantage of the vocabulary I have adopted is that any such specification of boundaries is irrelevant to issues of responsibility and liability.

ripen into injuries, they own the injuries, and the payment of damages serves to return those injuries to their rightful owners.

The notion of ownership involved in talk about various people owning various injuries and misfortunes is not the libertarian conception of full ownership, however. That strong idea of ownership must give way for the same reasons as did strict liability: The libertarian idea of ownership is indeterminate in a world of risks. The idea that people own themselves, or own various injuries, requires an independent and conceptually prior account of the normatively appropriate distribution of risks. Once that account has been provided, talk of people owning risks and misfortunes is simply a way of spelling out the idea expressed in such familiar idioms as "that's not my problem." Providing an account of a fair division of risks is the task to which we must now turn.

Chapter 3

A Fair Division of Risks

At the end of the last chapter, I suggested that the idea that a distribution can be justified by the process that produced it is too important to be left with libertarians. This chapter fills out one element of that idea by offering an alternative to strict liability in tort. The libertarian concern with strict liability arose out of the recognition that an account of justice that treats voluntary transactions as justice-preserving requires a way of undoing *wrongful* changes. The point of an historical account is that not all changes to a pattern of holdings disturb its justice. But some do. Thus, an account of fair terms of interaction must specify which changes need to be remedied, and the appropriate remedy when those changes occur.

Negligence is the primary basis of tort liability in Anglo-American legal systems. Negligence liability serves to undo those losses that result from a failure to take appropriate care. The intuitive idea is that my responsibility for my negligence extends only to the negligent aspects of my conduct. In failing to live up to a standard of care, I act as though the legally protected interests of others are mere things. In so doing, I make the risk to them part of my agency. Because the risk is mine, and whether or not it ripens is a matter of causation, causation fixes both the existence and extent of my liability. That is, the injuries I cause are mine because responsibility flows back to me through the effects of my deed; causation acts as a conduit for my agency. Damages then serve to make the notional transfer real, to place the injury with the person with whom it properly belongs. In tort, the magnitude of the plaintiff's loss is the appropriate measure of the magnitude of the defendant's liability, and it is the loss that must be returned to its proper bearer.

Standard treatments of negligence organize the issues under four heads: The duty of care, remoteness, the standard of care, and the measure of damages. The duty of care concerns the agents to whom care is owed. Thus, I have to look out for the risk that my fire will spread to your yard, but I do not need to look out for the chance that my business will lure customers away from yours. Questions of remoteness concern the injuries for which those who breach their duty of care are liable. The standard of care determines how careful I must be with regard to protected interests. Even if I must look out for your interest in avoiding bodily injury, I am allowed to ignore some risks to your safety. The measure of damages sets the remedy to which you are entitled If you are injured as a result of my failure to take appropriate care.

My interpretation of fault liability shares with libertarianism the view that rights and remedies must be defined together, but interprets it in light of the broadly Kantian idea that the boundaries of individual rights are given by fair terms of social interaction. Thus, the boundaries between persons are given by a concern for equal liberty and security for all. Taken together, these ideas lead to the conclusion that, for purposes of liability, the distinction between what someone does and what merely happens is a normative distinction. Provided I exercise appropriate care, the consequences of my actions are treated as though they merely happened. If I fail to exercise appropriate care, though, the risks I create are mine to bear, and if they ripen into injuries, I must bear the costs of those injuries. The distinction is for purposes of liability only. The person who exercises appropriate care still acts, but is not liable for the injuries those acts might cause.

The fault standard holds agents responsible in a way that aims to be fair to both the injurer and the injured party. Each has a liberty interest in going about his or her own affairs, and a security interest in being free of injury. Pursued to their limits, these interests are bound to conflict. An unlimited interest in security would prevent others from acting, because virtually all action creates a risk of injury. Conversely, an unlimited interest in liberty would make the security of one person hostage to the choices of others. Either of these approaches would violate the fundamental principle of equality, which requires that one party may not unilaterally set the terms of interaction. The solution is to find an *acceptable* level of risk, protecting the liberty and security of all equally. The only way such a solution can be provided is by resisting the libertarian's one-dimensional language of liberty in favor of the idea that people have legitimate interests in particular liberties, not in liberty as such.

3.1 DIVIDING RISKS

Virtually all activities carry some risk of injury. The fault system serves to divide those risks fairly. It does so by supposing that all have interests in both liberty and security. The interest in liberty requires a protected space for freedom of action, the ability to carry out one's purposes in the world. The interest in security requires that the limits be imposed on the actions of others. To make injured plaintiffs bear the full risk of injury would forego the interest in security, and return us to the Hobbesian state of nature in which each person's security is wholly vulnerable to the liberty of others. To make injurers bear the full risk would forego the interest in liberty, and we would return to the problem of strict liability, in which each person's liberty is wholly subject to the vulnerability of others.

The fault system avoids the extremes of strict liability and the Hobbesian state of nature by dividing the risks between potential injuries and those who are potentially injured. The basic strategy for dividing risks is to look to the interests in both liberty and security that all are presumed to share. If neither liberty nor security interests are to totally cancel the significance of the other, some balance must be struck between them. Rather than trying to balance those interests *across* persons – supposing, in some way, that one person's gain can make up for another person's loss – the fault system balances them *within* representative persons. By supposing that all have the same interests in both liberty and security, the fault system treats parties as equals, by allowing a like liberty and security to all.

The fault system serves to divide risks at two levels. On the one hand, the duty of care – the specification of the interests of others with respect to which one must exercise care – serves to define the equality of the parties. Not all interests are protected from the risk of injury. Only some forms of attachment to particular goods are protected; protecting all economic interests would place too great a burden on the liberty of others.[1] If I could not act unless I was sure that your financial position would not be adversely affected, I could not act at all. Which interests in liberty and security are protected depend on substantive views of the importance of various interests to the ability to lead a life of one's own. Moreover, not all otherwise protected

---

[1] Peter Benson, "The Basis for Excluding Liability for Economic Loss in Tort Law," in *Philosophical Foundations of Tort Law*, edited by David G. Owen (Oxford: Oxford University Press, 1995), pp. 427–58.

interests are protected from all risks. Instead, one must only take precautions against those risks that are "apparent to the eye of ordinary vigilance."[2] Although each person has a protected interest in being free of bodily injury, others need only take precautions with respect to certain ways in which bodily injury might come about. From the perspective of the injured party, all injuries are alike. But from the perspective of the reasonable person, injuries are differentiated in part on the basis of the burden to liberty that precautions against them pose. Each person accepts a certain level of risk in return for a measure of liberty; each accepts a restriction on liberty in return for a measure of security.

The standard of care – the amount of care one must exercise so as to avoid injury to protected interests – also expresses a conception of the parties as equals. Even where interests are protected, the risk of harm to them is divided between potential injurers and those who might be injured. The fault system does not require that unlimited efforts be taken to avoid injuring the protected interests of others. Instead, the risks are divided fairly, asking only that people moderate their activities in light of the interests of others.

Most liberty and security interests are utterly uncontroversial. Security from bodily injury is obviously important, as is the liberty to come and go as one pleases. In order to fill out the idea of protecting people equally, though, a more detailed account is required. The amount of care that is required of a person is set in relation to specific risks. In general, the fact that my activity might cause you some injury is not sufficient to require me to take care. Nor is the fact that my liberty is at stake sufficient to require you to bear risks. Instead, the question is whether or not I exercise appropriate care with respect to specific risks.

A fair division of risks requires that particular risks be assigned to particular activities, or, to be more precise, that they be assigned to activities in contexts.[3] This is a direct consequence of the idea that interaction is reciprocal. The fact that my hammer and your unprotected head meet is the basis of liability on a residential street, but perhaps not on a construction site. In determining where particular risks properly lie, it is important to remember that risks are the product of

[2] *Palsgraf v. Long Island R.R.*, 162 N.E. 99 (N.Y. 1928).
[3] Stephen Perry, "Responsibility for Outcomes, Risks, and the Law of Torts," forthcoming in *Philosophy and U.S. Tort Law,* edited by G. Postema (Cambridge: Cambridge University Press, 1999).

interactions, not of actions as such. This was, it will be recalled, the difficulty faced by the libertarian's attempt to articulate a general scheme of strict liability: No single deed could be identified as *the* cause of an accident, because many acts are necessary for any outcome. Thus, we might treat certain risks associated with driving differently than others, supposing that some are done at the driver's risk, others at the risk of those who might be injured. In so doing, we might think it wise, for example, to assign risks posed to other drivers differently than those posed to pedestrians.

Although patterns of interaction can ordinarily be thought of in terms of the interests of the two interacting parties, the appropriate distribution of risks may sometimes depend on the protected interests of other parties. For example, if a train has two types of brakes, and using one would be safer for its passengers but increase the risks to motorists at level crossings, whereas the other would protect motorists but endanger passengers, some balance must be struck between the railroad's duty to passengers and its duty to motorists.[4] One person cannot disregard the security interests of another simply because doing so would prevent an avoidable injury to some third person. To do so would make one person's vulnerability the measure of another's security, no differently than would generalized strict liability.

Parties engaging in potentially risky activities must show reasonable care for those who might be injured by those activities, not simply for the persons who turn out to be so injured. The abstraction of defining the standard of care in terms of the category of plaintiffs rather than the actual plaintiff follows directly from the requirement of treating the parties as equals. Each is required to show appropriate regard for the interests of others. Although fairness between the parties is the central issue in apportioning the risk, the relation between the parties is itself a microcosm of the more general relationship of equality in which all are supposed to stand. Sometimes injuries will still occur; allowing liberty its place requires that some risks lie where they fall. Provided that everyone takes only such risks as she is entitled to take, all injuries will properly lie where they fall. Here too the aim is to give expression to the twin ideas of moderating one's claims in light of the legitimate claims of others and of bearing the costs of one's own activities. Those who moderate their activities in light of the interests of others do not create increased

---

[4] *Lucchese v. San-Francisco-Sacramento R.R. Co.*, 289 P. 188 (California, 1930).

risks. The idea of responsibility thus carries with it an idea of responsible agency. In order to be a responsible agent, one must be able both to pursue one's own ends and to moderate one's claims in light of the legitimate claims of others.

That is, the fault standard defines a situation of equality between the parties, and the payment of damages restores that equality.[5] The defendant is selected to pay the costs because it is the defendant's deeds that have violated equality. That violation of equality is a problem because of its effects, and the appropriate remedy is to undo those effects. Provided that the more general relation of equality is preserved through each person's exercise of appropriate care, there is no need for any party to restore the losses of another. Again, if someone fails to exercise appropriate care, but no injury results, there is no need to compensate, because the failure does not affect anyone's holdings. The need for compensation only arises if an injury results from one party's failure to show appropriate care. In such circumstances, compensation serves, as far as possible, to undo the effects of that failure.

3.2   RISKS AND OUTCOMES

An account of the fault standard must do two things: First, it must offer a principled account of the kinds of behavior that are unreasonable. Second, it must explain why liability for damages is the appropriate remedy. In this section, I offer an account of both in terms of the idea that the person who exposes another to a risk "owns" the risk, and if the risk ripens into an injury, that person owns the injury. The basic idea is simple: In assigning liability, the fault system determines whose problem a certain loss is. When a risk ripens into an injury, the injury belongs to whomever the risk in question belongs. Reasonable

---

[5]   Although much of my account of the structure of negligence law follows Ernest Weinrib's important work in *The Idea of Private Law* (Cambridge: Harvard University Press, 1995), I do not seek to ground it in an account of the will, or articulate the equality of the parties to a tort in terms of the abstract capacity for self-determination with respect to which persons are in fact equal. Indeed, I do not mean to offer a "grounding" in that sense at all. Instead, the equality of the parties is defined in terms of the representative reasonable person, who has interest in both liberty and security. An abstract account of the concepts of both the will and the capacity for self-determination implicit in negligence law could perhaps be distilled from the account I offer. Far from providing a foundation for corrective justice, though, any such abstract account would be derivative of the justificatory apparatus of fair terms of interaction. On the derivative status of the will in Weinrib's own account, see Martin Stone, "On the Idea of Private Law," 9 *Canadian Journal of Law and Jurisprudence* 235 (1996).

risks – those risks the imposition of which is compatible with appropriate regard for the interests of others – lie where they fall. Unreasonable risks belong to those who create them; as a result, the injuries that result from unreasonable risk imposition belong to the injurers. Since they are the injurer's problem, the injurer must make them up. Hence, damages provide the remedy.

As I said at the end of the previous chapter, the vocabulary of ownership is potentially misleading here; my use of it is meant to draw attention to a familiar point. When confronted with an accidental injury, tort law asks whose problem it is. Just as we can say that an injury is one person's problem and not another's, so we can say that a risk is one person's risk and not another's. When a warning on an unattended beach says, "Swim at your own risk," no puzzling claims are being made about property rights in risks. When I speak of one person owning a risk, I mean nothing more puzzling.

The allocation of risks can be thought of as part of the specification of fair terms of interaction. As we saw in our discussion of the libertarian's distinction between patterned and historical theories of justice, distributive justice is best thought of not as a theory of particular holdings at a given time, but rather as a specification of fair terms of interaction prior to particular interactions. That requires the distribution of rights as well as resources. Thus, if a number of people start out with equal shares of material resources, and fair opportunities (whatever exactly that might mean), other things being equal, there seems to be no basis for objecting to the justice of the outcomes of any voluntary exchanges we might make. To be sure, other things are almost never equal. For the present chapter, the most important respect in which things are unequal is that accidents sometimes create losses. Other things are unequal in other ways as well. Indeed, I shall argue in Chapter 9 that periodic redistribution is necessary in order to protect the conditions of agency that are themselves the precondition of responsibility for the consequences of one's acts. Still, the idea that fair transitions from a fair starting point lead to fair consequences has considerable appeal, for it gives expression both to the idea that people should moderate their claims in terms of the legitimate claims of others and to the idea that people should bear the costs of their activities.

The fault system has two roles in filling out this idea of fair interaction from fair starting points. First, it gives content to the idea that people should moderate their claims in light of the interests of others. People should not, and cannot, avoid imposing some risks on others; the fault system serves to distinguish acceptable from unacceptable risks. Second, it provides the grounds for undoing the injuries that result from unacceptable risks.

Now imagine that as well as assigning rights and resources, we have also somehow determined where various familiar risks lie. As we saw in the last chapter, no assignment of rights and resources is possible except against the background of an assignment of risks. That is, in order to specify which interests are protected, we must also specify the risks against which they are protected. The risks that are assigned in this way are specific risks of particular injuries, rather than either total amounts of risk across a lifetime or some general schedule of benefits and burdens, discounted for their likelihood. The risk of bodily injury through negligence or of damage to one's property as a result of particular acts of others is assigned. The risk of having one's life go well or badly is not.

Such an assignment of risks must not be understood as the provision of a certain level of security to everyone in the society. Whatever might be said for such an approach to risk, and whatever might be done to make it workable,[6] this is not the suggestion I am making. Although everyone does enjoy the same protected liberty and security interests, their actual level of security may vary. Nor is it a matter of the libertarian's provision of a certain level of liberty to all. Nor is security protected only in cases where risk imposition is nonreciprocal.[7] Taken alone, the idea of reciprocity has no necessary upper bound, and might in principle allow important security interests to give way to unimportant liberties, provided that all are free to take them.[8] Instead, specific liberty interests and security interests are protected, based on a conception of their importance to leading an autonomous life. Thus, risks are distributed in light of the interests that all have in both liberty and security. Risks that result from the acceptable exercise of liberty lie where they fall; risks beyond that lie with those who create them.

The specification of important liberty and security interests and a fair division of risks generates a conception of the reasonable person.

---

[6]   Richard Abel, "A Socialist Approach to Risk," 41 *Maryland Law Review* 695 (1982). Abel argues that risks, including those associated with dangerous work, should be fairly and equally distributed in a society. Central to Abel's account is the claim that risks are not tradeable. Thus, the willingness to take on extra risks in return for money (as do both insurance companies and workers performing dangerous tasks) is ruled out on Abel's account.

[7]   George P. Fletcher, "Fairness and Utility in Tort Theory," 85 *Harvard Law Review* 537 (1972).

[8]   For example, driving at high speeds might threaten security without violating reciprocity, provided that people all expose each other to the same unreasonable risk.

The reasonable person is, as always, the person who moderates his or her actions in light of the legitimate claims of others. Applied to circumstances of risk, the reasonable person does not expose others to more risk than is reasonable in light of fair terms of cooperation. The basic strategy is the one I outlined in Chapter 1: We look to the liberty and security interests of representative persons – the reasonable person – and protect all equally with respect to those interests. To protect all equally requires weighing liberty against security, but any weighing is done within the representative reasonable person, rather than across persons. The point of weighing interests within a representative person is to avoid allowing the particularities of one person's situation to set the limits of another's liberty or security. Each of us is presumed to have the same interests in both liberty and security. People may disagree about the importance of various liberties and security interests. Those disagreements are about particular interests in liberty and security, not about the relative importance of liberty or security in general. The law does not, and could not, protect a general interest in liberty (understood as doing as one pleases) or security (understood as being free of the unwanted effects by others). Instead, certain specific interests are protected.

A fair distribution of risk is a general matter, but courts are called on to decide liability in specific cases. The reasonable person provides the standpoint from which the general distribution of risks can be applied to particular circumstances. Just as the background distribution of risk is tied to the importance of protected interests in both liberty and security, so the reasonable person moderates his or her behavior in light of the importance of those interests. Thus, in deciding liability, courts must decide whether a person showing appropriate regard would have taken a particular risk into account.

Suppose that given a background distribution of risks, one person behaves unreasonably by exposing another to some further risk. In such a situation, the person who imposes the risk can be thought of as doing so at his or her own risk. Just as I am responsible for my own injury if I take risks with my own safety, so your injury becomes my problem if I take undue risks with your safety. Either way, if an injury occurs, the costs of the injury properly lie with the person who created the risk. If no injury results, the risk imposer is just lucky, for there is no injury to make up. It is because the injury is the injurer's problem that the injured party has a right to repair. Should the injured party fail to seek damages, the loss will not be returned to the person to whom it belongs. This poses no problems from the point of view of risk ownership; the injured party need not exercise the right to be relieved of the loss (any more than anyone else need enforce their private rights against another person). The idea of risk ownership explains why there is a right the injured person may enforce, not why the injured person must enforce it.

Particular liberty and security interests are protected. As a result, only particular risks are distributed. As a result, only some consequences of risk imposition will be significant. If one person exposes another to a risk, and that risk ripens into an injury, the injurer is responsible for the injury, even if the injured party turns out on balance to gain some other benefit as a result. If the plaintiff meets a future spouse while hospitalized as a result of an injury, the benefit that the defendant accidentally conferred on her is irrelevant to the assessment of damages. Again, if a negligent driver causes someone to miss a plane, and the plane crashes, leaving no survivors, the negligent driver cannot claim to have conferred a benefit (a saved life) rather than caused an injury (a missed flight).[9] The risk of a plane crash was the ticket holder's risk, not the driver's, and the fact that the driver eliminated that risk is of no more significance to questions of liability than if the driver had made a large gift to the passenger some time before the accident.[10] The readiness to sue in such a case may reflect badly on the plaintiff's character. From the point of view of liability, such matters are irrelevant.

The idea that those who fail to exercise appropriate care own the risks they create accounts for the fault system's characteristic approach to questions about the duty of care, the standard of care, and the measure of damages. The duty of care is given by the fair background division of risks – our interests in both liberty and security determine where various types of risks lie. Some interests are not protected against injury, others are. The standard of care is set in the same way: Interests in both liberty and security serve to set the degree of care required in various interactions. When someone fails to take appropriate precautions, the new risk created belongs to them, so the measure of damages is set by the extent of the injury that results from the wrongful risk creation.

---

[9]   See the discussion of this issue in Ernest Weinrib, "Right and Advantage in Private Law," 10 *Cardozo Law Review* 1283 (1989), and Bruce Chapman, "Wrongdoing, Welfare and Damages: Recovery for Non-Pecuniary Loss in Corrective Justice" in Owen (ed.), *Philosophical Foundations of Tort Law*, pp. 409–26.

[10]   Someone who would turn around and sue someone who has conferred a benefit in that way may not be an admirable character, but that is a separate issue.

Understanding tort law in terms of ownership of risks and injuries lets us see why money damages would be an appropriate remedy to a wide range of injuries. Commentators have puzzled over how a sum of money can really serve to make up for a bodily injury, emotional loss, or pain and suffering.[11] The person who is injured and unable to work is entitled to money damages to make up for lost income. Missing work may have other social and emotional costs that do not fall under the head of lost income, costs that are at best very difficult to make up in monetary terms. As a result, money is an imperfect means of making it as though an injury had never happened. In that sense, though, nothing could make it as though the injury had never happened. Insofar as the costs of injury cannot be made up, money damages are problematic. But insofar as they enable a plaintiff to adapt to his or her situation, money damages are an appropriate way of transferring the loss so that it becomes the injurer's problem to decide how to deal with what is properly his or her loss. The idea that people should bear the costs of their choices requires that the defendant bear the costs of such adjustments as must be made.

Once we understand the fault system as an expression of fair terms of interaction in a world of risks, we can see why it imposes a general requirement on agents that they take into account the costs their actions may impose on others. The question is not whether I am being careful by the standards of what I am doing, but whether I am being appropriately careful in light of my neighbor's interests in security and mine in liberty. The importance of my particular activity enters into defining the appropriate degree of care, by fixing the degree of liberty appropriate to those engaged in that sort of activity. Only this conception of fault can provide an objective measure of the costs of my activity that will enable us to honor the principle that one should bear the costs of one's own activities.

3.3 SOME CONTRASTS

3.3.1 The Learned Hand Test

This understanding of the fault system is importantly different from Judge Learned Hand's influential test for liability, or at least the stan-

---

[11] See, for example, Margaret Jane Radin, "Compensation and Commensurability" 43 *Duke Law Journal* 56 (1994).

dard reading of that test. Hand emphasized the need to balance the costs of accident avoidance against the likelihood and extent of injury. In a case concerning a barge that had broken loose while unsupervised, he offered the following formula for balancing them: "[T]he owner's duty . . . to provide against resulting injuries is a result of three variables: (1) the probability that she will break away; (2) the gravity of the resulting injury, if she does; (3) the burden of adequate precautions . . . if the probability be called P, the injury L; and the burden B; liability depends upon whether B is less than L multiplied by P."[12] Although the test is often translated into monetary terms, it need not be – costs on both sides of the "equation" can include nonmonetary factors.

So understood, Hand might be thought of as pointing to the importance of both liberty and security interests. The dominant reading of Hand's test is at odds with the idea of a fair division of risks, though. On this economic reading, the standard of reasonable care is a standard of individual rationality, which justifies outcomes by their beneficial consequences for the decision maker. If compensating would be cheaper than taking precautions, the injurer is free to regard the costs to others as acceptable side effects of his activities. If it is cheaper to compensate, though, no compensation is needed, because the injurer has taken all of the precautions that *would be* justified by their costs. Those who fail to take more generous precautions are not liable if someone is injured as a result of that failure. This approach has two consequences at odds with the idea of fair division of risks. First, the costs of precautions to the particular tort-feasor are relevant to setting the standard of care he must meet. Thus, if a precaution is particularly difficult in the circumstances, that potentially counts as a reason not to take it. As a result, the security of others is subject to the costs precautions pose for particular injurers. Second, the anticipated extent of damages enters into setting the standard of care. If those who might be injured have smaller incomes to replace, for example, correspondingly less by way of precautions are justified by their costs. On the Hand test, care for the interests of others is only justified when the costs of taking care are less than the costs of compensating injured parties.

On the risk-ownership conception, by contrast, fundamental interests in both liberty and security are protected even in cases where

---

[12]   *United States v. Carroll Towing Co.*, 159 F.2d 169, at 173 (2d Cir. 1947).

compensation would be cheaper than precautions.[13] The idea of the reasonable person allows us to define both the duty of care and standard of care without reference to the extent of damages in any particular case. As a result, reasonable care is defined in terms of fair terms of interaction *in general*. If a security interest is protected against a certain type of risk, that protection is not lost because precautions would be more expensive than compensation on a particular occasion; if a liberty interest is protected, it does not need to be compromised, even if the cost of doing so is low. If injuring someone with a small income to replace would be cheaper than taking precautions, no liability would lie on the economic test, but it would on the reasonableness test. Conversely, my liberty interest in driving my car is protected even in those cases where driving it probably does not make my life any easier or less expensive. And if a security interest is not protected, no questions can even arise about the costs of protecting it.

The fault system thus provides a way of *measuring* costs across persons without *aggregating* them. On the economic test, tort liability serves two distinct purposes. First, it serves as an incentive to take appropriate precautions. Second, it serves to compensate those who are injured so as to provide them with an incentive to sue – thus underwriting the first incentive. Neither incentive is needed when injurers already take such precautions as are justified by their overall costs. Both are needed when the failure to take precautions increases overall accident costs. There is much that is puzzling about such a picture, notably its readiness to leave costs where they lie in just those cases where it would have been more expensive for *the injurer* to take precautions than for *the victim* to bear them. The risk-ownership conception avoids these difficulties because it ties liability to particular risks. Those who create wrongful risks are liable if those risks ripen, even if injuring others was less expensive than being careful would have been.

3.3.2   Insurance

For related reasons, the fault system's conception of risk treats considerations of insurance as secondary to questions of liability. Just as first-

---

[13]   The incentive effects of such an imbalance of costs might lead some to decide to injure and pay rather than take precautions, thus substituting private rationality for public standards of reasonableness. As I explain in Chapter 6, acting on the basis of such reasoning is not only negligent, but forms the basis for punitive damages, for it involves treating the rights of others as tradeable.

person insurance enables people to protect themselves against any losses that they might suffer, so liability insurance allows parties to protect themselves against losses they might be left with as a result of their negligence. Injuries occasioned by wrongful risk imposition belong to the people who wrongfully cause them. If others contract to assume those risks, such contracts and their terms are a matter between the defendant and those with whom such agreements are made, in which the law takes no interest. Conversely, if an insurer has indemnified a plaintiff against a certain loss, the insurer has a right of subrogation against those who negligently injure the plaintiff. Because the insurance contract passes the risk of injury onto the insurer, the insurer can collect from the person to whom the risk properly belongs. If, as is often the case, both plaintiff and defendant have made prior arrangements, litigation will involve the two insurers. That this should be so reflects the way in which the tort system supposes that risks can be owned and traded.

In part because so many suits directly involve insurers rather than the parties to an injury, insurance is sometimes thought to play a more fundamental role in tort liability. Judgments of liability are sometimes thought to rest on questions of which party was in a better position to insure against a category of loss. For example, the law's unwillingness to compensate for the sentimental value a plaintiff attaches to some injured object is sometimes explained in light of the fact that the plaintiff was in a better position to insure against such losses than was the defendant.[14] The idea of fair terms of interaction stands in the way of arguments of this sort on the same two grounds as it rejects the economic interpretation of the Hand test. Just as the Hand test makes judgments of liability depend on whether it would be rational for *this* plaintiff to avoid injuring *this* defendant, rather than asking about the importance of the liberty and security interests to reasonable persons, so insurance arguments look to whether it would be rational for plaintiff or defendant to insure against his kind of loss. The resulting inquiry looks to questions about both plaintiff and defendant that are both too idiosyncratic and too general. They are too idiosyncratic, because the extent to which the plaintiff's security is

---

[14]   See, for example, Alan Schwartz's argument that American product liability laws lead consumers to purchase more insurance than they want. Alan Schwartz, "The Case Against Strict Liability," 60 *Fordham Law Review* 819, 820, 832–40 (1992); "Proposals for Products Liability Reform: Towards a Theoretical Synthesis," 97 *Yale Law Journal* 353 (1988).

protected depends on the particular interests of the defendant who has caused the injury, and the extent of the defendant's liberty is fixed by the particular sensitivities of the plaintiff. Each party is limited in this way precisely because insurance allows parties to protect idiosyncratic interests. At the same time, they are too general, because whether it is rational for a particular person to insure depends on that person's general pattern of activities. Whether a defendant will insure against injuring a certain class of plaintiff depends on the overall likelihood of that defendant causing that type of injury. Those who repeatedly expose others to a similar risk of injury will insure; those who are repeatedly exposed to those risks will insure themselves against injury. Thus, both liberty and security are hostage to the overall patterns of activity of particular plaintiffs and defendants. Making liability turn on which of the parties is in the best position to insure rests on the idea that the loss is the common problem of both parties. Once the loss is thought of in this way, the liberty and security of each depend on the particular situation of the other.[15]

3.3.3   The Disproportion Test

But if the fault system does not reduce reasonableness to overall rationality by aggregating injury and avoidance costs across persons, it also does not require the "disproportion test" sometimes enunciated by English courts. That test supposes that security enjoys a special priority, and so looks only to the danger posed by various acts, and assigns a lesser weight to liberty interests. In *Bolton v. Stone,* Lord Reid, after conceding the importance of the likelihood and severity of injury to fixing the standard of care, said that he did "not think it would be right to take into account the difficulty of remedial measures."[16] Reid later qualified the test, acknowledging that precaution

---

[15] Insurance arguments sometimes take another form, which faces additional difficulties as well. Courts sometimes appeal to the availability of standard types of insurance in determining who should bear the costs of an injury. In *Lamb v. Camden London Borough Council* [1981] QB 625 (C.A.), Lord Denning pointed to the availability of homeowner's insurance to spread the costs of the damage to the plaintiff's home caused when squatters moved in after the defendant's negligence rendered it uninhabitable. Yet in order for such considerations to arise, the regime of legal rights needs to be determined. Insurance contracts ordinarily include a right of subrogation against tort-feasors; pointing to the availability of an insurance policy presumes the absence of liability.

[16] *Bolton v. Stone* [1951] App. Cas. 850, 867 (H. L.) (per Lord Reid). I presume "remedial" here means "risk reducing," rather than the cost of damages.

costs could be taken into account if the costs were large and the danger small.[17]

No such disproportion is appropriate when we consider that both liberty and security interests are always involved in setting the standard of care. Although we might agree with Lord Reid's sentiment that if cricket cannot be played safely, it should not be played at all,[18] other liberty interests may be important enough to justify exposing others to risks. Driving a car safely almost certainly creates greater risks than does cricket. So too do countless other activities. To be fair to Lord Reid, he concedes this, noting that "in the crowded conditions of modern life even the most careful person cannot avoid creating some risks and accepting others."[19] He also couches the disproportion test in terms of the risks a reasonable man would think it right to neglect. A reasonable man, or better, a reasonable person, would not think in the terms suggested by the Learned Hand test, weighing precaution costs against compensation costs. Instead, the reasonable person thinks from the perspective of equality, and takes such care as is required by a like liberty and security for all. Because the only way of increasing the sphere of liberty of defendants is to increase it for all, some genuine and avoidable risks may be disregarded by the test, not because they are mere possibilities or cost-justified, but because the liberty interest at stake is so important.[20]

---

[17]   *Overseas Tankship (U.K.) Ltd. v. The Miller Steamship Pty. Ltd (The Wagon Mound No. 2),* (1967) 1 App. Cas. 617, at 641 (P.C.). On appeal from Australia.

[18]   *Bolton v. Stone* at 867.

[19]   Ibid., at 807.

[20]   Both the Learned Hand test and the disproportion test are potentially misleading, because both talk about the risks that may be disregarded, as though negligence is a matter of consciously considering a risk and deciding whether to ignore it. But the standard of care in negligence law is not centrally concerned with the injurer's state of mind, only with outward behavior. Whether one exposes others to risks through one's voluntary actions is not in the first instance a matter of whether one pays attention to those risks. Instead, it is a matter of the risks one poses. Avoiding risks to others is my problem, but I need not adopt any particular solution to it.

If we think of liability in terms of the economic conception of the Learned Hand test, the difficulties attendant on paying attention would seem to be among the costs to be taken into account in determining the optimal level of precaution. Paying attention is a cost, and like other accident avoidance costs, its expenditure must be justified. However, if we think of liability in terms of a fair distribution of risk, the level of compliance is always incorporated into the standard of reasonableness. The fact that on some particular occasion someone has difficulty complying with a fair standard is not more significant than the fact that someone has difficulty repaying their debts. In each case, it is not up to the particular others with whom they interact to bear the costs of that difficulty.

3.4 EXPLAINING TORT DOCTRINE

In the remainder of this chapter, I show how the ideas of risk ownership and the reasonable person serve to make sense of six important
features of tort law. The first three are respects in which liability is
limited. First, when someone is careless, he is only liable for the injuries that are within the risk that makes his conduct negligent. Second, in certain areas, liability is supposedly "strict," yet it too is limited by the risks that subject the conduct to liability. Third, there is no
liability for risk imposition alone. The remaining three are respects in
which tort doctrine may seem cold and uncaring. First, tort law combines an "eggshell skull rule" according to which an injurer is liable
for the full *extent* of injuries, no matter how unusual such injuries are,
with an "ultrasensitive plaintiff rule" according to which an injurer is
not liable for unusual *types* of injury, no matter how severe those injuries are. Second, the standard of care in tort is objective, so that due
diligence is not a defense to a tort action. Third, tort doctrine draws
a sharp line between nonfeasance and misfeasance, as a result of
which there is no tort duty to rescue. In the next chapter, I use the idea
of reciprocity to explain the concept of responsibility that underlies
the idea of risk ownership. Foreseeability of injury is ordinarily a necessary condition for tort liability; I explain its role in terms of the idea
of publicity. I also explain the role of contributory and comparative
negligence, as well as the attendant distinction between intervening
causes and further links in a causal chain. Some of the explanations I
offer are briefer than others. My purpose in going through all of them
is to point to the explanatory power of the idea of risk ownership. My
discussion also aims to show the sense in which these tort doctrines
reflect an attractive underlying conception of fairness even when
they at first seem cold and unfeeling. Looked at from the perspective
of binary adjudication between two parties, that conception of fairness may appear to leave too many misfortunes where they lie, but,
as I explain in Chapter 9, a fuller application of the same conception

---

Fault liability is not a sort of queer hybrid between strict liability and recklessness (as suggested by Larry Alexander, "Foreword: Coleman and Corrective
Justice," 15 *Harvard Journal of Law and Public Policy,* 621 (1992). Although it is triv-
ially true that all cases of risk imposition involve agents who either did or did
not advert to the risk, it is the risk, rather than the advertense or nonadvertense
to it, that provides the basis for the liability. Negligence liability is defined in
terms of the appropriate distribution of risk, and as such is prior to questions
about the tort-feasor's mental state.

of risk leads to the conclusion that some of those misfortunes should be held in common as part of a larger pool.

3.4.1 The Risk Rule

The idea that those who expose others to risks are responsible for the outcomes they cause has considerable appeal. Kant says that those who do wrong "play a game of chance with the agency of others."[21] Hegel approvingly quotes a German proverb: "The stone belongs to the devil when it leaves the hand that threw it."[22] Hegel's formulation raises an obvious question: Just how much may the devil do with it?

The fault system answers that liability is limited to the risks that make the conduct wrongful. It thus explains why causation matters, and in so doing, it shows when it does. The libertarian view goes astray in supposing causation is sufficient for liability, but not in supposing it is necessary. What actually happens is crucial to tort liability, and causation fixes what does and does not happen. Causation matters because if I fail to exercise appropriate care, I expose others to risks. Since those risks are in some important sense mine, responsibility flows back to me for those risks: Whatever happens as a result is my misfortune. As long as we understand the boundaries between persons in terms of spatial metaphors, it seems as though any boundary crossing must open up unlimited responsibility. But if we understand the boundaries between persons as existing in moral rather than geometric space, we see that the fault system can coherently hold someone liable only for the losses that are within the risk implicit in the violated standard of care. If someone fails to exercise appropriate care with respect to some risk, he or she is liable for any harms following from that particular risk. Because different degrees of care are called for in relation to different activities and different risks, violating a standard of care is not enough to establish liability for consequences that result from unforeseeable causal chains. The particular risk is the basis of liability, and so also controls its extent.

The intuitive appeal of such a limitation on liability is summed up by Judge Hand: "[S]o long as it is an element of imposed liability that the wrongdoer shall in some degree disregard the sufferer's interests,

---

[21] Kant, "On a Supposed Right to Lie from Benevolent Motives," in *Immanuel Kant, Grounding for the Metaphysics of Morals*, translated by James Ellington (Indianapolis: Hackett 1993), pp. 63–7.

[22] G. W. F. Hegel, *Elements of the Philosophy of Right*, translated by H. B. Nisbet (Cambridge: Cambridge University Press, 1991), para. 119A, p. 148.

it can only be an anomaly, and indeed vindictive, to make him responsible to those whose interests he has not disregarded."[23] There is a clear intuitive line between what someone did and what merely happened, by accident, as it were. To hold someone liable for something that happened by accident just because they behaved badly in some other way is indeed, as Hand puts it, vindictive. It is also arbitrary, for liability for consequences unrelated to the wrongdoer's disregard of the sufferer's interests does not fit the wrong done.

The leading case in which this limitation on liability is played out is *Palsgraf*.[24] A platform attendant of the Long Island Railroad pushed a passenger up onto a moving train, while a conductor pulled him up. The combination of pushes and pulls dislodged the passenger's package, which fell onto the third (electric) rail. The package was filled with fireworks, and exploded. As a result of the explosion, a set of scales, at the far end of the platform, fell on the plaintiff, who was standing waiting for a train. The passenger disappeared into the resulting melee; whatever his liability might have been, he (literally) escaped it. The court found it clear that the railroad was not negligent either in failing to inspect all passenger parcels or in keeping scales on the platform. Some may wish to dispute these findings,[25] but I will not. Without them, the central issue does not come into focus. The court held that the railway was, at most, negligent in its treatment of the unidentified passenger. By pushing him, they failed to show appropriate care for his parcel. If he had lost a more ordinary parcel, he would have been entitled to damages for its lost contents. The question was whether the railway was liable for the injuries of Mrs. Palsgraf, to whom it was not negligent. The dissent, by Justice Andrews, held that the railroad was liable, on the grounds that the injury was direct enough to qualify as a "proximate" consequence of the carelessness.[26] Andrews saw that unlimited liability was both unworkable and morally unthinkable, but also supposed that courts are capable of making intuitive judgments about whether an injury was

---

[23] *Sinran et al v. Pennsylvania Ry. Co.*, 62 F. 2d 767 (2d Cir 1932).

[24] *Palsgraf v. Long Island R.R.*, 162 N.E. 99 (NY 1928).

[25] Prosser argues that the facts as described in the case were impossible, and that the scales were almost certainly knocked over by passengers frightened by the explosion. See William Prosser, "Palsgraf Revisited," 52 *Michigan Law Review* 1 (1953).

[26] For Andrews, "proximate" simply means "close enough to count." Andrews explicitly denies that there is a principled way of deciding which of the "ripples" of causation is actionable.

close enough to the wrongdoing. For Andrews, if the injury is close enough, liability lies with the negligent defendant.

Justice Cardozo, writing for the majority, held otherwise, arguing that liability must be limited by the risk that gives rise to the standard of care. As he put it, "negligence in the air" will not do. Negligence must always be directed at someone in particular. That is, the particular risk with respect to which the defendant is negligent is a risk of a particular sort of injury to a particular class of plaintiff. Those who are negligent to one person are not liable for the injuries their negligence nonnegligently causes others. The railroad had no duty to protect Mrs. Palsgraf from scales falling as a result of an explosion. Its breach of a duty to someone else cannot create a duty where there was none before. The force of Cardozo's argument is clear if we consider a variant on the facts of *Palsgraf*. Suppose the unidentified passenger had dropped his package, unaided and unjostled by conductor or platform attendant. It hit the rail and exploded, knocking the scales onto Mrs. Palsgraf. In such a situation, there is no negligence, and thus no liability. Alternatively, suppose the railroad had been negligent, but the package had not contained fireworks. This time there would have been negligence toward the passenger, but again, no liability to Mrs. Palsgraf. Cardozo's point can be summed up as follows: Although Mrs. Palsgraf was injured, she was not wronged by the railroad.

The ruling in *Palsgraf* concerns liability to an unprotected plaintiff. The idea of risk ownership extends the same idea to questions of remoteness, in a way that is consistent with the holding in *Palsgraf*, but not made explicit in it.[27] Liability must also be limited to the *type* of injury as well as the class of plaintiffs the standard of care is meant to protect. Hand's rationale (if not his wording) applies in just the same way: It would be vindictive to hold someone responsible for injuries to interests he has not disregarded, even if he has disregarded *some* security interests. The rationale can be put in any number of ways, but the simplest is a direct consequence of the idea of risk ownership:

---

[27] Cardozo cites *Polemis v. Furness Withy Co.* [1921] K.B. 560 (C.A.), with apparent approval in passing in his opinion. That case involved careless stevedores who dropped a plank, causing vapors in the hold of a ship to explode. Their handling of the plank was careless because of the risk of damage done by the physical impact of the plank. The explosion itself was not foreseeable. The court nonetheless held that the duty was owed to the ship's owners and so they were held liable. On both Cardozo and Hand's explicit formulations, duty is limited to the class of plaintiffs. On the broader construal of the underlying principle developed here, the duty is limited to the type of risk.

Fault differs from other sorts of moral failings because it links the careless person to the injury. By failing to take regard of dangers to you, I become liable for those dangers. Wrongdoers own the wrongful consequences of their deeds, that is, the consequences the risk of which make those deeds wrongful.[28]

Robert Keeton has explained this limitation of liability by pointing out that without a connection between the risk that makes the conduct faulty and the injury that ensues, fault becomes no different from any number of other moral failings.[29] Here the problem that plagued strict liability arises yet again. Almost any injury has causal antecedents that involve people who exhibit moral failings of one sort or another. Were all failings treated as occasions for liability, an adulterer, who drives carefully while on an illicit tryst, would be liable for any injuries accidentally caused, since those injuries would not have happened but for the adultery.[30] The driver who violated the speed limit earlier in the day would be liable for injuries caused later, since without the speeding she would have been elsewhere.[31] The person who gives a child a loaded gun which the child then drops, breaking his toe, would be liable.[32] Simply adding a dimension of moral evaluation as a necessary condition of liability does nothing to solve the problem.[33, 34]

---

[28] What is and is not a part of the original injury is a complicated matter, as we will see in the next chapter. For example, liability always extends to the reasonable responses of others to wrongdoing.

[29] Robert Keeton, *Legal Cause in the Law of Torts* (Columbus: Ohio State University Press, 1963), p. 21.

[30] This is a variant on the story of Sherman McCoy, doomed protagonist of Tom Wolfe's *Bonfire of the Vanities*.

[31] *Berry v. Sugar Notch Borough*, 43 A. 240 (Pennsylvania 1899).

[32] *Restatement (Second) of Torts*, s. 281, illustration 3, American Law Institute, Philadelphia (1965).

[33] Comparative moral evaluation faces other problems as well. It is not clear why the time frame for the evaluation should be limited to the period immediately preceding the injury, nor why the candidates should be limited to the parties to the injury. If the point of awarding damages is to punish the morally worse of the parties, it seems arbitrary to wait for an accident before awarding them.

[34] Kant offers what seems to be an extreme statement of the view that wrongdoers open themselves up to unlimited consequences in his essay "On a Supposed Right to Lie Because of Philanthropic Concerns," in Kant, *Grounding for the Metaphysics of Morals*. Kant considers the example of the person who lies to a murderer who is in search of his intended victim; by lying, the victim's would-be savior may well lead the killer to kill the wrong person by mistake, and, discovering his error, go on to kill the intended victim. In such circumstances, Kant insists that the liar is to blame for the innocent's death. On the other hand, if the lie saves the intended victim, the liar gets no credit. For Kant, the person who lies "plays a game of chance" with another's agency; as a re-

Keeton is right to conclude that the appropriate object of inquiry is the relation between the risk-creating activity and the injury. There is a shorter route to his conclusion, though. We need not isolate fault as a special moral failing. Instead, we can focus on the particular risk that leads to the injury. Those who fail to exercise appropriate care with respect to particular risks act at their peril *with respect to those risks.*[35] If an injury eventuates, it is the careless person's injury. In this sense, injuring others is no different from injuring oneself when engaging in some activity the risks of which lie with those who engage in them. The bungee-jumper acts at his or her own peril, and any injury that results is rightly the jumper's. In the same way, the careless driver acts at his peril with respect to that risk, and so is liable for injuries that result from that risk.

To sum up, the idea of risk ownership ties together questions of duty of care, remoteness, and standard of care. Those who fail to exercise appropriate care are responsible for the injuries of those to

---

sult, he is liable for the bad consequences of that game, including even unforeseeable ones. (In Kant's own example, it is not clear that the consequences could not be foreseen.) So put, the principle has some appeal, as it suggests that one protects oneself against the play of fortune by conducting one's affairs rightfully. And to be fair to Kant, his examples are concerned with deliberate deceit, not mere carelessness. So understood, it fares somewhat better. Deceit involves taking a risk with another's agency, not just with that person's interests; one lies in the hope of being believed. There is something wrong with trying to distance oneself, after the fact, from the consequences of one's deliberate wrongdoing by claiming that one had hoped for better consequences, since one had hoped to be believed by a rational agent who, as a rational agent, acts on his beliefs. Even so, Kant's principle seems too strong.

As a basis of liability, the strong Kantian position is probably also indeterminate in the ways in which strict liability turned out to be. Making those who fail to exercise appropriate care responsible for the full consequences of any wrongful activities makes too many people liable. This is hardly a problem for Kant's *moral* analysis – both the liar and the killer can be criticized on moral grounds.

35   This formulation allows us to repair a difficulty posed by Keeton's explicit formulation in terms of the type of harm the duty is supposed to prevent. As Richard Wright has pointed out, Keeton's formulation focuses on the harm that makes the conduct negligent, rather than on the negligence itself. Wright points to a number of ways in which what would be intuitively classified as coincidences fall within the scope of Keeton's formulation. If a truck carrying explosives causes an explosion by using a radio transmitter near an unmarked blasting site, the transport of explosives causes an explosion, yet plainly falls outside the risk that imposes strict liability for the transport of explosives. See Wright, "Causation in Tort Law," 75 *California Law Review* 1735, 1770 (1985).

The idea of risk ownership avoids these difficulties because those who fail to exercise appropriate care come to "own" the specific risks that make their acts wrongful. They do not face liability for some type of harm.

whom they owed a duty to be careful with respect to some particular risk. The basis of the tort-feasor's responsibility can be modeled on the idea that the risks (of particular types of injuries to a particular class of persons) created through his failure to exercise appropriate care are his, and he must bear the costs they impose.

3.4.2 Strict Liability

The pockets of strict liability that are found in fault-based legal systems can also be explained by the idea of risk ownership. Most of the familiar areas of strict liability can be understood as particular applications of the more general features of the risk ownership conception, even though they are not required by it. Certain recurrent situations of injury arise from activities that are very risky. Courts addressing those cases can be thought of as adopting conclusive presumptions of negligence when injuries ensue from such activities. The idea of fair terms of interaction helps to identify such activities, even though it does not compel classifying them as such. Statutes serve to create areas of strict liability in the same way. Driving above the speed limit, for example, is negligence per se, so that speeding drivers are liable for the injuries they cause. This is so even if the driver can show that he was being careful, even extraordinarily so.

Most areas of strict liability do not impose liability as a matter of supposed moral taint with respect to an injury. Nor is it a matter of simply having caused an injury to others. Instead, it is a matter of exposing the security of others to risk, as a result of which any injuries within that risk that ensue are the injurer's problem. Consider first *Rylands v. Fletcher*,[36] the case that has been taught to generations of torts students as the leading example of strict liability in the nineteenth century. In that case, the defendant's reservoir leaked into mine shafts under the plaintiff's property. The defendant was held liable despite the court accepting that he had exercised considerable care in constructing the reservoir. The decision was cast in terms of a distinction between natural and nonnatural uses, and imposed strict liability for noncustomary uses. Liability for mining or agriculture requires that the plaintiff establish the defendant's fault; liability for unusual activities requires a showing of causation but not negligence. Thus, the defendant can be liable even if he exercised reasonable, or even

---

[36] *Fletcher v. Rylands*, 34 L.J. Ex. 154 (exch) aff'd *sub. nom. Rylands v. Fletcher*, 37 L.J. Ex. 161 (H.L.).

exceptional, care. On second reading, though, the court's reasoning turns out to be considerably more subtle. A landowner must answer for the "natural and anticipated consequences" of keeping something mischievous on his property.[37] For certain types of activities, the danger is sufficiently high so that even extraordinary care cannot eliminate the risk. This is not the same as claiming that the defendant's conduct is wrong in a way that would justify a general prohibition on engaging in it, or even that it is wrong in a way that justifies granting injunctive relief to the plaintiff. Rather, engaging in the conduct is permissible, but any way of engaging in it imposes risks that the person engaging in it must bear. Thus, any costs resulting from the activity must lie with the defendant. The defendant's duty to the plaintiff is defined accordingly. The rationale is to be found in the relatively greater importance of the plaintiff's security interest than the defendant's liberty interest.

So understood, important areas of strict liability involve the same sort of judgments about the importance of various liberty and security interests as does the fault system. If the standard of care is supposed to protect people equally from each other, it cannot leave one person free to choose any activity and then exercise care in relation to that activity. The choice of activities may itself expose others to undue risks, which the risk creator must bear. That idea will sometimes map onto a distinction between customary and noncustomary uses. If almost everyone engages in the same activities, and all have important liberty interests in participating in them, customary ways of doing things will incorporate a standard of care. Noncustomary activities may impose uncharacteristic risks.

The same factors can limit the reach of strict liability in areas in which it is otherwise important. In *Williams v. RCA*, a security guard was injured because his walkie-talkie failed when he was seeking assistance to apprehend an intruder.[38] The court rightly distinguished a case in which the failure of a can of mace was grounds for liability because it was brought into the stream of commerce as a crime prevention device.[39] It held that the manufacturer of the walkie-talkie was not liable for a risk arising in a use for which its product was not designed. Here again, risks are allocated on the basis of various liberty and security interests. In this case, the court held that the defendant's

---

[37] *Fletcher v. Rylands* at 156, per Blackburn, J.
[38] *Williams v. RCA Corp.*, 376 N.E. 2d 37 (Ill. 1978).
[39] *Klagess v. General Ordinance Equipment Corp.*, 367 A. 2d 304 (Pennsylvania 1976).

interest in selling its product did not require it to indemnify all users against all possible risks, despite the general rule of strict liability. Again, consider a variant on *Rylands v. Fletcher:* If your land remains intact but my reservoir lures away the ducks who normally nest in your pond, I am not liable for the costs, even if you are no longer able to attract tourists to your inn.[40]

The limit of liability within the risk is thus not a matter of the wrongdoer being a morally bad person either in general or in the particular case, but rather a matter of her having taken a risk in such circumstances. Since she did not take other risks, the fact that her otherwise risky voluntary actions were among the causal antecedents of other injuries is beside the point. Liability is not a reflection of the wrongdoer's bad character, but of the negligent imposition of particular risks. If the tort-feasor wants to know why she has been selected to pay, we can tell her, "you took a risk with someone else's security and the risk, and its outcomes, are thus yours."[41]

3.4.3 Risks and Remedies: Why Wait?

The idea of risk ownership also serves to explain why no liability arises for the mere imposition of risk. Some have suggested that those who injure and those who merely impose risks are alike in all morally significant respects, and so should incur the same liability. We've already seen that tort liability does not properly reflect overall moral evaluations. Still, the idea that those who differ only by luck should fare equally well or badly is prominent, and its suggested implementation in tort law is worth considering.

---

[40]   *Keeble v. Hickeringill* [1809] 103 Eng. Rep. 1127 (Q. B.).

[41]   The liability of employers for the torts of their employees is also sometimes put forward as an example of strict liability. It is strict in a quite different sense than liability for ultrahazardous activities, however. Employer liability requires negligence; its supposed strictness flows from the fact that the employer cannot defend against a charge of negligence by showing that reasonable care was exercized in selecting the employee. Instead, the law treats the employee's acts as the employer's. That it should do so is not surprising; once we realize that tort liability carries with it its own conception of responsible agency, there is no barrier to supposing that a legal person can be made up of a number of biological persons. Since the duty of care applies to the legal person as a whole, the relevant inquiry about the standard of care looks to the biological person carrying out the particular task. The real puzzle about employer liability is why the law sometimes allows differentiation into several persons via contract. That is the apparent departure from the ordinary ways in which persons are expected to moderate their activities in light of the interests of others.

The most influential exponent of the argument that luck is irrelevant to moral evaluation is Thomas Nagel. Whether I injure you or have simply been careless depends on factors outside my control, and so should not, on Nagel's view, make a difference to my responsibility. Once I have acted, independent causal factors determine what happens. For Nagel, the pervasiveness of "moral luck" is deeply subversive of ordinary moral thought.[42] Although Nagel concedes that chance might be allowed a place in fixing legal liability, he finds its moral role problematic. One response to Nagel's concern is a general skepticism about responsibility; another, tamer response, supposes that people who differ only by luck should be treated alike by the tort system.

Whatever its implications for moral responsibility, more generally, the idea of risk ownership lets us see that Nagel's puzzle poses no problem for tort law. Nagel's argument gets its force from a powerful intuition about justice, the idea that people who are relevantly similar deserve equivalent treatment. So stated, the idea is difficult to resist. The nub of the matter, however, concerns the relevant respects in which people should be thought of as alike. There is a clear sense in which all risk imposers are alike. But whether they are alike depends on what else is at issue. In cases of tort liability, the wrongdoer is not selected to pay because he or she is a bad person, so the fact that others are equally bad is not the relevant basis for comparison. Others may create comparable risks without incurring liability, and others may be morally worse in countless ways while escaping liability. In this respect, negligence liability includes an unavoidable element of chance. As such it is importantly different from many plausible conceptions of blameworthiness, which suppose that the moral quality of an act derives from the agent's will, or perhaps the agent's character that it expresses. The reason is not that tort liability is amoral and arbitrary, but because it asks a specific question about each unwanted injury: Whose problem is it? The injuries that are the main province of tort law are things that nobody wanted to happen, and as a result, there is necessarily an element of luck involved. We can thus restate the question of liability with a question about whose bad luck an injury is. In answering that question, no inquiry into the agent's will or character is necessary, only one into his or her deeds.

The problem for Nagel-inspired proposals in tort law comes in

---

[42]   Thomas Nagel, "Moral Luck," in his *Mortal Questions* (Cambridge: Cambridge University Press, 1979), pp. 24–38.

explaining why the lack of care should be the relevant dimension along which similarly situated people are treated alike. Talk about carelessness and inadvertence may obscure this point, insofar as they suggest that the wrongdoer was thinking in the wrong way. But the standard of care is concerned with whether a person's acts show appropriate regard for the interests of others. The person who is careful may be careful without thinking, and the person who is careless may be so despite trying very hard. The standard of care does not depend on care in that sense, but only on respecting the boundaries of another's agency. Again, if our concern is with an agent's overall moral character, the standard of care is also an unlikely dimension of evaluation. Those who try equally hard may be morally alike in the requisite sense. Those who are equally careful are probably not. Again, if the concern is with the moral evaluation of an agent's will or character, motives would seem to be important. The quality of a tort-feasor's motives does not enter into the assessment of liability, nor would they on any of the proposals that would treat people alike on the basis of their degree of care.[43]

---

[43] Tony Honoré's approach to the supposed arbitrariness of chance merits brief comment. In "Responsibility and Luck: The Moral Issues of Strict Liability," 104 *Law Quarterly Review* 530 (1988), Honoré argues that although the operation of chance is arbitrary, it is not unfair because in the long run, liability for injury has the structure of a fair lottery. Although I may seem to lose disproportionally if I must pay large damages for an injury that I caused through no greater negligence than with which many other people are guilty, I also benefit in all those cases in which I expose others to risks and, through my good fortune, avoid injuring them. Since things tend to even out in the long run, there is, for Honoré, no unfairness in the imposition of liability in particular cases.

Honoré's solution faces two difficulties. First, we might wonder whether it rests on dubious empirical premises. We all know people who just seem to be unlucky and others who enjoy considerable good fortune. To say confidently that the good and bad effects of chance *in general* in a person's life are likely to cancel each other out in the long run is simply too optimistic. (For an example of such optimism, see Daniel Dennett, *Elbow Room: Varieties of Free Will Worth Wanting* [Cambridge, MA: The MIT Press, 1984].) Some people have talents, charms, and wealth. Although not all such fortunate persons end up with happy lives, some do, and even some of those who don't still "seem to have all the luck." In the more specific case of accidents, there are similar reasons to be wary of too much optimism about things evening themselves out. Those who pay large damage awards early in their lives may never get a chance to expose others to further risks. Those who are almost never careless may nonetheless cause a serious and expensive injury on rare occasions.

Second, even if Honoré's empirical assumptions were true, his account would not show that tort liability is to be preferred to any number of alternative regimes. As Joel Feinberg has remarked, Honoré's proposal is reminiscent of Augustine's claim that we are all sinners, so that those who are fortunate

74

3.4.3.1   Why Wait for Injuries?   Now it might be thought that the role of chance is unavoidable, but that if it were administratively feasible, risk creation should be sufficient for liability. In this section and the one that follows it, I argue that it is not. The argument of this section has two parts. I first show that cases in which risk appears to be the basis of liability are actually cases of liability for injuries associated with risk. I then examine a proposal to cancel the effects of chance on liability by holding all risk creators liable for the total injuries that result. I show that any such proposal escapes the supposed arbitrariness of chance by surrendering its ability to explain either why carelessness should be the basis of liability or why the plaintiff's loss is the measure of damages for negligence.

There are cases in which risk appears to be the basis for liability. If two hunters negligently shoot at the same time and one of them injures a third, though we do not know which one fired the injuring shot, it seems fair to hold both liable. If a number of manufacturers negligently market a hazardous drug that injures a number of plaintiffs, but it is not possible to identify the particular injurers with particular victims, courts have held that manufacturers should pay in accordance with their market share.[44] Such examples pose an apparent counterexample to the risk rule, for they suggest that when risks ripen, liability is proportional to risk imposition.

Some have taken these examples to show that the creation of risks is itself a harm, and so an appropriate basis for compensation.[45] There are, to be sure, some cases in which exposure to a risk causes an injury even if the risk does not ripen. In such cases, exposure to risk leads to further disadvantages. These disadvantages seem to fall

enough to be saved are so through grace. As for the rest, they have no grounds for complaint. Like Augustine, Honoré seems to suppose that arbitrary treatment of those who do wrong is acceptable. The problem is that the "rationale" for the fault system is less appealing than the system it is supposed to justify. See Joel Feinberg, "Sua Culpa," in his *Doing and Deserving: Essays in the Theory of Responsibility* (Princeton: Princeton University Press, 1970), p. 213. Consider a "no-liability" rule, on which all accident costs lie where they fall. Under such a system, nobody would have to pay for injuries to others, on the grounds that all benefit from escaping liability. Those who are injured may face enormous losses, but that is made up for by the fact that they avoided liability for injuries to others. Or consider a rule that makes all who are negligent contribute to a liability pool to compensate those who are injured. On Honoré's account, there is no argument of fairness for preferring the fault system to either of those alternatives.

44   *Sindell v. Abbot Laboratories*, 607 P.2d 924 (California 1980).
45   Richard Wright advances this suggestion in his account of the DES cases. See Wright, "Causation in Tort Law," p. 1819.

into two categories: Sometimes risks create reasonable fears; sometimes they lead others to treat me differently. Sometimes serious risks of serious harms will cause fear; in such circumstances, the creator of the risk may be held liable, but is liable not for the risk but for fear. Thus, the risk itself is not the harm; the fear would be just as genuine (and just as actionable) if the risk never materialized, or, for that matter, if the person creating the fear had made a mistake and wrongly informed someone that he was at serious risk. If the doctor tells me I was transfused with hepatitis-bearing blood, and have a 50 percent chance of developing the disease, any damages I might be due for the fear created will apply even if it turns out that the records were misfiled and I did not receive tainted blood at all. That is, if compensation is due, it is because an injury has occurred, not because of a risk.

Exposure to risk may seem to be harmful in another way. If others believe that I have been exposed to risk, they may refuse to hire me for some job, or refuse to insure me. Thus, the person who is at risk may suffer a diminution in her economic value – the price that the market would place on her, or her assets. Talking about the market valuing people may trouble some, and so distract us from the question at issue. So consider an alternative: Suppose you carelessly bump into my Ming vase. Miraculously, it survives, but as a result of the impact, it may be more likely to eventually crack if the humidity changes. Unfortunately, no nondestructive testing will determine whether or not it will survive. You have put the vase at risk; as a result, museums will be willing to pay less for it, so its value has decreased. Surely, you have harmed me in that sense. Because of your carelessness, my vase can no longer be sold for its prior value, except by fraud. But you have not broken it, and you may not even have harmed it. Yet you have decreased its economic value.

I want to suggest that even in such cases, the harm is not in the risk, but in the loss of a chance. The law has developed standard ways of evaluating lost chances. The person who is negligently passed over in a job competition is entitled to damages prorated for the likelihood of his getting the job.[46] Although this general approach has not been

---

[46] See, for example, Stephen Waddams, *The Law of Damages* (Toronto: Canada Law Book, 1983), p. 1078. Waddams discusses *Chaplin v. Hicks* [1911] 2 K.B. (a contract case in which the defendant failed to notify the plaintiff of the next stage in an audition process); *Prior v. McNab* (1976) 78 D.L.R. (3d) 319 (H.C.J.) (a case of solicitor's negligence in which the plaintiff was awarded the settlement value of a case that the court conceded he would probably not have won); and *Albion v. Cochrane* (1969) 4 D.L.R. (3d) 667 (a case in which a child lost a kidney

applied to all cases of lost chances, it can be applied to those cases where the risk appears to be an injury. The person who wrongfully loses another's raffle ticket might be held liable for the value of the ticket, which is in turn a function of the value of the prize and chances of success. (I imagine here that the loss of the ticket precludes its entry into the draw; if the ticket could still win, but I cannot claim the prize, the situation is different.) Applied to the dropped vase, the diminution in its value reflects its future market value. Although the loss cannot be calculated with certainty, it is in this way no different from the diminution in its value if you had placed a small stain, detectable only by experts, on its inside. These risk-related injuries are not injuries that are the result of the creation of a risk, but rather are injuries that consist in something that can only be valued in terms of chances. As such, they pose no special problems, and do not involve liability for the imposition of risks.

To claim that risks themselves are compensable harms, two things need to be shown. First, the imposition of risk needs to be an injury *apart from* any of the other injurious effects that might accompany it. Any of fear, or the inability to purchase insurance, or a decrease in the market value of my vase are injuries already, and so the risk is not itself the basis of liability. Second, the damages must be somehow proportionate to the imposition of risk. The second requirement is strong indeed, for it would seem to require that *all* who are exposed to the risk receive compensation, since all suffer the risk equally. No pooling of the costs of actual injuries among various risk imposers would satisfy this requirement, because the fortunate ones who are exposed to risks but not injuries would receive no compensation.

It is difficult to isolate the various factors in such a proposal, so I will construct a hypothetical case. Suppose then that a particular risk will take years to ripen. Is exposure to the risk itself a wrong?[47] For example, exposure to certain chemicals substantially increases the risk

---

and was awarded damages based on the extra precautions he would need to take to protect his other kidney).

[47] Stephen Perry has argued that the idea of liability for risks rests on an epistemic notion of risk, that is, on the idea that risk is tied to the available knowledge, especially about the future. But, Perry contends, so characterized risks simply reflect the fact that injuries are unknown, and so are not a separate type of injury. There may well be probabilities that need to be characterized objectively at the quantum mechanical level, but these do not prevent macro phenomena from being characterized deterministically. See "Risk, Harm, and Probability," in *Philosophical Foundations of Tort Law,* edited by David G. Owen (Oxford: Oxford University Press, 1995), p. 337.

of cancer. May a manufacturer who in the past negligently exposed workers to the chemical go out of business without either compensating them or at least insuring them against later injury? To avoid the easy solution of requiring some sort of actuarial pool of those who are exposed to the risk, I stipulate further the numbers are too small to be certain that anyone will in fact develop cancer.[48] The company that winds up its business without taking any such precautions is plainly doing something morally troubling.

Those who create risks and then abandon them behave badly. But we need not appeal to the idea of liability for risks to explain what is wrong with such behavior.[49] There is an alternative explanation. Those who knowingly walk away from unripened risks take advantage of an uncertainty they have wrongfully created. Consider again the example of the two hunters who negligently fire toward a third at the same time, as a result of which the third loses an eye. By ordinary standards of proof, neither can be shown more probably than not to be the cause of the injury. Yet courts have held the plaintiff should still recover. This is not because they both have wrongfully exposed him to risk for which they must compensate. Were that the rationale, they would owe him compensation even if it *was* known who had injured him, and the amount of compensation would not depend on whether the injury actually ensued. Instead, the compensation is tied to his injury, not the risk. In circumstances in which they have created the uncertainty, the negligent hunters are not entitled to the benefit of a rule designed to break a tie when evidence between plaintiff and defendant is equally matched.[50] Ordinary rules of proof require that a plaintiff

[48] I am grateful to Scott Brewer for this example, and the sharpened formulation of it.

[49] A further consideration is also perhaps relevant here. Limited shareholder liability is a familiar feature of modern corporate law. Although shareholders stand to benefit from the full gains of a corporation, regardless of its proportion to their initial investment, their liability is limited to the value of their investment in the company. Shareholders' other assets are protected if a company goes bankrupt, even if the bankruptcy is the result of wrongdoing by the company. Thus, those who expose others to risks that are greater than the total value of the company's assets are able to protect themselves from full liability for the consequences of their acts. The merits of a corporate law that protect investors in this way are matter of debate; I mention them here to suggest that the unripened risk case is not unique.

[50] Ordinarily, the requirement that plaintiff prove defendant's responsibility on the balance of probabilities makes sense because, ordinarily, the misfortune appropriately lies with defendant if, and only if, it does not lie with plaintiff. In cases with multiple tort-feasors, that assumption no longer holds. I explore strategies for dealing with these issues in a paper coauthored with Benjamin

show that it is more likely than not that the defendant's negligence caused the injury. Where it is clear that one of the defendants caused the injury, and the undisputed negligence of multiple defendants makes it impossible to show which one caused it, the defendants are not entitled to the benefit of the ordinary procedural rule. The point is not that they are being punished for creating the risk. It is rather that they must forego the procedural benefit that results from their carelessness. They are not held liable for their risk imposition, but they must forego the procedural benefits that risk imposition affords them. As a result, ordinary burdens of proof are suspended in just those cases in which they would reward wrongdoing.

The general principle at work in this sort of case is one of "unclean hands," and is familiar in a variety of legal contexts. Consider the case of the person who breaches a contract, as a result of which some business cannot operate. In calculating the damages, it may be unclear whether the business would have lost money overall had the contract been completed. As a result, it is not clear that the party breaching the contract did not actually *advantage* the other party overall. Yet there is something untoward about someone who breached a contract raising such an argument.[51] The underlying principles are complex in their application, and the identification of the procedural benefits that might be thought to accrue from wrongdoing is a thorny issue. But the underlying intuitive ideas of fair play go a considerable distance toward explaining what is wrong with leaving someone hanging when there is a risk of injury, quite apart from any claims about risks themselves counting as injuries. The problem is one of benefitting from an uncertainty one has created. The creation of that uncertainty is not itself a wrong, any more than is the creation of any other risk. But the existence of that uncertainty cannot be allowed to prevent the plaintiff from proving his or her case. In the same way, if the hunters create an uncertainty through their wrongdoing, they are not allowed to benefit from it. The manufacturer who winds down his business without seeing to the security of those who he might have injured does something similar. I do not know if any court would stop such a person from winding down the business. Indeed, I am not sure whether a court should stop such a person, nor about the sort of priority the person

Zipursky, "Corrective Justice in an Age of Mass Torts" in *Philosophy and U.S. Tort Law*, edited by G. Postema (Cambridge: Cambridge University Press, forthcoming).

[51]   *Anglia Television v. Reid* [1972] 1 QB 60 (C.A.) at 64 per Lord Denning, M.R.

exposed to risks ought to have in relation to other creditors should the company declare bankruptcy. The example is meant only to suggest that the intuitive source of trouble in such behavior is not that the creation of a risk is itself a harm, but rather that the manufacturer is benefitting from a problem of proof that he has created through his negligence. Such behavior does not necessarily harm, but it offends against intuitive ideas of fair play.

3.4.3.2 Risk Pools. Christopher Schroeder has defended a liability-for-risks scheme on the grounds that it realizes the ideal of corrective justice.[52] According to Schroeder, the concept of corrective justice imposes three requirements on liability. First, liability must be tied to agency. Second, victims of injury must be compensated. Third, financing must be internal – compensation must come from wrongdoers. The second and third conditions are compatible with traditional tort doctrine. For Schroeder, the first condition is defeated if chance is allowed a role, because two agents alike in their agency will differ in their liability. Instead, all who are equally careless should shoulder an equal burden when it comes to compensation. Particular agents who impose risks on others are not liable to the particular people on whom the risks are imposed. Instead, those who create undue risks should pay into a pool, the funds from which will serve to compensate those who are injured by risks.[53]

Rather than identifying liability with outcomes, then, Schroeder would have those who create risks bear the costs of those risks by paying in proportion to their risky behavior. To return to an earlier example, if two hunters fire at the same time and injure a third, they should share in liability. If a number of manufacturers produce a toxic

---

[52] Christopher Schroeder, "Corrective Justice, Liability for Risks, and Tort Law," 38 *UCLA Law Review* 143 (1990) . See also Jeremy Waldron, "Moments of Carelessness and Massive Loss," in Owen (ed.), *Philosophical Foundations of Tort Law,* pp. 387–408.

[53] Such a scheme may well face insurmountable administrative difficulties, given the problems of both identifying types of risks to pools and identifying those who create risks that do not materialize. I want to put those worries aside for two reasons. First, local pools may be easier to identify. Indeed, creation of an at-fault pool is sometimes claimed to be the basis of liability in cases of mass torts involving multiple manufacturers and plaintiffs. Second, tort law as it currently exists has countless administrative problems of its own, and an imperfect substitute might still do a better job of compensating plaintiffs and of following the dictates of the conception of corrective justice that underlies it. What we must do, then, is look at the conception of justice to see whether it is adequate.

product, they should pay for injuries in proportion to their sales, even if the pattern of injuries imperfectly reflects the pattern of sales. In both of these examples, the principle seems to have the right intuitive feel. This raises two questions. First, is Schroeder's account able to explain these results? Second, is its appeal in such cases grounds for generalizing the approach? With regard to the first question, Schroeder's account fits the cases: Those who impose risks are made to pay in proportion to the likelihood that they caused injuries. However, there are a variety of competing explanations for the results, and Schroeder's explanation creates as many difficulties as it solves.

Schroeder's concern for the arbitrariness of luck leads him to distinguish several questions that the idea of risk ownership treats as integrally related. One concerns the boundaries of reasonable behavior. The second concerns who should pay for the results of unreasonable behavior, and the third the appropriate sanction for unreasonable behavior. The idea of risk ownership (and traditional tort doctrine) supposes that those who fail to exercise appropriate care must make up those losses that they so cause. Schroeder's proposal supposes that the costs of negligent behavior should be borne by people who are negligent. As an account of cases involving multiple tort-feasors, Schroeder's account shows something they have in common. In order to succeed as a more general account, though, it needs to explain why the relevant similarity is between various people who are negligent, rather than between those who injure, or those who are injured.

Schroeder's argument proceeds by classifying negligent people as relevantly similar, and concludes that given that similarity, it is arbitrary to make the liability of similar people turn on causation. Yet we need some explanation of why that is the relevant classification. We've encountered one difficulty already: The failure to exercise appropriate care is one moral failing among others, and some explanation is required of why it is the relevant respect in which people should receive like treatment. The need for some rationale for classifying various people as relevantly similar is all the more pressing given Schroeder's concern with negligence. Negligence is a failure of conduct. Unlike the intention to deceive or injure, which might plausibly be supposed to be wrongful regardless of what comes of them (and so perhaps to merit sanctions), negligence is normatively significant *because* it makes injury more likely. The purpose of corrective justice is not to ensure like treatment of all bad behavior – as Keeton points out, negligence just isn't bad enough to single it out for such treatment – but to undo the effects of unreasonable behavior by re-turning those losses to those who are responsible for them.

Although Schroeder emphasizes the fact that people can control their carelessness, that does not yet serve to delimit the pool in the right way. Consider the case of self-injurers. As I've suggested, a his-torical account of justice in distribution treats wrongful injuries to others as on a par with self-injury: Those who wrongfully injure oth-ers bear the costs as though they have injured themselves. Schroeder does not include people who injure themselves through their own carelessness in the pool of those who are to receive compensation. Nor does he include those who are careless with regard to their own safety among the contributors to the compensatory pool. Yet the role of chance is just as arbitrary in shaping the fate of self-injurers as it is in shaping the fate of those who injure others. Now it may be that we do not think that any ideal of corrective justice requires compensat-ing self-injurers, in the way that corrective justice arguably does re-quire compensating those who are injured by others. Yet that is pre-cisely the difference that needs to be explained. If the claim is that people's lives should not depend on chance, self-injury is indistin-guishable from injury to others. If liability for risks is tied to an agent's carelessness, or what could have been controlled, self-injury is again indistinguishable. Indeed, forced risk pooling for self-injurers meets Schroeder's three criteria of corrective justice: Responsibility is tied to action, injuries are compensated, and the financing is internal.

If we focus on the need to compensate innocent people, careless self-injury can be distinguished from careless injury to others. Those who carelessly injure themselves are perhaps not wholly innocent in that respect. Yet if compensation is the point, we need some basis for distinguishing between innocent accident victims who are injured by others' negligence and those injured merely by chance. They are alike in their inability to avoid injury, and in their need for compensation.[54] If we accept Schroeder's claim that the difference between negligent injurers and negligent noninjurers is simply a matter of luck, and so morally irrelevant, we might well wonder why such a morally irrel-evant factor is employed to pick out the class of persons entitled to compensation. The difference, no doubt, is that in cases of negligence,

---

[54] Schroeder concedes that his scheme's failure to compensate for injuries and ill-ness that are not the result of negligence is arbitrary, but goes on to suggest that such arbitrariness is not a concern of corrective justice. See "Corrective Justice," at 159. In "Causation, Compensation, and Social Responsibility," in Owen (ed.), *Philosophical Foundations of Tort Law,* he takes this worry more seriously.

one person *did* injure another. Thus, the injured party has grounds for complaint in a way that people who injure themselves do not. But the only person against whom the injured party has grounds for complaint is the actual injurer. That is why Schroeder's internal financing requirement makes sense. Severed from a focus on what actually happened, though, it provides no rationale for connecting careless people with injured people. Causation connects particular risk imposers with particular injuries. If causation is deemed irrelevant, failure to exercise appropriate care bears no obvious relations to membership in a compensatory pool. Those who fail to exercise appropriate care behave badly. But so do many other people, without incurring liability on Schroeder's scheme.[55]

The difficulties with Schroeder's scheme does not mean that some sort of mandatory risk-pooling scheme is never acceptable. Certainly voluntary arrangements to contract around tort rules are acceptable, so that a group of persons might decide to insure each other. A democratic legislature may choose to implement such an arrangement in certain kinds of cases in order to facilitate mutually advantageous cooperation.[56] For example, mandatory automobile insurance and worker's compensation schemes might be justified by the combination of two features. First, those who engage in risky activities do so voluntarily and knowingly. Second, those engaging in the activities may not have the resources to meet their financial obligations in case of injury.[57] In such cases, those engaging in the activity can be required to insure themselves, and the economics of such insurance can be allowed to define the actuarial categories. Over the longer term, risk-pooling schemes may even approximate the results corrective

---

[55]   Jeremy Waldron has offered an account that is similar to Schroeder's but which focuses on spreading the costs of accidental injury among people who differ only by luck. Like Schroeder, though, Waldron offers no explanation of why only those misfortunes brought about by carelessness are to be compensated in this way. In the attempt to avoid the supposed arbitrariness of chance, Waldron, like Schroeder, finds himself embracing the genuine arbitrariness of selecting candidates for compensation based on how they came about while simultaneously denying the relevance of how they came about. See Waldron, "Moments of Carelessness and Massive Loss, " in Owen (ed.), *Philosophical Foundations of Tort Law*, pp. 387–408.

[56]   In the same way, it might subsidize public transit in order to get those who prefer private transportation to bear some of the cost of the benefits of uncongested roads they receive when others use public transport.

[57]   In the same way, a society that finances medical care might require people engaging in dangerous activities such as hang gliding to insure themselves against injury. The point is not to assert a moral equivalence among all hang gliders, but to make sure that all are in a position to bear the costs of their activities.

justice would have reached. But such schemes do not get their rationale from the fact that they avoid the arbitrariness of causation.

Schroeder's approach starts with the idea that causation is morally arbitrary because two people can be alike in their behavior, yet one ends up with huge liability and the other ends up escaping it. The problem is with the initial classification. The idea of risk ownership acknowledges that the effects of chance cannot be eliminated. It supposes instead that those who have a fair chance to avoid liability are not treated arbitrarily if they are held liable even if they might have had better luck. It is luck all right, but it is *their* bad luck, and as responsible agents, they must accept its consequences, just as responsible agents must accept the consequences of foolish choices they make for themselves. That is, careless self-injury and careless injury to others are alike in these respects. The duty to compensate is not only the result of an injured person's need for compensation, but of the fact that the loss properly belongs with the person who imposed the risk. On the risk ownership conception of liability, then, chance is allowed a role, but that role is not arbitrary.

3.4.4 Reasonableness and Objectivity

The idea that those who create unreasonable risks are responsible for them shows why the idea of fault must be objective in a strong sense of that term. The fact that someone was trying their best does not excuse them from liability. The classic illustration of this point is the nineteenth-century case of *Vaughan v. Menlove*.[58] Menlove, who had limited mental abilities, left a rick of hay on the edge of his property, close to Vaughan's barn. The hay spontaneously combusted, taking the barn with it. Vaughan sued for damages. Menlove's lawyers argued that because he was not intelligent enough to understand that hay was susceptible of spontaneous combustion, he should not be liable for the resultant damage. The court rejected the argument, for reasons that have broad significance. Because of the binary structure of adjudication – because it had to be somebody's bad luck – the court had to decide whose it was. Here nobody could in fact have controlled the outcome, but the bad luck must be borne by someone. If we relieve Menlove of responsibility for something he cannot control, we saddle Vaughan with a cost the origins of which *he* could not control. There is no way to retreat to equating responsibility with control.

[58] *Vaughan v. Menlove* (1837) 132 E.R. 490 (C.P.).

Yet the decision is not just an administrative one in a situation in which nobody could control the loss.[59] Rather, holding Menlove liable is the only way to treat the parties as equals, by protecting them each from the activities of others, and leaving each with room to pursue his or her own purposes. The only way one can be exempt from the need to bear the costs of one's activities is to not be an agent at all. Had the court relieved Menlove of responsibility, and treated the bad luck as Vaughan's, they would have been treating Menlove himself as a mere natural thing rather than as an agent. At the same time, had they refused to make Menlove bear the costs of his activities to others, they would have been treating Vaughan as less than an equal, making him bear the costs of a broader range of others' activities than they must bear of his own.[60]

Put slightly differently, although we hesitate to blame Menlove for his incapacity, we hold him liable because the risk that he imposed on Vaughan was rightly his. We hold him liable without supposing him to be morally tainted because a fair distribution of risks requires that the risk lie with him. His liability can also be restated in terms of his responsibility to moderate his activities in light of the legitimate claims of others. Those who engage in the activities of ordinary life have a responsibility to take account of the dangers their activities pose. Those who are genuinely incapable of assessing risks and taking precautions – incapable, that is, of moderating their pursuit of their own ends in light of the legitimate claims of others – cannot be held responsible for the consequences of their deeds, but they also can be prevented from exposing others to those risks. Those who have the requisite capacities cannot excuse themselves on those occasions on which they fail – for whatever reason – to exercise them adequately. That is, the general capacity for responsible agency is the capacity both to pursue one's ends and moderate one's claims in light of one's duties to others. In the next chapter, I will say more about how that capacity is specified. For now, the crucial point is that those who have the general capacity are required to moderate their behavior in light of the

---

[59] It is not merely administrative for two reasons: First, it does nothing to prevent future losses, for those in Menlove's situation are *ex hypothesis* incapable of appreciating the risks. Second, it is plainly administratively simpler to let losses lie where they fall, unless there is some pressing reason to do otherwise.

[60] Holding Menlove liable is just the flip side of a principle we have already seen. If you injure me in spite of taking reasonable care, you are not liable, even if I injure easily. To hold you liable in such circumstances would mean that you could only act subject to my idiosyncrasies. In just the same way, Vaughan's interest in security cannot be made to depend on Menlove's lack of intelligence.

interests of others. The extent to which that capacity must be exercised is given by those interests. In the case of accidents, it is thus given by the standard of reasonable care. Menlove cannot both claim incapacity in a particular case, yet also insist on the liberty to engage in risky activities. Insofar as he escapes responsibility, his liberty can be constrained for the safety of others.

The details of *Vaughan* have led some commentators to suggest that it is a misleading example of the principle for which it is supposed to stand. The defendant had been warned of the dangers, and declared that his stock was insured and he was "willing to chance it." This might suggest that he really was in control of the situation and could have avoided the injury, but chose not to.[61] Certainly, if we broaden the time frame, there must be some precautions that he could have taken – selling his land and moving to the city, if nothing else.[62] But the problem of limited foresight recurs even on this broader time frame. His failure to recognize the seriousness of danger would have prevented him from taking further precautions. Moreover, the question of whether he is responsible for the earlier failure to take precautions is objective in just the same way. He did not realize further inquiries were necessary; the question remains whether he should have.

Vaughan v. Menlove is a particularly dramatic example of a far more general principle. The same requirement of treating parties as equals by holding them responsible for the risks they have created regularly plays itself out in more mundane examples. Rather than asking everyone to expend the same degree of effort, thus leaving each person's security dependent on who their neighbors happen to be, the law demands the same degree of care from everyone and protects all to the same degree. If I am tired or distracted, and carelessly injure you as a result, I am not excused because at the time of the accident I could not control its outcome. Nor am I excused because I didn't realize the activity was risky. My inattention may itself be a reflection of my preoccupation with higher things, it may be the result of exhaustion because I busied myself with good works, or it may simply reflect inappropriate priorities on my part. From the point of view of liability, none of these things properly matters, because none of these things

---

[61] I am grateful to George Christie for pointing this out to me.
[62] Because of the land law governing entails in England at the time, even this may not have been an option.

entitle me to put you at risk. Likewise, I am not excused if I didn't know of the dangers of my activity, quite apart from any questions of what, if anything, else occupied my mind. In each case, I remain liable even though I was doing my best at the time, for the alternative would be to make your security dependent on my capabilities. As was the case with *Vaughan v. Menlove*, it is always possible to widen the time frame and ask if I could have taken precautions earlier. To answer that question, though, we must ask about my duties, not my efforts.

The same principle requires that those who do not try their best – those who can see that some accident is possible or even likely – do not always incur liability. By driving an automobile carefully, I may know that if I drive frequently enough I am likely to injure others. Nonetheless, I can drive and even injure others and escape liability. In such cases, I avoid liability because I exercise the care required of me. It may be that I could have driven even more carefully and reduced the risk of injury still further. Indeed, in the case of automobiles, this is plainly possible. Driving at three miles per hour is very safe, however annoying it might be to other drivers. Yet the person who drives much faster is not liable. In the same way, the person who is just attentive enough avoids liability, even though by being more attentive, risks could have been reduced further.

The outcome in *Vaughan* may nonetheless strike some as unfair. If so, it is perhaps because they suppose that the costs of Menlove's lack of intelligence should not be borne by him alone. Though the general idea is surely appealing, it does not lead to the conclusion that Vaughan should not be allowed to recover. If we wish to distribute the costs of Vaughan's misfortune, it is difficult to see why Vaughan in particular should bear a disproportionate share. We might wonder instead whether those costs might be treated as everyone's bad luck. That question is a political one, because the only *kind* of answer it can receive will depend on our view of the importance of various types of activities. I will return to these matters in Chapter 9.

3.4.4.1 A Clarification About Objectivity. Talk about objective standards makes some people uneasy. The idea of objectivity may suggest that such standards are somehow eternal and exist quite apart from questions about which interests people have and how important they are. Any such conception of objectivity might well raise suspicions that it is little more than a smokescreen for interests that are already well-entrenched.[63] But I mean something considerably more modest. Precisely because the fault standard turns on substantive views about the importance of various activities, its contours will always be open to debate. It is objective in a negative sense, inasmuch as it is not subjective, so that the limits of liability are not fixed by the views, interests, or abilities of either of the parties to a tort action. Instead, it protects the interests in both liberty and security that everyone is assumed to have. On the basis of those interests, it asks whether a reasonable person is entitled to have a particular interest protected. The importance, and even existence, of particular interests is often controversial, and the common law has sometimes been indifferent to what now seem significant interests, and concerned about insignificant ones. Clear examples of such indifference can be found in the absence, until recently, of any legal recognition of the interest that women have in being free of sexual harassment. But the very possibility of identifying the problems shows the way to the appropriate response to them: Moving to a more nuanced objective standard.[64]

In cases in which parties are asymmetrically situated with respects to information, power, or vulnerability, risks must be divided accordingly. The law never had conceptual difficulties taking account of such asymmetries in cases of professional negligence. The fact that a physician exposed patients to risks to which patients do not expose physicians leads to a different sort of division of risks. Still the law has not always been good at understanding such asymmetries, and there are cases, most notably around issues of gender, in which its misunderstanding of power relations has been appalling. A particular objective standard is always an expression of particular views about the importance of various interests. As a result, in an important sense, it is always political, and in principle subject to contest. It is also political in a less appealing sense, inasmuch as it expresses power relations in the society. Yet in this sense, no way of ordering any aspect of social life can be free of such effects.

---

[63] See, for example, Catherine A. MacKinnon, *Toward a Feminist Theory of the State* (Cambridge, MA: Harvard University Press, 1989). For a discussion of MacKinnon's views, see Sally Haslanger, "On Being Objective and Being Objectified," in *A Mind of One's Own*, edited by Louise Antony and Charlotte Witt (Boulder, CO: Westview Press, 1994), pp. 85–125.

[64] See, for example, Susan Estrich, "Sex at Work," 43 *Stanford Law Review* 813, 842 (1991), for an exploration of the possibilities of a reasonableness standard in sexual harassment cases that recognizes the seriousness of women's interests and the limited importance of men's interests in harassment.

3.4.5 Unusual Sensitivities

The converse of the refusal to make special accommodations for those trying their best is tort law's lack of solicitude for plaintiff's with unusual sensitivities. It too is a direct consequence of the idea of risk ownership. If an interest is not protected, the fact that someone's conduct foreseeably may injure it does not create liability. The law of nuisance is fully explicit on this point. If my singing in the shower gives my neighbor headaches, it may be awful of me to continue, but my neighbor cannot enjoin me to desist. In the extreme and leading case, a church was allowed to ring a bell that caused a neighbor to suffer seizures.[65] The example is striking because the injury was extreme and certain. In cases of negligence, the situation is only slightly more complicated. The person who fails to take care when someone may be injured in an unusual way does not incur liability if they are injured. Suppose you get a severe allergic reaction from the plants in my garden. I do not need to compensate you for your injury unless it is a sort against which I ought to have taken precautions.[66] On the other hand, if I keep plants known to be toxic to humans, I may be liable. The basic principle is that the risk of certain idiosyncratic injuries lies with those who are injured. The fact that others cause them is not more relevant than the fact that various acts of careful people may be causal antecedents of an injury. This is, of course, just another application of the general principles of duty and remoteness: One can only become responsible for a particular risk if one has a duty to others to avoid injuring them in some particular way.

But if unusual types of injury do not create liability, unusual extent of injury does. The idea of risk ownership explains what is called the "eggshell-skull rule." If I injure you through my negligence, and unbeknownst to me, you have an unusual susceptibility so that the extent of your injury far exceeds the ordinary extent, I am nonetheless liable for your entire injury. The parallel with lost income is instructive here: If I injure you and must make up the income you lose as a result, the amount I must make up depends on your earning capacity, whether or not I was aware of it. Having taken a risk with some aspect of your security, I own the full extent of the injuries connected

---

[65] *Rogers v. Elliott*, 15 N.E. 768 (Mass. 1888).
[66] This extends even to American products liability. An unusual sensitivity, rather than a failure to warn, is treated as the proximate cause of an allergic reaction. *Adelman-Tremblay v. Jewel Cos.*, 859 F.2d 517 (7th cir. 1988).

with that aspect. Just as I escape liability if, by good fortune, you are not injured, so I am liable for the extent of the injury that is within the risk that makes my conduct negligent. That is, the thin-skull rule only applies if the injurer was behaving unreasonably with respect to the risk in question. At the same time, if I am careless with respect to one aspect of your security and, because of your unusual susceptibility, I injure you in some other respect, the thin-skull rule does not apply. Because liability is tied to the creation of particular risks, my failure to show appropriate care with respect to one risk does not lead to liability any more than it would if different people were involved, as in the *Palsgraf* case.

The idea of risk ownership lets us see that, far from being opposed principles, the thin-skull rule and the ultrasensitive plaintiff rule are actually expressions of a single underlying principle. My liability does not depend only on what happens, but rather on the risks to which I expose you. If you are sensitive in unusual ways, the injuries that come out of that sensitivity are yours. Were others liable for them, their liberty would be subject to your security, which would be no more acceptable than if your security was limited by the good-faith efforts of others. The boundaries of reasonable care depend on interests in both liberty and security. The problem with making defendants liable for unusual injuries is not that it would create crippling liability – that may or may not be the case – but rather that it would encumber liberty too much, as people seeking to avoid wronging others would need to moderate their activity to too great an extent. By contrast, liability for the full *extent* of injury, no matter how surprising, places no burden on liberty. For no extra precautions are required to avoid severe injuries than are required to avoid less severe ones. The standard of reasonable care is not a proxy for the price of injury. The relation between the thin-skull rule and ultrasensitive-plaintiff rule thus illustrates the difficulties of economic approaches to tort liability, which collapse unreasonable risk imposition into expensive risk imposition. As long as these are kept distinct, the thin-skull rule and ultrasensitive plaintiff rule can be seen as complementary. From the point of view of the reasonable person, the relevant risks are those of injury, not of being out-of-pocket.

In each of these three cases – thin skulls, ultrasensitive plaintiffs, and those who try their best – a fair distribution of risks allows some plaintiffs to collect from a defendant who wasn't morally bad, and bars other plaintiffs from collecting from defendants who were. The result may make tort law seem like a cruel and cold system, a shocking illustration of why Hume described justice as a "jealous virtue." In particular, it allows someone to knowingly expose another to injury, standing narrowly on his or her right to do so, and utterly lacking in compassion. Although such concerns are not without force, it is important to remember that the underlying issues are not about blame but about coercion and equality. A kinder, gentler regime of individual responsibility would lead to even less appealing results. To require each person to limit their activities because others might be made worse off by them is to give up on both the idea of individual liberty and the idea of people moderating their activities in light of the legitimate claims of others. If all of a person's vulnerabilities limit the liberty of others, none is free to go about their own affairs.

3.4.6   Misfeasance and Nonfeasance

The law's lack of solace for unusually sensitive plaintiffs whose vulnerabilities are known is of a piece with the legal distinction between misfeasance and nonfeasance. The distinction between misfeasance and nonfeasance is not the same as that between acts and omissions, nor even as that between harm and benefit. Tort duties are often breached by omission – the failure to take precautions is the most obvious example – and when people occupy special roles or stand in special relations, liability can follow on the failure to confer a benefit. Instead, the distinction between nonfeasance and misfeasance is the distinction between unreasonable behavior that injures and reasonable behavior that does. The most striking consequences of this distinction is the absence of a tort duty to rescue. There is surely a moral duty to rescue in some situations. The failure to fulfill such a moral duty might be enforced through a criminal penalty, but does not provide the basis for tort liability. Now it might be thought that if anything is reasonable in such cases, it is to take small easy steps in order to aid another. But although there is a clear sense of the word "reasonable" on which this is true, it is a sense that is foreign to tort law and the idea that particular risks belong to particular people. The fact that you are in peril, and I know of your peril, does not make that risk mine. As a result, if it ripens into an injury, it is not my loss to make up. The idea of risk ownership offers a simple explanation: Mere knowledge of another's needs, no matter how pressing, is not enough to shift a risk from one person to another. To shift risk in this way would be unduly burdensome to liberty, because it would always require people to give up what they were doing whenever they had a prospect of aiding others in distress.[67] Moreover, those who failed to aid would be responsible for the full extent of the other person's injury.

Now it might be thought a more moderate tort duty to rescue is appropriate, such as a duty that was limited to *easy* rescues. As morally attractive as such a proposal might be, it would sit uneasily with the rest of tort doctrine. In cases of misfeasance, the existence of duty of care does not depend on the ease with which it can be discharged in the particular instance. Instead, it depends on the significance of the relevant interests in liberty and security. Once account has been taken of those, the costs of care to the defendant counts for nothing. Put differently, rights in tort law are not defined in terms of prices or welfare. That is why the frequency with which someone engages in an activity is irrelevant to questions of reasonable care. The same point applies to any imaginable duty to rescue: If the existence of the duty depends on the ease with which it is discharged, it would fail to express the idea of reciprocity, because it would make the security of those in peril depend on considerations about the welfare of those positioned to rescue them. Conversely, it would make the liberty of those in a position to rescue others depend on the welfare of others. The point is not just that this would import an element of chance into the situation. That much is inevitable, since the opportunity to rescue is largely a matter of being in the right place at the right time. From the point of view of risk ownership, the real problem is that who owned which risks would be tied to shifting welfare considerations. Here again we see the difference between a conception of tort law that focuses on fair terms of interaction and one that focuses on costs. From the point of view of costs, the costs of discharging a duty on a particular occasion might well be relevant to whether there was such a duty. From the point of view of fair terms of interaction, they are not.

Although the absence of a duty to rescue may seem yet another example of a cruel and unfeeling doctrine, it is important to recognize that it does not stand in the way of considerable mandatory redistribution. Many misfortunes can and should be held in common. The distinction between misfeasance and nonfeasance is simply the requirement that a particular misfortune not be shifted from one person to another.[68]

---

[67] McCauley's "Notes on the Indian Penal Code" in *Works*, Vol. 7 (New York: Longmans Green, 1897), p. 497.

[68] Still, if a tort duty to rescue is difficult to justify, criminal sanctions for failure to make easy rescues is not. Joel Feinberg offers the example of a statutory duty to report fires to the fire department. ("The Moral and Legal Responsibility of

the Bad Samaritan," in *Freedom and Fulfilment* [Princeton: Princeton University Press, 1992], pp. 175–96.) Such a duty would appropriately be limited to easy reports, and failure to report might be punishable by a fine. Feinberg's example is illuminating in this context because the penalty that would appropriately attach to such a crime would be nowhere near that attached to arson, quite apart from the magnitude of the fire. Instead, the duty to report could be thought of as a piece of public welfare legislation. With this model in hand, Feinberg suggests a parallel duty of easy rescue in emergency situations. Such a duty would fall randomly, though presumably not in an unfair way, and its burden would be small. Yet it surely would not be appropriate to make liability for the full extent of the fire or injury fall on the person who failed to report it.

Chapter 4

Foresight and Responsibility

In the last chapter, I explained basic features of tort liability in terms of the idea of reciprocity. In this one, I explicate the conception of responsibility implicit in that idea. Any account of responsibility limits its purview to the sorts of beings who can be responsible, who have such capacities as are required to moderate their activities. An account of why certain changes in holdings must be undone can only apply to agents who are capable of moderating their activities in light of the interests of others. The capacities that are relevant to tort liability are thus themselves identified in terms of reciprocity and fair terms of interaction. As I suggested in discussing *Vaughan v. Menlove*, those who are free to exercise their liberty must take responsibility for the costs they impose on others, even if on particular occasions they are unable to live up to the standard of care.

Perhaps the most important of the capacities that is requisite to tort liability is the capacity for foresight. As a result, it is the central focus of my discussion. Negligence liability is ordinarily limited to those consequences of wrongdoing that are foreseeable. If an injury is not foreseeable, it is not compensable. The requirement that injuries be foreseeable may look like a competing principle, in tension with the risk rule and the idea of reasonableness, because foresight appears to be an epistemic feature, definable apart from any question of fair terms of interaction. The central claim of this chapter is that foresight is neither a matter of what is in fact foreseen nor of what could ideally be foreseen. Instead, it is a matter of what a reasonable person would foresee. Thus, the duty of care is defined in terms of standards of reasonableness. As Lord Atkin put it in *Donoghue v. Stevenson*, I owe a duty of care to "persons who are so closely and directly affected by my act that I ought reasonably to have them in contemplation as being so affected when I am directing my mind to the acts or omissions which are called into question."[1] As we shall see, both closeness and directness are fixed by fair terms of interaction.

I begin by considering, and rejecting, an argument that seeks to explain the importance of foresight in terms of a more general conception of moral responsibility. That is Stephen Perry's argument that foresight is relevant to liability because an agent is only morally responsible for things that he or she can foresee. Perry's account is important because it applies an intuitively powerful idea about moral responsibility to tort law. I show why Perry's account fails to make sense of the objectivity of the foresight requirement. I then offer an alternative account of foresight in terms of reasonableness. Just as the standard of reasonable behavior is not given by whether a person engages in a process of reasoning, so the requirement that injuries be foreseeable is not tied to an independent idea of foresight. Instead, it reflects a normative conception of appropriate foresight – the requirement that people look out for the protected interests of others. As a result, it gives expression to the idea that people should moderate their claims in light of the interests of others. It also gives expression to the related idea of publicity, the idea that people should be in a position to know what they may do without fear of legal sanction.

I illustrate my positive account with some examples of intervening agency, either by the injured plaintiff or a third party, that courts have held to be within the risk of wrongful behavior. These include the intervening acts of rescuers and people defending themselves, as well as those who fail to mitigate their losses based on religious convictions. I argue that these cases can be brought within the purview of an account of foreseeability in light of the idea that reasonable behavior is always foreseeable. This idea follows directly from the idea of reciprocity implicit in the reasonableness standard: Fair terms of cooperation require that people take the interests of others into account, including their interest in behaving reasonably.[2] A proper

---

[1] *Donoghue v. Stevenson* [1932] 1 A.C. 562 (H.L.).

[2] The converse point applies to cases of pure economic loss. Although tort law supposes people to have special attachments to things that they own, no such attachments are presumed to things that people merely use. As a result, economic losses that are foreseeable in the sense that little effort would be required to discover them – if defendant's negligently steered barge destroys only the bridge access to the plaintiff's factory – nonetheless do not lead to liability. See *Rickards v. Sun Oil Co.*, 41 A. 2d 267 (New Jersey, 1945) and the excellent discussion in Peter Benson, "The Basis for Excluding Liability for Economic Loss in Tort Law," in Owen, *Philosophical Foundations of Tort Law,* edited by David G. Owen (Oxford: Oxford University Press, 1995), pp. 427–58.

understanding of foreseeability thus enables us to see why reasonable behavior typically does not give rise to liability when done in response to wrongdoing, even though it does when done in response to a natural peril. A further benefit of this approach to foreseeability is that it also explains why those who respond reasonably to natural perils are strictly liable for the cost of their reasonable responses.

4.1 FORESIGHT AS A CONDITION OF AGENCY

In this section, I examine a proposal that ties foresight to a more general idea of moral agency and responsibility. The appeal of such an account should be apparent: The assessment of tort damages is a response to wrongful agency, and so should depend on some significant aspect of the agent's wrongful act. It is tempting to suppose that a person is properly held liable for an injury *because* he is responsible for it, and that the underlying idea of responsibility applies apart from whatever considerations of reciprocity might shape the degree of care we owe each other. The general approach is also interesting because it introduces an element of specifically moral assessment into tort law while avoiding Keeton's challenge to attempts to link tort liability to a moral assessment of the defendant. Keeton's argument, it will be recalled, was that a moral assessment of the defendant's act raises the question of why carelessness is the only element of assessment introduced into the moral comparison of the parties. Both plaintiff and defendant might be bad (or good) in any number of respects: Why focus only on the question of whether defendant was careless about plaintiff's safety? The approach we are considering avoids the force of Keeton's challenge by treating injuries as a result of moral agency, and so as bearing a special relation to it. The focus on moral agency makes a person's acts, rather than her character, the focus of attention. Thus, the account narrows and sharpens the familiar judicial idea of choosing between an innocent plaintiff and a negligent defendant.[3] Those who find themselves faced with such a choice understandably prefer the innocent over the blameworthy party. But, I will contend, any such account needs to explain the normative basis for presenting a court with that very choice. It also needs to explain the requisite senses of negligence and innocence that underwrite the choice.

---

[3]   H. L. A. Hart and Tony Honoré, *Causation in the Law*, 2d ed. (Oxford: Oxford University Press, 1985), p. 267; W. Page Keeton et al., *Prosser and Keeton on the Law of Torts* (St Paul, MN: West, 1984), p. 287.

4.1 Foresight as a Condition of Agency

4.1.1 Perry's Account

Stephen Perry has probably done the most to articulate this line of thinking.[4] Perry's work is interesting because he combines two initially attractive views about foresight: The idea that the relevant sense of foresight is tied to ordinary human abilities to foresee some things but not others, and the idea that foresight is relevant to liability because of the significance of control to moral responsibility. Although I will conclude that both of these views require considerable recasting and qualification to explain tort doctrine, Perry's work repays careful attention. The idea that someone could have avoided some outcome is, without further qualification, too open-ended to explain liability, because almost any outcome could have been avoided, provided that other conditions are satisfied.[5] Perry offers a narrower notion of responsibility, which is identifiable and morally interesting apart from questions of political philosophy, but robust enough to underwrite impositions of liability. Perry is not alone in this ambition. I focus on his account because it is the strongest formulation of a plausible view. As a result, it shows both the possibilities and the limits of explaining tort law in those moral terms. Perry's account incorporates elements of both causalist and voluntarist understandings of agency, avoiding what appear to be the unsatisfactory elements of each. Yet it ends up running into the problem that is common to both voluntarist and causalist accounts.

Perry explicates the core idea of responsibility in light of the idea of "outcome responsibility" developed by Tony Honoré.[6] Honoré argues that in a world of risk, every action involves an implicit gamble. How those various gambles turn out is constitutive of a person's agency. How things turn out is crucial to our sense of who we are. When things go well, the credit redounds to us. When they turn out

---

[4] Stephen R. Perry, "The Moral Foundations of Tort Law," 77 *Iowa Law Review* 494 (1992), and "Responsibility for Outcomes, Risks, and the Law of Torts," *Philosophy & U.S. Tort Law*, edited by G. Postema (forthcoming Cambridge: Cambridge University Press, 1999).

[5] See, for example, Guido Calabresi's approach to foreseeability. Calabresi recasts the idea of foreseeability as the idea of something that can be taken into account. Thus, the concept is always forward-looking – an injury is foreseeable just in case precautions could be taken against it in future. See Calabresi, "Concerning Cause and the Law of Torts: An Essay for Harry Kalven, Jr.," 43 *University of Chicago Law Review* 69 (1975).

[6] Tony Honoré, "Responsibility and Luck: The Moral Issues of Strict Liability," 104 *Law Quarterly Review* 530 (1988).

badly, we are responsible for the bad results.[7] As a body, my boundaries may end at my skin; as a person, I am responsible for my deeds,
and those deeds are always in the world. As a result, agency is defined
at least in part by its consequences.

Like the causalist accounts of responsibility we saw in Chapter 2,
outcome responsibility focuses on the way things turn out. It differs
from those accounts in two respects. First, outcome responsibility is
a moral notion through and through. The consequences of an action
are expressions of agency; as such, they also provide further agent-
specific reasons for action. But not everything a person causes is a
consequence in the requisite sense. Thus, the libertarian's problems
of indeterminacy do not arise. Second, Perry's account of outcome responsibility fixes what is and is not a consequence in terms of a requirement of control. That is why foresight is central to the analysis.
One can only control what one can take into account, and one can at
most be responsible for things within one's control. At the same time,
neither foresight nor moral responsibility is a sufficient condition for
liability. In cases involving unusual sensitivities, for example, an injurer may be responsible, but not liable. Again, someone who exercises the required level of care, but could have been more careful may
be responsible for the injury that results, but he too escapes liability.
On Perry's view, law properly incorporates this idea of responsibility.

Outcome responsibility enters Perry's account as the normative
foundation of tort liability, and is supposed to explain the relation between two fundamental features of tort doctrine, the duty of care and
the duty of repair. The duty of care reflects the fact that only agents
who have the capacity for foresight can take account of others, and so
only they can be responsible for their failure to do so. The measure of
appropriate regard is the foreseeability of injury, because ordinary
powers of foresight are part of agency. Thus, agents are responsible
only for those outcomes they had both the capacity and the opportunity to avoid. Unforeseeable injuries are not things that people can be
expected to take into account in making their way in the world; as a

---

[7] Bernard Williams develops a similar account of responsibility. See his "Moral
Luck," in his *Moral Luck* (Cambridge: Cambridge University Press, 1981), pp. 20–
39. Williams does not offer his view as an account of legal or political morality.
Indeed, he suggests "no conception of responsible agency can match exactly an
ideal of maturity because, among other reasons, to hold oneself responsible only
when the public could rightly hold one responsible is not a sign of maturity."
See his "Voluntary Acts and Responsible Agents," in his *Making Sense of Humanity* (Cambridge: Cambridge University Press, 1995), pp. 22–34.

result, such outcomes are not expressions of a person's agency.[8] Unforeseeable outcomes do not express agency, even when the conduct that produces them foreseeably threatens others in some other way. In *Polemis*,[9] a plank handled negligently by stevedores caused an explosion because of unforeseeable vapors in a ship's hold. On Perry's analysis, such cases do not call for liability because unforeseeable outcomes are not a reflection of the injurer's agency, and so do not give rise to reasons for action.[10]

Injury gives rise to a duty to repair in light of a more general responsibility for outcomes. Since the injury is the result of the wrongdoer's agency, it gives him or her a subsequent reason for action. Depending on the nature of the injury and its relation to the injurer's agency, the appropriate response to having injured another may run anywhere from apologizing, through seeking help, to repairing the loss.

4.1.2 Objectivity and Moral Agency

Perry's account thus enables us to see both the duty of care and the duty to repair as expressions of a unified conception of moral agency. To explain tort law, Perry's account needs to explain why the basis of liability is not whether or not an agent actually foresaw the injury, but rather the foresight of a reasonable or ordinary person. Those who lack the general capacity for foresight are not subject to either a duty of care or a duty to repair, for they cannot be outcome-responsible for the consequences of their actions. But those who have that capacity can be outcome-responsible even on occasions on which they fail to exercise it.

I now want to argue that an objective conception of foresight and Perry's account of agency and responsibility form an unstable combination. The very factors that make his view of agency appealing as

---

[8] Perry offers a related, but distinct, account of the particular interests protected by tort law. Like the idea of outcome responsibility, it makes the idea of autonomy central. Since the harm is a harm to the victim's autonomy, and the risk was itself a risk to that autonomy, Perry limits the reach of the principle of repair to cases in which the defendant's moral failing constitutes a threat to the plaintiff's interest in autonomy. Failure to show appropriate regard for the autonomy interests of others gives rise to a subsequent reason to repair those injuries. If one person's agency interferes with another's, the person responsible must make amends.

[9] *Polemis v. Furness Withy & Co.* [1921] 3 K.B. 560 (C.A.).

[10] Perry, "Moral Foundations," p. 504.

an account of our first-person experience of moral agency[11] make it an unsuitable basis for an account of tort liability. The core of my argument is that the objectivity of the requirement of foreseeability in tort cannot be reconciled with what is essentially a first-person perspective on agency. Nothing in Perry's account precludes combining it with an idea of objectivity at the level of both the interests that are protected by tort law and the standard of care, that is, the amount of care people are required to take with respect to those interests. It cannot, however, be combined with the idea that the duty of care is itself objective, in the sense that someone can be responsible for something that he did not himself foresee.

The root of the problem is that the idea of foresight relevant to outcome responsibility depends on its actual exercise. A person's agency is expressed in her *actual* exercise of her capacities. That she, or some other, hypothetical person might have exercised them differently does not change what of her *was* expressed in the deed. A special case of this feature of outcome responsibility is that moral agency is expressed in what a person did know.

[11] It is not clear that Perry's account of responsibility and reasons for action even succeeds on its own terms. Williams ("Moral Luck") introduces his account of agent regret with the example of a lorry driver who, despite taking all due precautions, runs down a small child. Williams suggests that the driver ought to feel terrible about what he has done, and that he has a special obligation to seek help, apologize to the child's parents, and so on. Williams is surely right that some degree of regret and response is appropriate in such circumstances. Although a bystander ought to feel dreadful witnessing such an event, the driver, it seems, should feel even worse. The driver's agency is implicated in the situation, even though he could not foresee it.

The idea that one's situation gives rise to reasons for action probably even reaches to cases in which agency is not implicated at all. This should not come as a surprise; a prominent theme in broadly existentialist writings has been the way in which one finds oneself "thrown" into a world not of one's own choosing. Whereas Jean-Paul Sartre, for example, sometimes writes as though one's situation imposes no constraints, others in the broad tradition running from Pascal through Heidegger recognize that found possibilities create the space within which one makes one's way in the world. Consider an example. In a Raymond Carver short story, incorporated into the film *Short Cuts,* a group of men decide not to interrupt their fishing trip when they find a dead body. Worse, none seems bothered by the decision. The story gets its force from the callousness of both their behavior and their attitude toward it. Watching their indifference, it strikes us as callous because we suppose being so closely associated with death should be troubling, even if one hasn't caused it. At the very least, finding a dead body should ruin their day. It may even create some special obligation to notify the appropriate authorities. It does not, however, reflect an idea of outcome responsibility. Their situation is found, not made, but they are responsible nonetheless.

4.1 Foresight as a Condition of Agency

The way in which Perry's account of responsibility turns on actual foresight generates two sets of problems. One centers around extra knowledge, the other around the negligent lack of knowledge. Take extra knowledge first. If you continue to talk after I tell you your talking in an ordinary voice gives me terrible headaches, you are outcome-responsible for my injury. After all, you hurt me, knowing perfectly well what you are doing. As a result, my injury is an unproblematic expression of your agency. Perhaps outcome responsibility would only give rise to reasons to apologize (preferably in writing!), but not to tort liability. If so, though, some further explanation is needed of why the duty is so limited, given that my injury is both serious and foreseen. Courts have been unanimous in refusing to award damages to plaintiffs with unusual sensibilities, while awarding damages to those whose injuries are unusual in their extent. Yet by an agent-relative account of foresight and outcome responsibility, injuries to unusual sensitivities that are known are expressions of agency, whereas the unknown extent of injury is not.[12] The person who fails to curb his activities once he learns of the unusual sensitivities of others may be morally worse than the person who inadvertently causes a severe injury. The law's response to the two cases suggests it employs a different understanding of responsibility. As we saw in the last chapter, that understanding can be understood in terms of the more objective idea of taking particular risks, rather than the agent-specific idea of foreseeing certain outcomes.

Next, consider lack of knowledge. Perry's focus on the ways in which actions express agency is difficult to reconcile with the idea that persons are responsible for what they ought to have foreseen, measured in terms of reasonable or ordinary foresight. Perry allows that an agent may be liable for something that he or she did not actually foresee, provided that a person of ordinary capacities would have foreseen it. That is fair enough as a representation of tort doctrine. If our concern is with moral agency, though, it is puzzling that potential foresight should be its measure. If I failed to foresee something I should have foreseen, any injury that results is only problematically an expression of my agency. It may be my bad luck – if it has

---

12 These difficulties are magnified in cases of intervening agents. The law treats rescues as foreseeable responses to injury, even though they are unusual and so not predictable. The law also treats those who explode in anger in response to real or imagined injuries as intervening causes even though anyone with much experience of the crowded conditions of modern life knows to expect such behavior. I discuss these issues later in this chapter.

to be somebody's bad luck, it is presumably mine. But if I didn't even consider the possibility, it is hard to see why whether it is related to *my* agency should turn on whether *others* exercising ordinary capacities for foresight would have foreseen it. After all, the unit of outcome responsibility is *my* agency, not ordinary agency. Alternatively, if the unit of outcome responsibility is ordinary agency, we then need some explanation of why it gives *me* in particular reasons for action.

These examples might be thought to miss Perry's point. Outcome responsibility is supposed to be a necessary condition for a moral duty to repair, not a sufficient one. But the claim that outcome responsibility is a necessary condition of liability conceals an ambiguity. On the one hand, it might be the comparatively weak claim that only agents who have the general capacities to moderate their behavior can be held liable. On this first, weaker, reading, the requisite capacities do not provide a moral basis for the imposition of liability apart from the general considerations of fairness across persons we considered in the last chapter. Instead, they set out the boundary conditions against which the idea of fairness across persons has application. In this sense, the defendant in *Vaughan v. Menlove* is liable, even if he was unable to exercise the requisite capacities on a particular occasion, because any other result would be unfair to the plaintiff, not because the burned cottages were expressive of his agency in any further sense.

Alternatively, the idea that outcome responsibility is a necessary condition for a duty to repair might be read more robustly as a claim about why damages are the appropriate remedy in cases of negligent injury.[13] On the stronger reading, though, the problems of over- and underinclusiveness are serious. The problems of overinclusiveness are serious because these are cases in which the moral basis for liability is present, but liability is absent. The problems of underinclusiveness are more serious for Perry's account, because they are cases in which liability is imposed in the apparent absence of moral responsibility. We do violence to the conception of agency that gives

---

[13] On Honoré's original formulation, in "Responsibility and Luck," outcome responsibility gets its relevance as part of a practice of holding others responsible. As a result, perhaps Honoré could reply that standards of ordinary foresight are part of the practice, and not unfair because on balance people benefit from them as frequently as they lose out from them. No such route is open to Perry, however, because his account is supposed to generate reasons for action in response to one's deeds, and so to apply *apart* from any ongoing social practice, and justify the creation of such a practice.

102

rise to reasons for action from a first-person point of view when we require payment where no agency is expressed. Something cannot be an expression of *my* agency if it played no part in my practical deliberation, even if others might have thought of it.[14]

Outcome responsibility can only fill the explanatory role Perry sets for it if it is a monadic property of agents, that is, a property that does not depend on factors outside the agent. Monadic properties thus contrast with relational ones. Being six feet tall or able to do a handstand are monadic properties in the relevant sense; being employed or indebted, by contrast, are relational. Only if outcome responsibility is monadic is it expressed through an agent's deeds, and only if it is monadic in this way does it give rise to reasons for action. The monadic version of foresight sits uneasily with tort doctrine though, because it makes actual foresight the appropriate basis of responsibility. Thus, it generates moral responsibility for injuries to known ultrasensitive plaintiffs and excludes it for risks unknown to the injurer. If we construe outcome responsibility relationally, though, we lose the connection to reasons for action. Without some independent account of how and why the protected interests of others are always already implicated in a person's agency – the idea of risk ownership, for example – any appeal to the boundaries of the self will fail to explain why those boundaries are given by the capacities of others.[15]

All of these difficulties for Perry's account can be restated in terms of coercion. If I do something that gives me a reason to apologize, or

---

14   Dennis Klimchuk reminds me that the failure to take into account various important things may be expressive of one's character, and so of one's agency. What I didn't think of may well say more about me than what I did. Indeed, what I failed to *do* may also be expressive of who I am. In that sense, one may be accountable for failure at a legal or moral duty one didn't even consider. Klimchuk's reminder is of no help to Perry, however, because it requires an independent account of why the agent should have taken account of that thing. A character-based account of responsibility also needs more to turn it into an account of responsibility for outcomes. A character-based account also seems to depend on the agent's actual capacities for foresight at the time, not on the ordinary capacities of others.

15   There are other ways of implicating the interests of others in a person's agency. For example, in *The Idea of Private Law* (Cambridge, MA: Harvard University Press, 1995), Ernest Weinrib seeks to ground both the duty of care and the duty of repair in the capacity of persons to abstract away from any possible object of choice. If this grounding were to succeed, we would have an explanation of why the interests of others are implicated in agency as such. But it does not. I look at the difficulties with the general project of grounding duties in the capacity for choice in discussing the first of three difficulties with Hegel's account of the distinction between mistakes of fact and mistakes of law in Chapter 6.

puts me in a special position to seek aid, I ordinarily cannot be coerced to act on those reasons. Likewise, if I fail to take account of your unusual sensibilities, your hurts count on my moral ledger, but I can neither be enjoined from my activity nor made to pay damages. By contrast, if I injure someone through my carelessness, and should have foreseen that injury, I can be forced to make appropriate amends, as judged by a court of law. We need some explanation of why coercion is legitimate for some cases of outcome responsibility but not others. The idea of risk ownership gives a straightforward account: I am not coerced as an added inducement to my own better self. I am coerced in my capacity as a legal person. If I wrongfully injure you, you have the right to demand that I restore you to the position you would have been in if not for my carelessness.[16]

4.2 AN ALTERNATIVE ACCOUNT

Still, Perry is right to emphasize the role of foreseeability in both liability and responsibility. Foreseeability needs to be explained in light of a different conception of agency than is appropriate to first-person moral evaluation. I now want to argue that what is foreseeable is a matter of what a reasonable person would foresee if in the circumstances. To understand foresight in this way is to understand it as a preliminary test for liability, in the way that Lord Reid deploys it in *Bolton v. Stone*.[17] On this understanding, if an injury was unforeseeable, there is no further question of liability to ask, because the defendant could not have taken account of the risk that it would happen. Once the test of foreseeability has been passed, the further inquiry is fixed by questions of duty and risk. Foresight still has a role, because it rules out liability for certain injuries. But that role is performed by a test that is normative rather than epistemic.

---

[16] The point about coercion can also be put in terms of the distinction between nonfeasance and misfeasance discussed in the preceding chapter. Tort liability is limited to the consequences of misfeasance, that is, wrongful injury to the protected interests of others. It does not extend to nonfeasance, the failure to confer a benefit on another, even in cases in which a substantial benefit, such as saving a person's life, could be conferred at very little cost. I explained that distinction in the preceding chapter in terms of the idea that knowledge of another person's vulnerability is not sufficient to shift a risk from one person to another. If we look at outcome responsibility in terms of the idea that someone can only be responsible for an outcome they foresaw, the distinction between nonfeasance and misfeasance is invisible.

[17] [1951] App. Cas. 850 (H.L.).

Our discussion of Perry reveals that the appropriate idea of foresight is neither the strong requirement that the consequences actually have been foreseen, and generate reasons, nor the very weak requirement that it has been possible in principle – even if after the fact – to have foreseen them. The first is too strong, because it would make one person's security depend on another's state of mind. The second reduces fault to strict liability, because, except for the most bizarre of coincidences, everything is in principle foreseeable, and everything that has happened as a result of natural forces is in fact foreseeable. In place of these extremes, we find the intermediate and normative requirement that consequences are foreseeable if a person showing appropriate regard for the interests of others would have taken them into account. Limiting liability to actually foreseen consequences would expose some to the thoughtlessness of others, and in so doing import an undue element of subjectivity. Conversely, the chance of an injury is not enough to require precautions, and the fact that someone didn't think of the dangers is not sufficient to excuse the failure to be careful. Instead, the reach of liability is set by reasonable foresight, the foresight of a person who takes appropriate care for the interests of others.

On the view I will defend, foresight is not required because it is a general condition of agency. Instead, it is implicit in the idea of fair terms of interaction. The point can be put in either of two ways. The first of these is that people can only moderate their behavior in light of those interests of others of which they can take account. It makes no sense to ask that someone exercise care with respect to the risk of a coincidence, and so it makes no sense to say that some act creates a risk of a coincidence. The other way of putting the same point is to say that fair terms of interaction require publicity. That is, agents need to be able to know which actions can be performed without fear of legal sanction, and, more to the point, the interests of others of which they must take account. The limitation of liability to foreseeable injuries is an expression of the idea that people must be in a position to know their rights and the rights of others. *Reasonable* foreseeability is required rather than actual foresight because it is public in the right way, that is, accessible in principle both to those who might injure others and those who might be injured by them.

The effect of looking at foreseeability in this way is not to reduce responsibility to liability. We can still say that someone is held liable because he is responsible. But judgments of responsibility depend on the exercise of capacities that are relevant because they are prerequisite to fair interaction, not because they have some independent moral status. Coercive institutions properly take an interest in responsibility and foresight because of its significance for a social world in which persons interact on terms of reciprocity, not because foresight is somehow enmeshed in self-creation.

If we understand foresight as the precondition of people moderating their behavior in light of others, we see why it would function only as a preliminary test of liability. Only if the class of plaintiff and type of injury would be foreseen by a reasonable person can the further question of care arise. If an injury was foreseeable, the further question of whether care should have been taken can arise; if it was not, that question has no purchase, because care could not have been taken.

So foreseeable risks are those of which a reasonable person would take account, whether or not they have in fact been taken into account by a particular person on a particular occasion. Liability is limited to foreseeable injuries because liability for injuries that neither could be foreseen through ordinary efforts nor found out about through inquiries appropriate to the activity in which an agent is engaged would demand that people do more than take the legitimate claims of others into account. Thus, it would fail as an interpretation of liberty and equality, because it would fail to be public in the appropriate way.

Reasonable foresight extends further than wrongful risk imposition does. Natural causal forces turn risks into injuries, so injurers are liable for the natural consequences of their risky behavior. A fair distribution of risks puts the onus on agents to take the natural consequences of their acts into account. Still, whether something is foreseeable, like whether something is reasonable, is determined by a normative conception of the person. Just as the reasonable person is not necessarily engaged in any process of reasoning,[18] so foreseeable injuries are not the result of the exercise of a psychological capacity for foresight. The reasonable person is, as I've said, the person who displays the appropriate amount of care for the interests of others. In terms of foresight, the reasonable person only tries so hard to consider the interests of others. Having ascertained what the possible effects of my action might be, I then need only go so far in moderating my behavior. Although a moment's reflection might convince me that

---

[18] Joshua Cohen, "Moral Pluralism and Political Consensus," in *The Idea of Democracy* edited by David Copp, Jean Hampton, and John E. Roemer (Cambridge: Cambridge University Press, 1993), pp. 270–91.

my activities will end up costing you money, I can often simply disregard that concern.[19]

Many people with ordinary capacities for foresight may fail to think ahead in a particular situation. The question of liability does not turn on whether they did think ahead, but whether they should have. Whether they should have, in turn, is not a matter of whether they could have at that very instant (whatever exactly such an inquiry would involve or discover), but rather of whether they are in general capable of foresight, to the degree that they can carry out their projects as others carry out theirs. Those who have less capacity for foresight than is typical may need to try harder, but to ask less of them is to make the security of others turn on their efforts.[20]

The capacity for reasonable foresight is thus what John Rawls has called a "range property."[21] Rawls illustrates with the example of different points within a circle. All points within the circle are equally within it, even though they vary along other dimensions, such as closeness to the center. Rawls suggests that the capacity to be a subject of justice is a range property in this sense. I want to appropriate Rawls's image to make sense of tort law's idea of responsible agency. As long as one fits within the ordinary range of human capacities, including the capacity to foresee the consequences of one's action, one can be both entitled to the solicitude of others and be held responsible for the costs one's conduct imposes on others. At the same time, being a responsible agent is a range property in another respect as well. One must also have adequate resources and

---

[19]   Benjamin Zipursky has shown the pervasiveness of what he calls "triangular torts," in which a wrongful injury to one party might also inflict epistemically foreseeable losses on third parties that are nonetheless noncompensable. Tort law only protects some reactions and relationships. See Zipursky, "Rights and Recourse," 51 *Vanderbilt Law Review* 1 (1998).

[20]   The one apparent exception involves children, who are held to the degree of foresight typical for those at their developmental stage. The adjustment for age marks not the introduction of a subjective standard, but rather the recognition of the necessity of development to achieve full agency. Infants are not responsible agents but merely natural things; as children grow up, they become increasingly responsible. The risks associated with childhood thus lie in part with the child and in part where they fall, as they would with any other unowned natural objects. Judicial statements capture the underlying idea in some memorable turns of phrase: "Nothing could be more ordinary or normal than to be aged 15," *D.P.P. v. Camplin* [1978] A.C. 705 per Lord Diplock; and "Childhood is not an idiosyncrasy," *McHale v. Watson* [1966] A.L.R. 523 (Austr. H.C.) per Owen, J., at 532.

[21]   John Rawls, *A Theory of Justice* (Cambridge, MA: Harvard University Press, 1971), p. 508.

opportunities in order for the consequences of one's deeds to be fairly imputed.

4.2.1 Intervening Agents

The acts of intervening agents illustrate the meaning, and limits, of the idea of foreseeability. In some circumstances, intervening agency serves to break the causal chain between agent and outcome; in others, it simply continues it. Intervening agents also provide concrete illustrations of the ways in which particular liberty and security interests are valued. The deeds of intervening agents sometimes count as natural consequences, but other times they do not. Yet the classification of intervening acts as foreseeable or otherwise does not depend only on ordinary psychological capacities. Some outcomes are foreseeable *as such,* that is, things of which agents can always be expected to take account, no matter how unlikely they are.

Not all voluntary acts in response to wrong continue the chain of liability. When riding my bicycle in traffic, I occasionally harbor punitive fantasies toward inconsiderate drivers. When a car cuts me off in traffic, I cannot speed merrily along the sidewalk, disregarding the safety of pedestrians, secure in the knowledge that my risky behavior will at worst be expensive for the driver who started it. Nor, for that matter, can I neglect the injury someone else has caused me, secure in the knowledge that my injurer will be responsible for any resulting costs. The requirement that I bear the costs of my choices does not go away once someone else has behaved negligently toward me or anyone else. I am still responsible. The difference that an injury makes is that some of the things that I do – the reasonable ones – count as costs of the injurer's activity, not mine. That there are some such responses is often explained under the rubric of causation. I focus instead on foreseeability, because they illustrate the special nature of its implicit idea of publicity. What can be foreseen – indeed, what must be foreseen – needs to be understood in light of the idea of fair terms of interaction. Reasonable responses to injury can always be taken into account, even when they are surprising.

Reasonable responses to injury count as foreseeable because people are presumed to know that others will behave reasonably. That presumption reflects the idea that free and responsible agents act within a world of other free and responsible agents. In that sense, the principle that reasonable acts are always foreseeable is an analogue of the distinction made by the criminal law between mistakes of fact and mistakes of law. Mistakes of fact may provide the basis for an excuse[22] to a criminal charge, but mistakes of law do not.[23] Agents are presumed to know the rights of others, and to take them into account in deciding what to do. In the same way, if some injury could not in fact have been foreseen, the injurer will avoid liability for it. But a failure to foresee that others will behave reasonably does not limit liability, because people are presumed to know the rights of others and to plan their activities accordingly. Among those rights is the right to respond reasonably to injury. As a result, reasonable responses to danger are conclusively presumed to be foreseen by all agents, even if unreasonable responses are more common. What does and does not count as a reasonable response is itself a substantive question of political morality, and so people may in fact fail to anticipate the reasonable responses of others. Because those responses are reasonable, though, those who fail to anticipate them cannot claim that they could not have known about them. For to allow those who fail to anticipate reasonable responses to escape liability would effectively make their beliefs the measure of the liberty of others. If whether one behaves in a particular way at one's peril depends on whether some other person in particular believes one's actions to be reasonable, one's freedom is limited by the beliefs of others.

The basic principle governing intervening causes is deceptively simple: If the voluntary act of another agent intervenes between my act and your injury in such a way that the natural course of events is interrupted, my liability is eliminated. Ordinarily, intervening intentional human actions are sufficient to break the causal chain between a deed and its consequences. If you leave a fire unattended, and I pour gasoline on it, I have caused the resulting fire. Here what typically happens is part of the story – people have a responsibility to take certain precautions against the predictable wrongful acts of others, even though the wrongdoers are ultimately responsible for their deeds. Given those dangers, people must protect others against them, even though they have no duty to protect themselves.

Consider some further examples: Adolescents in California have taken to playing a game of "chicken," seeing who will wait the longest before jumping off railroad bridges ahead of oncoming trains.

---

22   Reasonable mistakes about victim consent or the necessity of defensive force justify rather than excuse. I explore these matters in Chapter 6.
23   There is an exception in the case of regulatory offenses, to which officially induced error may be a defense.

Railroads can foresee a danger, though they can do little to prevent it. Should engineers be required to slow down in case track jumpers stand in their way?[24] Again, suppose that a tavern posts a sign saying "drunks crossing." Do drivers acquire an increased duty of care, once they have been informed that they may confront pedestrians unable or unwilling to take responsibility for their own safety? Conversely, is the injurer who did not, and could not know, that the person he injured would refuse medical treatment, responsible for the full extent of injuries that proper treatment could have avoided?

Courts have dealt with cases like the track jumpers with doctrines of contributory and, more recently, comparative negligence. Under the older contributory negligence regime, the plaintiff's negligence was a complete defense to liability. Under more recent comparative negligence rules, the injured party's assumption of the risk of the plaintiff's negligence reduces the injurer's liability in proportion to the risks taken by each. A full discussion of the merits and demerits of contributory and comparative negligence schemes is well beyond the current inquiry. For present purposes, both are alike in treating a victim's activity as relevant to the existence of a particular risk, and so as relevant to the question of where the resulting injury rightly belongs. They also share a single underlying rationale from the perspective of the idea of risk ownership. Although there is nothing wrongful about taking risks, including substantial ones, with one's own safety, one cannot wholly displace the costs of those risks onto others, even if those others are negligent.[25]

---

[24] I owe this example to Gregory Keating, "The Rational and the Reasonable in Negligence Theory," 48 *Stanford Law Review* 311, at 368 (1995) (citing John M. Glionna, Trestle-Jumping Fad Puts Youths in Path of Danger, *L.A. Times*, Aug. 10, 1992, p. A1). The example is made more interesting because extra caution on the part of railroads would deprive track jumping of much of its appeal. Keating notes that the example is also complicated because the optimal railroad behavior from the point of view of the jumpers is to go quickly and then slam on the brakes, which would endanger lives and property on board the train.

[25] One advantage of comparative negligence is that it does not lead to judicial doctrines that undermine the overall rationale of tort liability in order to avoid injustice in particular cases. For example, the doctrine of "last clear chance" allowed the plaintiff's contributory negligence to be overridden in cases in which the defendant (usually a railroad) had opportunity to avoid injury after the plaintiff had acted. The problem with such doctrines is that they allow plaintiffs to shift the full costs of their lack of caution onto those who injure them simply by making them aware of their situation. For example, the last clear-chance rule would make railroads liable to track jumpers. Although their knowledge of the track jumpers might make them outcome-responsible in Perry's sense, they would not be liable.

Legal rules governing both contributory negligence and intervening causes can be explained by the idea of risk ownership. Once one
person has put another at risk, the risk continues to flow if the plaintiff acts reasonably; the risk created includes the risk of others acting
reasonably either in response to the danger or in a separate causal
chain that intersects with the wrongful risk creation. Thus, people who
fail to care for their own safety are not treated as foreseeable, but people who do take appropriate care are foreseeable. So put, the principle
has a nice Kantian feel to it. Kant's second formulation of the categorical imperative proscribes treating another person as a means. Thus,
wrongfulness is understood in terms of treating another's agency as a
mere instrument of one's will. As Kant puts it, those who do wrong
"play a game of chance" with the agency of others. As a result, it becomes a conduit for that will. Those who do so are responsible for the
consequences of the reasonable behavior of others. Those who create
perils through their failure to exercise appropriate care thereby make
the reasonable responses of others part of their deeds.

4.2.2   Some Special Cases

Before turning to intervening causes, it is worth noting that the idea
that reasonable behavior is foreseeable helps to explain why tort law
supposes that disabled plaintiffs are foreseeable, unusual though they
might be. Consider the seemingly increased duty of care that drivers
and those obstructing walkways owe to blind persons. Many American jurisdictions have enacted statutes requiring drivers to slow down
where blind pedestrians make themselves visible. The standard does
not depend on what the driver knows, but rather on what he or she
knows or ought to know. Thus, if the pedestrian makes his difficulties apparent to a reasonable person, a driver is liable, whether or not
the driver attended to those difficulties. In Britain, the same result has
been reached without a statute.[26] Drivers and those obstructing walkways are presumed to know that there are blind pedestrians, and to
take the risks to them into account. On the British model, blind pedestrians are not thought of as ultrasensitive plaintiffs, nor even as ordinary plaintiffs whose security is entitled to extra care. This may seem
puzzling until we realize that the duty of care always includes the responsibility of adapting to changing circumstances. Part of what it
means to exercise reasonable care while driving is to be attuned to

---

[26]   See, for example, *Haley v. London Electricity Board* [1965] AC 778 (H.L.).

111

one's circumstances, to slow down if traffic is heavy, visibility bad, or roads icy. These are not changed duties but the same duty. In the same way, care required in the presence of blind pedestrians is not a matter of either a special duty to an unusual class of person or of an increased duty because of extra knowledge.[27] Instead, it is a matter of the reasonableness of blind pedestrians exercising their liberty interest in being out on the streets.[28] If I wear a reflector as I ride my bicycle at night, I do not create an extra duty of care in drivers, but simply provide them with information that enables them to live up to that duty.

On the other hand, the tavern that posts a sign warning that drunks are crossing in front of it creates no extra liability even though it makes drivers foresee certain types of injury. To be sure, like a sign that says "bridge freezes before road surface," such a sign warns drivers of the existence of conditions, against which they already need to take precautions. Yet the presence of the sign does not shift the risk of accident from the careless drunk to careful driver. Likewise, if I post a sign announcing that I intend to play "chicken" with cars on the street in front of me, I cannot impose a legal duty on them to drive at two miles per hour in case I spring out in front of them. Of course, any driver who sees me will need to make reasonable efforts to stop. But drivers had a duty to do that much already. I cannot create a new duty where there wasn't one before simply by informing others that I will not look out for my own interests. To allow me to create liability for others by warning them of my vulnerabilities would enable me to

---

[27] Parallel reasoning explains the rules governing the contributory negligence of children. In cases of contributory (or comparative) negligence, the standard of care is adjusted to both the child's age and his or her actual level of development. The general policy of a sliding standard can be seen as a reflection of the fact that childhood is an inevitable stage on the way to responsible adult behavior, the risks of which are properly borne by each person as an adult rather than as a child. The actual level of development test might appear to import a subjective test. Yet it can be understood in terms of the standard to which the tort-feasor can be held. The presence of children of a variety of developmental stages is something that people creating risks can be expected to foresee. Since the sliding scale of foresight is tied to developmental stages, it does not matter at what age one reaches a particular stage, for it is the stage, rather than the age, that makes the difference.

[28] This example may appear to be in tension with my endorsement of the objective standard of *Vaughan v. Menlove*, discussed in Chapter 3. The conflict is only apparent, however, because the blind pedestrian's limited ability to protect him or herself does not expose others to risk. Indeed, a blind pedestrian who used neither a cane nor a guide dog would not be able to recover. Further, as I will explain below, reasonable responses to perils created by other agents are different from shifting an ongoing peril to others.

displace the costs of my activities onto others by forcing them to take extra precautions. It would thus allow one party to unilaterally shift the rights of another.[29]

These examples may seem misleading because the inebriated patrons of the tavern presumably would be judged to be contributorily negligent. But, indeed, that is exactly the point. Warning of one's carelessness with regards to one's own safety does not shift the burden of precautions to others.[30]

4.3 BOUNCING BALLS AND EXPANDING ACTS

Intervening acts of others work in roughly the same way as does contributory negligence. The basic principle is that reasonable responses to wrongdoing are treated as though they were simply parts of the natural order. Put in the vocabulary of foreseeability, those who unreasonably expose others to risks are expected to foresee that others will behave reasonably in response to those risks. As a result, reasonable responses will count as part of the initially unreasonable act, and the consequences will continue to flow through them. Reasonable responses to wrongdoing act as a conduit for the wrong – it flows directly through them, back to the wrongdoer. What counts as reasonable in such contexts of course will depend on the importance assigned to various interests and activities. But however such matters are decided, their consequences will be among the costs associated with the risk-creating activities that cause them. Thus, they will count as foreseeable in the requisite sense, even if they are statistically uncommon.

---

[29] A parallel creation of new rights in virtue of new information is a feature of the doctrine of coming to the nuisance, prominent in U.S. law. The rationale is supposed to be that the latecomer had the opportunity to take the nuisance into account, and that it probably was factored into the price of the land. That rationale cannot be right as it stands, for the land price will only reflect the nuisance if the latecomer has no right to enjoin the nuisance. If it comes with a right to an injunction, the value of the land will not be affected.

[30] On the other hand, if someone with a severe peanut allergy asks a waiter if some dish contains peanuts, the situation is different, though not because the announcement created an extra duty of care. Instead, the restaurant patron is entering into a specific voluntary interaction with the waiter, one into which the waiter can decline to enter if he or she is unwilling to take the risk. The quasi-contractual nature of this interaction explains why it is a case in which extra knowledge gives rise to extra liability, and thus why it is like medical malpractice cases, but unlike cases in which a person's extra skill as a driver does not give rise to a higher standard of care. See, for example, *Fredericks. v. Castora*, 360 A.2d 696 (Pennsylvania 1976).

As we've seen, for purposes of assigning responsibility, the consequences of an action can be identified only against the background of
some specification of duties among persons. Intervening causes reflect
the same kinds of normative judgments, though in somewhat different ways. Whether something counts as an intervening cause depends
on whether the intervening agent was behaving reasonably. If the intervening agent behaves reasonably, responsibility flows back through
her to the previous agent. This sort of reasonableness is a bar to liability in cases of intervening causation, but not in cases in which the
agent is responding to a natural event rather than someone else's act.
That this should be so may at first seem puzzling, but makes sense
once we recall that tort law serves to determine whose problem various injuries are. If someone behaves in a way that would incur liability, and someone else reasonably protects herself from an injury
and in so doing injures another, the person who was the initial cause
of the injury is liable. But if the second person is instead trying to reduce a loss that would otherwise lie with her, the costs of so doing
must still lie with her.

The basic principle I want to explore is illustrated by *Scott v. Shepherd*.[31] Shepherd threw a burning squib into the market stall of Yates,
from which Willis, to protect himself and Yates's goods, threw it into
the stall of Ryall, who immediately tossed it away from himself. The
squib finally exploded in Scott's stall, costing him his eye. Why was
Shepherd, rather than Yates or Ryall, liable for Scott's injury? After
all, one might reason, each of them injured Scott through his voluntary act. Why take the first person in the chain, rather than, for example, the last? The immediately tempting answer is that Shepherd
was the one who started it. That answer won't do on its own, though,
because, as we've seen, every event has antecedents, and virtually
every voluntary human action has other voluntary human actions
among its antecedents. Again, we may want to say that Shepherd alone
was *acting*, whereas the others were merely *reacting*. Although more
promising, this response needs to explain how acting and reacting
differ here. Another obvious candidate, of course, is that Shepherd
was the only person who did anything wrong. Combining the two,
we get: The distinction between acting and merely reacting depends
on the whether someone was behaving reasonably.[32]

---

[31] *Scott v. Shepherd* (1773) 95 E.R. 1124 (K.B.).
[32] The case is complicated by the fact that *Scott v. Shepherd* was decided under old
common law forms of action, according to which the injurer was liable for di-

DeGrey, C.J., suggested that once the squib had left Shepherd's hand, it made no difference whether it had bounced or been passed from hand to hand. Another version of the same principle, also offered by DeGrey, was the "no man contracts guilt in self-defense." As we shall see, this principle requires qualification. But for now, we can say: Responsibility flows through the defensive acts of innocent parties. The lesson of *Scott* is that when one treats others as mere things without rights, in an important sense they become instruments – conduits through whom responsibility flows back to the agent who failed to respect their agency. Just as I cannot evade liability because it was my car rather than my body that hit you, so if I turn another person into my tool, I am liable for whatever havoc he wreaks. The analogy is imperfect, because those who react to my wrongdoing retain their capacity for agency despite the fact that I use them. Thus, if Willis, rather than simply protecting himself and Yates, seized on the opportunity provided by the squib to ambush his sworn enemy Scott, he, rather than Shepherd, would properly have been liable.[33] But the fact that the responses of Willis and Ryall were reasonable allows liability to flow through them.

There may be some temptation to suppose that Willis and Ryall escape liability because their actions were instinctive, and that the real rationale for treating their acts as a conduit for Scott's wrong is that they could not help what they did. Yet their responses need not have been instinctive; rather, they were appropriate to the circumstances. Indeed, the greatest difficulty with the idea that they were not acting is that their behavior so obviously makes sense in the circumstances. Moreover, had they had time to think, the result should be the same.[34]

rect injuries apart from fault. Officially, at least, this meant that the only question for the court was whether or not one party hit the other party directly. No questions of wrongdoing even came up. This led Blackstone, J., to reason that since Shepherd's guilt would have been irrelevant had the squib injured Willis, Scott's recovery was barred because the injury wasn't direct. Blackstone's reasons for so thinking grew out of the forms of action through which a case could be made at that time. We can leave those issues aside for now, because our concern is with what makes an injury suitably "direct." As the other judges saw, but Blackstone did not, the issue concerns how intervening agency affects initial liability, however that initial liability was established. Of course, to modern eyes, Shepherd's wrongdoing seems highly relevant. But the central issue is how liability, however established, is interrupted by the deeds of others.

33   That is, assuming there was a safe way to dispose of it. If Willis had faced a choice between injuring himself and injuring Scott, his malicious motives would not have made him liable.

34   A similar point is made in *Haynes v. Harwood* [1935] 1 K.B. 146 (C.A.), in which

The fact that they did so without a moment's thought is not significant.

Willis and Ryall avoided injury to themselves. We do not know how serious those injuries would have been. As a result, their defensive acts may well have increased the overall extent of injury. That is, from the point of view of the overall wealth of society, their acts might have been irrational. They are nonetheless permissible, not only because they could not be expected to make the calculation in the circumstances, but more importantly because their responses are reasonable as a type of act, not only in specific situations in which the consequences are likely to work out favorably.

In what sense is acting to preserve oneself reasonable? To do so is plainly rational – protecting oneself is prerequisite to continuing to pursue one's private ends. It is also reasonable, because fair terms of social cooperation do not simply demand that agents moderate their claims in light of the claims of others. They also leave agents space within which they can do as they please in pursuit of their own ends. Self-preservation is the sort of liberty that is protected, for it is so obviously an important security interest.

What other things do and do not qualify as reasonable in these circumstances? Preserving one's life is a clear and easy case, because it is so plainly an important interest. We'll also see that the law can treat other interests in parallel fashion, even if they are not comparably important. But before turning to that question, it is essential to note that reasonableness in reacting to danger only limits liability in certain circumstances. In particular, reasonableness limits liability in just those cases in which liability can flow back to someone. Although reasonable responses to danger may allow injury to be shifted from one person to another, they do not allow liability to be shifted.

The underlying principle in *Scott* is not that it is reasonable to transfer one's own perils to another. The principle is rather that the peril properly belonged to Shepherd who created it by throwing the squib. As a result, the injury also belongs to him. The eye cannot be

the court argued that the law must protect those who act bravely as well as those who act without thinking.

There may be cases in which something readily characterized as panic leads us to doubt that the person was acting at all. In such circumstances, it is conceivable that the reaction be thought of as no action at all, in the way that some courts have treated an epileptic's first seizure if it takes place while driving. See *Cordas v. Peerless Transp,* 27 N.Y.S.2d 198 (1941). At the same time, some understanding of a fair distribution of risks would need to be invoked, in order to distinguish such a case from that of the person who falls asleep while driving.

replaced; the only question is how best to cope with the loss. When Scott asks why he should be the one without an eye, we have no answer to give him. It is simply his misfortune that he was the one injured by Shepherd's deed. Plainly, he would much prefer to have his eye back rather than the small sum Shepherd is likely to cough up. In that sense, the loss is irrevocably his, and something about which a court of justice can do nothing. But in another sense, the payment of damages, here as elsewhere, serves to transfer the loss back to the person to whom it properly belongs. Money damages make this possible, not because it can make Scott entirely whole, but instead because they are the best means available to make Shepherd properly confront the magnitude of the loss.

In the two centuries since *Scott* was decided, legal doctrine has evolved in one important way. Shepherd's injury can still be treated as Scott's act, but the fact that Scott initiated the chain of events leading to Shepherd's injury does not foreclose the possibility of Shepherd recovering from Ryall. Ryall, in turn, could recover from Willis, who can in turn recover from Scott. Alternatively – and according to Shepherd's choice – he could recover directly from Scott. That is, the cause of action between Shepherd and Ryall does not depend on how Ryall found himself confronted with the squib. Each member of the chain owes a duty of care to the susequent members; liability can flow back up the chain, but if Scott cannot afford to pay damages, or disappears into the melée, Willis would be left bearing the cost of Scott's injury, just as he would have been left with his own injury if Scott had been unreachable and the squib had exploded before he was able to toss it.

4.3.1 Natural Necessity

Consider a variant of *Scott*. Suppose that rather than a squib, Yates had found himself besieged by a bit of flaming pitch, caused by a bolt of lightning that struck the thatched roof of his market stall. (Put aside worries about the liability of stall owners for using flammable materials. Make it a meteorite if you prefer, as long as it can somehow be passed from hand to hand. Or provide the parties with cricket bats, borrowed from *Bolton v. Stone*, to facilitate moving small objects in sometimes unpredictable directions.) Willis, acting quickly, threw the flaming parcel away, directly into Ryall's stall. Ryall threw it away, where it caused the plaintiff his injury. Whose problem is it? Notice that Willis and Ryall behaved no differently than they had in the original case. We might think that, as a result, they do not "contract guilt in their own defense." Instead, we might suppose, responsibility simply flows through them, back to the bolt of lightning, leaving poor Scott injured and without a remedy. Since it would have been Scott's problem if the lightning had hit his stall directly, and the intervening agency was reasonable, we might conclude that the loss must lie where it falls. Then again, we might conclude that since Yates would have been injured if not for Willis's acts, he should bear Scott's loss.

So far as I know, *Scott II* (as I shall call it) never happened as I've described it, but equivalent cases, albeit with fewer steps, often have. The most prominent of these is *Vincent v. Lake Erie Transportation*.[35] Suppose, either over your protests or simply without your permission, I tie my boat to your dock in a storm, in order to reduce damage to it. My action saves my boat, but at the cost of considerable damage to your dock. Suppose that the only way to save my boat, or at least a reasonable guess as to the only way to save it, was by tying to your dock. I behaved reasonably – it was the only way to secure my boat. If the storm had damaged your dock in my absence, it would simply be your problem. May we conclude that it is still your problem, given that I was acting reasonably? Again, suppose I break into your cabin in a storm, reasonably[36] believing that doing so is the only way to keep myself alive. Do I nonetheless need to pay for the furniture I burned and the food I ate? Or does the fact that I was behaving reasonably make it as though the storm had consumed the food and furniture directly? Each of these cases is a version of *Scott II*. The chain of agents is shorter, but the basic facts are the same: One agent injured another in order to spare himself injury. In each case, injury was averted, at considerable (though typically lesser) costs to others. Should this make a difference?

In cases like *Scott II*, we find another expression of the principle that I suggested underlies all of traditional tort liability. That is the principle that people should bear the costs of their choices rather than displacing them onto others. If the defendants in *Scott II* were allowed to get off scott free (sorry), they would essentially be allowed to displace risks they face onto others. Although it is difficult to object to their use of the property of others to reduce their potential losses,

---

[35]   124 N.W. 221 (Minnesota 1910).

[36]   In the technical sense of the term. My grounds for so believing do not involve adopting a self-serving perspective on the risks I face. Any reasonable person would agree about the risks I face.

there is an important difference between using the property of others and taking that property.[37] In circumstances of necessity, the right to exclude others from one's property is limited. Insofar as I act to protect myself, I do not need to secure your consent any more than I need to secure your consent before behaving carelessly. However, having failed to secure your consent, I bear the full risks of my act. If, by tying my ship to your dock, I destroy both, my liability is not limited to the amount I saved (in this case nothing) or even should have expected to save.

It may seem unfair that I should bear the full costs of the storm that took me by surprise. Why make the fact that I was the person the storm randomly "chose" the decisive factor? If the storm had destroyed your dock, or the flaming pitch landed directly on Scott, the losses would have lain where they fell. Yet it is no less true that if your dock or cabin (or Scott's stall) had not been available, the losses would have lain where they fell. That is, too many counterfactual cases are available to allow any one to determine what is acceptable in the actual circumstances.

In his discussion of *Vincent*, Richard Epstein has suggested we can solve these problems by supposing that both boat and dock were owned by the same person, or in some analogous way in the other cases. Epstein's reasoning is that if we do so, we will realize that the decision about whether to remain moored would be made on the basis of some sort of cost–benefit calculation. As a result, whether the ship moored or not would depend on which course of action would cost the least. From this, Epstein concludes that the cost should be borne by the active party.[38] Yet the possibility of unifying the parties in a thought experiment tells us nothing about which aspects of that union are appropriate in the actual circumstances. We might use the same reasoning to judge that the costs should be borne by the party best positioned to minimize them,[39] or, for that matter, divided equally. But the difficulties with Epstein's approach point the way to a better account. If the shipowner also owned the dock, the damage

---

[37]   Discussing a case of duress, Holmes remarks, "And it may well be argued that although he does wisely to ransom his life as best he may, there is not reason why he should be allowed to intentionally and permanently transfer his misfortunes to the shoulders of his neighbors." Oliver Wendell Holmes, *The Common Law* (Boston: Little, Brown, 1881), p. 148.

[38]   Though, of course, he might have concluded instead that the costs should be borne by both, since that would have been done if the dock and boat had been owned by the same person.

[39]   Guido Calabresi, *The Costs of Accidents* (New Haven: Yale University Press, 1970).

to it would be his alone to bear. Yet there would be something wrong if he could reduce his losses because he didn't own the dock, but merely borrowed it without the owner's permission. The fact of peril makes it legitimate for him to borrow it, but in borrowing it, he gains no advantage he wouldn't have had if he owned it.

In cases of extreme peril, the peril suspends the rules of trespass and conversion that ordinarily allow people to exclude others from using their property. The temporary suspension of those rules does not thereby entitle the user either to keep the goods in question or to destroy them, however. The court in *Vincent* makes this point with an example: If the boat had required new lines to secure it, the defendants would have been free to use them because of the necessity of the situation. Yet the defendant would also need to compensate the rope owners for their value.

We have already seen that if I carelessly injure you, the point of damages is to make that injury belong to me, to make the notional transfer of the injury real. In the *Scott II* cases, the use of another's property does not change the fact that the injury, whatever its magnitude, properly belongs to the person it initially befell. Thus, they differ from *Scott*, where the injury properly belongs to the person who wrongfully created it.

4.3.1.1 Digression: Necessity and Mistake. Cases like *Vincent* are striking in two respects. The first is that rules of trespass are suspended by peril; the second that injurers are nonetheless liable for actual damages. I've suggested that *Vincent* differs from *Scott* because the risk imposed by a natural peril properly belongs to the person it first befalls. It remains for me to explain one legal aspect of the case. Why is necessity *both* a defense to trespass *and* a basis for liability? Trespass does not ordinarily require a showing of harm. Instead, damages in trespass serve to protect the autonomy interests of property holders, apart from and in addition to any losses they might suffer. Thus, nominal damages are awarded even in the absence of harm. If anyone could use another's property whenever they supposed it served their purposes to do so, provided only that they were prepared to pay for its use, the idea of things belonging to particular people would lose its sense.[40] Damages for losses serve to return the costs of an injury to the injurer; nominal damages for trespass serve to protect and

---

[40] Cases in which the use of another's property is intentional generate further problems. I touch on these issues in Chapter 5.

vindicate the rights of property owners.[41] As such, damages for trespass share important features with both punitive damages and criminal punishments. It is thus no coincidence that both criminal charges and damages for trespass are both suspended in circumstances of peril. Both punishment and damages for trespass are forward-looking warnings in a way that damages for injury are not. Interests in deciding what to do with one's own property do not lose their importance in circumstances of peril. But no remedy, either criminal or tort, could serve to protect them.[42] Because the peril is temporary, there is no need to vindicate the property owner's rights after the fact; because it is a peril, the prospect of punishment or damages would not stop the boat owner from acting.[43] Although the record in *Vincent* does not mention passengers or crew aboard the boat, they were presumably aboard, and thus at risk. (Sending an unmanned freighter into a storm would have imperiled more than the boat.) Because the risk was to persons as well as property, the threat of damages or criminal penalties would not have deterred the boat's master.

If we understand the absence of trespass in *Vincent* in terms of the impossibility of deterrence, we can see also why liability for injury would be a natural concomitant of exemption from liability for trespass. Suppose I take your (identical) raincoat instead of my own. In such circumstances, it might be said that the mistake was one that anyone could have made. Or it might be said that my mistake is imputable to the circumstances instead of anything I have done wrong. Yet I still need to return your raincoat. I even need to return it if my taking it is your doing, not mine; if, for example, the dry cleaner mixed up our orders; or my mistake was the result of your earlier mistake in taking mine. I have done nothing to which damages for conversion would be an appropriate remedy.[44] Nonetheless, I do not thereby acquire a lasting property interest in your coat. And if I damage it while

---

[41]   *Restatement (Second) of Torts*, s. 163 (Philadelphia: American Law Institute, 1979).

[42]   I discuss this issue at length in Chapter 5, in explaining necessity as a criminal defense.

[43]   The absence of trespass also explains the result in *Ploof v. Putnam,* 75 A.277 (Vt. 1910), in which a dock owner was found liable when his servant sent a boat out in a storm. Because the emergency meant that the defendant was not entitled to either an injunction or damages for trespass, his act exposed the plaintiff's boat and its passengers to the risks of the storm. Thus, his act was negligent with respect to the plaintiff's interest in security, and he was liable for damages within the risk of that negligence.

[44]   A parallel example involving mistakes can be found in W. Page Keeton et al., *Prosser and Keeton on the Law of Torts* 95. (St. Paul, MN: West, 1984).

I have it, I still need to repair it, even if the damage to the coat was not my fault.

In legal terms, my use of your raincoat is a bailment – the possession of one person's goods by another. In cases of bailment, liability is strict, precisely because the possession, but not the ownership, of the thing shifts temporarily. As a result, it must be returned in its original condition. If you had loaned me your raincoat, and I had spilled coffee on it, I must return it to you in the condition in which I received it. *The very thing that makes my use of the coat acceptable also makes me strictly liable for any damage to it.* Otherwise, your gracious loan of the coat would enable me to shift my problems – problems that are my problems, even if they are not my fault – to you.[45]

Like mistakes, circumstances of necessity enable me to claim that the circumstances, rather than my act, are responsible for my disregard for the rights of others. In that sense, the natural necessity flows through me, as it might if I exercised appropriate care in other settings. When my use of the dock (or raincoat) is imputed to the circumstances, no quasi-punitive response to my mistake is appropriate. So my borrowing of each without your permission is excused. But that doesn't mean that I thereby come to own the dock to which I have moored my boat. Precisely because the circumstances excuse my *use* of your goods, when I must restore them to you after the emergency ends or the mistake is discovered, they must be in the condition in which I borrowed them. The fact that it was an honest mistake does not change the fact that it was *my* mistake. In the same way, the fact that it was a genuine emergency does not change the fact that it was *my* emergency.

My privilege to use your goods in circumstances of necessity is incomplete; I cannot paint your dock in the storm. I can only use your goods in the ways that I must if I am to avoid the dangers I face. Put differently, my decision to tie up my boat may be imputable to the circumstances in which I find myself; my decision to paint your dock is not. (If anything, my decision to do so undermines my claim to be reacting to the circumstances.) In cases of negligence, I am only re-

---

[45] Ernest Weinrib has suggested to me that this point can be put in terms of unjust enrichment: If I spill coffee on your coat, I am using it beyond the ways in which the original loan (or mistake) makes legitimate. As a result, I must give up the benefit of the further use. Thus, in our examples, my allowable use of the coat was wearing it; the unauthorized further use of the coat was as a receptacle for spilt coffee; the boat owner's allowable use of the dock was as a mooring in a storm; the further use was as an impact absorber. Those uses must be paid for, even though they are accidental concomitants of excusable uses.

sponsible for the damage I do that is within the risk that makes my conduct wrongful; in cases of necessity, I only avoid doing wrong in response to those risks that make my action necessary. Any other harm I do is wrongful. Although the wrongfulness of my deed is limited by the risk, my liability for damage that I do is not. But to the extent that I can use those goods, I must return them as I found them. Had I torn my own raincoat, or damaged my own dock, the problem would still be mine, regardless of how careful I had been.[46]

The apparently strict liability for acts done in conditions of necessity gets its rationale from a different source than does strict liability for engaging in dangerous activities discussed in Chapter 3. If I borrow your raincoat or your dock, I am liable for the damage I do to it, no matter how freakish. By contrast, if I engage in ultrahazardous activities, my liability is limited to the very risks that make my activity hazardous. If I use explosives, I am only liable for the harms that characteristically result from their use, not for all of the harms that result from their use in this particular case. The more stringent rule of necessity protects the injured party against a greater range of injuries, because the defendant's privilege to use another's property in an emergency requires that it be returned in the exact condition in which it was taken.

4.3.2 Rescuers

Now consider another variant on *Scott*, which I will call *Scott III*. Suppose that the squib posed no danger to Willis, but he rushed into Yates's stall, hoping to protect the latter. He succeeds in protecting Yates, but injures himself in the process. Whose problem is his injury? If he hadn't leapt to the rescue, Yates might have been seriously injured – but that injury would have belonged to Shepherd. Once again, we

---

[46] Liability for losses occasioned by natural perils may seem a harsh, even cruel doctrine. The boat owner did no wrong, yet bears the burden of a substantial loss. Had the boat been destroyed, and the dock damaged in the process, the boat owner would have been left with the cost of both. It is important to identify the source of the difficulty, though. The harshness of the doctrine – like the harshness of leaving Vaughan with the full costs of his limited intelligence – comes from the default rule that losses lie where they fall. In cases of either limited capacity or natural peril, it may be appropriate to hold the losses in common. Such responses to large scale natural disasters is common in modern societies, and, as I will argue in Chapter 9, there are reasons for a broader pooling of losses. Any argument for a broader pooling of losses needs to be distinguished, however, from a license to displace losses onto someone in particular who happens to be available.

don't know what the extent of that injury would have been. It may be that Willis's act actually increased the overall extent of injury. Should he be liable as a result? Or should he escape liability on the grounds that protecting the life of another – even a stranger – is just as reasonable as protecting one's own life? Neither is so reasonable as to be mandatory – we probably wouldn't blame the original Willis if he simply faced the danger, or this imagined Willis were he to stand idly by as Yates was injured. Demanding that people behave in a certain way is one thing; supposing it is reasonable for them to so behave quite another.

When courts have confronted cases like *Scott III*, they have held the initial injurer was liable for the full extent of the rescuer's injuries. In one such case,[47] a man leapt into the path of an oncoming train, pushing his drunken friend out of its path. He misjudged the force required to dislodge his friend, and as a result, his leg remained in the train's path, and was severely injured. The railroad tried to avoid liability by insisting that the rescuer had contributed to his own injury. The court held that this was irrelevant, on the grounds that he was acting to protect life. Had the rescuer rolled across the track in front of the train in other circumstances, perhaps on a dare, and misjudged in a way that cost him his leg, the court would have held that he contributed to his own injury. The only thing that makes a difference is the fact that he is acting to protect life. In virtue of that fact, his misjudging his own abilities becomes the railroad's problem. That is, because of the railroad's negligence, the reasonable response to danger became part of the railroad's act.[48]

---

[47] *Peyton v. Texas and Pac. Ry.*, 6 So. 690 (Louisiana 1889).

[48] Rescuing others is no different from rescuing oneself. If I injure you in a negligent attempt to rescue you from some natural disaster, under common-law rules, I will be liable for your injury, in spite of my commendable motives. Many jurisdictions have introduced statues that modify the common-law rule, in the hope of encouraging, or at least not discouraging, would-be rescuers who fear liability from a botched rescue. Such initiatives are typically limited in their reach, only indemnifying against injury to the party being rescued, not to third parties. Even so, the sense of the traditional rule is not hard to grasp: Think of the person who drives at high speeds while attempting to effect a rescue, let alone the person who imagines himself capable of performing surgical procedures he has seen on television. Limiting liability in such cases may make some sense, though if it does, it is because we suppose that the rescuer is simply trying to reduce the problems of the rescued, rather than to displace any problems from one person onto another. When negligence shades over into recklessness, as it perhaps does in the case of an amateur surgeon, the would-be rescuer might well be thought to be displacing the costs of heroic fantasies onto some injured person convenient for the purpose, and so to be liable.

What is the basis of liability in such cases? One suggestion can be found in *Haynes v. Harwood:* "It seems to me that if horses run away it must be quite obviously contemplated that people are likely to be knocked down. It must also, I think, be contemplated that persons will attempt to stop the horses and try to prevent injury to life or limb."[49] The idea of contemplation here must not be misconstrued. Hart and Honoré ask, "When must this be contemplated, and what would be the point of contemplating it?"[50] Failure to restrain horses is already negligent, even if nobody comes to the aid of the injured. For the same reasons, we do not suppose that railroads are prohibited from speeding in stations because rescuers aiding drunks in their path may take too great a risk and get injured. If we were confident that nobody would ever risk a rescue, limits on railroad speed would be no less legitimate. Conversely, limits on railroad speed do not earn any extra warrant because some daredevils will play chicken, jumping from railway bridges.

The reason that rescuers are treated differently than others who jump onto railroad tracks is that rescuers are behaving reasonably. In *Wagner v. International Railway,* Cardozo explains liability to rescuers on the grounds that rescuers are a foreseeable outcome of danger, and those who create danger call forth rescuers: "Danger Invites Rescue. The cry of distress is the summons to relief. The emergency begets the man. The wrongdoer may not have foreseen the coming of a deliverer. He is liable as if he had."[51] Because the reasonable actions of others are always foreseeable, their injuries are compensable. One does not need to take into account the chance that others will behave badly, but one does need to take into account the possibility that they will

Even where good Samaritan statutes limit the liability of would-be rescuers, they can be liable to third parties. In *Buck by Buck v. Greyhound Lines Inc.,* 783 P.2d 437 (Nevada 1989), a passing driver took charge of a vehicle that had stalled in the process of making a U-turn on an isolated Nevada highway. Rather than pushing the stalled car off the road, the would-be rescuer instructed the driver to turn off her lights, and blocked the other lane of traffic with his car, shining his headlights into oncoming traffic. A bus, the driver of which was temporarily blinded by the lights, ran into the stalled car, severely injuring the passengers. Since the would-be rescuer's bad judgment was the cause of the accident, the question arose of whether the Nevada good Samaritan statute protected him from liability. The court held that it did not on the grounds that no emergency existed at the time of the "rescue."

49 *Haynes v. Harwood* [1935] 2 KB 240, per Finlay J. at 247, aff'd (1934); [1935] 1 K.B. 146 (C.A.).
50 Hart and Honoré, *Causation in the Law,* p. 266, n. 43.
51 *Wagner v. International Railway Co.,* 133 N.E. 437 (N.Y. 1921).

behave well. In that sense, one "must" contemplate the presence of rescuers, even in the most unlikely places.

Like other reasonable responses, rescues are foreseeable regardless of their frequency. Rescues are comparatively uncommon, whereas carelessness in angry response to negligence may be more so. Many people, particularly men, explode in rage when they are injured. Many people who have had a "close call" become careless because distracted. Comparatively few people expose themselves to peril when they see strangers facing it. Indeed, many governments give awards for unusual bravery in such circumstances. The rescue is foreseeable because it is reasonable, not vice versa.

Cardozo's dictum "danger invites rescue" suggests that the duty to avoid exposing rescuers to risk is owed to the rescuers themselves, not to the person being rescued. Thus, liability does not depend on an Andrewslike principle that would make the negligent party liable for injuries caused, even outside of the risk. Since the rescuer's response to peril is reasonable, it is foreseeable, and others must take it into account. If it leads to injury, those who create the risk of injury during rescue are liable. One consequence of this account of liability to rescuers is that it explains the otherwise surprising fact that someone who is rescued by another is liable to the rescuer for the rescuer's expenses. That liability follows directly because the duty to protect rescuers from risks is owed to the rescuers. Creating a peril invites rescue, whether one places oneself or another in that peril.[52] At the same time, creating a peril may also invite onlookers, but one is not liable for their injuries, because their actions are not considered reasonable, even though they are presumably more common than rescuers.

The same rationale that underwrites liability to rescuers explains the liability of an initial injurer for the further injuries caused through negligent medical care. Seeking medical care is a reasonable response to injury, as is providing it.[53] Even where the medical care is carried

---

[52] Thus, liability to rescuers is doctrinally related to the idea of an "attractive nuisance" in comparative fault cases involving children. Those who keep swimming pools or concrete pipes where children might play in them and be injured are liable for the injuries. See, for example, *Terranella v. Union Bldg & Const. Co.*, 70 A.2d 753 (N.J. 1949). In the same way, those who create risks to themselves or others are liable for the injuries of the rescuers they attract.

[53] "Doctors, being human, are apt occasionally to lapse from prescribed standards, and the likelihood of carelessness, lack of judgment or of skill, on the part of one employed to effect a cure for a condition caused by another's act, is therefore considered in law as an incident of the original injury, and, if the injured party has used ordinary care in the selection of a physician or surgeon,

out negligently, it is treated as foreseeable, because the risk of medical malpractice on that particular occasion is created by the original wrongdoer. Such liability has its limits, just as it does in the variants of *Scott:* if a physician intentionally inflicts an injury, or performs an unrelated operation, the original injurer is not liable, just as Shepherd would have avoided liability if Ryall had used the squib to settle an earlier score.[54]

The point here is not that it is good public policy to promote either rescues or the provision of medical care in this way. It is difficult to know whether rescuers expect to be injured, or give any thought to questions of compensation if they are. Emergencies that invite rescue are so infrequent that comparatively few people ever find themselves in a position to effect a rescue. As a result, it is not easy to assess whether liability to rescuers has any incentive effects. In the same way, most people who are injured will seek medical care quite apart from considerations of liability. The important point concerns the way reasonableness standards operate in the rescue cases. Whether an activity counts as reasonable for the purposes of transferring responsibility depends on views about the importance of that activity. If a reaction counts as reasonable, it gains its importance in a particular way. Preserving life only allows one to increase costs to those who endanger it, not to impose them on uninvolved third parties. A policy that favors a particular sort of activity only favors it in certain situations. The advantage of looking at policies promoting rescue in terms of the principle of *Scott v. Shepherd* is that we see that goods can play an essential role without being subject to anything like a utilitarian calculus. In rescues, the interest at issue is formally parallel to the interest in *Scott*. Whatever it might cost others, it is important that people be able to act in ways that will protect themselves and others.

So far, we have seen two kinds of cases in which an injurer's liability can be increased by the acts of others. In *Scott,* the initial thrower of the squib was liable for the defensive acts of those who found themselves in its path; in *Peyton,* the railroad was liable for the acts of those who rescued those it placed in danger. In both of these cases,

---

any additional harm resulting from the latter's mistake or negligence is considered as one of the elements of the damages for which the original wrongdoer is liable." *Thompson v. Fox,* 192 A.107, at 108–109 (Pennsylvania 1937).

[54] The same principle does not apply to negligent repair to damaged property, though it is difficult to see why it should not, provided the injury is suitably related to the problem being repaired. See *Exner Sand & Gravel v. Petterson Lighterage & Towing Corp.,* 258 F.2d 1 (Second Circuit, 1958).

the acts of others are deemed to be at the tort-feasor's peril, even though those same acts would be the occasions of liability if done in response to a natural peril.

4.3.3 Liability for the Consequences of Plaintiff's Religious Beliefs

Just as a tort-feasor can acquire liability for the reasonable acts of victims before and during a dangerous incident, so can liability be acquired for the reasonable acts of victims after such an incident. The classic examples involve accident victims who fail to mitigate their damages on religious grounds – for example, by refusing lifesaving treatments – whose heirs sue for wrongful death. That is, in many jurisdictions, religious belief is a respect in which injurers must take their plaintiffs as they find them. The cases are revealing both because the plaintiffs are often treated like constructive hemophiliacs, and because they illustrate that although protected security interests are objectively defined, those who have different priorities can sometimes be allowed to act on those priorities even though it will cost others money. The general line of the American cases holds that a plaintiff need not abandon religious commitments in order to save a negligent plaintiff money.[55] Those cases are controversial, and not all jurisdictions accept them. The controversy stems from disagreement about how best to classify religious belief, whether it is to be thought of on the model of hemophilia or on the model of an expensive preference. The disagreement does not concern the abstract structure I have been describing, but only where religious beliefs fit into it.

In treating religious beliefs as the equivalent of self-protection, courts are making a substantive decision. Ordinarily, failure to mitigate one's losses reduces the damages accordingly, even if the plaintiff's failure can be traced to what is otherwise an important liberty interest. For example, if I delay seeking medical treatment because I do not want to miss an important meeting or a vacation that I have long anticipated, or because I am afraid of doctors, it is my decision, for which I cannot expect others to bear the costs. The person who puts off a visit to the doctor because he worries a small cut may be serious does not recover from his injurer if the cut festers and his leg must eventually be amputated. Although I have a liberty interest in

---

[55] See, for example, *Lange v. Hoyt*, 159 A.575 (Conn. 1932), as well as the cases discussed in Guido Calabresi, "The Beliefs of a Reasonable Person," in his *Ideals, Beliefs, Attitudes and the Law* (Syracuse: Syracuse University Press, 1985), pp. 45–68.

being able to decide whether to go on my vacation, or in deciding how to manage my personal health, you do not need to take that possibility into account in deciding whether to expose me to risks. Like the voyeur who gets too close to an accident and is injured in the process, I act at my own peril. What makes the difference? In each case, I would be liable if I injured someone else *de novo*. If either my vacation plans or my religious beliefs caused an injury to another – either my campfire or ceremonial candles burn you, say – I would be liable. And I cannot displace the costs of either onto anyone else – I cannot commandeer your car for my vacation or pilgrimage. The reason for treating the person who fails to mitigate on religious grounds differently is not that the belief is deeply held, nor that it is widely held. It is rather that the law supposes that that particular category of belief is so important that it is reasonable to act on it. That is, the injurer cannot unilaterally require the plaintiff to bear the costs of conscience where the injurer's wrong has made conscience costly.[56]

The general principle from *Scott* is that tort-feasors are liable for reasonable responses to their deeds; the religion cases show that acting on religious beliefs can be thought of as reasonable. But nothing in the general structure of liability requires that they be thought of in that way. Consider a slightly different example. Suppose a racist refuses a transfusion for fear that the blood will be from a member of a despised race.[57] Suppose further that the racist's views are sincere, and related to deeply held religious views.[58] In the example, the question of reasonableness is pulled in two directions. On the one hand, the fact that it is a profound matter of conscience means that an important liberty interest is at stake. On the other, the religious view

[56] The scale of importance here is given by a broader understanding of freedom of religion. To recognize religious belief as important does not, by itself, demand conclusions about its relevance to questions of tort liability. Those conclusions rest on views about the importance of conscience to fair terms of interaction. I will not try to articulate, let alone defend, those views here; the point of the example is that if religious belief is thought of as important in a certain way, the failure to mitigate losses on religious grounds must be thought of as reasonable, and so foreseeable.

[57] Guido Calabresi offers this hypothetical case in *Ideals, Beliefs, Attitudes and the Law*. Calabresi finds it obvious that a court would treat the racist's choice as an intervening cause.

[58] See *Bob Jones University v. United States*, and Robert Cover, "Foreword: Nomos and Narrative," 97 *Harvard Law Review* 4 (1983). In *Bob Jones*, a religious university lost its tax exemption because it forbade interracial dating on the basis of its interpretation of scripture. As Cover points out, the depth of religious commitment was questionable, since the university abandoned its policy in order to regain the exemption.

runs contrary to the idea of equality underlying fair terms of interaction. My own view is that the competing pressures are not even, and that equality should win out in such a case, so that the racist's choice is treated no differently than an idiosyncratic individual preference. Still, the fact that there are competing forces at work in the definition of reasonableness shows that the problem here is one of specifying the requisite liberty and security interests.

4.3.4 A Counterexample?

I close this chapter by considering a putative counterexample to my claim that the reasonable acts of others are always foreseeable. In some circumstances, patently unreasonable acts are also treated as foreseeable. In *Dorset Yacht v. Home Office*,[59] borstal boys (juvenile delinquents) were inadequately supervised. They escaped and did considerable damage to the plaintiff's yacht. The negligent guards were held liable, and could not claim that the actions of the borstal boys were an intervening cause, despite the fact that they were intervening human actions. Here the situation appears to be precisely the opposite of that in *Peyton* and *Scott* – liability flows through the unreasonable activities of others. The difference is easy to explain, though. The risks that made negligence in guarding the borstal boys wrongful was that they would escape and do damage. In fact, *Dorset Yacht* differs from *Peyton* and *Scott* because in both *Peyton* and *Scott*, the reasonable reactions of others are not part of what made the initial act wrongful. Instead, the initial act is rendered wrongful in each case by the dangers that it poses; the reasonable intervention of others simply transfers a prior peril. By contrast, the peril in *Dorset Yacht* is created by unsupervised borstal boys.[60]

Other cases share the general structure of *Dorset Yacht*.[61] For ex-

---

[59] *Dorset Yacht Co. v. Home Office* [1970] A.C. 1004 (H.L.).
[60] See for example, *Wierum v. RKO General*, 539 P.2d 36 (Calif. 1975), in which a pedestrian recovered from a radio station because the station's contest led drivers to drive recklessly in a race to an announced location for a prize. In both *Wierum* and *Dorset Yacht*, the plaintiff presumably had a cause of action against the direct injurers also, but could recover from the person who created the risk of unreasonable behavior. Unlike *Dorset Yacht*, however, *Wierum* does not depend on the idea that the radio station was somehow charged with caring for dangerous things.
[61] Some American cases go one step further and hold a defendant liable for creating conditions in which others act negligently. In some cases, a defendant who has negligently obstructed a pedestrian plaintiff's view of traffic has been held liable for injuries caused by a negligent motorist. See, for example, *Boese v. Val-*

ample, a mental institution may be held liable for injuries caused by negligently released patients.[62] In some jurisdictions, a driver who leaves keys in a parked car is liable for injuries brought about by car thieves.[63] In each of these cases, the wrongful risk is thought to consist in the foreseeable bad behavior of others. The only danger connected with leaving keys in a parked car comes from the intervening acts of others, just as the point of supervising borstal boys is that they are likely to do damage if left on their own. The case of mental patients may be slightly different, at least in those cases in which their condition prevents them from being responsible agents at all. In such cases, the severity of their illness may mean that for legal purposes, they do not count as acting at all. If they do not count as acting, then they are treated in the same way as are dangerous animals. Those in charge of them are responsible for protecting others from them.[64]

4.4   CONCLUSION

The idea of reasonable foresight serves to explain the extent to which fair terms of cooperation require each person to take account of the interests of others. Just as risk can always be reduced further by taking extra precautions, so risk can be better foreseen by checking more carefully. Because the law of tort aims to protect liberty no less than

---

ley Farm Dairy Company, 300 S.W.2d 453 (Missouri 1953). In other cases, the driver's negligence has been held to break the causal chain between the defendant's negligence and the plaintiff's injury. In some of those cases in which the initial defendant is found liable, its liability is a matter of contributory negligence. So they can be seen to parallel *Scott* after all. Ordinarily, the negligent driver would be able to reduce his liability by pointing to the plaintiff's comparative negligence. In this case, however, the plaintiff can argue that walking on the road was a reasonable response to the negligence of those obstructing the sidewalk. Responsibility flows through reasonable actions and relieves the plaintiff of comparative fault.

[62] See, for example, *Homere v. State of New York*, 48 A.2d 422 (N.Y. 1975).
[63] See, for example, *Ross v. Hartman*, 139 F. 2d 14 (D.C. Cir. 1943).
[64] The same principle applies to objects, such as weapons, that are only dangerous if used. What counts as a sufficient danger will depend in part on how important the liberty and security interests involved are thought to be. In the United States, the right to bear arms seems to count for too much to allow liability in the case of guns. To hold the gun owner liable depends on treating firearms as the English courts have treated borstal boys, and thus on rejecting the NRA's claim that guns don't kill people. Guns do kill people, and those who keep them must take appropriate precaution in light of that fact. If a thief takes an unlocked weapon and injures somebody else, the injured party has a claim against the homeowner, even if the homeowner could in principle recover from the thief.

security, there is a limit to the amount that reasonable persons are required to foresee. Conversely, some things must be taken into account, no matter how unusual they are. Whether the reasonable act comes before, during, or after the wrongdoing, it can be thought of as allowing liability to flow through an agent. Because free agents act within a world of other free agents, reasonable responses to wrongdoing count as foreseeable parts of the natural causal order.

Chapter 5

Punishment and the
Tort/Crime Distinction

This is the first of four chapters extending the ideas of reasonableness and risk to problems of the criminal law. The criminal law is the area in which the interest in responsibility is perhaps most pressing. Various proxies for the tort system may be the best way of imperfectly realizing corrective justice; proxies for the criminal law are cause for concern about miscarriages of justice. Those who cause injuries ought to pay, but if someone else offers a voluntary payment instead, the injured party has no grounds for complaint. Since the injury is the injurer's problem, how can the injured party complain if someone makes what is in effect a gift to the injurer? In the case of crimes, however, there is a strong and legitimate retributive sentiment, which demands that wrongdoers "pay" for their deeds, though in a different sense. I think the basic apparatus introduced in our discussion of tort helps to make sense of this retributive impulse, and goes some distance toward justifying it.

An account of responsibility in the criminal law must do at least four things. First, it must identify the type of acts that generate criminal culpability, and explain the grounds for criminalizing certain types of behavior. Second, it must explain the general requirement of a guilty mind for criminal culpability. Tort law's negligence standard measures conduct, apart from any questions about the defendant's thoughts; criminal culpability requires more. Third, an account of the criminal law must explain why punishment is an appropriate response to criminally culpable behavior. That is, it must explain why punishment is an appropriate response to the specifically criminal form of responsibility. Fourth, it must explain the conditions under which otherwise criminal behavior is not punished.

Different theorists have explained these factors in different ways, and on many views, their answers do not come as a package. Instead, they reflect a variety of disparate social policies and concerns. Some theorists opt for a pluralist view on principled grounds. H. L. A. Hart, for example, supposes that preventing harm is the basis for criminal behavior, that intent is required because liability to criminal sanction should be within an individual's control, that punishment serves to deter, and that otherwise wrongful behavior is excused just in case committing the crime lay outside the control of the accused.[1] For Hart, both the requirement of intent and the familiar excusing conditions express the general theme of allowing wrongdoers a fair chance to avoid criminal sanctions. The other parts of Hart's account receive independent justifications, though. Others, such as Joel Feinberg, share Hart's emphasis on harm as the basis for criminalization, but maintain that punishment is fundamentally expressive.[2] And still others, including many, if not most, sitting judges, speak of the multiple purposes of punishment, without relating them systematically to the other elements of the criminal law.

In this and the next three chapters, I offer a more unified approach to issues of criminal culpability and punishment. In broadest outline, the account runs as follows. The criminal law serves primarily to protect and vindicate fair terms of interaction. Tort liability is appropriate when someone *takes* a risk with the security of others; criminal liability is reserved for the narrower class of cases in which someone *chooses* a risk (or result). The requisite notion of choice is explicated in terms of the distinction between the rational and the reasonable: Criminal acts are those acts in which one person seeks to substitute private rationality for public standards of reasonableness. Intent or recklessness is an essential element of core areas of criminality because a person must be aware that the rights of others are in jeopardy if his action is to count as such a substitution. Punishment is required in order to address the wrongful substitution. It takes the form of hard treatment because it addresses itself to the putative rationality of the wrongful deed. Otherwise wrongful conduct is excused in those cases in which the criminal act is a response to circumstances, because in such circumstances, punishment fails to address the wrong.

Like my discussion of tort liability, my account combines political theory and the constructive interpretation of legal practice. Unfortu-

---

[1] H. L. A. Hart, *Punishment and Responsibility* (Oxford: Oxford University Press, 1968).

[2] Joel Feinberg, Vol. 2: *The Moral Limits of the Criminal Law, Harm to Others* (New York: Oxford University Press, 1985); "The Expressive Function of Punishment," in his *Doing and Deserving* (Princeton: Princeton University Press, 1970), pp. 95–118.

nately, legal practice in the criminal context speaks with even more voices than it does in tort. This should come as no surprise. Crime is a serious matter, because on the whole it involves intentional wrongdoing. Punishment is also a serious matter, because it involves the deliberate and considered infliction of hard treatment. As a result, the criminal law is almost guaranteed to be a source of constant proposals for reform. Although I admire some such proposals, and make some myself, I fear others are the result of the dangerous combination of good intentions and bad philosophy. In particular, the tendency to understand punishment in terms of subjective blameworthiness has led to some decisions that my account must regard as unacceptable. Despite the impossibility of explaining all decisions, I think that my account can explain much that is familiar and appealing in settled areas of the criminal law. To those who find the account less appealing, I offer it at least as an example of how far an account of the criminal law can go without making it a special case of a more general account of either human action or moral blameworthiness. Rather than being a special case of either of these things, the criminal law is best understood as part of a political theory of the legitimate occasions of coercion. At the very least, I hope to show that significant areas of criminal doctrine express a unified, but specific, underlying conception of responsibility. As such, the scope of my claims is limited in the same ways that the scope of my earlier account of corrective justice was limited. I do not think it is possible to show that some other standard of responsibility, external to settled legal practice, could not be used instead; I show only that no such standard need be used. The aspects of the criminal law that are widely, if not universally, admired express a conception about the legitimate occasions for the use of coercion.

5.1   TORTS, CRIMES, AND AGENCY: SOME COMPARISONS

In important respects, the criminal law employs the same conception of agency as does tort law. Standards of responsibility are objective, in the sense that what a person thought he was doing is often not sufficient to exculpate him. That objectivity is understood in a specific way: Anglo-American criminal law employs a number of reasonableness tests to determine culpability. For example, if someone makes a mistake about the danger posed by another and claims self-defense, or makes a mistake about someone else's consent, his beliefs only serve to exculpate if they are reasonable, that is, if they are compatible with showing appropriate respect for the interests of others. Where tort law uses reasonableness standards to divide the risks associated with ordinary activities, criminal law uses reasonableness standards to divide the risks of mistakes in the application of justifications.

Criminal law also shares tort law's treatment of responsibility for consequences. Attempted crimes are treated as less serious than completed crimes; having done wrong, the seriousness of the wrong depends on what happens. Criminal wrongdoing also flows back through reasonable actions, just as misfortunes did in tort. If I carelessly dispose of a dangerous object, I am liable for the injuries it causes even if those injuries are in part the result of somebody else's reasonable, but unsuccessful attempt to protect himself from it. Although more than carelessness is required in order for a crime to be committed, once one has been committed, responsibility flows back to the wrongdoer through the reasonable acts of others. An extreme example can be found in the notorious doctrine of felony murder, whereby a person committing a felony using a firearm is responsible for the death of anyone who dies violently in the course of the crime. Milder examples can also be found, in which another agent's intervening action is treated as a natural consequence of a wrongdoer's deed. If an assailant injures someone and death ensues because of the incompetence of the attending physician, the assailant still commits murder.[3] On the other hand, if death ensues because the physician refuses to treat the victim, the assailant does not commit murder.[4] In each case, whether the intervening agency of another breaks the chain of causation depends on the reasonableness of the intervening person's act.

In the criminal law as in tort, the distinction between what someone does and what merely happens depends in part on appropriate norms of conduct. The person who hopes to kill, wound, or take the property of another is culpable if, through no further fault of his own, he kills, wounds, or steals from somebody else instead. The intention to do wrong can be transferred by chance events, just as the person who intends to hit someone in the head is still culpable if, as a result of clumsiness or chance, he hits the same person in the arm instead. Actions do not demand a single description, and which description is chosen depends on other features of the situation. Which conse-

---

[3] This applies only if the physician was acting in good faith.
[4] H. L. A. Hart and Tony Honoré, *Causation in the Law*, 2d ed. (Oxford: Oxford University Press, 1985), p. 361.

quences count a part of the action is given by the features that make the act wrongful. Intending to kill Smith is wrongful because it is intentional killing, not because it is Smith; intending to hit Smith in the arm is wrongful because of the hitting, not the arm, and so on.

Attempt liability expresses the idea that those who choose to do wrong open themselves to the consequences of chance. In so opening themselves, though, they do not thereby open themselves to unlimited chance. Instead, the type and extent of chance to which they are open reflects the same kind of factors as does the risk rule in tort. Crimes always involve violating a specific protected interest of others. Whatever protected interest it is that makes intentionally performing a particular type of criminal act wrongful opens those who perform criminal acts to the risks of those wrongs. Indeed, the reason the felony murder doctrine can be described as notorious is that its relation to the risk rule is so ambiguous. For example, the person who uses a loaded firearm in the course of a robbery adverts to (and so chooses) the possibility that others may die. Indeed, that is presumably the *point* of using a weapon to make threats. As a result, the person who makes the threats cannot disown them. In some such cases, there is a clear parallel between the person who makes such threats and the person who, meaning to kill one person, misses and kills another. In both cases, the person wrongfully employed deadly force to carry out his purposes. In both cases, the person did not want the particular death that actually occurred. In both cases, though, the person cannot plausibly claim to have not realized that there was a risk of death. Other cases are far more difficult, though. The person who merely carries a firearm, even if it is not loaded, is also within the reach of many felony-murder statutes. Such a person presumably meant to deceive rather than threaten. Parties to crimes, who are implicated via standard and plausible doctrines of complicity, may be in a similar situation. The person driving the getaway car may not have realized that the gun was loaded, or may even have thought that he had convinced his accomplice to leave the bullets behind.[5] In these cases, there is a lack of fit between the wrongfulness of the deed and the seriousness of the crime. In other circumstances, resulting deaths seem too remote to count as within the risk compassed by the wrongful intent. If the police shoot at escaping felons and kill one, the remaining

---

[5]   These were the facts of *R. v. Vaillincourt* [1987] 47 D.L.R. (4th) 399, which led Canada's supreme court to strike down a felony-murder statute on constitutional grounds.

felon falls short of murder. The issues are difficult, and their difficulty is parallel to difficult questions of foreseeability in tort. The hard cases are hard precisely because they depart from the paradigmatic case of felony murder.

These parallels suggest that the same conception of agency defined in terms of equality and reasonableness is at work in criminal law as in tort. Rights are defined in terms of the reasonable person, and for purposes of explanation, the boundary between what someone does and what merely happens is given by the amount we can reasonably expect of others in the circumstances.

Despite the parallels, though, there are four significant differences between the areas of law. The first is the requirement of intent or recklessness in the criminal law; the second is the role of punishment. The requirement of a mental element and the purposes of punishment are widely (and in my view correctly) thought to be closely related. Their relationship poses an apparent challenge to the type of view I hope to defend. I must show how the relationship between guilt and the hard treatment of wrongdoers can be spelled out in terms of the same sort of considerations of reasonableness to which I appealed in earlier chapters.

The third respect in which criminal law is different from tort is in the role of excusing conditions. In tort, the injurer who has behaved reasonably is not liable, whereas the injurer who has behaved unreasonably is liable. In the criminal law, there are two types of defenses, justifications and excuses.[6] Some of the features of agency familiar from tort law reflect aspects of justification, others aspects of excuse.

Justifications exculpate by showing that an apparently wrongful act was not wrongful. As a result, the theory of justifications is part of the theory of crimes. If an act is justified, none may use force to prevent it, and others may aid in its execution. That is, the theory of justification, like the theory of crimes, is above all the theory of the rights of private citizens with respect to each other.[7] Just as the criminal law

---

6 There are also other ways in which punishment might be blocked, such as the defense of entrapment. Entrapment stands as a bar to conviction because of the role of the state in producing the crime. Unlike a justification, a defense of entrapment requires that what the accused did was wrong; unlike an excuse, a defense of entrapment is only available if the inducement to do wrong came from the state.

7 There are some small exceptions to this generalization. Automatism, for example, can serve as an excuse in some jurisdictions because the accused was not acting. Thus, it excuses because an element of the crime was absent, namely, a voluntary act.

presumes that people know what it proscribes, so too does it presume that people know the contours of justifying conditions. On most views, an agent must be aware of the justification of an act at the time of an offense in order to appeal to it. Victim consent justifies many otherwise illegal actions, and self-defense justifies the use of force by private citizens. In each of these cases, reasonableness tests serve to define the rights of the parties – for reasons to be explored in what follows, reasonable beliefs as to consent and imminent danger exculpate, even where they are mistaken. Reasonableness tests for justifications confer a general right to act on appearances.[8]

Excuses, by contrast, presuppose that the person who is excused has committed a wrong. In that sense, the theory of excuses is not part of the theory of crimes; in order for an act to be excused, it must be wrongful. Wrongdoers who are excused cannot be punished, however. The theory of excuses is properly part of the theory of punishment, that is, the theory of when, and to what extent, the state may use force after the fact against wrongdoers.[9] Because excusing conditions speak to the state, but not to wrongdoers, excuses differ from justifications in that people need not be aware of excusing conditions in order to avail themselves of them. As a result, my discussion of excusing conditions will be reserved for my discussion of punishment.

Fourth, in almost all jurisdictions, criminal law is explicitly codified in a way that the common law of torts is not. I offer no explanation of why this should be so, but take note of it here because statutes tend to have an "either/or" quality to them. As a result, a well-drafted statute can draw important distinctions between crimes, and a poorly drafted one can collapse them. For example, in the next chapter, I argue that those who make sincere but unreasonable mistakes about the need for defensive force or the consent of others should not be excused for the crimes they commit. At the same time, a statute might well view those who use (what they suppose is) defensive force unreasonably as less culpable than those who use force without any beliefs about the dangers they face. Such distinctions are important to the task of codification. Although I acknowledge their importance, I say almost nothing about them in what follows, because my concern is with the general structure of fair terms of cooperation.

---

[8]   "The defendant, under necessity of determining at once whether it was necessary to defend himself, had a right to act on appearances." *Hughes v. State*, 10 N.E.2d 629 at 633 (Indiana 1937).

[9]   See Meir Dan-Cohen, "Decision Rules and Conduct Rules: On Acoustic Separation in Law," 97 *Harvard Law Review* 625 (1985).

Just as my account of tort liability began with an account of why fair terms of interaction require damages to be paid in cases of wrongful injury, so my account of the criminal law begins with an account of punishment, that is, an account of why certain types of wrongful behavior require more than the payment of damages. That account can be developed by looking only at cases of criminal liability that are familiar and largely uncontroversial. With it in hand, we will be in a better position to understand the contours of the fair terms of interaction.

5.2 PUNISHMENT

Punishment involves the intentional infliction of hard treatment. Like other coercive forms of social control, it bears a substantial burden of justification. Some other methods of control, such as curfews or quarantines, may be more difficult to justify. Unlike punishment, they may fail to take seriously the claims of those on whom the hard treatment is inflicted. Punishment is different, because it is addressed specifically to wrongdoers after they have done wrong. Punishment is thought to be deserved, not just expedient, and the punishment deserved is supposed to be proportional both to the seriousness of the wrong and the intention of the wrongdoer. An adequate theory of punishment needs to make sense of these features.

Prominent accounts of punishment are usually classified as either deterrent or retributive. Deterrence theories insist that punishment should be solely forward-looking, tailored to preventing future wrongdoing. Retributive views suppose it should be backward-looking, and serve to respond to past wrongs. Each view, taken alone, is open to familiar objections. After rehearsing some of those objections, I offer an alternative account.

The account I will offer combines retribution and deterrence. It treats punishment as above all an expressive act, meant to denounce serious wrongs. Punishment is a response to crime, which is understood as the criminal's substitution of the pursuit of his or her private ends for public standards of reasonableness. Punishment serves to vindicate those public standards by addressing the private perspective from which the criminal acted. It takes the form of hard treatment because that is addressed to the private perspective from which the wrongdoer acted. It seeks to cancel the crime by canceling its apparent advantage from the point of view from which the criminal acted. I sometimes describe that perspective as one of the wrongdoer's rationality. By that I mean only that the wrongdoer is pursuing his or her ends from a private perspective, intentionally giving insufficient regard to the legitimate interests of others. Punishment is scaled to the seriousness of the wrong rather than the expected advantage of the crime because it treats the denial of the victim's rights as the measure of the wrongdoer's gain. That loss is in the form of a loss of rights; the wrongdoer's putative gain is represented in terms of advantage because the wrongdoer treated the victim's rights in terms of advantage.

Like most philosophical accounts of punishment, my discussion may at times seem to suggest that the paradigmatic criminal is the cold and calculating embezzler, who carefully weighs the risks and possible benefits of crime. Many criminals do fit such a model, but of course many do not. The examples of crime most prominent in the public mind involve menacing figures who act from motives that are more difficult to comprehend. Some crimes are thought of as "crimes of passion" in which the criminal is somehow out of control. Others are thought of as expressions of deep depravity. Yet what all of these images of crime have in common is the fact of the criminal's intentional actions. The abusive husband who loses self-control does not literally dissociate into a frenzy; instead, he acts rationally from his own point of view, typically hurting his wife but not destroying the room. The depraved rapist does not hurl himself off a bridge, but takes out his rage on his victims. More generally, many people get uncontrollably angry, though those who do seldom become violent. Violent loss of self-control is typically the prerogative of the stronger, those who are able to act without fear.[10] Those who are smaller and weaker than others they might attack manage to restrain themselves. Of course, there are important exceptions. Children often act out of anger without regard to consequences. That is part of the reason they are not thought of as fully responsible agents. Among adults, though, the situation is different. Those who direct their anger at others can be understood as substituting their private rationality for public standards of reasonableness, for they too are prepared to regard the legitimate claims of others as so many obstacles in pursuit of their own ends, however transient those ends might be. There may well be some circumstances in which a provocation is so severe that we might conclude that anyone would have lost self-control and reacted in similar ways. But, as I shall suggest at the end of this chapter, if there are such

---

[10]   See Jeremy Horder, *Provocation and Responsibility* (Oxford: Oxford University Press, 1992).

circumstances, they are extremely rare, and need to be understood in terms of a more general account of excusing conditions, rather than as expressing the idea that crimes of passion are less serious. After discussing the excuse of necessity, I offer an account of the ways in which hot blood might properly be seen as partially mitigating the seriousness of crimes.

5.2.1 Deterrence and Retribution

Accounts of punishment that emphasize deterrence offer an account of why hard treatment is a necessary part of punishment, but underplay the role of responsibility and blameworthiness too much. Much unwelcome behavior might be deterred, but not all of it merits punishment. Any deterrence theory begins from the assumption that increasing the costs of an action will lead rational people to avoid it. Any such account will thus concede that deterrence is sometimes possible for nonintentional wrongdoing.[11] As a result, it needs to explain why intentional wrongdoing merits a particular punitive response in a way that mere carelessness does not. A theory of deterrence also needs to explain the widespread view that the severity of punishment should be tied to the seriousness of the wrong, rather than the temptations of the crime.

Sophisticated deterrence theories make punishment contingent on the criminal having had a fair chance to avoid the penalty. Sometimes this point is made in terms of consent; other times, in terms of opportunity.[12] As H. L. A. Hart puts it, penalties announced in advance allow individuals to give effect to their own choices as a result of which "the pains of punishment will for each individual represent the price of some satisfaction obtained from breach of the law."[13] Although

---

[11] This point is familiar from economic analyses of tort law. Although such analyses go wrong in tracing the justification of liability to its effects, they are right about those effects.

[12] See, for example, Hart, *Punishment and Responsibility;* Carlos S. Nino, "A Consensual Theory of Punishment," 12 *Philosophy and Public Affairs* 289 (1983); T. M. Scanlon, "The Significance of Choice," in *Equal Freedom: Selected Tanner Lectures,* edited by Stephen Darwall (Ann Arbor: University of Michigan Press, 1995).

[13] Hart, *Punishment and Responsibility,* p. 47. Hart goes on to illustrate his account by reference to wicked legal systems, such as those of Nazi Germany and South Africa. I must admit to being puzzled by his choice of examples. They suggest that on Hart's view, the legitimacy of punishment is something quite apart from the legitimacy of the laws, since in each case, we can trace it to the choice of the person being punished.

perhaps a step in the right direction, Hart's account abandons the notion of wrongdoing in favor of the very different notion of having a fair chance to avoid something unpleasant. Fair notice of criminal liability may be a necessary condition of liability to punishment. Once it is satisfied, there is some temptation to say that the person punished cannot complain, provided that the punishment serves some useful purpose. But more is required in order to show that the wrongdoer *deserved* the punishment. Those who volunteer for dangerous or unpleasant public tasks cannot complain either, yet they seem to be in an entirely different category from those who deserve hard treatment.

Now it may be that Hart and those who follow him are eager to abandon the notion of desert in favor of other, clearer ideas. Although there is much to be said for revising obscure concepts in the process of clarifying them, the ideas of price and of a fair opportunity to avoid unpleasant consequences may not be the best alternatives. The idea that someone should only be punished if he has had a fair chance to avoid punishment may have some application to nonpunitive forms of social control, explaining, for example, why someone who has been convicted of a crime might be prevented from ever again occupying positions of trust. It could perhaps even be extended to explaining the practice of informing neighbors when a convicted sex offender is released into their community. These cases share an important feature: The extra cost imposed on the wrongdoer comes after the punitive sentence is complete. Whether or not they are defensible, such responses to crime are best understood as protective rather than punitive. (Although some of their advocates may suppose that standard punishments are inadequate, and hope to enhance punishments after the fact.) These nonpunitive responses treat the crime as predictive of future dangerousness, and seek to insulate the public from the consequences of that danger. If they can be defended at all, it is because the dangers are real, and the wrongdoer had a fair chance to avoid the protective response. Important as these responses to crime may be in the public mind, they do not seem to be paradigmatic cases of punishment. Their similarities with other practices obscure rather than clarify what is specifically punitive about punishment.[14]

Retributive theories, on the other hand, do well at explaining the

[14]   In particular, such responses seem to fit with what John Rawls once described as a "summary conception of rules." The general practice of punishment does not seem to justify its instances, but rather to inherit its justification from them, and to necessarily admit of exceptions when the instance fails to have the desired consequences.

specifically blaming aspects of punishment. They conceive of punishment as a backward-looking response to intentional wrong, which aims to right that wrong by responding to it in kind. Retributivism is sometimes understood as simply a negative constraint on punishment, the requirement that only the guilty should be punished. But it is sometimes also put forward as a positive claim to the effect that punishment must be addressed to the wrongfulness of the deed, rather than to the accomplishment of broader social purposes. It is this latter, more robust sense that is of more interest.

Where earlier retributivists supposed that injuring an injurer somehow undoes a wrong,[15] recent retributive views have emphasized the expressive dimensions of punishment, and seen it as denying the wrongdoer's claim about the irrelevance of the victim's rights. I shall suppose that expressive views capture the core of the retributive idea. Joel Feinberg suggests two fundamental respects in which punishment is expressive. First, punishment allows society to distance itself from the wrongful deed. Second, it allows society to authoritatively declare and vindicate (i.e., uphold) the claim of law. It lets society distance itself by making it clear that it does not regard such behavior as acceptable. The pattern of punishments speaks volumes about what is and is not considered acceptable, and how seriously various types of unacceptable behavior are taken. By distancing itself from particular wrongs, society makes it clear how seriously it takes the various parts of its codified law.[16]

Jean Hampton has developed Feinberg's approach by suggesting that punishment is expressive because crime itself is expressive. The criminal, by intentionally or recklessly violating the victim's rights, expresses a denial of the victim's value. In substituting private rationality for public standards of reasonableness, the criminal declares the victim's rights irrelevant. On Hampton's account, punishment serves to deny that declaration, and in so doing vindicates the victim's rights. Failure to punish leaves the criminal's declaration intact, and so implicitly endorses it.[17]

Hampton's account is more nuanced than my brief summary suggests, and has much to recommend it. It faces two difficulties, how-

---

[15] I briefly discuss Hegel's version of retributivism in the next chapter.
[16] Feinberg, "The Expressive Function of Punishment."
[17] See Jean Hampton, "The Retributive Idea," in Jean Hampton and Jeffrie Murphy, *Forgiveness and Mercy* (Cambridge: Cambridge University Press, 1988), pp. 111–61; "Correcting Harms and Righting Wrongs: The Aim of Retribution," 39 *UCLA Law Review* 1671 (1992).

ever, both of which are common to expressive views of punishment. First, because punishment is thought of as expressive, and so akin to blaming, it needs to explain why allowing different parties to inflict repeat punishments for the same crime is so obviously unjust. In non-punitive instances of blame, both interested parties and others are entitled to blame those who do wrong. The person who disrupts a dinner party can be blamed by all present, and those absent who subsequently learn what went on. The person who breaks a promise can be criticized by people other than the promisee. Having been criticized once, the promise breaker is not thought to be immune from further criticism, or, if criticism seems excessive, it is not excessive because it is undeserved. Punishment seems different, though. Those who have already been punished can still be blamed, but they cannot be legitimately punished again. The idea that those who are punished thereby pay their debt to society may not be entirely clear, but it captures an intuitively important difference between punishment and other types of blame. Once a crime has been punished, it cannot be punished further. It does not follow, though, that it has been forgiven.[18]

The second difficulty is related to the first. Expressive views need to explain why hard treatment is the appropriate vehicle for denouncing crimes.[19] As T. M. Scanlon has asked, why not say it with flowers, or better still with weeds?[20] The two difficulties are related, because the inappropriateness of repeat punishment reflects the fact that it involves hard treatment. Having received appropriate hard treatment, the criminal has received as much as he or she deserved. But why hard treatment at all? Comparative hard treatment is not difficult

---

[18]   The way in which punishment seems to demand quantification also creates puzzles for other versions of the expressive view. In *Philosophical Explanations* (Cambridge, MA: Harvard University Press, 1982), Robert Nozick suggests that punishment serves to connect the criminal with the correct values: Having made a mistake about the world of value, the wrongdoer must be answered. So understood, punishment seems to be required only when the criminal has not repented on his own. Those who have repented and acknowledged their errors have presumably reconnected themselves with the world of value. As a result, no further public communicative act would seem to be necessary. By contrast, those who have not repented after their punishment would seem to need further punishment, until they see the error of their ways.

[19]   Feinberg concedes that in other societies, something other than hard treatment (e.g., a highly ritualized condemnation) might serve the same expressive purpose. See his "The Expressive Function of Punishment." Although Feinberg is probably right about the role of particular forms of hard treatment, such as prisons, I will argue that the ability of a ritual to denounce is tied to the way in which it is unwelcome and generally feared.

[20]   Scanlon, "The Significance of Choice," p. 102.

to explain: If some crimes are denounced by hard treatment, then others will not be denounced at all if they receive only a verbal rebuke. Just as crimes admit of ordinal comparisons of seriousness, so prison terms admit of ordinal comparisons of length. But the question remains as to why any wrongdoing should be responded to by hard treatment. Other responses can equally well be scaled. For example, a public statement that the victim has been grievously wronged might allow society to both distance itself from the deed and declare the supremacy of the victim's rights. An official condemnation of the wrongdoer might achieve those aspects of punishment that make it a special case of more general practices of blaming.

It is sometimes suggested that hard treatment provides a form of expression that a criminal cannot help but recognize. Although perhaps true, this suggestion seems to underscore the differences between punishment and blame more generally. Ordinarily, the legitimacy of blaming is not dependent on its efficacy. The fact that someone might dismiss another's blame does not undermine the blame itself; conversely, the fact that the wrongdoer acknowledges the wrong makes it unnecessary to communicate with him in particular. Expressive views need some explanation of why punishment must address itself to the criminal in a particular way.

The difficulties of explaining hard treatment and who gets to inflict it reflect an undercurrent in many expressive accounts. When the expressive aims of blaming and vindication are achieved through hard treatment, it looks as though something more than reprobation is being expressed, something akin to anger or outrage at the criminal. The desire to hurt those who hurt or anger us runs deep in the human psyche. For all that, though, we hesitate to yield too much space to it. Yet expressive views of punishment have difficulty keeping it under control. As a result, they come perilously close to Stephen's claim that punishment "gratifies a natural public feeling."[21] There is plainly something to Stephen's remark, at least as an explanation of popular views of punishment. On its own, though, it is a counsel of barbarism, like his claim that "it is a morally good thing to hate criminals."[22] Such thoughts are in need of more domestication than Stephen offers by comparing the relationship between punishment and revenge to that between marriage and sexual appetite. If social

---

[21] Sir James Fitzjames Stephen, *History of the Criminal Law* [1883] (New York: B. Franklin, 1964), 3:311.
[22] Ibid., 3:82.

institutions are to be stable, they must be compatible with fundamental human emotional responses. Yet the way they do so must be sensitive to considerations of fairness. Not all public feelings deserve to be gratified, and if the feeling remains ungratified after punishment, a second try is not acceptable.

Just as deterrent theories make punishment one among many behavior-shaping practices, so expressive theories make it one among many blaming practices. As such, the two approaches are alike in needing to appeal to some other criterion to determine why criminal activity in particular should be the object of sanctions. They are also alike in that they take the fact of criminal activity as the occasion for society as a whole to use the perpetrator to satisfy its own wishes.[23]

Still, deterrence and denunciation theories each seem to be right about something. Crimes really do need to be denounced because of what they express, and denouncing past crimes really is an appropriate occasion for preventing future ones. A plausible view of punishment should show its relation to the two central aims of criminal law: Punishing the guilty and protecting the innocent. The problem is to reconcile them.

5.2.2   Torts and Crimes: Damages and Punishment

Any account of punishment needs to explain why punishment is sometimes required in addition to compensation, as well as why intentional acts are the appropriate occasions for that additional response. I begin by suggesting that crimes are torts with something added. Once we see what is added, we see why punishment is the appropriate response to that extra thing.

---

[23] There is a long and distinguished tradition of combining deterrence and retribution by representing punishment as part of a social contract. For Rousseau, for example, among the articles of the general will is a schedule of punishments for various departures from the other articles. On this view, people coming together to form a state agree to forbid various serious harms to each other, and provide each other with the further incentive of threats should anyone fail to live up to their commitments. As Rousseau puts it, "it is in order to avoid being killed by a murderer that one consents to die should one become a murderer." Jean-Jacques Rousseau, "The Social Contract," Bk. II, Chapter 5, in *The Basic Political Writings*, translated by Donald Cress (Indianapolis: Hackett, 1987), p. 159. There is plainly something to such accounts, but they require further elaboration. In particular, they need some independent account of why they attach deterrent punishments to intentional wrongdoing and why they are keyed to the seriousness of the wrong rather than, for example, the temptations of wrongdoing. People coming together to protect themselves would presumably want to protect themselves against injuries rather than wrongs.

Not all wrongdoing, nor even all serious wrongdoing, merits punishment. Although crimes are intuitively more serious than torts, the scale of seriousness needs to be specified carefully. A carelessly discarded cigarette may have the same consequences as deliberate arson, and there are obvious similarities between a leg broken by a gangster and one broken by a careless driver. The difference is not in the results. Crime victims can ordinarily recover in tort,[24] but even after they have recovered, or even if the criminal has been caught in the act before anything was done, the crime remains.

On this view, then, a criminal act has two kinds of consequences. As a private (legal) person, each has rights against suffering wrongful losses. Those rights are protected by the right to receive damages in the event of a wrongful loss. I will call these rights against injury. As a person from the point of view of criminal law, each has further rights against having one's rights as a private person be treated as tradeable. I will call these rights against insult. By treating a person's rights as tradeable, crimes add insult to injury. We can think of punishment in terms of protecting the victim's latter set of rights. Punishing crimes serves to both vindicate the system of rights as a whole and to vindicate the particular victim's rights.

To call these two sets of rights is perhaps misleading, for all of the interests protected against crimes *mala in se* are also protected by tort law. The burglar is liable for the broken window, the assailant for the assault, and the murderer for wrongful death.[25] In each case, the criminal has performed one wrongful act, not two. The point of distinguishing them is that the losses cannot be traded against each other. The payment of damages (including whatever damages might be appropriate to make up the victim's emotional and other suffering) is no replacement for punishment, and inability to pay damages is not an appropriate reason for increased punishment.[26] As a private

---

[24] Though criminals are often financially insolvent, so the right to recover is infrequently exercised. Many jurisdictions have set up victim compensation funds as a result.

[25] There are cases in which criminal culpability obtains although a tort action is barred because of victim consent such as mutual combat. See W. Page Keeton et al., *Prosser and Keeton on the Law of Torts*, 5th ed. (St. Paul: West, 1984), p. 122.

[26] I appreciate that this comment is at odds with the widespread practice of considering restitutionary payments to crime victims as a mitigating factor in punishment. Insofar as prosecutors and judges may legitimately consider a wrongdoer's remorse to be a mitigating factor, such payment might be thought of as a form of remorse. But although the willingness to make restitution may be legitimately taken into account, it is difficult to see why the ability to do so is relevant to sentencing.

person, the victim of a crime has an interest in reparation. As a victim of crime, that same person has a legitimate interest in having his or her rights vindicated, but not in the wrongdoer's suffering as such.[27] Punishment thus differs from revenge in that the wrongdoer's suffering is not desired for its own sake. Instead, it is required to right the wrong.

To sum up, a crime differs from a tort because it involves a denial of the victim's rights. To shift only the factual costs of crime back to the criminal would leave the criminal's claim to subject the other's rights to his own will unchallenged, and so the victim's rights would be as the criminal claims them to be. Without punishment, the criminal would in some sense be right. Punishment provides the remedy necessary to vindicate those rights.[28] The next question is, why does vindication require some particular form?

5.2.3   Interlude: Punitive Damages

To see why the rights of victims of crime must be vindicated, and how they can be, consider the suggestion that tort damages would be an adequate response to crime. The privatization of response to crime has been a prominent theme in recent libertarian writing, and its failings are instructive. Randy Barnett has advocated one version of the libertarian privatization account.[29] Barnett's account focuses on restitution rather than damages, but the basic principle is the same. Criminal punishment is thought to be ineffective and costly as a deterrent, and to give excessive power to the state. In its place, a regime of restitution is said to provide a less costly and morally appropriate response to crime. I will illustrate the problems with the restitutionary account in two stages. First, I will show why there are some cases in which restitution alone is not an adequate tort remedy.

---

[27]   See *Eacret v. Holmes*, 333 P.2d 741 (Oregon 1958). Parents of a murder victim sought an injunction to prevent the governor of Oregon, who opposed capital punishment, from commuting the death sentence of their son's killer. The court held that the parents lacked standing to raise the issue.

[28]   Some have claimed to find this view in Hegel. See David E. Cooper, "Hegel's Theory of Punishment," in *Hegel's Political Philosophy: Problems and Perspectives*, edited by Zbigniew A. Pelczynski (Cambridge: Cambridge University Press, 1971), pp. 151–67. Cooper attributes to Hegel the view that American Constitutional scholars have dubbed "no right without a remedy." Cooper's Hegel is silent on why punishment should be the particular form the remedy takes, rather than, for example, damages.

[29]   Randy Barnett, "Restitution: A New Paradigm of Criminal Justice," 87 *Ethics* 279 (1977).

I will then go on to show why private remedies are generally inadequate as a response to crime.

Consider first a category intermediate between tort damages and criminal punishments, punitive damages. Punitive damages do more than make up a plaintiff's loss. Aggravating circumstances surrounding a tort may lead to aggravated damages, for they can be seen as aggravating the plaintiff's injury.[30] Punitive damages do more. They are reserved for precisely those cases in which the defendant's conduct is so outrageous that it merits something more than compensation for the injury.

Punitive tort damages are a controversial topic, and debates about them typically reflect underlying views about punishment. For example, deterrence theories, with or without the added proviso that wrongdoers should have a fair chance to avoid sanctions, will likely welcome punitive damages in just those cases in which their deterrent effects outweigh their costs. Thus, deterrence theories should have no difficulty with punitive damage awards for negligent, or even strict liability torts, provided that the tort-feasor was in a position to take extra care to avoid liability.

I want to avoid contemporary controversies and focus on an earlier rationale for punitive damages. It can be found in the old English tort of trespass against minerals and nineteenth-century American cases of conversion of natural resources. In *Wooden-Ware,*[31] the defendant purchased logs that had been illegally cut from plaintiff's lands, and transported them to a mill. The taking of the logs came to light, and the plaintiff sued for conversion. The ordinary remedy for conversion is a forced purchase of the converted object at its value at the time it was taken. If one person inadvertently takes another's goods, the one who took them must pay the value they had when taken. If that were the only remedy in this case, though, the defendant would effectively have forced the plaintiff to sell the logs at their market price. In so doing, the defendant would have deprived the plaintiff of one of the central rights of ownership, namely, the right to *refuse* to sell something at its market value. The court responded to this situation by allowing a further remedy: The defendant was required to pay the full value of the wood, and not allowed to deduct

---

[30] Some American states explicitly address damages to the plaintiff's feelings of outrage. See Keeton et al., *Prosser and Keeton, on the Law of Torts,* p. 9. It is not clear why such damages would be tied to the defendant's intentions.

[31] *Wooden-Ware Co. v. United States,* 106. U.S. 432 (1882).

the transport and milling costs. The portion of the damages above the market value of the logs is punitive. It serves to punish the defendant's intentional taking of the logs; without the punitive portion, the plaintiff's right to refuse to enter into transactions would simply have become part of the cost of the defendant's business. The court also spoke of the need to deter such poaching of logs. The two rationales are at bottom identical: The only way to vindicate the plaintiff's property rights is to make sure that violating them does not pay.

In *Wooden-Ware*, the additional damages are not compensatory. At the same time, they do serve to make up something that is in some sense the victim's loss, namely, the loss of the right to refuse to sell. That right is not compensated; the value of the logs has already covered it. Although the victim suffered an additional dignitary loss, and the punitive damages serve to address that loss, their purpose is not to compensate for it. Indeed, their point is precisely that the dignitary loss is not compensable. They serve instead to vindicate the right.

A similar approach survives in the judgments of English courts. They are far more sparing in their use of punitive damages than are U.S. courts. Lord Diplock summarizes the category that is of interest to us here:[32] "[T]hose in which the defendant's conduct has been calculated by him to make a profit for himself which may well exceed the compensation payable to the plaintiff. . . . Where a defendant with a cynical disregard for a plaintiff's rights has calculated that the money to be made out of his wrongdoing will probably exceed the damages at risk, it is necessary for the law to show that it cannot be broken with impunity. This category is not confined to moneymaking in the strict sense. Exemplary damages can properly be awarded whenever it is necessary to teach a wrongdoer that tort does not pay."[33] The rationale is that damages in excess of those needed to compensate tort victims are appropriate in those cases in which the tort-feasor has not simply failed to take adequate account of the victim's interests but has *considered* those interests and willfully acted against them, regarding them as simply an obstacle to the pursuit of his or her own ends.

Such situations sometimes come about because damages are calculated in economic terms. Thus, there are some cases in which someone might regard wrongful injuries to others merely as a cost of going about their own affairs, perform a cost–benefit analysis, and decide that they will do better to injure others and pay than to exercise

---

[32]   The other category is arbitrary or oppressive government action.
[33]   *Rookes v. Barnard* [1964] A. C. 1129 (H.L.) per Lord Devlin.

appropriate care.[34] In a leading English case, a publisher knowingly published a libellous book in the hope that the libel proceedings would increase sales.[35] In so doing, the publisher treated the plaintiff's rights against libel as something offered for sale.[36] In so doing, the publisher substituted his or her own private judgments of rationality for public standards of reasonableness.[37] It is that substitution that makes punitive damages appropriate.

In both of these examples, a punitive response is necessary, because without one, the wrongdoer would have succeeded in treating the other party's rights as part of the cost of pursuing his or her own ends. The punitive response cannot just take the form of a solemn public declaration, though. If it did, the wrongdoer would have gotten away with the wrongdoing, for he or she would have been right about the costs and benefits of doing wrong. Something more is needed to reject the perspective from which the wrong was done. Imposing an extra cost does so because it rejects the wrongdoer's deed from the perspective within which it purportedly made sense, namely, that of private advantage.[38]

On this account, punitive damages reveal the relation between

---

[34] On the Learned Hand test for tort liability, increasingly influential in American courts, people are expected to make exactly such a calculation.

[35] *Cassel & Co. v. Broome* [1972] A.C. 1027.

[36] The most famous example is probably the Ford Pinto case. Ford knew of the dangers of the Pinto's exploding gas tank, and that the problem could be corrected for about $10 per car. They nonetheless decided against making the necessary modification. One jury awarded punitive damages in the amount of the savings Ford had hoped to realize, although these reduced by the trial judge. See *Grimshaw v. Ford Motor Co.*, 174 Cal. Rptr. 348, 389 (1981). For a skeptical view, see Gary T. Schwartz, "The Myth of the Ford Pinto Case," 43 *Rutgers Law Review* 1013 (1991).

[37] As Jules Coleman and Jody Kraus note, economic analyses of tort damages have difficulty explaining the sense in which tort remedies are supposed to protect legal rights. "It is surely odd to claim that an individual's right is protected when another individual is permitted to force a transfer at a price set by third parties. Isn't the very idea of a forced transfer contrary to the autonomy or liberty thought constitutive of rights? Jules L. Coleman and Jody S. Kraus, "Rethinking the Theory of Legal Rights," 95 *Yale Law Journal* 1335 at 1339 (1986).

[38] Punitive damages are irrational in economic terms. After all, if one person can harm another, compensate them fully, and still come out ahead, we might think that his activity is efficient. By the standard criterion of Pareto efficiency, the victim is no worse off, and the tort-feasor is better off. By the standard of Kaldor-Hicks efficiency, the act is wealth-creating, and punitive damages undermine its rationality. What this inefficiency shows, I think, is that individual rights are not structured to promote economic efficiencies, but rather to protect important interests.

152

public reasonableness and private rationality. The sense of rationality involved here is not that the wrongdoer acts prudently or successfully in pursuit of his own advantage. That may or may not be the case. From the perspective of punitive damages, the essential feature is that the wrongdoer acts in pursuit of his or her ends by intentionally exposing others to injuries or unreasonable risks. Punitive damages serve both to denounce such behavior as unreasonable and to ensure that it is irrational, by shifting the cost-benefit analysis so that the apparent advantage disappears.[39] They denounce by denying the claim that other people's rights are merely prices.

Making intentional wrongs more costly may seem to affirm the perspective from which the wrongdoer treated the plaintiff's rights as tradeable. After all, a prohibitive price is still a price. Yet by imposing punitive damages, the court is able to effectively denounce the deed in the two ways to which Feinberg drew our attention. First, it serves to authoritatively distance society from the deed, by making it clear that it is not something with which people can get away. Second, it serves to vindicate the rights of the plaintiff. Had the wrongful deed merely been criticized, the criminal would have gotten away with the crime, for the victim's rights would have been tradeable after all. By making the wrongdoer pay more, the court makes the plaintiff's rights a real barrier to wrongdoing.

Punitive damages also deter. That is because the denunciation of the wrongdoing is not possible except by imposing a substantial cost that will more than cancel the expected gain. Deterrence is the inevitable by-product of condemning the deed in this way.[40] They will also teach the wrongdoer that tort does not pay, because they will make it painfully apparent.

In cases in which the wrongdoer hopes to gain by disregarding the plaintiff's rights, but things do not work out as planned, some punitive

---

[39]   As Galanter and Luban observe of punitive damages in a predatory pricing case, "Only when the punitive damages far exceed BFI's gain from predatory pricing will the company be tempted to turn its eyes away from its balance sheet and toward the law." Marc Galanter and David Luban, "Poetic Justice: Punitive Damages and Legal Pluralism," 42 *American University Law Review* 1393, at 1430 (1993).

[40]   In the United States, juries have largely unlimited discretion in setting the amounts of punitive damages. Although controversial, such discretion has enormous deterrent potential because wrongdoers may be unable to assess the private rationality of their deeds if they know that the damages they pay will be the result of a jury "spinning the big wheel."

damages may still be appropriate. Acting on the prospect that wrong-ful behavior pays is sufficient.[41] If the libellous publisher had miscal-culated the increase in sales, or the manufacturer in *Wooden-Ware* had lost his goods in a fire, it seems appropriate that the damages still ex-ceed the plaintiff's factual loss. In each case, some response is needed to the wrongdoer's readiness to treat the plaintiff's rights as tradeable.

Punitive damages show why compensation is not an adequate re-sponse to certain kinds of serious wrongdoing. They nonetheless pro-vide an incomplete model of punishment, because they are the result of a private right of action, and although they are awarded by a court, they do not involve prosecution by the state. The replacement of punitive damages for conversion with criminal penalties for theft is surely a good thing.[42]

Punitive damages may be troubling for other reasons. Procedural

[41] *Cassells & Co. v. Broome*, A. C., at 1130. The rationale is that limiting them to the magnitude of the plaintiff's actual loss would enable defendants to conclude that at worst they had nothing to lose by engaging in such behavior. If the pub-lisher only has to pay punitive damages if the book is a success, he may dis-count the likelihood of breaking even if a suit is brought against the chances that a suit will fail despite its merits. Lord Diplock also notes that the calcula-tion need not have been made. All that is required is that the defendant con-sidered the risk and decided to commit the tort anyway.

[42] They have other limitations as well. Punitive damages are awarded to the in-jured party, because a tort action is private. We might wonder whether this is appropriate, since the initial victim turns out to be better off as a result of the other person's wrong. Certainly, neither party can object that such an arrange-ment is unfair, even though the injured party is not entitled to the benefit re-ceived. (Were this problem solved by making them payable to the state, their size would need to be announced in advance.)

Punitive damages provide an incomplete model of punishment for other reasons also. Their size is often tied to the wealth of the defendant, particularly if it is a wealthy corporation. Although perhaps partly the result of juries look-ing to transfer wealth from rich to poor, tying punitive damages to corporate wealth may be required to ensure that the costs are genuinely punitive, that the denunciation is real and not just another cost. Because of their varying size, though, punitive damages are at odds with standard practices of sentencing, which both announce penalties in advance and seek to ensure proportionality of the punishment to the crime, rather than a set amount of suffering on the part of the wrongdoer. In general, subjective dissatisfaction of the offender is not necessary for punishment. The wrongdoer who is happy in prison still gets a prison term. On the unusual occasions when dissatisfaction does not result, the punishment does not thereby fail. Instead, for reasons I shall explain in what follows, punishment is addressed to the rationality of the ordinary per-son. The extent to which a given prison term will be especially onerous for a given offender may well be a mitigating factor in some cases. But the point of sentencing is not to tailor punishment to some predetermined level of dissat-isfaction.

features of the system of private litigation make their application unfair. Those features pull in two different directions, though not in a way that inspires confidence that one cancels the other out. First, punitive damages may be assessed with an insufficient showing of wrongdoing, because the standard of proof in a civil trial is merely the balance of probabilities.[43] That standard is appropriate for compensatory damages because they make up a loss that uncontroversially already exists. As a result, it is appropriate to leave that loss with the person with whom it more probably belongs. The question of whether a *punitive* response is appropriate, though, is inseparable from the question of whether there was an intentional wrong. A higher standard of proof ensures that punishment not create a new cost simply to impose it on an innocent party. Whether punitive damages are legitimate without the higher standard, punishment by the state plainly is not. Second, punitive damages may not be assessed when they should be, because they are not mandatory, but within the (reviewable) discretion of the jury.[44] Thus, there is a danger of the proportionality of punishment to crime being lost from either of these directions. If wrongs are serious enough, the punitive response must be mandatory, and announced in advance. A sporadic pattern of punishment would fail to vindicate the rights of victims. I do not doubt that the sympathies of prosecutors, judges, and juries often lead to such failures. An adequate account of punishment should allow them to be identified.

Still, whether or not practices involving punitive damages are wholly defensible, they are a promising place to begin an account of punishment. Properly understood, they capture the idea of denouncing the substitution of private rationality for public standards of reasonableness by denying it. That denial takes the form of undermining their rationality.

---

[43] Galanter and Luban argue that this does not pose a problem for punitive damages, because the "beyond reasonable doubt" standard is appropriate largely to balance the massive disproportions in resources between the powerful state and the accused. (Observers of the recent O. J. Simpson trials may wonder about that disproportion.) "Poetic justice," another important difference, which Galanter and Luban do not note, is that compensatory damages make up a loss that already exists; punishment is only appropriate if there is a wrong, which depends in part on what the accused can be shown to have done.

[44] For reflections on the significance of this fact, see Dorsey D. Ellis Jr., "Fairness and Efficiency in the Law of Punitive Damages," 56 *Southern California Law Review* 1 (1982).

5.2.4 The State

Next, consider nonviolent crimes against the public order – everything from fines for traffic violations to penalties for tax evasion or failure to call the fire department in an emergency. There are difficult questions, both in general and in detail, about how the public order should be constructed; I put those to one side and presume, perhaps contrary to fact, that we are dealing with a public order that is largely just, so that no questions arise about the legitimacy of its demands. Fairness requires that people adjust their behavior to those demands. What would justify punishment of those who fail to do so?

Punishments for crimes *mala prohibita* is best seen as a response to those who regard the rules of public order as merely natural facts to be worked around. Punishments for such crimes serve to uphold the laws that were broken. As such, they can be seen as a form of punitive damages owed to the state. If a tax evader simply must repay the taxes owed, the view that the tax system is merely a parameter in light of which one may take risks is confirmed. Adding an official rebuke while demanding only that penalties be repaid is insufficient as an answer, because the wrongdoer who does not care about obeying the law will be confirmed in his judgment. Adding a substantial penalty condemns the attitude that the law is merely a parameter to be exploited by denying it its own terms, that is, by denying its claim to rationality. Punishment is thus an appropriate response to behavior that treats the protected interests of others as mere expenses.

The role of the state in punishing crimes *mala prohibita* is clear. It is, after all, an interested party. There is typically no particular victim other than the state, and so we might suppose that the state alone has an interest in punishing wrongs against it. Yet the parallel with punitive damages does not go so far. The state's claim to punish wrongdoing extends to cases in which there is a victim. The person who unilaterally sets the terms of interaction with others both wrongs his or her particular victim and commits a wrong against the public order. Because the public order is violated, the state has an interest in vindicating it; because that public order is in part one of individual rights, the order itself can only be vindicated by vindicating the victim's rights. At the same time, the victim's rights can only be vindicated by a practice that vindicates them as rights that everyone has.

5.2.5   *Malum in se*

Crimes against persons and property are slightly different. A fine that is added to the tax owing in order to make tax evasion fail to be rational achieves its purpose because the tax evader acts in pursuit of monetary gain. By converting the intended gain to an actual loss, the fine upholds the tax system. In so doing, it also protects it, by deterring others who might be tempted to evade.

Crimes *mala in se* involve more than treating the basic rules of social order as parameters around which to plan in pursuit of private ends. They also involve a particular feature of those public standards, namely, their protection of individual rights. Most of the rights protected by the criminal law rest on the idea that one person may not take it upon himself to make important decisions for another. That is why consent provides a complete defense to most criminal charges. The criminal who ignores the victim's right to decide has denied the rights of the victim in particular. The thief who takes another's property deprives his victim of the right to decide who can use it. The assailant violates the victim's right to decide how she may be touched, and by whom. Consent is not a defense to murder, but the law of murder too serves to protect against one person deciding to end another's life. Both the law's claim to protect people equally and the victim's claim to decide his or her own boundaries are violated by crime. As a result, the appropriate response to the crime must both vindicate the law and vindicate the rights of the victim in particular.

5.2.6   Damages, Again

To see how punishment serves to vindicate rights, consider an alternative arrangement. Suppose that a scheme of restitution of losses occasioned by crime was to be adopted in place of a system of punishments. No doubt, any such scheme would face serious problems with the details of its implementation. The losses of crime are difficult to quantify or commensurate: How does one make up someone's death, or a broken limb, let alone a sexual assault? These practical problems are real, but with current arrangements, victims are entitled to recover civil damages from criminals in such cases. The calculations of those damages are a problem, but not an insurmountable one. Collecting damages may also be a problem, since most criminals lack the resources to pay them. But even this might be overcome.[45]

More serious than either of these practical problems is that even where damages are readily quantifiable, they are insufficient as a response to the specifically criminal aspects of crime. Consider an example in which damages would be easy to calculate. Suppose I refuse to lend you my car, and you decide to "borrow" it anyway. If my only remedy was that you were required to pay me damages – perhaps you return the car with the damaged locks repaired and a full tank of gas, plus an allowance for my out-of-pocket expenses for taxis and some reasonable depreciation fee per mile that you drove it – my refusal to consent to the use of the car is irrelevant. Something more needs to be done in order to vindicate my right to decide who uses it. Your payment of something like a rental fee makes up my material loss, and some further fee might make up for my distress at your high-handed behavior. In addition to both of these things, punishment is needed to make up the loss of my right to refuse.[46]

Indeed, without some further vindication, there is an important sense in which the victim's rights would not be real. A right that can be knowingly violated with impunity is no right at all.[47] A right to govern one's own affairs that can be violated provided the violator simply makes up the right-holder's actual losses is not a right to govern one's own affairs. If you can use my car at will provided you pay me damages, I do not have a right to decide how it will be used. Something further must be done to uphold my right, or I do not have a legal right at all. The only way to uphold the victim's right after the fact is to undermine the rationality of the crime – to make the crime not pay, that is, to make it clear that the wrongdoer did not get away with the crime.

Where something is readily replaceable, and most people would be willing to sell it for some price or other, a forced sale is less seri-

---

45 Richard Posner argues that punishment is required as a deterrent for those crimes for which civil damages would fail to deter because most offenders are indigent. Where damages would deter, Posner argues that they are sufficient. See Posner, "An Economic Theory of the Criminal Law, 85 *Columbia Law Review* 1193 (1985).

46 By contrast, intentionally breaching a contract does not constitute a crime because both parties to the contract have already consented to treat its subject matter as tradeable.

47 I do not mean to deny that rights protected only by civil action are still rights. They are rights because they give rise to enforceable claims. Moreover, they cannot be violated with impunity because doing so invites a punitive response.

ous than a forced sale of something that is not saleable. A scheme of restitution for violent assaults would essentially leave assailants free to force others to sell them the right to injure them, at some market rate. However exactly that market rate was set, victims of assaults would be grievously wronged. Punishment may or may not satisfy the victim in such cases; it is needed to make it clear that society will not allow the insult.

We can put this point in terms of elements of Feinberg's account of the expressive function of punishment. Punishment vindicates rights by upholding them, and so establishes their status as something other than prices. It also serves to authoritatively distance society from the crime, by making it clear that the criminal did not succeed in treating the victim's rights as mere prices. Kant makes the same point in insisting that a society disbanding itself must still punish criminals.[48] To fail to punish is to acquiesce in crime, for the failure to punish means that the criminal's assessment of the significance of the victims's rights was correct. Because punishment is a response to something a person has done, it is not justified by its effects. At the same time, it can only succeed if it will normally have deterrent effects, because any condemnation that was not unpleasant would leave the wrongdoers assessment of the relation between his advantage and the rights of others intact.

Once we see that the expressive elements of punishment can only be accomplished by hard treatment, we see also that punishment expresses something importantly different from blame. In particular, disavowal and vindication can only be expressed once. Once it is clear that the criminal has not gotten away with the crime and the victim's rights are secure, further punishments are without point. At the same time, further *blame* may still be appropriate, because blame does not serve to right a wrong.

Just as it differs from blame, so punishment differs from revenge. Often, those who thirst for revenge want also to be the agents of that revenge. It is essential to punishment as a response to crime that *someone else* other than the aggrieved victim does the punishing. Punishment does not allow the victim to hurt the criminal, any more than it expresses the victim's understandable urge to humiliate the criminal.

---

[48]   Immanuel Kant, *The Metaphysics of Morals*, translated by Mary Gregor (Cambridge: Cambridge University Press, 1991), p. 142. Kant's remark focuses on executing murderers, though the specific issue of capital punishment is not essential to this part of his view.

Instead, it serves to placate an entirely different demand of the victim, that *others* not simply allow the wrong to go unchallenged. Since punishment is not a substitute for revenge, it is not surprising that it does not always quench the thirst for it. The public purpose of punishment is to make it clear that wrongdoing is unacceptable to the society.

Put slightly differently, just as tort damages serve, insofar as it is possible to do so, to make it as though the injury had never happened to the victim, by treating the costs of injury as the tort-feasor's problem, so punishment serves, as far as it is possible to do so, to make it as though the victim's right to autonomy had never been denied. It does so not by repairing the victim's life, but by redressing the criminal's denial of right. This is not to say that other measures, such as restoring the well-being of victims of crime, are not also appropriate ways of canceling the effects of crime. They are plainly justified, for they too serve to distance society from the crime, and to reassert the victim's dignity. Taken alone, though, they do not redress the specifically wrongful aspects of the deed. By placing the insult with the wrongdoer, punishment cancels the rationality of the criminal's deed by standing as an obstacle to the wrongful pursuit of it. As a threat, it stands as such an obstacle in advance; as a response, it serves to annul the competing claim of private advantage.[49]

5.2.7 The Scales of Justice

Punishment gives expression to the intuitive idea that righting a wrong is a matter of restoring a balance. The balance in question is not part of some cosmic order according to which wrongdoers must suffer the exact harms they inflict. Nor is it a balance of advantages between criminal and victim. Instead, punishment serves to restore

---

[49] Other forms of deterrence are acceptable on quite different grounds, though subject to certain constraints. For example, random police patrols may well stop people from committing crimes for fear of apprehension and/or failure. Such deterrent measures raise no interesting issues of justification, since the person who had planned to commit a crime has no grounds for complaint in being thwarted in his efforts, even if it should turn out that others succeeded in similar crimes while he was being arrested. If the police patrols are nonrandom, perhaps targeting members of a particular group, the situation is more complicated, though not because of its deterrent effects. Deterrence raises difficult issues only insofar as one person is made to suffer in order to influence the behavior of others. Being prevented from breaking the law is not suffering in the relevant sense.

the victim's rights, and put the criminal's calculation of advantage where it properly belongs. The victim's rights can only be restored by punishment, but in order to do so, punishment must be part of a system, for the victim's rights in particular are an instance of the structure of rights that punishment serves to uphold. Far from simply restructuring incentives, then, the punishment restores fair terms of cooperation by canceling the claim that private advantage takes precedence. The hard treatment imposed on wrongdoers thus vindicates the reasonable by canceling the advantage the wrong promised *from the point of view from which the wrongdoer acted*. In so doing, it also vindicates the rights of the victim in particular.

5.2.8 Some Contrasts

The balance restored by punishment is not a matter of distributive justice. Herbert Morris once suggested that the purpose of punishment is to restore a distributive balance of advantages across a society.[50] On Morris's view, punishment serves to cancel the advantage that the criminal takes in relation to others. As many critics have pointed out, it is not clear that ordinary law-abiding citizens lose anything by being prevented from stealing from or killing others. Other defenders of similar approaches have suggested that criminals enjoy an unfair advantage other people miss by exercising a lower level of self-control.[51] The problem with this and similar proposals is that loss of self-control, like killing and stealing, do not seem to be the sort of things of which there are fair distributive shares. It is not as though people are allowed a certain amount and wrongdoers take more than their share. Instead, no one is allowed any. Further, the criminal who is disadvantaged in terms of other distributive shares does not seem to be less worthy of punishment simply because he is at a distributive disadvantage in other ways. Although judges and juries may sometimes make such judgments, taking into account misfortunes unrelated to the crime, it is difficult to see this as anything different from a more general tendency to be lenient with people they find sympathetic.[52] Such

---

[50] Herbert Morris, *On Guilt and Innocence* (Berkeley: University of California Press, 1976).

[51] Wojciech Sadurski, "Distributive Justice and the Theory of Punishment," 5 *Oxford Journal of Legal Studies* 47 (1985).

[52] See Harry Kalven Jr. and Hans Zeisel, *The American Jury* (Boston: Little, Brown, 1966), and Elaine H. Walster et al., *Equity: Theory and Research* (Boston: Allyn & Bacon, 1978).

unpleasant exceptions aside, punishments are not tradeable across time. Nor are they transferrable, as we might expect distributive shares to be. And even if these difficulties could be avoided were the distributive principle limited to crimes and punishments, the punitive response has a temporal direction. The person who has been wrongfully imprisoned does not gain a license to commit the appropriate crime after the mistake comes to light. Nor should someone who finds themselves with several months free be able to bank some time in prison for future use.

Morris's view goes awry in making punishment an acknowledgment of advantages of crime. In fact, it is just the reverse – a denial of those advantages. Punishment does not serve to restore a fair balance of benefits and burdens across a society. Instead, it serves to cancel the wrongdoer's implicit claim that the crime was advantageous. Thus, the victim's rights are vindicated by denying the crime's *claim* to rationality. Whatever the criminal is actually thinking, the crime is treated as driven by the criminal's private perspective. No acknowledgment is made of the benefit of the crime in real terms; only the benefit from the wrongdoer's particular point of view is denied.

5.2.9 Clarifications and Qualifications

Several further clarifications and qualifications are necessary. First, although punishment aims to denounce the wrong in the wrongdoer's own terms, not every act that denounces a wrong will be taken to do so by the wrongdoer. Some people may simply fail to recognize that their deeds were irrational. Others may think of themselves as "principled" wrongdoers, breaking what they regard as unjust laws. The principled wrongdoer might be indifferent to any punishment because he purported to be acting from either a higher morality or from a position beyond morality.[53] Now there are plainly cases in which people genuinely occupy a moral high ground in relation to the criminal law. When they do, punishment is unjustified. But the inappropriateness of punishment in such cases does not flow from the fact that the lawbreaker refuses the law's demands. Part of the idea of the rule of law is the idea that the public order has political

---

[53] Civil disobedients typically make claims of the former sort. When those claims are legitimate, punishment becomes problematic. For now, I limit myself to cases in which they are not. Claims to civil disobedience are usually addressed to laws that fail to protect individual rights, not to laws that protect the rights of others.

morality more or less right, and that individual claims about a higher (or post-) morality, when they interfere with the rights of others, are to be treated simply as attempts to replace public reason with private rationality. Of course, the principled wrongdoer rejects such a description, but allowing wrongdoers to set the standards by which they are judged is no different from simply allowing them to do wrong. Although the principled wrongdoer's sincerity may separate him from the ordinary run of criminal, the law need not take that into account. Where the wrongdoer's principles violate the rights of others, they can be treated as merely subjective preferences and denounced as such. The principled wrongdoer may insist that he didn't suppose that crime paid, only that something the state proscribed should not be a crime. To state such a contrast is already to reveal its incoherence. By disregarding the rights of others, the principled wrongdoer supposes himself entitled to act as though they didn't exist, and so to act on the basis of his own point of view. Part of condemning that perspective is denying its claim to occupy a moral high ground.

The point of returning the wrong to the wrongdoer is not simply to make him see the error of his ways. The wrongdoer might come to see the error of his ways with or without punishment. He might apologize and feel genuine remorse. Punishment is still required because the wrong cannot simply be taken back voluntarily. The wrongdoer's consent is irrelevant to the punishment because a punishment that depended on the wrongdoer's consent would *confirm* his view that the boundaries of others' rights are up to him. Although subjective remorse is not an untoward or even a selfish motive, it is still very much a matter of the wrongdoer's own individual will, and in that sense a matter of private advantage rather than public reasonableness. In the same way, some crimes may be motivated by hatred or spite; in such cases, the wrongdoer expects to gain nothing, and may be willing to sacrifice a great deal. Even in such cases, we measure the wrongdoer's gain by the victim's loss. The wrongdoer's factual gain is beside the point, for the wrongfulness of the deed lies in the advantage the wrongdoer sought to gain over and above the injury to the victim through the denial of the victim's rights.

5.3   JUSTIFICATIONS AND EXCUSES

I now turn briefly to the role of excuses in the criminal law. Questions of justification are part of the theory of crime; excuses are part of the theory of punishment. J. L. Austin observed that justifications involve accepting responsibility but denying the act was bad, whereas excuses involve admitting that an act was bad but refusing to accept full, or even any, responsibility.[54] Legal excuses are slightly different. In the legal context, excuses differ from justifications in that a justification shows an act to be rightful, whereas an excuse concedes the act was wrongful, but denies that the agent can be punished. Wrongdoers may be excused from punishment; they may or may not escape blame. For example, crimes committed under circumstances of extreme necessity or duress are wrongful but excused. In those cases, the explanation of the deed lies as much in the circumstances as the agent. Because excuses limit punishment only when an act is wrongful, excusing conditions do not change the contours of the offense. Indeed, if the accused acts in part because he knows his act will be excused, it vitiates his claim to have been compelled by the circumstances.[55] Only if the prospect of punishment is irrelevant is the act excused. The same point is sometimes put in terms of the irrelevance of the agent's character to the explanation of the crime. Where circumstances would compel anyone to do the same, there is a sense in which the deed does not reflect on the wrongdoer. As a result, there is no reason for singling out the wrongdoer in particular for punishment.

One prominent view of excuses sees them as the law's response to human infirmity. George Fletcher suggests that there is a "moral equivalence" between an excused act and no act at all.[56] Although Fletcher is right about the equivalence, his explanation of it in terms of infirmity leads him to the conclusion that excusing conditions should be individualized. Particular people are infirm in particular ways. As a result, any concessions to infirmity must look at how individual wills respond to circumstances in deciding whether to excuse. Whatever its moral appeal, Fletcher's account sits uneasily with the law's traditional excusing conditions, which only apply when an ordinary person, similarly situated, would have responded in the same way. It is also important that excused acts may still be blameworthy. The person who uses defensive force against an innocent aggressor – a child firing a gun, for example – properly escapes punishment, even though

---

[54] J. L. Austin, "A Plea for Excuses," in *The Philosophy of Action,* edited by A. R. White (Oxford: 1968), p. 19.

[55] Compare with George Fletcher, "The Individualization of Excusing Conditions," 47 *Southern California Law Review* 1269, 1303 (1974); and Meir Dan-Cohen, "Decision Rules and Conduct Rules" (arguing that whereas justifications are addressed to agents, excuses are addressed to courts).

[56] George Fletcher, *Rethinking Criminal Law* (Boston: Little, Brown, 1978).

we might think it morally blameworthy to prefer one's own life to that of an innocent person. (Certainly there is moral space for the child's parents to blame the killer.)

A further difficulty for an account of the excuses that views them as a response to infirmity is that human infirmity reveals itself in responses to offers as well as threats. The person who faces the prospect of a huge sum of money if a crime is committed may well succumb to temptation, just as the person caught in a storm may well succumb to fear for her life. Both display human infirmity; only the latter is excused from punishment.

An account of punishment that emphasizes denunciation through deterrence offers a different explanation of excusing conditions. Kant makes the general point explicit when he remarks that acts done under necessity are culpable but not punishable; they cannot be punished because they cannot be deterred. On this view, necessity is a paradigmatic excuse because any attempt to punish acts done in circumstances of necessity will fail. Consider some famous cases: Shipwrecked without food or water for twenty-one days, Dudley and Stevens kill and eat the cabin boy, Richard Parker.[57] The court concedes that anyone would have done the same, but insists that necessity does not shift the boundaries of people's rights. As a result, it finds Dudley and Stevens guilty of murder. Yet the same court that said that the law must set standards that people may be unable to meet goes on to urge the crown to commute their sentence. Again, survivors trapped in the overturned hull of the ill-fated *Herald of Free Enterprise* save themselves from an icy death in the North Sea by pulling into the water a man who, paralyzed by cold or fear, blocked their route to safety. The inquest into the disaster takes note of the information, but doesn't even bother to record the names. Instead, the man on the ladder is simply treated as one of those who perished in the sea.[58]

These cases share a common theme, which Kant makes explicit in his discussion of Cicero's example of two shipwrecked sailors struggling over a plank that can support only one. Kant notes that anyone faced with a choice between immediate and certain death and the prospect of subsequent punishment (including execution) would choose the latter. As a result, the threat of punishment has no deterrent

---

[57]   *R. v. Dudley and Stevens* (1884) 14 Q.B.D. 273 (C.C.R.); A. W. B. Simpson, *Cannibalism and the Common Law* (Chicago: University of Chicago Press, 1984).

[58]   This example is described in J. C. Smith, *Justification and Excuse in the Criminal Law* (London: Stephens, 1989).

force. To punish someone who acts in such circumstances would be pointless, because it would do nothing to undermine the deed's rationality. Kant is not simply saying that the sailor was not deterred. That much is clear in this, as in any other case of punishment. Kant's claim is rather that even if punished, the sailor's deed remains rational from the point of view of both the agent and the ordinary person. The sailor did wrong, but punishment cannot right that wrong. In such circumstances, crime pays, even if it is punished. Hence, punishment has no point.

Put in slightly different terms, in cases in which a person's will is overborne by circumstances, punishing the agent will do nothing to denounce the act. The idea of a person's will being overborne and that of the impossibility of denunciation may seem to be two distinct criteria, but they are equivalent. Some responses to circumstances are privileged because we suppose that nobody else would have acted differently. Although not exactly compelled by the circumstances, we treat the behavior as if it is – it is, as Blackstone puts it, morally involuntary, so we treat it as though the agent wasn't involved at all – and explain the behavior by reference to the circumstances rather than any particularities of the agent. If the circumstances serve to explain the behavior, it follows that the behavior could not have been deterred. The point is not that it is rational to break the law in such circumstances – for extraordinary fortitude is surely not *ir*rational – but that punishment fails to denounce it if the circumstances made the person do it (as measured by whether an ordinary person would have done it), because in such circumstances, the deed remains rational, even after the fact. As a result, it cannot be denounced. In overbearing the wrongdoer's will, the circumstances also overbear both the law's ability to demand conformity and its ability to denounce wrongdoing.[59]

Cases in which someone chooses a lesser evil also fit this model of excuses. The person who violates traffic laws to rush an injured person to the hospital is sometimes thought to be justified in his or her action. In the case of minor statutory violations, we may well presume that the statute carries an implicit exception for emergencies, and so suppose that such a person does the right thing. A simpler view is

---

[59] It is worth noticing that *revenge* may still appeal to victims of crimes committed in circumstances of necessity. Punishing Dudley and Stevens accomplishes nothing, but if Richard Parker's family desires revenge, the dire circumstances of the crime need not rob that revenge of its satisfactions. (As it turns out, Parker's family forgave them. See Simpson, *Cannibalism and the Common Law*.)

that such lawbreaking could not be deterred by any punishment proportional to it. Anyone confronted with a choice between rushing an injured person to the hospital and avoiding a fine of a few hundred dollars would choose the former. A more serious penalty might deter, but would be disproportionate to the wrongfulness of driving above the speed limit.[60]

Now it might be thought that a purely vindicating sentence – a finding of guilt, with no further punishment – is the appropriate response to crimes committed in circumstances in which they could not have been deterred. A purely vindicating conviction might keep the distinction between justifications and excuses clear, because it would make it clear that a wrong had been done. Whatever its appeal, such a proposal would fail to vindicate the rights of the victim. Even a solemn declaration that a wrong has been done is in part a punishment; it is just not enough of a punishment to successfully denounce a serious crime. Where more severe punishments would fail to right a wrong, a less serious punishment must also fail.

5.3.1   Objective Standards, Again

Not every case in which someone commits a crime in response to circumstances is excused. The person who breaks the law out of fear in circumstances in which others of ordinary fortitude would have resisted is punished. Such a person was presumably not deterred by the threat of punishment. We may even suppose that he genuinely believed his act to be necessary to preserve his life. The act is still treated as his, rather than the result of his circumstances, because an ordinary person would have been able to resist. Thus, the question of whether the crime is the result of agency or circumstance depends on a line between the two that is drawn in moral terms. The question is not whether the wrongdoer could have resisted (since he plainly didn't), but whether an ordinary person could have. Whether an ordinary person could have resisted depends on the available alternatives, the degree of diligence in seeking them out, and the amount of fortitude we expect of others.

Why punish someone who wasn't deterred, just because others would have been? Such a person's acts can be successfully denounced

---

[60]   It is worth recalling that someone who drove recklessly in an emergency and injured another person would be both culpable and liable, even if he supposed himself to be, on balance of probabilities, avoiding a more serious evil.

because the agent failed to avail himself of alternative courses of action that others would have followed. To prefer one's own advantage to the rights of others where alternatives are not unduly burdensome is to substitute private rationality for public reasonableness. As a result, the act must be denounced, its rationality contested. The availability of alternatives makes it possible to contest the rationality of the act. The sense of the word "could" in which the law takes an interest concerns whether an ordinary person could have been deterred. If the prospect of punishment would have deterred others, punishment can successfully denounce the crime.

Objective tests for excuses thus look to whether or not a person of reasonable or normal fortitude would have been able to conform his behavior to the law's demands. Unlike reasonableness tests for justifications, which, as we shall see in the next chapter, grant the accused "the right to act on appearances,"[61] tests for excuses do not divide the risk between accused and victim. Acts that are excused plainly violate the victim's rights. Instead, objective tests for excuses suppose that in circumstances in which a person of ordinary fortitude could not have been deterred by the prospect of punishment, the act is properly attributed to the circumstances rather than to the agent.

Still, objective tests for excuses do share one important feature with reasonableness tests. In order to set the appropriate standard of self-control, the law has no choice but to consider the importance of substantive goods. In particular, the onerousness of circumstances can only be assessed in relation to views of the seriousness of various burdens the lawbreaker might face. Most assessments of onerousness are fairly easy, because they involve threats to life and limb. In other cases, judgments of onerousness may be more controversial. What we make of the claims of the person who succumbs to threats to his family,[62] or the person who claims necessity in saving his own life at the expense of an innocent person[63] depends on how important we suppose care for one's family to be, and how much greater self-restraint we think appropriate when human life is at issue. The dependence on such factors is appropriate, for the issue is one of moral involuntariness. But although such moral factors appropriately enter into setting the standard of self-control, their role is not to make the act morally

---

[61] *Hughes v. State*, 10 N.E. 2d 629 at 633 (Indiana 1937).

[62] *R. v. Langlois* (1993) 89 C.C.C. (3d) 28 (Quebec C.A.) (A prison guard helps prisoners smuggle drugs into prison because of credible threats to his family.)

[63] See Smith, *Justification and Excuse in the Criminal Law; R. v. Dudley and Stevens;* Simpson, *Cannibalism and the Common Law.*

innocent. Instead, they serve to set the limits of deeds that are beyond the reach of punishment. The law can only ask for so much by way of fortitude and diligence, but the amount it can ask for is not set by how much particular offenders are able to give.

On this understanding of necessity, it provides a bar to punishment, but does not rest on the total absence of agency. Unlike sleepwalking or epilepsy, the excuse of necessity involves intentional actions of a responsible agent. Yet precisely because the person who cannot be punished was nonetheless acting in light of his or her own ends, he or she may still be liable for damages in tort. The hiker who breaks into another's cabin to save his own life cannot be punished, but must pay for the broken window and the food eaten. Although the use of the cabin could not have been deterred, the costs of using it properly lie with the person who created them.[64]

5.3.2   Hot and Cold

Looking at the structure of excuses enables us to see why punishment makes sense even in cases in which people act in ways that cannot easily be characterized as expressions of the wrongdoer's private rationality. In this section, I briefly return to the issue of crimes of passion. Many crimes are committed in "hot blood," and involve deeds that the wrongdoer would surely repudiate in a quieter moment. As I suggested earlier, such crimes can still be understood as expressions

---

[64]   There are some circumstances in which the defense of necessity is unavailable even though an ordinary person would not have been deterred. Those who wrongfully get themselves into dangerous situations may have difficulty claiming necessity. The person who breaks into a cabin when in the woods while escaping after committing a crime may have a claim of necessity, even if the earlier wrongdoing leads him to be in a situation in which he could not have been deterred. By contrast, the person who finds himself with no choice but to break the law because his only alternative would involve abandoning some illegal activity in progress has no claim of necessity. The availability of a legal alternative always qualifies as a reasonable choice in the relevant sense. Here we see still another illustration of the risk rule familiar from torts. Ordinarily, finding oneself in circumstances of peril is not within the risk that makes committing a crime wrongful. As a result, those who commit crimes do not become outlaws, unable to avail themselves of a defense of necessity. If the necessity is within the risk of the original wrong, though, he loses the right to necessity. The person who carelessly leads another to fear for his life, even if he has no intention of harming the other cannot claim necessity in responding to the other's use of defensive force. Such a person perhaps could not have been deterred at the time he acted, but his initial wrongful deed is both culpable and punishable, and responsibility flows back to him through the dangerous acts of others that make his behavior wrongful.

of the wrongdoer's agency inasmuch as they display the ability to act purposively in relation to the victim, as opposed to total loss of all self-control. Punishment is a response to an intentional deed, not to the motives that produced it, and so the person's anger seems not to the point.

Still, there are some cases in which hot-blooded criminals are widely thought to deserve less serious treatment than do those who act in cold blood. The law of provocation illustrates this. A successful defense of provocation serves to reduce a charge from murder to manslaughter. Whereas murder usually carries a mandatory sentence, various mitigating factors can enter into sentencing those convicted of manslaughter.[65] The person with an unusually short temper does not receive special solace from the law. Instead, only where an ordinary person would have lost self-control can the fact that the particular accused did be treated as simply a matter of chance. The person with an unusually short temper counts as a murderer because he has failed to live up to a minimal standard of self-control.

The defense of provocation is in some ways troubling. One problem is that it focuses on those losses of self-control that result from anger, rather than, for example, greed or lust.[66] This may reflect the idea that emotions other than anger are never acceptably expressed through violating the rights of others. Yet this makes the problem more, rather than less, severe. It is hardly appropriate to express anger through violence. Worse, expressing one's anger in violence toward others is typically the prerogative of the stronger. Those who are physically weak, like those who find themselves in the presence of a police officer, seem to have much more self-control when angry. Thus, there is reason to worry whether there really is a standard of

---

[65] The defense had its origins in the refusal of common-law juries to convict those who killed in the heat of passion. The defense of provocation was introduced to steer jurors toward a more nuanced response to such killings. Not all killings done in anger were excused. Originally, the defense incorporated something close to an Aristotelian model of virtue: Acts explicable as the results of legitimate outrage were excused. On this view, the victim in some sense "asked for it." By the nineteenth century, killing in hot blood was thought of as a loss of self-control. By the middle of that century, the standard of the reasonable person had made its way from tort law to the defense of provocation. Although the standard seems to have first been employed evidentially, by early in this century, it played a substantive role. The basic principle is that the accused is not a murderer if the death resulted from a loss of self-control and a reasonable person would have lost self-control in similar circumstances. For discussion of these issues, see Jeremy Horder, *Provocation and Responsibility* (Oxford: Oxford University Press, 1993); Dennis Klimchuk, "Outrage, Self-Control, and Culpability," 44 *University of Toronto Law Journal* 441 (1994).

[66] Horder, *Provocation and Responsibility*.

170

acceptable self-control apart from the ability to act with impunity, which is itself a matter of self-control, not its lack. There are also hard questions about which things would lead an ordinary person to lose self-control. Like the parallel standard of fortitude in cases of necessity, any acceptable standard will inevitably rest on substantive views about the burdens imposed by various provocative events. However great the burdens are, the use of physical force in response to them is out of proportion to them. Here again we face the difficulty that attacking others in anger is the prerogative of the stronger: Most of those who claim to have been provoked would not have acted had a police officer been standing at their elbow, or indeed if their victims had been more powerful. This may suggest that most provoked killings could have been deterred. But that is just to say that they involve the pursuit of private ends in the face of public standards of reasonableness.

5.4 CONCLUSION

In this chapter, I have outlined the difference between torts and crimes at the level of remedies, and have offered an explanation of why criminal liability both requires a mental element and merits punishment. I have said very little, however, about the fair terms of interaction the criminal law seeks to uphold. It is to that task that I now turn.

Chapter 6

Mistakes

In this chapter, I develop an account of the ways in which the criminal law upholds fair terms of interaction. My emphasis is on the idea of *interaction*. As a result, my central focus will be on the two kinds of cases in which the rights of two people are at issue, namely, self-defense and consent. Where they are applicable, both self-defense and victim consent provide complete defenses to criminal charges. They are also the two areas in which reasonableness tests apply to mistakes. I will explain the underlying idea of reasonableness, and thus the role of those tests, in light of the ideas of fair terms of interaction I developed in my account of tort. Where the criminal law employs reasonableness tests, they are sometimes thought to rest on an evaluation of the plausibility of the accused's beliefs, given available evidence. The burden of this chapter is to show that reasonableness tests are deeper, indeed constitutive of the rights the criminal law protects. Here, as elsewhere, the reasonable person is the one who interacts with others on terms of reciprocity.

6.1 MISTAKES

Mistakes enter the criminal law in two distinct ways. Sometimes, mistake is an excuse, regardless of how stupid the mistake might be. If one person takes another's raincoat, genuinely mistaking it for his own, no matter how stupid his mistake, he commits no crime. Again, the person who kills another person by firing a gun she believes to be unloaded commits at most manslaughter, not murder. More generally, when it comes to factual circumstances, a person is excused from punishment if she would have committed no crime had the facts been as she took them to be. The rationale is simple: Honest belief negatives intent.[1] If I was not aware of some risk, or feature of my act that

[1] *R. v. Tolson* (1889) 23 Q.B.D. 168 (C.C.R.). Edwin R Keedy, "Ignorance and Mistake in the Criminal Law," 22 *Harvard Law Review* 75 (1908).

172

jeopardizes the rights of others, I did not choose that feature or risk. Hence, I do not commit an intentional wrong. On this understanding, the only possible role for reasonableness tests is evidential: In assessing whether the accused actually had the purported belief, one piece of evidence is whether a reasonable person would have believed such a thing in the circumstances. If I claim to have mistaken your coat for my own despite them having almost nothing in common, a jury might well doubt my claim to have believed it.

Mistakes enter the criminal law in a second way as well, in those circumstances in which mistakes concern the significance of another person's act. Beliefs about the need for defensive force must be reasonable in order to exculpate; in many jurisdictions, so too must beliefs about whether someone has consented to some interaction. One of my primary purposes in this chapter is to explain why the two categories of mistake are treated differently. I will do so by considering an influential view according to which all mistakes should be treated alike, because whenever someone acts under a mistaken belief about the factual situation in which he finds himself, his mind is innocent.

6.2   SUBJECTIVISM

The idea that mistakes always exculpate is sometimes put forward as part of a broader package of views about criminal culpability that is generally referred to as "subjectivism." Unfortunately, the words "subjective" and "objective" are used in so many different ways that it is difficult to isolate a central set of claims. Still, the views that are often thought to come as a package seek to separate questions of culpability from questions about either circumstances or consequences of a crime. So characterized, subjectivism has been prominent in England for the last few decades, due in large measure to the influence of Glanville Williams. It has also had considerable influence in the United States, where the drafters of the American Law Institute's *Model Penal Code* incorporated a variety of subjectivist provisions. Thus, a common thread in subjectivist writings is the idea that a person accused of a crime should be judged on the basis of the facts as he sincerely believed them to be. This position is supposed to apply to all circumstances of a crime, so that no reasonableness tests apply to a person's beliefs about the need for defensive force or the consent of the complainant. Another thread, which we will take up in our discussion of attempts in Chapter 7, denies the relevance of the consequences of wrongdoing to punishment. The threads overlap, but are analytically distinguishable, and not everyone who accepts the view of mistakes accepts the view of consequences. My concern for now will only be with the subjectivist account of mistakes.

The subjectivist argument gets part of its force from the idea that criminal law differs from civil law precisely in the fact that in a civil dispute, the problem in question must end up being borne by someone. If my behavior falls below the standard of care and you are injured, one or the other of us will end up bearing the cost. The fact that I made a mistake is not the end of the story. Again, if I mistakenly agree to purchase something from you, I cannot renege on our agreement simply because I discover that I had misunderstood the terms of the agreement. In each case, to excuse me is to burden you. But, the subjectivist maintains, that is not true in the criminal law. If my mistake is unreasonable, I may still be liable in damages. But if I do not go to prison, you do not end up in prison instead.

Subjectivism is sometimes defended in terms of an idea of voluntariness. The idea that only voluntary acts merit punishment is itself uncontroversial in the criminal law. It has been recognized at least since Aristotle, who notes that a person who hits another because a third has grabbed his arm is not responsible for the hitting. The same requirement underwrites a variety of criminal defenses, including sleepwalking and insanity: Those whose acts are involuntary are not responsible. (Indeed, there is some temptation to say that they do not act at all.) In the same way, such defenses as necessity and duress, which are available when the actor is thought to have had no real choice about whether to obey the law, are also sometimes modeled on involuntariness. The subjectivist does not simply embrace this commonplace about voluntariness, however. The subjectivist interprets it in a specific way: An act is only voluntary with respect to some circumstance or consequence if that circumstance or consequence came before the agent's mind.[2] The person who intends to kill kills voluntarily; the person who recognizes the substantial risk of breaking a window and acts anyway breaks the window voluntarily.

Subjectivists have offered three broad rationales for their view.

---

[2] This account of voluntariness bears superficial affinities to Kant's moral philosophy, according to which the character of an action is given by the maxim according to which the agent wills it. Kant's legal thought steers clear of this conception of voluntariness, since he supposes law to be concerned with outward action. For Kant, the maxim under which an act is willed is fixed by the noumenal self, not the empirical self. Thus, the agent's conscious self-description is not at issue in Kant's moral thought.

174

6.2 Subjectivism

One account supposes that an agent can only be deterred if he is consciously attending to the nature of his act. A second supposes that guilty minds are the real objects of punishment. The third account supposes that punishment is only appropriate in cases in which the wrongdoer was aware of doing wrong. My main concern will be with the third account. I should say a few words, though only in passing, about the first and second. According to the first account, subjectivism is required on grounds of the efficacy of the criminal sanction. Since Bentham, defenders of deterrence models of punishment have been drawn to subjectivism on the assumption that an act can only be deterred if it comes before a person's mind. Glanville Williams has been a prominent contemporary exponent of this view (although many of his specific arguments seem to rest on considerations of fairness). The assumption that only those acts that come before a person's mind can be deterred has been roundly criticized, most notably by H. L. A. Hart, who pointed out that the threat of punishment can lead people to attend to things that they otherwise wouldn't.[3] Traffic laws lead people to drive more carefully, even if they don't intend to drive carelessly, and there is every reason to believe that severe criminal sanctions could have comparable effects. Whether subjectivism strengthens or undermines the efficacy of the criminal sanction is a question of fact. Williams places great store in the ability of prosecutors to give wrongdoers "a hot time in the witness box,"[4] and so discover their true thoughts. Yet, as Hart points out, a requirement of subjective guilt might lead some to suppose that they can escape punishment by claiming to have not realized what they were doing. Even if zealous prosecutors could convict in every case of actual subjective guilt, persons contemplating crimes might well suppose that they would succeed in concealing their thoughts, and so commit crimes. The issues here concern matters of fact, and the evidence is at best mixed.

My central concern in my discussion of subjectivism is with the argument about the distinctive nature of the criminal sanction. If the subjectivist is right, the conception of responsibility familiar from tort law that I pointed to in the preceding chapter has no place in a decent and humane criminal law. It reflects a barbaric urge to punish people for things for which they are not to blame.

---

[3] H. L. A. Hart, "Legal Responsibility and Excuses," in his *Punishment and Responsibility* (Oxford: Oxford University Press, 1968), p. 42.

[4] Glanville Williams, "The Unresolved Problem of Recklessness," 8 *Legal Studies* 74 at 77 (1988).

For the subjectivist, anything that shows that the wrongdoer did not mean to do wrong serves to exculpate. Thus, mistakes, including unreasonable ones, show that the accused lacked a "guilty mind" in the requisite sense. And the person motivated by fear, including unreasonable fear, is innocent because he too lacks a guilty mind. The person who subjects others to excessive risks but honestly believes himself to be expert enough to manage them is likewise blameless. So too is the person who loses self-control. In each case, the act is involuntary, and so the agent is not culpable. On subjectivist accounts, tests of reasonableness serve at most evidentially, to determine whether the accused really did have the belief or fear in question.[5] If the belief is unreasonable enough, the trier of fact might conclude that the accused did not believe it all. But that is a question of fact extrinsic to the definition of culpability. Not surprisingly, subjectivists also regard the law's treatment of attempts as irrational. J. C. Smith, for example, laments the fact that chance cannot be removed entirely from the criminal law.[6] Since the attempter and successful criminal differ only in their luck (whether good or bad), the subjectivist supposes they should be treated alike.

The subjectivist account of crime and punishment has significant implications for doctrine. Subjectivism is a defendant-centered view of responsibility. The only questions of fairness that arise concerning punishment are matters between the state and the wrongdoer. Subjectivists theories of mistakes have led to some deeply troubling results. In *Morgan*, an R.A.F. officer invited a number of men under his command home to have sexual intercourse with his wife. Morgan told them that his wife would heighten her own pleasure by pretending to resist. When she resisted, they proceeded anyway, and at their trial claimed that they believed that she had consented. They were found guilty because their beliefs were unreasonable. A majority of the House of Lords held that the jury instruction concerning the requirement of reasonableness had been in error, and that a sincere but unreasonable belief in the victim's consent is a complete defense to a charge of rape. The court's reasoning was impeccable from a subjectivist point of

---

[5] Ibid.; some subjectivists allow reasonableness tests in defining recklessness: Whether an act is reckless depends on whether it poses an unreasonable risk. But whether recklessness is culpable depends on whether the accused adverts to the risk in question.

[6] J. C. Smith, "The Element of Chance in Criminal Liability" [1971], *Criminal Law Review* 63.

view. Rape was defined at the time as nonconsensual sexual intercourse. If a rapist believed, however unreasonably, that his victim
consented, he did not intend to have nonconsensual intercourse. If he
did not realize he was committing a wrongful act, he committed no
crime, so he cannot be punished. If the defendants' story were believed, they differed from ordinary men only in the accident of having made a mistake. In the *Morgan* case itself, the court found that the
beliefs the defendants claimed were so manifestly unreasonable that
they could not have sincerely held them. Still, the results are ominous
for the idea that the law protects people equally, for they make the
wrongfulness of a deed depend on the wrongdoer's beliefs about the
victim. Thus, the victim's ability to consent seems to be beside the
point. The subjectivist need not deny that what occurred was wrongful. The subjectivist claims only the law should only take an interest
in an act if the agent knew it was wrong. The subjectivist view that
the defendant who makes a mistake lacks a guilty mind, coupled with
the idea that a guilty mind is an element of the offense, leads inex-
orably to the conclusion that no crime was committed. Something
happened that should not have, but it is not the sort of unfortunate
thing in which the criminal law should take an interest. For the subjectivist, an unreasonable mistake about consent does not merely excuse what would otherwise be a crime. It makes it no crime at all.

Glanville Williams defended the *Morgan* decision on the grounds
that if a man makes an unreasonable mistake about victim consent, it
can only be because he is stupid, yet "to convict the stupid man would
be to convict him for what lawyers call inadvertent negligence – honest conduct which may be the best that this man can do but that does
not come up to the standard of the so-called reasonable man. People
ought not to be punished for negligence except in some minor offenses established by statute."[7] Williams's smooth transition between
unreasonableness, negligence, and inadvertence is striking. It is a transition from a culpable failure to behave in keeping with minimal standards to an innocent intellectual failing. Other subjectivists put their
doctrine forward as though it were a logical consequence of simple
definitions. J. C. Smith described the decision as "a victory for common sense" and that there was an "inconsistency" in imposing a reasonableness test on mistakes as to consent in cases of rape.[8]

7   Glanville Williams, Letter to *The Times* (London), May 8, 1975, p. 15.
8   J. C. Smith, Letter to *The Times* (London), May 7, 1975, p. 17.

6.2.1 Some Problems with Subjectivism

Subjectivism has been criticized on a number of different grounds. I will explore some of these in detail in the discussion of consent and of attempt liability, which follows. For now, I limit myself to a passing remark and two criticisms. The first criticism raises the question of whether the subjectivist position can be stated in such a way as to avoid either expanding or effacing the category of crime. The second looks to the subjectivist's apparent readiness to leave victims of crime out of an account of culpability.

First, the passing remark. A curious feature of much subjectivist writing is its appeal to what are taken to be obvious deliverances of either "common sense" or logic. Yet its view of intention is not found either elsewhere in the criminal law or outside of it. The subjectivist account of intent supposes that one can only intend something that comes before one's mind. Such a view has been subject to devastating critiques in philosophy at least since Wittgenstein, and sits well with neither legal nor ordinary usage. Intending always takes place against a background of beliefs about the world, and covers more than what comes before a person's mind. Again, Antony Duff has pointed to the striking parallel between the subjectivist account of intention and empiricist accounts of perception, according to which we perceive only our sense impressions, not the world. The perceptual argument has been the object of severe criticisms, as has the more general conception of mind on which it rests.[9] I will not develop those arguments here, because I take it to be a worthwhile venture to develop an account of responsibility and agency that is specific to legal contexts. Failure to comport with philosophical accounts of responsibility and agency more generally need not disqualify a view of culpability. Although the subjectivist purports to speak from the standpoint of commonsense morality, the same account can be read as specific to the criminal law. It is in that light that I will examine subjectivism for the remainder of this chapter. I mention Duff's argument only because the leading statements of the subjectivist account claim the authority of common sense and logic. Commonsense morality often stands ready to criticize those who were not thinking as they act. The subjectivist position does not reflect commonsense views, and must be

---

[9] The *locus classicus* of the criticisms is Wilfrid Sellars, *Empiricism and the Philosophy of Mind* (Cambridge, MA: Harvard University Press, 1997; originally 1956). Sellars also discusses the parallel between "seeming" and "trying" in that work.

judged by the standards of political morality. Here too they will be found wanting.

I think that Duff's arguments about the nature of intention are all successful on their own terms, and succeed in undermining a significant, if philosophically naive, argument for subjectivism. I will not engage those issues, because in another way, Duff's arguments fail to make contact with their intended target. For what Duff sets out to show is that the concept of intention is essentially public and essentially normative. He shows that by showing that aspects of intention and action that appear to be private are conceptually derivative of their more public counterparts. In arguing that our concepts of the private, the inner and the subjective are derivative, he does make it seem odd that the criminal law would take an interest in such things. Whatever one makes of those arguments, though (I, for one, find them convincing), they do not show that the criminal law *could* take no such interest. Headaches, for example, are private and inner even if our ability to describe them is ultimately parasitic on our understanding of public things. Duff's arguments also fail to show that the relevant normative basis of the concept of intention is the very norms of reasonableness that are employed by the criminal law. Only an independent normative argument, one that does not look to abstract considerations about action, could show that norms of reasonableness are appropriate in legal contexts.

6.2.2   Mistake of Fact and Mistake of Law

The subjectivist account of the exculpating role of mistakes is supposed to apply only to mistakes of fact, not mistakes of law. Holmes (among others) has argued that a consistent subjectivism would exculpate those who think that their conduct is morally faultless.[10] Holmes's objection can be put in terms of the subjectivist account of voluntary action: Any act is only voluntary with respect to the characteristics of the act that the agent considers. The idea of voluntariness underwrites a plausible view of mistakes of fact: If I am not aware of some circumstance in which I act, my act is involuntary with respect to that circumstance; it does not matter why I am unaware, or whether my mistake is reasonable. Holmes's point is that this conception of voluntariness reaches too far: If I act without realizing that murder or theft is wrong, give no thought to the moral or legal status of my act,

---

[10]   Oliver Wendell Holmes, *The Common Law* (Boston: Little, Brown, 1881), pp. 41–3.

or believe myself to be exempted from some law, my act is also involuntary with respect to that wrong.[11] The same point can be put in terms of the purposes of punishment. It is precisely the fact that nobody needs to be punished – that the victim ends up materially no worse off if the accused is excused – that opens up the subjectivist to Holmes's challenge. For the person who makes a mistake of law will still be civilly liable to those injured as a result of that mistake. The question is whether such a person merits punishment, since that person did not intend to act contrary to the law, even though what he did intentionally was contrary to the law.

Put slightly differently, Holmes's objection is that a consistent subjectivist must treat mistakes of fact and mistakes of law in the same way. One of the central principles of the criminal law is that ignorance of the law is no excuse. The distinction between fact and law is a normative distinction, rather than a factual one; the classification of matters of fact and as matters of law are the conclusions of legal arguments. Still, most cases are uncontroversial. People are presumed to know such basic principles as that they are not entitled to take another's property, and that consent is required in order for various interactions to be legitimate. The idea that ignorance of the law is no excuse can be restated as the general requirement that people are culpable for their failure to know the basic principles governing the rights of others and the principles that legitimate what would otherwise be boundary crossings. The person who does not know that it is illegal to take another's property is still a thief, as the person who thinks that the fact that someone is a family member confers a right to assault them is still an assailant.[12] The challenge is to explain why the accused's beliefs matter in some cases, but not in others.

---

[11] Subjectivists sometimes appeal to the idea of willful blindness to identify culpable mistakes. An agent is willfully blind if he takes steps to maintain his ignorance of some fact. The concept of willful blindness presumably applies to both mistakes of fact and mistakes of law.

[12] Since Holmes's day, two exceptions to this general rule have emerged, both of which only apply to regulatory offenses. Neither has been interpreted as applying to crimes *mala in se*, so they do not really make contact with Holmes's objection. One is a defense of due diligence in complying with regulatory statutes: If someone does everything she can to comply with a regulation, her conduct is excused even if she misunderstood the regulation. See, for example, *Lambert v. California*, 335 U.S. 419 (1957). The second is the defense of officially induced error, which acts as a bar to punishment in those cases in which the accused has relied on an official statement as to the law. See, for example, *Cox v. Louisiana*, 379 U.S. 559 (1965). In the first sort of case, the behavior is excused because the accused was beyond the reach of the law's deterrent effect. In the

6.2   Subjectivism

The subjectivist maintains that if I mistake your smile for an invitation, or use defensive force when there is no real danger, I have made a mistake of fact. If I suppose I am entitled to injure you or take your property without your permission, I have made a mistake of law. The subjectivist would exculpate all those who make mistakes of fact, no matter how unreasonable. The difficulty comes in justifying such exculpation without thereby also exculpating those who make mistakes of law.[13]

Although Holmes himself offered his objection in support of a utilitarian account of culpability, the issue it raises is of broader importance. Any account of the broad features of the criminal law must explain why mistakes of fact and mistakes of law are treated differently; more importantly, it must explain how various mistakes are to be classified.[14]

If mistakes of law were to exculpate, one person would be able to unilaterally set the terms of his interaction with others, for one person's

second, the operative principle is akin to estoppel: Having made a representation to the accused, the state cannot disown that representation in prosecution. The representation does not thereby entitle the accused to an acquittal. Instead, it disentitles the state to a conviction.

[13]   Bernard (not Glanville) Williams has made a similar point about moral blame. Williams's argument is complex, but its basic point can be put simply. He suggests that blame is puzzling if we think of it in terms of what he calls "external" reasons, that is, reasons not related to the agent's existing motivational set. Many types of criticism have nothing to do with an agent's motivating reasons, but Williams suggests that blame is different. Although his aim is to show that the idea of blame is itself obscure, Williams's argument serves to show the natural resting place of a consistent subjectivism. As long as we think there is something troubling, either morally or metaphysically, about holding someone responsible for things to which he did not attend, we are left with, at most, the agent's own internal resources for criticism. We thus might sum up the subjectivist's position with the slogan: No criticisms without (sincere) self-criticism. See Bernard Williams, "Internal Reasons and the Obscurity of Blame, " in his *Making Sense of Humanity* (Cambridge: Cambridge University Press, 1995), pp. 35–45. For an argument that even self-criticism requires external resources, see John Broome, "Can a Humean be Moderate?" in *Value, Welfare, and Morality*, edited by R. G. Frey and Christopher W. Morris (Cambridge: Cambridge University Press, 1993), pp. 51–73.

[14]   The law/fact distinction is potentially misleading here, so I offer a few words of clarification. Strictly speaking, the relevant distinction is between mistakes that are relevant to culpability and those that are not. That distinction, in turn, is reflected in the procedural distinction between the element of an offense that the prosecution must prove and those that can be assumed. For example, the prosecution need not prove that taking another's property is against the law. But if someone seizes another person's car, believing himself to have a mechanic's lien against it, his mistake is one of law, but his belief may excuse him because it is about a particular lien.

freedom would depend on what another person takes to be the appropriate limits to that freedom. To be sure, tort damages might still be assessed against such wrongdoers, assuming they had the resources to pay them. But, as I suggested in the last chapter, damages are not a sufficient remedy. Failure to punish such wrongs would make the rights of victims tradeable, and so in that sense subject to the will of others. At the same time, the question is not only philosophical: Many serious crimes involve criminals who suppose themselves to be justified in their deeds. Crimes motivated by racial animus often fit into this category, as do all crimes in which the criminal thinks the victim's rights insignificant.[15]

Holmes's objection has invited a variety of responses. In principle, the subjectivist might concede that Holmes is right, and that punishment should only be carried out where the wrongdoer does acknowledge the wrong, thus reserving it for the occasions on which an omniscient God would punish.[16] One compromise solution just short of this extreme will not work. The subjectivist cannot concede that the agent's beliefs about the law also matter, and go on to insist that allowing such people to harm others is simply too dangerous.[17] Any such account must explain why the line of compromise should be drawn so as to insulate all mistakes of fact, however unreasonable, and no mistakes of law. Those who make unreasonable mistakes of fact may well pose more, rather than less, of a peril to others than those who make mistakes of law. Unreasonable mistakes of fact are at the very least a sign of disregard for the legitimate interests of others; mistakes of law may simply be the result of confusion.

---

[15] Of course, not all laws are just, and it might be thought that mistakes of law ought to exculpate in cases of unjust laws, for such mistakes would be reasonable in the appropriate sense, since the lawbreaker's belief would be in keeping with fair terms of interaction, whereas the law was not. But the reason those who violate unjust laws ought not to be punished is surely not that they failed to realize that a law was in place. Instead, it is the injustice of the law. Whatever standard of treatment is appropriate to those who mistakenly break unjust laws also applies to those who are aware of the unjust law in question.

[16] George Fletcher has pointed out that many religions suppose that God would enforce more objective standards. Fletcher, *Rethinking Criminal Law* (Boston: Little, Brown, 1978), p. 507.

[17] Glanville Williams suggests this explains the law's unwillingness to treat drunkenness as a defense. See Williams, *Textbook of Criminal Law*, 2d ed. (London: Stevens, 1983), p. 471.

6.2.3 A Hegelian Solution?

Some have claimed to find a response to Holmes's argument in Hegel.[18] The details of the Hegelian argument may or may not be in Hegel, but the general form of argument is familiar. The basic strategy is to demonstrate that there is a categorical difference between mistakes about the rights people have and mistakes about particular facts. That difference is said to reside in the idea that one need not know *any* particular facts in order to know about basic rights. The Hegelian version of the argument draws this distinction in terms of the abstract concept of agency, but the same distinction might be drawn on quasi-Hobbesian grounds in terms of the necessary conditions for mutually advantageous cooperation,[19] or even on utilitarian grounds in terms of the general rules with long-term benefits. Since Hegelians, Hobbesians, and utilitarians are in broad agreement about the content of those rules, and differ only as to their philosophical underpinnings, the same kind of distinction between fact and law can be deployed by any such position. A broadly Kantian view that emphasizes fair terms of interaction, such as the one developed here, can, indeed must, draw the same kind of distinction. I focus on the Hegelian argument for two reasons. The first is that it makes the *normative* distinction between fact and law into an *epistemic* distinction between things that can be imputed regardless of what a person is aware of and things that cannot. If successful, such an argument is extraordinarily powerful. It is not successful, however, and its failures are instructive. Once the a priori nature of the argument is abandoned, it does yield a categorical difference between mistakes about matters of fact and mistakes about the rights of others (i.e., about fair terms of interaction), but it leaves unreasonable mistakes on the wrong side of the subjectivist divide. I will argue that, properly understood, unreasonable mistakes about justifying circumstances are mistakes of law, not fact.

The Hegelian argument constructs the distinction between mistakes of fact and mistakes of law by claiming that the nature of wrongfulness *malum in se* is inherent in the concept of agency, so that

---

18 Alan Brudner, "Agency and Welfare in the Penal Law," in *Action and Value in Criminal Law,* edited by Stephen Shute, John Gardner, and Jeremy Horder (Oxford: Oxford University Press, 1993), pp. 30 ff.

19 See David Gauthier, *Morals by Agreement* (Oxford: Oxford University Press, 1986).

all implicitly know that certain acts are wrongful.[20] If successful, the Hegelian argument would seem to allow the subjectivist to distinguish mistakes of fact from mistakes of law. By this reasoning, no mistake of law is ever exculpating and all mistakes of fact are exculpating, so there is no room for any tests of reasonableness.

Hegel's derivation turns on the idea that to be an agent is already to implicitly understand the conditions of one's own agency. To commit a crime is to intend to undermine the conditions of another's agency. To act at all, one must be self-conscious and capable of reflection on one's ends. Without this capacity for reflection, animal behavior may be possible, but not responsible agency. Responsible agency requires the ability to stand back from particular ends and decide which ones to pursue, and to understand oneself as so reflecting. As a result, to act at all, one must already implicitly know the conditions of one's own agency. Thus, to act at all, one thereby must also know the conditions of agency as such. Since crimes *mala in se* involve intentional invasion of another person's reflective capacity to choose *his* own ends, anyone who acts cannot but realize that certain acts are wrongful. The criminal thus implicitly knows the wrongfulness of the wrongful deed. The criminal does not, by contrast, necessarily know the factual situation, and the person who is mistaken about the factual situation does not intend to do wrong, inasmuch as that person is not aware of the type of deed it is.

The root idea for Hegel, then, is that a criminal wrongdoer differs from a tort-feasor, because the criminal acts intentionally in a way that is contrary to the intersubjective basis of the criminal's own will. Hegel writes that "force or coercion is in its very conception self-destructive because it is an expression of a will which annuls the expression of determinate existence of a will."[21] When I act, I put my will *as a will* into things; as a result, I act under the idea of willing, and so when I use my will to violate another will, I do wrong. So, for example, if I steal something, I claim it as my own, that is, I claim a right to exclusive use, and so claim a right. More generally, when I injure others, I implicitly claim a right to do so without interference, and so at once both affirm the existence of rights and deny them. Punishment is not a response to the wrong in the world – that is, for Hegel, a "nullity" anyway – but rather is supposed to correct the inner con-

20   Brudner, "Agency and Welfare in the Penal Law," p. 36.
21   G. W. F. Hegel, *Philosophy of Right*, translated by H. B. Nisbet (Cambridge: Cambridge University Press, 1991), para. 92, p. 120.

tradiction in the wrongdoer's will that results from his simultaneous affirmation of the basis of *his* will and denial of the importance of the capacity for willing as such. The point of so conceiving crime and punishment is that it enables us to say that the criminal is being punished for the sake of ends that he already accepts. He is already committed to the basic principles of the criminal law in virtue of having a will at all. This approach is also supposed to explain why the difference between mistakes of fact and mistakes of law is so important. Those who merely make mistakes about facts are not at odds with their own wills, for if the world were as they took it to be, they would do no wrong.

Ingenious though it is, the argument goes wrong in seeking to reduce wrongdoing to the incoherence of the wrongdoer's will and punishment to the restoration of that coherence. The idea that the criminal has violated his own commitments rests on an ambiguity in the idea of a "basis" for the will. I suggested in Chapter 1 that such concepts as agency and choice get their meaning in legal contexts from their relation to legal principles. The same goes for the idea of the will. Although there is no real harm in talking about agents willing certain outcomes, there is a danger in supposing that the concept of the will gives some sort of explanatory leverage in understanding issues of responsibility.

Even if we could make sense of Hegel's supposed derivation of the concept of wrongfulness from that of agency, though, it is no help to the subjectivist. The account faces three distinct problems. The first source of trouble comes from the difficulty in finding an account of the conditions of agency that is both thin enough for all agents to be committed to it, and thick enough so as to require particular actions in concrete cases. The second problem is that even if some implicit commitment to the minimal conditions of interaction could be shown, a further step is needed to get from implicit commitment to the sort of explicit awareness that the subjectivist requires in other contexts. That step is sure to be treacherous, because if the subjectivist allows *implicit* commitments to be imputed as conscious states, all manner of objective standards might be imputed to agents, leaving subjectivism without content. The third, and most serious, source of trouble for the subjectivist appropriation of Hegel is that even if the argument were to succeed in deriving the concept of wrongdoing from that of agency, and awareness from implicit commitments, it needs to show that reasonableness standards are not part of the implicit concept of agency. My main focus will be on this third difficulty, because it is what gives the Hegelian argument its interest. Far from defending subjectivism against Holmes's challenge, the argument shows that unreasonable mistakes about justifying conditions are mistakes of law. I examine these difficulties in ascending order of seriousness.

The first difficulty is with the sort of implicit commitment to the basic principles of the criminal law that all are supposed to have simply in virtue of their capacities for reflection. The problem is not simply that recognizing one's *own* agency says nothing about respecting the agency of *others*. Even if we grant that connection, though the deeper problem is that any concept of respect for the agency of others thin enough to be presupposed by all action will be incompatible with every action. On the face of it, the criminal who decides on reflection that his commitment to his gang is more important than any commitment not to take the lives of strangers has done something awful, but has not *contradicted* himself. If we presume (as the argument requires) that the criminal's commitment to respecting agency as such flows from the fact that he acts for reasons that he recognizes, then whatever he decides to do, he will end up honoring it. (Or if he does not, his act will show that it is after all possible to act without that commitment.) In order to show that some implicit commitment has been violated, the commitment must both be implicit in every act, and yet violated in criminal acts. The question for the subjectivist is not whether or not the agent could be made aware of the law, but whether he was aware of it at the time of the offense.[22]

The second difficulty for the argument is that even if we grant that all agents are implicitly aware of the conditions of their agency, and that that implicit awareness implicitly commits them to a recognition of the wrongfulness of certain acts, that awareness needs to be made explicit. Given the subjectivist's readiness to excuse mere inadvertence about matters of fact, why not also excuse inadvertence about one's implicit commitments? It is a familiar feature of ordinary life that people often forget about commitments they have explicitly made. Whether or not forgetfulness is always an adequate *moral* excuse for a missed appointment or broken promise, it is difficult to see why the subjectivist would not excuse those who forgot, or misun-

---

[22] Moreover, if reflection is a formal feature of thought, seeking a stable point of reflection is a possible content for thought. Seeking the natural stopping point of reflection is not a precondition of reflection, and so not presupposed in all agency.

derstood, their implicit commitments. Like those who make mistakes of fact, they did not realize they were doing wrong. As a result, their actions were not voluntary with respect to their wrongdoing.

The third difficulty for the Hegelian argument goes deepest. I've suggested that the argument does not succeed in showing that we are all implicitly aware of the basic principles of the criminal law. For Hegel, crime differs from tort inasmuch as the criminal acts against the category of right, whereas the tort-feasor merely violates the rights of others. In order for this conception of wrongdoing to lead to subjectivist conclusions, though, the category of right itself must exclude considerations of reasonableness. Now talk of acting against the category of right is similar to my own preferred vocabulary of substituting private rationality for public reasonableness. Put in the latter vocabulary, though, the nub of the problem becomes clear. Fair terms of interaction in a world of risks include reasonableness tests to divide risks. The category of right against which the criminal acts already includes the distinction between reasonable and unreasonable mistakes. The latter part of this chapter develops this point in detail by looking at the two cases in which reasonableness tests apply to mistakes, namely, consent and self-defense. They illustrate a fundamental point: The relevance of an offender's thoughts depends on the fair terms of interaction that the criminal law seeks to uphold.[23]

In order to make unreasonable mistakes of fact exculpate, but unreasonable mistakes of law inculpate, the subjectivist must provide a conception of agency that does two seemingly incompatible things. It must both incorporate some account of reciprocity into the very concept of agency, yet at the same time remain monadic. It must incorporate reciprocity because if it does not, the conditions of agency will fail to implicate the protected interests of others. If it fails to incorporate the interests of others, it will lack the grounds to distinguish mistakes of fact from mistakes of law, because the very possibility of acting will not implicitly include knowing the rights of others. At the same time, the account of agency must not be too reciprocal, for otherwise it will incorporate reasonableness tests, that is, tests that seek to be fair to both parties in situations of risk. For the argument from

---

[23]   Other kinds of examples might be developed to make the same basic point: The person who takes another's property, believing that he is entitled to do so as long as he puts it to a more efficient use than the owner might claim to have simply misapplied the widely available defense of lesser evils; the racist who denies that his victim is a person protected by law might claim to have simply made a mistake of classification.

187

agency to lead to subjectivist conclusions, agents must know the rights of others and those rights must not include the right to have others only violate their apparent interests on reasonable grounds. No amount of analysis of the concept of intention could establish such a thing.

This difficulty illustrates a point that came up in our discussion of risks and causation in Chapter 2. Any account of corrective justice or of punishment that ignores the fact that the world is always uncertain will be unable to articulate an ideal of impartiality that has application in a world of risks. The core idea of impartiality requires that neither party may unilaterally dictate the terms of interaction. Both the libertarian of Chapter 2 and this chapter's subjectivist give up on this idea because they eschew the concept of reasonableness. The libertarian eschews it in order to cast a broader net of tort liability. Yet by ignoring the existence of risks, the libertarian runs into difficulty in finding a single agent to be the cause of an injury. As a result, the net is cast too wide, with too many agents liable for too many injuries. The subjectivist eschews reasonableness tests in order to narrow the net of culpability. Because risks are ignored, though, the subjectivist is unable to make sense of the idea of treating parties as equals, and thus unable to make sense of the idea of showing appropriate regard for the interests of others. As a result, the net of culpability is cast so narrowly as to disappear, for the subjectivist is unable to distinguish between mistakes of fact and mistakes of law.

The appeal to agency thus needs to be supplemented to constitute a defense of subjectivism. It needs a definition of the conditions of agency that does not implicitly incorporate any reasonableness tests. Put slightly differently, the subjectivist account of voluntariness needs to be supplemented with an account of how it is that people know who has which rights.

I do not suppose that these considerations are fully conclusive against the subjectivist. I suspect that the only way to effectively refute subjectivism is by providing an attractive alternative to it. That is what I now propose to do. The first thing I must do is show how a description of legal rights in terms of reasonableness provides a clear account of large amounts of settled law. In the next chapter, I will show its application to the law of attempts.

6.3 MISTAKES AND REASONABLE BOUNDARIES

One of the core claims of the subjectivist position is that reasonableness tests are at most evidential rather than substantive. I now turn to the task of explicating the role of reasonableness tests. As in tort law, the reasonable must deal with drawing boundaries between persons in a world of risks. Because the criminal law is concerned with intentional violations, it protects against a much narrower class of risks than does tort law. Talk of a risk of intentional wrongdoing may seem paradoxical. Such a risk can arise in situations involving mistakes about justifying conditions. Someone may break into the wrong house,[24] believing herself to have permission, mistake a smile for an invitation, or mistake an approach for an attack. Respecting the security of potential victims requires that reasonable steps be taken to look before acting; protecting liberty requires that some error be allowable.[25] In each case, there is a question about where the risk should lie.

Risks enter into the criminal law in two distinctive ways. One, parallel to the sorts of risks found in tort, involves outcomes with respect to which the wrongdoer might be reckless. In *Shimmen,* the accused demonstrated his ability at martial arts by kicking within an inch of a plate glass window. Unfortunately, the kick ended an inch on the wrong side of the window, and he was convicted of recklessly damaging property.[26] His act was reckless with respect to a risk, and he was culpable for the damage that occurred. Risks enter the law in a similar way in the punishment of attempts, the topic of the next chapter.

The second type of risk is slightly different, because the risk is not of some outcome that may eventuate, but of a mistake about some justifying condition. The risk is built into the structure of wrongdoing. Where consent would justify an act, those who are reckless with respect to it are not risking some further outcome. Instead, they suppose themselves to be justified when they are not. The person who uses defensive force without reasonable grounds for believing it is necessary engages in wrongful aggression, even if he believes he is acting defensively.

I want to illustrate the way risk enters into the structure of rights by looking more carefully at the two paradigmatic cases in which risks of mistake are greatest. The first is self-defense, the second those

---

24   See, for example, *R. v. Jaggard and Dickinson* (1980) [1981] Q.B. 521 (D.C.). (The accused had permission to break into a friend's house, but, because she was drunk, broke into the wrong one.)

25   Many jurisdictions include some strict liability offenses in their criminal codes. The Supreme Court of Canada declared such offenses unconstitutional in *Reference re s. 94(2) of the Motor Vehicle Act (British Columbia)* [1985] 2 S.C.R. 486.

26   *Chief Constable of Avon and Somerset Constabulary v. Shimmen* (1986) 84 Cr. App. R. 7.

crimes against persons and property to which consent provides a complete defense.

I focus on self-defense and consent for two reasons. First, they are the sites of legal and scholarly controversy regarding the status of mistakes. Second, and underlying the first reason, consent and aggression are the two ways in which the rights of parties can shift. If you are attacking me, your attack entitles me to use force. If you invite me into your home, your invitation entitles me to visit you. In both cases, *your* deeds shape *my* rights.

Self-defense and consent might be thought to be fundamentally different, in that self-defense is a defense to a criminal charge, whereas the absence of consent is an element of the crime. Although I do not mean to deny these procedural and definitional differences, I want to insist that the similarity between them is more important than their differences: Consent and self-defense are alike in that they are both ways in which one person's action licenses another to act. That is why both self-defense and consent are uncontroversial defenses to a tort action for battery. To show that another consented, or that one's use of force was defensive, is to show that, despite the physical events, no wrong has been done. Consent and self-defense thus differ from other defenses to a criminal charge in that the successful defense will also be sufficient to defend against a tort action. They are also alike, or so I shall argue, in incorporating reasonableness standards. A consistent subjectivism requires abandoning reasonableness tests for both consent and self-defense, for it must suppose that any mistake an accused might make about another person is a simple mistake of fact that undermines the intention to do wrong. Indeed, under the influence of *Morgan*, reasonableness tests are now rejected for self-defense as well as for consent in England.[27]

I turn first to self-defense.

6.4 SELF-DEFENSE

Self-defense provides the most pressing example of risks and reasonable mistakes. For those activities that are wrongful unless consent is first secured, a general requirement of looking before you leap

---

[27] See *Williams (Gladstone) v. R.* [1987] 3 All E.R. 411 (C.A.) (1983) 78 Cr App R 276, which applies *Morgan* to conclude that all mistakes "negative" intention. The decision in *Gladstone Williams* was approved by the Privy Council in *Solomon Bedford v. The Queen* [1988] 1 AC 130 (P.C.).

can be imposed – one must take additional steps, or appeal to conventional signs, to make sure the situation is as one supposes it to be. In cases of self-defense, such an approach is sometimes too risky. As Justice Holmes observed in *Brown v. United States*, "Detached reflection cannot be demanded in the presence of an uplifted knife."[28] The only fair alternative is to consider whether the defender's belief about the danger is reasonable. Almost all criminal codes impose just such a requirement.

The traditional law of self-defense sets two requirements. One may take the life of another only if one has reasonable grounds for fearing death or imminent bodily harm, and no reasonable opportunity to get out of harm's way. In each case, the accused's beliefs about the dangers faced and alternatives available must be reasonable. The *New York Penal Law* formulation is representative. It holds that someone is justified in using force when "He reasonably believes that such other person is using or is about to use deadly physical force . . . or he reasonably believes that such other person is committing or attempting to commit a kidnapping, forcible rape, forcible sodomy or robbery."[29,30,31,32] Those circumstances justify the use of force; when

[28]   *Brown v. United States*, 256 U.S. 335, 343 (1921).
[29]   *New York Penal Law* §35.15.
[30]   The *Model Penal Code* takes a slightly different approach, deleting the word "reasonable" from the New York provision, but adding a general requirement of reasonableness for a complete defense. "When the actor believes that the use of force upon or toward the person of another is necessary for any of the purposes for which such belief would establish a justification . . . but the actor is reckless or negligent in having such belief or in acquiring or failing to acquire any knowledge or belief which is material to the justifiability of his use of force the justification afforded by these sections is unavailable in a prosecution for an offense for which recklessness or negligence, as the case may be, suffices to establish culpability" (*Model Penal Code* §3.09[2]).
[31]   The *Canadian Criminal Code* formulation includes two subsections:
   34(1)   Every one who is unlawfully assaulted without having provoked the assault is justified in repelling force by force if the force he uses is not intended to cause death or grievous bodily harm and is no more than is necessary to enable him to defend himself.
   34(2)   Everyone who is unlawfully assaulted and who causes death or grievous bodily harm in repelling the assault is justified if (a) he causes it under reasonable apprehension of death or grievous bodily harm from the violence with which the assault was originally made or with which the assailant pursues his purposes (b) he believes, on reasonable grounds, that he cannot otherwise preserve himself from death or grievous bodily harm.
[32]   Some jurisdictions allow the accused to use self-defense in his home, without considering the possibility of retreat. See, for example, *People v. Shields*, 311 N.E. 2d 220 (Illinois, 1974), and *People v. Collins*, 11 Cal. Rptr. 504 (1961). In some

it is used, it must be no greater than is required in order to prevent the attack.

The test incorporates both a subjective component and a reasonableness component. Both are necessary, and together they are sufficient. The subjective test requires that, as a matter of fact, the accused really did believe that the other was about to use deadly physical force or commit one of the enumerated crimes. The subjective requirement expresses a plausible conception of guilt: The person who uses deadly force without believing his life is in danger was prepared to use that force without being in danger. Since the danger is irrelevant to his use of force, such a person is no different from the person who kills in the absence of danger. As a result, he should not be able to avail himself of self-defense.

The reasonableness requirement, in turn, ensures that the accused really was protecting her rights, not just that she thought so. Although some criminal codes make no explicit mention of the absence of alternatives, the existence of alternatives shapes the requirement that beliefs about danger be reasonable. To take an extreme example, the person who needs only to close a door to get out of an aggressor's way cannot claim to have had a reasonable fear for her life. Questions about reasonable alternatives are always questions about how great a risk the accused must take, and what else must be sacrificed in deciding whether to defend herself. The mere fact of being afraid does not justify the use of lethal force. Here again, the reasonable person in this sense is not the typical or average person, but the person whose actions display appropriate regard for both her interests and the interests of others.

It is important to both the law and morality of self-defense that the subjective and objective requirements not be combined in the wrong way. The two requirements are separate; one requires that the person claiming that her use of force was justified, believed the use of force to be justified when using it; the other is a requirement that the force be justified – that it be reasonable in the circumstances. Thus, there is no supposition that the fact that someone believed themselves to be justified itself serves to justify their deed. George Fletcher suggests that a belief, even a reasonable belief, can never serve to justify an ac-

cases earlier this century, the same rationale was extended to a person defending his place of work. See, for example, *Brown v. United States*, 256 U.S. 335 (1921), *State v. Francis*, 112 S.E. 2d 756 (N.C. 1960). The significance of this exception is discussed in what follows.

tion.[33] Of course, the fact that something is believed cannot, on its own, justify an action. But the requirement of reasonable belief does not depend on any such idea. To construe the requirement of reasonable belief in this way is like supposing that a true belief cannot justify an action because it is a belief. But although the fact that it is believed does not justify the action, the fact that it is true does. The agent can only appeal to that justification if he or she was aware of it at the time of the act because only if it was believed can he or she claim to have acted on it.

To look to questions of reasonableness is not a concession to the defender's particular limitations; it is the only way to treat parties as equals in a world of uncertainty. Asking whether the assailant really did pose a threat is a separate and misleading line of inquiry. Suppose I come at you, firing a loaded gun. Unbeknownst to either of us, the remaining bullets in the chamber are flawed, and will not fire. Such an attack must pass any test of reasonable fear, even if chance events make it turn out that I do not pose a mortal danger to you. To put the point differently, we might say that imminent attacks do not always materialize. Rather, an attack is imminent if it is sufficiently likely to happen, even if, for reasons unknown to the parties involved, it would not actually have happened.

The question of whether or not the accused's fear was reasonable is thus a question of the amount of risk he or she should take. For legal purposes, the reasonableness of a belief is not simply a matter of the evidence the accused has concerning the attack; it depends crucially on the other alternatives available to her. The prospects and dangers associated with those alternatives may make the same response to an attack more or less appropriate. And just as the risks of attack must be divided between the parties, so too must the risks of the accused making a mistake about the seriousness of an attack be so divided. The fact that the accused believed something cannot justify her acts, but the reasonableness of her behavior can.

Assessing whether or not the use of force was reasonable depends on assessing whether it is reasonable to ask the accused to bear the risk of a perceived attack, or to make the apparent aggressor bear the

---

[33]   George Fletcher, "The Right and the Reasonable," 98 *Harvard Law Review* 949, 972 (1985) ("mere belief cannot generate a justification"). Fletcher supposes this to show that reasonableness cannot generate a justification either. However, once reasonableness is understood properly as dividing the risk between parties, it turns out to be a perfectly objective phenomenon, and thus capable of both defining legal rights and generating justifications.

risk that the accused was mistaken. In answering such questions, we must first fix the boundary of each party's rights. A requirement that someone who believes her life to be endangered by the attack of another hold off from using deadly force would abolish the law of self-defense; the entitlement to avoid all perceived risk would justify the taking of life whenever risk of harm was subjectively perceived. Neither alternative is acceptable. The former would make the initial attacker's will the measure of the accused's security; the latter would make the accused's level of fear the measure of the perceived attacker's security. The alternative to these extremes is to divide the risk between the parties, protecting the accused against unreasonable threats, and exposing the attacker only to reasonable self-defense. Exactly where the line of reasonableness is drawn depends on specific judgments about who should bear how much risk. Such judgments are unavoidable, for either the attacker or accused will end up bearing the risk. It is only once such judgments have been made that the question of whether the attack was "really" unavoidable is answered.

Still, substantive views about reasonableness moderate the avenues of escape the accused is required to consider. In general, the availability of a third choice, other than killing or being killed, is sufficient to deny one the right to use lethal force. In other circumstances, though, if the third way involves too great a cost, one may be entitled to disregard it. Just as tort law allows people to disregard possible safety precautions, depending on what else is at stake, so the criminal law allows those defending themselves to ignore unreasonable alternatives. For example, many jurisdictions do not require a person to give up his or her home to an intruder. In such circumstances, the accused is not allowed to take another's life to protect property; instead, abandoning one's home is an unreasonable avenue of escape to require of someone defending themselves.[34,35] The exception for defending

---

[34] In those jurisdictions that waive the duty to retreat in the case of defending one's home, the exception is sometimes explained in terms of an entirely different view of self-defense, according to which if the accused is "a true man without fault" in a "place where he has a right to be." George Fletcher, *Rethinking Criminal Law* (Boston: Little, Brown, 1978), p. 866, citing *Beard v. United States* 158 U.S. 550 (1895). The underlying idea is one of private vindication of rights. Although the exception is part of the law, in many jurisdictions, its different rationale has important implications. In particular, the accused need not attempt to call the police before acting, and the defense cannot be invoked if one comes to the aid of another. In contrast, the main thrust of the law of self-defense is that individuals can use self-help only when the state is not available to protect their interests and vindicate their rights. Still, the perceived threat must be imminent and the perception of it reasonable. Although this

one's home may seem dated. In modern urban settings, safety and help are usually not far from one's home. Still, it illustrates a more general feature of reasonableness tests. Many things are always at risk, and reasonableness tests take all of them into account. If the only way to safety is moving to Australia and assuming a false identity, one need not do that much in order to protect an aggressor's life. There is a duty of diligence in making sure one is not mistaken about the dangers posed. But that duty is limited by the defender's other legitimate interests.

What is reasonable is thus always a matter of relations between the parties involved, rather than an individual's own perspective and history. Features of my situation may shape what is reasonable – if I am physically weaker than you, that may change the danger you pose and the appropriateness of my response to it. Again, the accused's history and characteristics apart from interactions with the deceased are not relevant to the danger perceived, but the history of interaction between the parties may be. If I frighten easily, that does not entitle me to respond any differently to your aggression, regardless of how I became so timid. But if I find myself alone in a stalled elevator with the person who has threatened me, or whose attack I had narrowly escaped in the past, the situation is plainly different. The difference is not that we know each other in the latter case but not the former, but that in the latter I have extra knowledge, rather than extra fears. So this concept of reasonableness is not equivalent to notions of reasonableness that might be used by, for example, psychiatry, where "reasonable" means something close to "explicable in terms of the patient's past."[36] Dividing the risk does not introduce an element of subjectivity, but rather avoids both subjectivity and strict liability. In doing something that might reasonably be perceived as an attack, I take a risk that I will be killed or wounded by the reasonable defensive measures of another.[37]

strand in the law of self-defense is difficult to deny, a more unified and coherent view emerges if we suppose that the right to stay in one's home marks the boundary of reasonable retreat.

[35]   Admittedly, these strands may be difficult to separate in particular cases, as the primary interest of intruders is typically in property. But if a threat to property escalates into a threat to life, the homeowner need not give up the home.

[36]   See, for example, Mira Mihajlovich, "Does Plight Make Right: The Battered Woman Syndrome, Expert Testimony, and the Law of Self-Defense," 62 *Indiana Law Journal* 1253, at 1277 (1987).

[37]   Not all dangers are posed by malevolent aggressors. There is a substantial philosophical literature about innocent threats. See, for example, Robert Nozick,

Because the reasonable marks the boundaries of wrongful conduct, the person who behaves in a way that others would reasonably take to be life-threatening is posing a threat to that person's life.[38,39,40] As a result, defensive actions against such a person are justified, both by the person to whom that threat is posed and by third parties. Consider a prominent, if controversial, example. Young intervened in an ongoing struggle between two middle-aged men and a youth. In the resulting struggle, one of the men was injured, and drew a gun, announcing that he and his partner were plainclothes police officers making a lawful arrest.[41] Young was charged with assault. His defense was that he had reasonable grounds for supposing that he was preventing an assault. If we understand self-defense in terms of the reasonable person, the fact that the officers were *in fact* making a lawful arrest is of no consequence. Their failure to identify themselves to Young – even though they had already identified themselves to the youth – would lead a reasonable person to suppose they were committing simple assault, and so Young did no wrong.[42]

> *Anarchy, State and Utopia* (New York: Basic Books, 1974); Judith Jarvis Thomson, "Self-Defense," 20 *Philosophy and Public Affairs* 283 (1991); Michael Otsuka, "Killing the Innocent in Self-Defense," 23 *Philosophy and Public Affairs* 74 (1994); and J. C. Smith, *Justification and Excuse in the Criminal Law* (London: Stevens, 1989). Self-defense against innocent threats is a special case of necessity, discussed in Chapter 5.

[38] By contrast, the person who is threatened with death unless they carry out an execution is not justified in taking a life. Although such a person acts from an understandable desire for self-preservation, his victim has not acted in a way that makes defensive action reasonable. Instead, a third party has acted in a way that makes aggression rational.

[39] Compare Kent Greenawalt, "The Perplexing Borders of Justification and Excuse," 84 *Columbia Law Review* 1897 (1984). Greenawalt worries that allowing reasonable mistakes about aggression to justify defensive force would preclude defensive force by someone who knows themselves to be only an apparent aggressor, on the grounds that one is not justified in resisting justified force. On the view defended here, the person who, by their intentional acts, leads others to reasonably believe that they are in danger *is* an aggressor, and so not entitled to invoke a right to self-defense any more than is any other aggressor. That "defensive" force might be excused in such murky circumstances is in no way incompatible with supposing that the limits of justification are determined by risks.

[40] If, for example, in the midst of rehearsing a play in a public park, I mistake you for another actor, and fire a starter's pistol at you, I pose no genuine danger to you, but considerable apparent danger. You are justified in defending yourself, even though the threat is not real, because your right to use force is a right to act on appearances.

[41] *People v. Young*, 229 N.Y.S.2d 1 (1962).

[42] To be sure, exculpating Young might make the jobs of undercover officers more difficult. Yet it is far from clear that they should not be difficult in *that* respect.

That is, the question of reasonableness is neither one of what the person under attack believed, nor of the perceived attacker's real intentions. Instead, it concerns the appropriate division of risk. Whether or not someone is an aggressor depends on whether a reasonable person would so take them to be, and so is not changed by their private intentions to the contrary.[43]

6.4.1   A Paradox?

If we look at the reasonableness requirement in terms of a division of risk, we escape the paradox that some have claimed follows from treating self-defense as justified rather than excused in cases of reasonable mistake. It is widely accepted – with the notable exception of Hobbes – that one is not entitled to resist a justified attack, but is entitled to resist an attack that is merely excused.[44] If resisting an attack about which one is mistaken is justified, it seems to be possible for two people to both reasonably but mistakenly believe themselves to be under attack, and thus both be justified in resisting. George Fletcher offers a hypothetical case in which a shopkeeper who has just been the victim of looting reasonably mistakes a police officer for an intruder.[45] The police officer, pinned by gunfire, reasonably believes that he must use force to defend himself. Yet on standard models of justification, both cannot be justified. Fletcher claims the puzzle is generated by "putative self-defense" – reasonable but mistaken belief. As a solution, he advocates treating putative self-defense as an excuse rather than a justification.

Fletcher appeals to a principle according to which a justified action is one that others are not entitled to use force to resist, and in support of which others are entitled to use force to render aid. Others may not resist a justified action because the agent has a right to perform it; others may aid for the same reason. I will not quibble with the general principle, which is merely an inference from the idea that if an act is justified, the use of force is not wrongful.

---

[43]   Fletcher, "The Right and the Reasonable," p. 976, points out that it is essential to justification that "Struggling parties should, in principle, be able to determine for themselves whose conduct conforms to the Right and whose does not." Although Fletcher takes this to show that reasonable mistakes do not justify self-defense, in fact, it shows that a person's status as an aggressor is given by how others would properly take him, not by his private intentions.

[44]   See, for example, Paul H. Robinson, "A Theory of Justification: Societal Harm as a Prerequisite for Criminal Liability," 23 UCLA Law Review 266 (1975); Fletcher, Rethinking Criminal Law, p. 759.

[45]   Fletcher, Rethinking Criminal Law, p. 765.

The allure of the principle to which Fletcher appeals becomes clear if we consider the views of Hobbes, who (largely) rejected it. Hobbes's theory of crimes is part of his more general political theory. For Hobbes, the state's monopoly on the use of force is justified because it is able to provide protection to its citizens. One consequence of this view is that when the state is unable to protect the life of a citizen – in particular, when it is the source of the threat to the citizen – the state returns to a state of nature with respect to that citizen. The citizen (or, strictly speaking, threatened individual) is free to use such force as is necessary to preserve his life and liberty. Thus, for Hobbes, if a person finds his life in danger because the state is making a lawful arrest, he is entitled to use force to defend himself. Those in danger from the state retain this right even when they unambiguously created the situation that endangers them. For Hobbes, the rationale of the right of nature is clear – self-preservation ranks above all other considerations. Because the right of nature is central, though, Hobbes's account lacks the resources to distinguish between justifications and excuses. Although some might wish to excuse those who prefer their own lives to the lives of others regardless of how they found themselves in the situation, the details of how they found themselves make a difference to whether their acts are justified. Those who find themselves in dire circumstances can perhaps be forgiven for preferring their own interests to the interests of others, even when the interests are in life itself. Yet few, other than Hobbes (and Hobbes himself only some of the time), would wish to say that someone in such circumstances is *justified* in using force. The wrongdoer who defends himself against the legitimate response of others cannot be said to be justified.[46] Two people may both be justified in pursuing their conflicting purposes – you and I rush toward the last seat on the subway – yet both are not justified in using force to get their way, and third parties are surely not justified in using force to take sides.

From the conclusion that the use of force against wrongful force is not itself wrongful, it is a short step to the conclusion that justifica-

---

[46] Modern conceptions of justification conclude that if a person is justified in using force, then others may rightfully use force in his aid. Hobbes must reject this view. To suppose that third parties are justified in using force to aid a wrongdoer in resisting legitimate force designed to stop him is to put everyone back in the state of nature, and the absence of legitimate authority. If all responsive force is justified, all are equally vulnerable to the violence of others provided one person uses violence to begin with. The idea that the limits of justification are the limits of the legitimate use of coercion seems to have slipped away.

tions apply to anyone, not just the person whose life is in danger. Thus, aiding it is legitimate – one may aid others in doing what one could have done oneself anyway. Again, one may not use force to resist a justified act because there is nothing wrongful in the act. Principles of excuse operate very differently. The person who prefers his or her own life to that of another may be beyond punishment or reproach, but the excused act is still not justified. I suggested earlier that the only alternative is Hobbes's view, which treats all defensive force as justified, even that by an aggressor. If we limit rights to those claims that may be coercively enforced, these paradoxical implications of Hobbes's view can be avoided. We are also left with Fletcher's general principle.

If the general principle is right, though, it does not serve to establish Fletcher's point about reasonableness. Fletcher's principle works in just the same way, whether we suppose that justification is fixed by what is actually going on or by what is reasonably taken to be going on. In either case, for the principle to operate, rights must fill the entire available space. Where one person's rights begin, another's must end. You and I cannot *both* be justified in defending ourselves against the other. The only question is whether our respective claims to justification depend on what was actually happening or on what a reasonable observer would believe was happening. Fletcher's example is meant to show that two reasonable people might both be mistaken about the dangers posed by the other, and so that reasonableness can lead to conflicting justifications.

Fletcher's diagnosis is that reasonable beliefs, being beliefs, are too subjective to confer justifications.[47] But it is important to see that, strange as it may sound, reasonable beliefs are not psychological states at all. Reasonableness is a description of the world from a particular perspective – the perspective of equality – and the requirement of belief is the further (and independent) requirement that those availing themselves of justifications know of the features of the situation that justify their acts. I'm not entitled to claim self-defense if I didn't think you were attacking me. But reasonableness is an objective test of the adequacy of the belief: If the belief is reasonable, it can serve to justify the use of force, even if it turns out not to be true.

The real source of Fletcher's paradox lies elsewhere. As Fletcher describes the case, the shopkeeper's defensive action was not justified, because the police officer posed no danger. Yet we hesitate to blame

---

[47]   Fletcher, "The Right and the Reasonable."

the shopkeeper. Why is that? It is not that his belief was reasonable but mistaken, but rather because he made a particular kind of mistake, a mistake of identity. Mistaken identity has received little discussion in the legal literature, but examples of it are not hard to think up. Suppose my sworn enemy has been threatening me, and I find myself confronted in the men's room by his identical twin, who reaches up, *Godfather* style, into the tank above the urinal. Fearing for my life, I shoot the twin, who turns out to be completely innocent, having been separated from his brother at birth. The twin didn't do anything that he ought to have known was menacing. Thus, he did nothing that gave me a *right* to defend myself. He simply did something that, in the circumstances, I cannot be blamed for mistaking for an imminent threat. Again, to switch to a tamer and friendlier example, if I let myself into the wrong house because of an innocent mistake (I mistook ambiguous directions in a perfectly natural way, found the key just where it was supposed to be, and so on), I may not be guilty of breaking and entering, but I am certainly not justified either. Once my mistake is discovered, I must leave. To take a tamer example still, if we have identical raincoats, and I take yours by mistake, I shouldn't be charged with theft, though I must give it back once the mistake is discovered, and as I suggested in the last chapter, I must also clean it if I spill coffee on it. And if I tow away your car, mistaking it for the one against which I have a lien, I commit no theft, though of course I must absorb the costs of the inconvenience I cause.

In each of these cases, a mistake of identity is a mistake of fact, not about the rights of others. As a result, the accused is rightly judged on the facts as he or she took them to be. In each case, the accused commits no crime, but we do not conclude the act to be justified. Instead, we conclude that the accused did not recognize that other people's rights were at issue. Beliefs about the status of an act must be reasonable; beliefs about the identity of the actor need not.

Once the role of mistaken identity is clear, Fletcher's paradox dissolves. We must consider whether the police officer's well-meaning activity gave signs that a reasonable person would take to be exposing the shopkeeper to more danger than he rightfully had to bear. If so, then the police officer ought to have known that he would create reasonable fear in the shopkeeper. As a result, the shopkeeper is justified in using defensive force. If so, we might still want to excuse the police officer. But if, as seems more likely, the shopkeeper simply made an excusable mistake of identity in the circumstances, the police officer is justified in resisting his force. Having done nothing that he could

200

be expected to know would lead to reasonable fear, the police officer is entitled to act on appearances, and suppose his life is in danger. In either case, only one party can be justified, not because reasonable mistakes of fact never serve to justify, but because mistaken identity never justifies, but at most excuses. Who is justified and who is merely excused in such a situation depends on the facts of the situation, which must be understood in light of the idea of the reasonable. Such questions may be difficult for a judge or jury to resolve, but answering questions of reasonableness is the only way to be fair to both parties.[48] Again, were an ordinary citizen caught in cross-fire, he would be entitled to use defensive force against the party posing the clearest danger to him, even if he believed that party to be justified in defending himself against the third party.[49,50]

In this section, I have argued that the law of self-defense needs to be understood in terms of a requirement of reasonableness. On this view, the right to use defensive force applies just in case a reasonable person would believe such force to be necessary. Just as the standard of care in tort law seeks to divide the risk of injury fairly, so the requirement that beliefs about dangers be reasonable divides the risks of mistake. In so doing, it gives expression to the idea that the law serves to protect people equally from each other in a world of uncertainty.

6.5   CONSENT

I now turn to the role of reasonableness tests for consent. Such tests should be understood in the same way as are reasonableness tests in self-defense. Here too the problems come up because of the risk of mistake. The person who knows that his victim has not consented

---

[48]   Of course, were Fletcher's approach adopted, the trier of fact would need to ascertain whether the excusing beliefs were reasonable.

[49]   In so doing, he would be in a situation no different from cases of necessity discussed in Chapter 5.

[50]   By contrast, Fletcher's proposed solution of appealing to the truth of the defender's beliefs does not dispel the paradox. Two parties could find themselves in a situation that had escalated to the point that both were in fact correct in believing that they could only preserve themselves by the use of force. Suppose the shopkeeper had fired on intruders and, at the same time, the police officer had fired on a sniper hiding above the shop. The firing escalates, and the policeman and shopkeeper find themselves on opposite sides of a gunfight. Each poses a mortal danger to the other. Are both justified? If, as Fletcher maintains, true beliefs about dangers and the intent of one's adversary are the mark of justification, such a conclusion is difficult to resist.

and acts wrongfully anyway has plainly committed a crime. The person who in fact secures consent before acting does no wrong. If the victim believes himself or herself to have consented, no wrong is done. The difficult cases arise when someone supposes himself to have secured consent, but the victim does not suppose himself or herself to have consented. Has the victim consented? Most jurisdictions use a reasonableness test to decide such cases. If the accused's belief about consent was reasonable in the requisite sense, then the victim has consented. If it was unreasonable, there is no consent.

I will argue that consent and self-defense are parallel. Both aggression and consent seem to be independent facts about which a person's beliefs are straightforwardly factual. A psychological fact about the victim might be thought to fix the truth or falsity of the accused's beliefs about consent, reasonable or otherwise. On this apparently natural way of looking at the matter questions about the reasonableness of beliefs are secondary to questions about their truth. I want to suggest otherwise, and to suggest that here too boundaries are defined in terms of reasonableness. Both consent and aggressive force turn on the practical status of a responsible agent's act. Just as one is entitled to act on appearances in the law of self-defense, so is one entitled to act on appearances regarding consent. The question of what is reasonable will, as always, depend on the liberty and security interests involved.

6.5.1 Consent and Cooperation

Consent provides a complete defense to many tort actions and criminal charges. A defense of consent protects interests in both liberty and security for both parties to cooperative activities. Those who wish to cooperate with others have a liberty interest in being able to do so; they also have a security interest in being free to refuse to cooperate on particular occasions. Moreover, both parties have a security interest in being able to make arrangements.

Consent is sometimes thought to be important because it constitutes a sort of waiver of rights, as a result of which no wrongdoing takes place. If we focus on the ideas of reasonableness and reciprocity, however, consent can be understood as having a different role: It enables people to enter into cooperative activities. Consent is a complete defense to a charge of theft or assault, and a defense to most charges of battery. Treating consent as a defense in these cases does not simply reflect an exercise of autonomy on the part of the person who would have been robbed or assaulted. Equally significant is the way in which a defense of consent allows others to engage in cooperative activities with them, receiving gifts, touching, or performing surgery. Consent allows both parties to act together by allowing the participants to participate without fear of legal sanction. They are able to do so because, by consenting each takes responsibility for the activity. Since both are responsible, neither has legal grounds for complaining that the activity was unreasonable. Absent consent though, the person who draws another into his projects has pursued his own ends in the face of fair terms of interaction.[51]

If we look at consent in terms of reciprocity and cooperation, we also see why it would not be a defense in certain cases. Consent is not a defense to wounding, except in cases of sport, because sport is a cooperative activity. Wounding, by contrast, is not a cooperative activity, even when consensual. Again, children who have not reached the age of reason cannot consent except to the extent to which they can engage in cooperative activities. Consent is not a defense to a charge of murder because murder is not a cooperative activity. The cases in which we are most likely to think consent should be a defense – cases of physician-assisted suicide of terminally ill patients – are cases in which the deceased needs the physician's help in carrying out a plan together. The consensual nature of this activity is not unlike the consensual nature of surgery, for example. What would have been wounding is not, not simply because the patient was willing, nor even because the patient benefits. Instead, consent is a defense because the patient needs the physician in order to carry out a common purpose. (Only a physician can do so because of general rules of public policy limiting the practice of medicine.) Some of these classifications of activities may seem forced, arcane, or arbitrary. Perhaps they are. A

---

[51]   That is why the law is concerned about consent in cases in which the complainant did not seem to care about the liberty interest questions in the usual way. Jeffrie Murphy regards it as puzzling that the rape of a prostitute should be a serious crime, given the prostitute's unusual attitude toward her own sexuality. Murphy, "Women, Violence and the Criminal Law," in *In Harm's Way: Essays in Honor of Joel Feinberg* edited by Jules Coleman and Allan Buchanan (Cambridge: Cambridge University Press, 1995), pp. 209–30. But a requirement of consent does protect some ideal of sexuality; instead, it protects the right to decide about important matters. The subjective magnitude of the injury of nonconsensual interaction may be relevant to the extent of tort liability, but the absence of consent alone is relevant to criminal culpability. Forced interaction is wrongful, whatever purposes might lead people to voluntarily cooperate with others.

further advantage to looking at consent in terms of protecting cooperative activities is that any such arbitrariness is highlighted.

Consider some examples:[52] Surgery is an essentially consensual activity; without consent, it is battery. Visiting is an essentially consensual activity; without consent, it is trespass. Philanthropy is an essentially consensual activity; without donor consent, it is larceny. And sexual intercourse is essentially consensual; nonconsensual sexual intercourse is rape. To say that these activities are essentially consensual is to make a claim about their legal status: Those who engage in them are not engaged in self-regarding activities in which they need to take care not to accidentally impinge on the rights of others. Instead, they are engaged in activities that are legitimate only with, indeed because of, the voluntary participation of others. Those who fail to properly check for consent *cannot* have simply made an inadvertent mistake, because they intend to engage in a consensual activity.[53]

Once we see that consent enables cooperation, we also see why reasonableness standards would be relevant to determining whether or not a person has consented. Cooperative activities involve both parties, and both have interests in being able to cooperate when they wish to, and in being able to avoid cooperation when they so choose. At the same time, both parties also have an interest in pursuing their interests in cooperative activities free of state sanction. The only way that these interests can be reconciled is by means of a public standard, one that both parties can recognize. Like other reasonableness standards, such a standard serves to divide the risk of mistakes between the parties.

The factors that enter into fixing such boundaries include the ease with which consent can be secured, the liberty interest to be exercised through consensual activity, and the significance of the victim's protected interest. Although all of these factors are always appropriately in play, the burden of securing consent will always lie almost entirely with the accused for two reasons. First, the costs of securing consent are almost always low – one can always, after all, *ask*. Second, the pro-

---

52 These examples are drawn from Susan Estrich, "Rape," 95 *Yale Law Journal* 1087 (1986).

53 As Estrich points out, it is hard to imagine a surgeon successfully defending against a charge of battery by saying, "I didn't think the patient meant it when he said he didn't want the operation; I thought he was just too proud to openly acknowledge that he needed surgery," ibid., p. 1126. The point is not just that it is difficult to imagine anyone sincerely believing such a thing. It is rather that it is not even a candidate for sincere belief.

tected liberty interest of those wishing to engage in consensual activities is an interest in engaging in those activities consensually, not in engaging them regardless of the other person's attitude.[54] The actor has no protected interest in engaging in the activity per se. As a result, the reasonableness test does not seek to strike a balance in the accused's interest in, say, taking another's property, and the victim's interest in keeping her property.

Understanding consent in terms of cooperation explains also why questions about whether someone has consented are not questions about what was going through that person's head. For example, if the definition of theft requires that the accused take the thing in question without the owner's consent, whether it is satisfied depends on what the owner has said and done, not on what is going through his mind. As a result, the accused's beliefs about what is going through the owner's mind are not relevant. If you hold a gun to my head and relieve me of my movable goods, the fact that, even as I tremble with fear, I secretly regard it as a blessing – perhaps I think that armed robbery is the only thing that will finally give me the strength to take a vow of poverty – does not entitle you to the goods.[55]

That consent does not depend only on whether the victim is pleased or displeased with the result reflects the way that the criminal law protects rights – including the right not to engage in various interactions – rather than welfare. The emphasis on rights parallels a feature of tort law that we saw in Chapter 3. If one person's negligence injures another, but also confers a benefit, the tort-feasor cannot appeal to the benefit in order to reduce the damages she must pay. In the same way, whether or not the wrongdoer has conferred an unsolicited benefit on the victim is irrelevant to criminal culpability. Since conferring a benefit is irrelevant, a mistaken belief about benefits conferred cannot excuse. The assailant or thief who has a belief about the victim's inner thoughts rather than outer acts has a belief that is at

---

[54]   This point is frequently forgotten in discussions of consent to sexual relations. In dividing the risk of mistake, the accused's putative liberty interest is *not* in engaging in sexual intercourse, but rather in engaging in *consensual* sexual intercourse. See Celia Wells, "Swatting the Subjectivist Bug" [1982] *Criminal Law Review* 209; and Antony Duff, *Intention, Agency and Criminal Liability*, p. 169.

[55]   As Onora O'Neill points out, victims may want the same results as do their coercers, but that is not the same as sharing those ends, for someone who is coerced, even if pointlessly, is not pursuing, nor therefore sharing, those ends at all. See Onora O'Neill, "Between Consenting Adults," in her *Constructions of Reason: Explorations of Kant's Practical Philosophy* (Cambridge: Cambridge University Press, 1989), p. 113.

most relevant to the victim's welfare. *If* the criminal law sought to protect welfare against intentional invasions, then it might be appropriate to excuse those who, reasonably or otherwise, believed their actions to be compatible with that welfare, including both those who made mistakes about consent and those who were aware of nonconsent, but believed themselves to be acting in the best interests of the victim. Such a criminal law would regard those who consent to engage in cooperative activities as passive rather than active. Perhaps we can imagine such a system. But a criminal law that protected welfare in this way would look very different from any known system of criminal law, for it would welcome individuals to make decisions for others. Thus, the fact that such a legal system – if indeed something that granted individual citizens so much discretion in making decisions for others can be called a legal system – would treat unreasonable mistakes about consent as exculpatory is irrelevant.[56]

6.5.2 Public and Private

Consent enables people to make their own arrangements. To do so, it must be public: Whether a person consents is a matter of what they say and do. The person who openly and voluntarily acquiesces while secretly saying "no" has consented, and the person who openly refuses while secretly agreeing has not consented. Hence, the role of reasonableness tests: The right to refuse to consent is a right to give signs that a reasonable person would take to be signs of nonconsent.

The public nature of consent reflects the publicity of standards of reasonableness that set fair terms of social interaction. Publicity requires that people be able to know how they may act without fear of legal sanction. Where victim consent is a defense, consent must be something that others can identify. That alternative would make one person's rights depend on another's secret thoughts.[57] One's duty is to ascertain the other's consent, not to read the other's mind. That is,

---

[56] We can also imagine a variant on such a system, in which whether an act was wrongful depended on whether the victim welcomed it. This system might also be made to lead to the subjectivist's result. Such a subjectivist view could be consistently stated. The difficulty comes in motivating an account that makes inner thoughts, rather than public acts, a way of shifting the rights of others.

[57] To be sure, consent can be illusory if it is coerced, either by force or fraud. In such circumstances, the standard of reasonableness applies to the coercion, not to the consent. Those who make what others will reasonably take to be threats subject the autonomy of their victims to their own will no less than if they ignore outward signs of consent.

it is the duty to take the other person at his word (except in circumstances where one knows oneself to be exploiting a situation of power so that the other person's word is coerced). In this sense, consent is entirely on the surface. It is also zero-sum: Consent marks the boundary of whether something is up to one person or to someone else.

Beliefs about consent are thus beliefs about the ways in which one person's actions can confer rights on others. As a result, they are practical beliefs.[58] The contrast between theoretical and practical beliefs can be brought out by considering Peter Strawson's distinction between adopting a theoretical attitude toward a human being, and adopting a practical attitude toward a person.[59] To adopt a theoretical attitude is to think of him as a natural system, the behavior of which can be explained in terms of, or modeled on, the natural sciences; to adopt a practical attitude is to think of him as a responsible agent, whose actions are subject to evaluation.[60] Matters of fact are matters that are ascertainable and determinate from a purely theoretical standpoint; matters of law are essentially practical. Ordinary human interactions involve both; in understanding your words and deeds, I both view you as a responsible agent and form broadly speaking theoretical hypotheses about various events and circumstances. If you tell me something, I both regard you as a responsible person who can be held accountable for misrepresentation, *and* have beliefs about the things to which you refer. Again, if I mishear you make a promise, I both adopt a practical attitude toward your action *and* have beliefs about the words you said.

In suggesting that beliefs about consent are practical, I do not mean to deny that something is going through a person's mind when they consent, or refuse to consent. The point is rather that when the law appropriately takes an interest in consent, it is an interest in

---

[58]   See Christine M. Korsgaard, "Creating the Kingdom of Ends," in her *Creating the Kingdom of Ends* (Cambridge: Cambridge University Press, 1996), pp. 188–222.

[59]   Peter Strawson, "Freedom and Resentment," in his *Freedom and Resentment* (London: Methuen, 1974), pp. 11–25.

[60]   Strawson's distinction follows Kant's distinction between theoretical and practical reason. I do not think that Kant is right to suppose that there is only one possible practical standpoint. Not only does commonsense morality contain elements of voluntarist, causalist, and reciprocity-based conceptions of responsibility, but there are also different ascriptions of responsibility within a reciprocity-based account. What I called (in Chapter 1) the liberal "separation strategy" makes room for someone to be responsible for something in one context but not in another. Nonetheless, *all* conceptions of responsibility arise from the practical standpoint, so that relevance of any distinctions within that standpoint is not relevant here.

whether a person has publicly signaled a willingness to engage in some cooperative activity. Those who enter into cooperative activities are responsible for those activities; to believe that someone has consented is to think of him as a responsible agent who has taken responsibility for his role in the interaction to follow.

Consent is a defense in both private law and criminal law for the same reason. It serves to make cooperative activities among responsible agents possible. Beliefs about consent are practical beliefs about what responsible agents are entitled to do. An unreasonable belief about consent is not a factual belief about an independently ascertainable fact, but rather a normative belief about the ways in which one person's actions may affect the rights of others. To consent is, in part, to take responsibility for one's role in some cooperative endeavor. To make an unreasonable mistake about another's consent is to hold that person responsible for something on inappropriate grounds. In this respect, consent and self-defense are parallel: The legitimacy of an action depends on what another person has done; beliefs about what the other person has done are beliefs about the acts of responsible agents presumed to understand the legal implications of their deeds.

The difference between consent and another defense to a charge of assault, namely, death, underscores the practical nature of beliefs about consent. If the victim of what would have been an assault is dead at the time of the act, the would-be assailant may be guilty of interfering with a corpse, but does not commit assault. Although the case law is full of examples in which someone attempts to assault someone who turns out to be dead,[61] it is not easy to come up with the opposite sort of example, in which someone assaults a living person, believing themselves to be interfering with a corpse. In such a case, in order to assess the accused's guilt, his or her beliefs about whether the victim was dead or alive need to be considered. It is unsettling, but, I think, also uncontroversial, that such a person is not guilty of assault. The beliefs in question are *theoretical* beliefs. The subjectivist argument goes wrong in assimilating mistakes about consent to mistakes made from a theoretical point of view.

---

[61] See, for example, *People v. Dlugash,* 363 N.E.2d 1155 (NY 1977), in which the accused shot a man who was probably already dead. The jury found that he believed the victim to still be alive, and so attempted murder. Had the accused's own story been accepted, presumably he would not have been found guilty of murder.

6.5.3   Mistakes

If I intend to enter your house as a guest, but don't take reasonable steps to find out whether I'm welcome, I've misunderstood the nature of consent.[62] That is, I've missed the fact that something only qualifies as consent if you use conventional means to convey your invitation.[63] Your consent confers a right on me because you are exercising your right to exclude me. With your permission, my entry does not violate that right, but confirms it. Not only do my beliefs about your consent fail to confer such a right; my failure to take reasonable steps to ascertain your consent shows insufficient regard for your right to exclude me.[64]

On the other hand, if I hastily help myself to the assumption that you are consenting, I am measuring your rights by my will no less than if I mistakenly think that the fact that we live on the same street entitles me to enter your home as I please. That is, if my mistake is unreasonable, it isn't a mistake about whether or not a standard form

---

[62]   The requirement of reasonable steps is explicit in the *Canadian Criminal Code;* see s. 273.2:

> It is not a defence to a charge under section 271, 272 or 273 that the accused believed that the complainant consented to the activity that forms the subject-matter of the charge, where
> (a)   the accused's belief arose from the accused's
>   (i)   self-induced intoxication, or
>   (ii)   recklessness or willful blindness; or
> (b)   the accused did not take reasonable steps, in the circumstances known to the accused at the time, to ascertain that the complainant was consenting.

[63]   There may be cases in which language problems complicate matters. Two comments are in order: First, "radical translation" of signs of consent and especially nonconsent is often comparatively easy. Second, in cases in which there is doubt about the other party's consent, it is almost always open to the party seeking consent to presume nonconsent and await evidence to the contrary.

[64]   This argument draws on several discussions of the role of mistakes in the law of rape; see E. M. Curley, "Excusing Rape," 5 *Philosophy and Public Affairs* 325 (1976); Estrich, "Rape," Mark Thornton, "Rape and Mens Rea," *Canadian Journal of Philosophy,* Supplementary Volume 118 (1982); Wells, "Swatting the Subjectivist Bug," Toni Pickard, "Culpable Mistakes and Rape: Relating *mens rea* to the Crime," 30 *University of Toronto Law Journal* 75 (1980).

The idea of a duty to advert to risks when engaging in risky activities is summed up by Alan Mewett: "All that is required is the acceptance of a principle that some activities create a high degree of risk that certain surrounding circumstances may exist and that to carry on those activities without taking reasonable steps to insure that those surrounding circumstances do not exist necessarily means that in choosing to act the actor chooses that risk." "The Reckless Rape," 18 *Criminal Law Quarterly* 418 (1975–6).

of justification applies in this case, but about whether some novel thing is a form of justification. The person who fails to take adequate care to ensure that another has consented yet believes the victim has consented arrogates to himself, rather than his victim, the right to judge whether consent has been secured. In so doing, he treats the victim as someone without the right to refuse consent.[65] Because the boundaries between persons are given by what a reasonable person would take them to be, those engaging in activities that are only legitimate if consensual can be presumed to know, as a matter of law, that there is a risk of mistake and that they must take reasonable steps to ascertain whether consent has been given. Those who fail to exercise appropriate diligence in such matters ignore their victims' right to consent.[66] It may well be that such persons *believe* themselves to be appropriately diligent. If so, the mistake is one of law, not fact.

Unreasonable mistakes about consent are in this way of a piece with recklessness with respect to consent, because the person making the mistake must intend to perform the deed with the thought that it is being done with the permission of the person who is to decide. To intend to do something that is only legitimate if consensual without taking reasonable steps to ascertain consent involves making one's own beliefs about another's consent the measure of that person's consent, that is, to make one's will the measure of another's

---

[65] Cases of mistaken identity complicate matters because the person who is mistaken for someone else who has consented has not done anything to invite the accused's behavior, but the accused may have done all that anyone might expect of them. This type of case is illustrated in *R. v. Jaggard and Dickinson*. Beverly Jaggard had her friend's permission to break into the friend's house. Having had too much to drink, Jaggard broke into the wrong house. Imagine a variant on Jaggard: You see me on the street and invite me into a house that, as it turns out, is not yours. In these cases, the wrongdoer makes a mistake about identity, and as a result makes a mistake about the range of consent. Jaggard's friend could not consent to her entry to the house she did in fact enter. Mistakes of identity will often be mistakes about consent, because consent is the basic way in which a person's identity determines the rights of others with respect to them. Still, they arise in other places as well – if I mistake your raincoat for mine, I have made a mistake about identity that changes the legal status of my deed. In each of the cases, the mistake is about whether or not this is the person who consented in the past.

[66] Antony Duff offers a homespun example of how failure to notice something can be straightforwardly culpable. Suppose a groom misses his own wedding, and later explains to his abandoned bride that the wedding had simply slipped his mind. On subjectivist grounds, he would seem to be blameless, since he meant no wrong. But plainly when important things are at stake, one can be blamed for failing to consider them. Duff, *Intention, Agency and Criminal Liability*, p. 162.

rights. Those who make that supposition are criminals precisely because they suppose that it is up to them to determine another's freedom.[67] If we understand the boundaries between persons in terms
of reasonableness, the person who makes an *unreasonable* mistake
has made a mistake about the rights of others. The mistake is not
simply about how those rights apply in a given case: It is a mistake
about the kind of thing that counts as consent. Those who make *reasonable* mistakes, by contrast, make mistakes about how rights apply
in a given situation; as a result, their mistakes are mistakes only of
fact.[68]

6.5.4 Why "No" Means "No"

The publicity of consent does not mean that it is conventional. Although people will for the most part use conventional signs to indi-
cate consent, the underlying idea of publicity has room for the possibility of parties reaching their own understandings in unconventional
but publicly accessible ways. Consent is essentially communicative;
as such it need not conform to any *particular* ritual in order to be expressed or understood. But that is just to say that there are many public ways in which consent or nonconsent can be expressed. Anyone
who can regard another person as a *person* with whom cooperative
activities can be engaged in must also regard him as capable of expressing or withholding consent.

The publicity of consent means that it is in principle possible for

---

[67] This account of consent may seem to introduce an asymmetry between criminals and victims, inasmuch as the victim's consent may seem to fix the boundaries of the criminal's freedom of action. The asymmetry is only apparent. Consent serves as a general justification, because one person's consent changes the
rights of others to do things to them. Consent can expand another person's liberty, but nonconsent cannot contract it. That is, my consent changes your rights
with respect to me, but does not change my rights with respect to you.

[68] This point can be made in terms of Aristotle's distinction between mistakes
about particulars and mistakes about universals. The subjectivist position is
that mistakes of fact are mistakes about particulars, and so nonculpable, whereas
mistakes of law are mistakes about universals, and so culpable. The idea that
mistakes about universals are culpable whereas those about particulars are not
is plausible enough. The real question is whether unreasonable mistakes about
consent concern universals or particulars. The view I have defended is that reasonable mistakes are mistakes about particulars, and so do not reflect on the
agent's culpability. Unreasonable mistakes, by contrast, are mistakes about how
to classify particulars. Such mistakes are not merely mistakes about particulars. Instead, they are mistakes about universals governing fair terms of interaction.

someone to consent to something by mistake. Just as some people become lost by telling someone to turn right when they mean to say "left," so someone in an unfamiliar setting might say something with a public meaning very different from what they had intended. Such cases are difficult to formulate, because consensual cooperative activities are ordinarily ongoing, and so usually provide opportunities to quickly correct the mistake. If I misspeak and invite you into my home, I can withdraw my invitation immediately. In the few seconds of misunderstanding, though, not only do you commit no criminal trespass; you commit no tort of trespass. My words, rather than my thoughts, are what counts.

In this respect, consent is parallel to self-defense: Whether the apparent assailant's act is one of aggression depends on the public nature of the act, not his or her private thoughts. No doubt the innocent and merely apparent assailant – the actor rehearsing a play, for example – would want an injunction to descend from heaven to protect him against the use of force by another. Yet that wish is not enough to require the law to privilege *his* preferred description of the act. The same goes for consent; my private thoughts about what I have said or done enjoy no privilege with respect to the rights of others. Although I might wish for an injunction from heaven as I invite you in, you have a right to rely on my words.

If we think of consent in this way, we can see both why in ordinary circumstances, "no" would mean "no," but also how there might be specific circumstances in which "no" means "yes." Boxing is one such example: Ordinarily, if one person resists another's blows, that resistance is a sign of nonconsent. In a boxing ring, however, signs have different meanings. Perhaps even explicitly saying "no" in the midst of a match does not count as withdrawing consent. In such cases – and there are no doubt others – things are abnormal in significant ways. They are abnormal because they involve an activity that can only take place if consent is given in advance, and not withdrawn in ordinary ways in the midst of the activity. In the world of boxing, suiting up and entering the ring is the occasion on which consent is given. (The person who does not understand boxing and finds himself in the midst of a fight, and continues without realizing what is going on, might be said to consent by mistake.) The striking feature of this example is that not only does "no" mean "yes" in this case; "yes" also does; indeed, while one is in the boxing ring, virtually everything counts as saying "yes."

The example of boxing is instructive, because it sheds some light on the debate about whether "no" means "no" in cases of sexual assault. "No" uncontroversially means "no" in cases of surgery, philanthropy, or visiting. Those who think that "no" means "yes" in cases of sexual overtures suppose that sexual encounters should be modeled on boxing matches, that a woman who accepts a man's dinner invitation is like a boxer entering the ring, and that her subsequent actions are to be understood in that light. On this view, saying "no" is part of a ritual, and so need not be taken as nonconsent.[69] At the same time, saying "yes" is also a way of giving consent, as is struggling. *Everything* a woman does in such a situation counts as consent. Although there may be people who subscribe to such a view of sexuality, there is no basis for the law to suppose that this must be the nature of sexual encounters, and so no reason for the law to presume that in the case of sexual encounters, the public meaning of "no" is really "yes."[70] The idea that "no" means "no" – that people can express their consent or nonconsent in simple and unambiguous ways – is the necessary background assumption to the idea that consent provides a way for people to voluntarily enter into cooperative activities. Departures from that assumption are possible, but must themselves be well marked and explicit. The idea that encounters between men and women are such a departure, let alone that men may assume them to be such a departure as *a matter of law* supposes that sex is like boxing, that sexual interactions would be impossible if there were any sort of turning back once some sign of interest has been given. Such a view requires giving up on the idea that women have a liberty interest in deciding about sex in particular cases. I doubt that many people

---

[69] In the second edition of his *Textbook of the Criminal Law,* Glanville Williams endorses this view, and says that many women "welcome a masterly advance while putting up a token resistance" (p. 238).

[70] Some recent antifeminist writing has suggested that spontaneity is lost if men must secure verbal consent from women. See the work discussed in Douglas N. Husak and George C. Thomas III, "Date Rape, Social Convention, and Reasonable Mistakes," 11 *Law and Philosophy* 95 (1992). Some people may have such an impoverished view of spontaneity. If they do, a requirement that they take care may get in the way of their enjoyment, as it might get in the way of those who want to act out rape fantasies. It is difficult to see why such considerations would lead the law to favor the liberty interest of those who want to engage in such activities over the security interest of those who do not. (Husak and Thomas defend a reasonableness test for mistakes, but their understanding of reasonableness turns on the existence of social conventions rather than on considerations of equality. As a result, they suppose that the fact that an accused accepts widespread stereotypes should undermine his culpabaility.)

would explicitly endorse such a view of sexuality; to reject it is to accept that the public meaning of "no" is "no."

6.6 CONCLUSION

In this chapter, I have outlined an account of the nature of criminal wrongdoing and of the ways in which reasonableness tests properly enter into questions of justification. For purposes of the criminal law, what someone is doing with respect to another person's rights depends on what a reasonable person would take him to be doing. Far from being either a concession to human fallibility or an unwarranted intrusion of tort principles into the criminal law, reasonableness tests reflect the idea that the law must protect people equally from each other.

APPENDIX: UNKNOWN JUSTIFICATIONS

Victim consent is a complete defense to any charge to which it is a defense, whether or not the accused adverted to the consent. If you suppose my sincere invitation to be sarcastic and enter my home anyway, you commit no trespass, for I have consented. In this respect, consent is like ownership of property: If I transfer title to you just as you are about to angrily smash my window, you have a complete defense to a charge of criminal damage, because no wrong is done. You also have a complete defense to a charge of attempted criminal damage. In the same way, you cannot steal your own umbrella, or even attempt to steal it. In each case, you also have a complete tort defense.

In most jurisdictions, however, self-defense is only available if the accused actually believed his or her life to be in danger. Thus, the person who uses deadly force against another who, unbeknownst to him, was in fact about to attack, commits murder.[71] The person who attacks another but does not believe him or herself to be in danger cannot claim self-defense.[72] The purpose of this appendix is to ex-

---

[71] In England, the *Criminal Law Act* (1967), s. 2, appeared to allow unknown justifications. The law commission's *Draft Criminal Law Bill* (1993), clause 27, explicitly precludes unknown justifications.

[72] Some have argued that allowing unknown aggressors to justify the use of defensive force also leads to paradox, as whichever of two people intent on killing the other shoots first would turn out to be justified on such a view. See Russell L. Christopher, "Unknowing Justification and the Logical Necessity of the *Dadson* Principle in Self-Defence," 15 *Oxford Journal of Legal Studies* 229 (1995).

plain how this difference is compatible with the structural parallels between consent and self-defense.

Paul Robinson has argued that this distinction is indefensible.[73] Since the act turns out not to be wrongful, Robinson contends that the killer's beliefs about it are not at issue. The beliefs of the accused are only at issue when a crime has been committed. Robinson's approach follows naturally from a picture of the criminal law that drives a sharp wedge between conduct elements and fault elements in the definition of crimes. Wrongful conduct is a necessary condition for criminal activity, and must be specified apart from any questions of the accused's fault. Those questions come in at a second stage of analysis, when determining whether or not the wrongful conduct is blameworthy. On Robinson's analysis, self-defense could *only* justify the use of force if the justification is independent of the beliefs of the person using it.

Robinson's argument proceeds in what appear to be a series of analytic steps. The first is the claim that the act requirement for criminal culpability must be objective, that is, defined independently of the actor's state of mind. On its face, the claim seems unobjectionable: We only inquire into a wrongdoer's state of mind if he has invaded some legally protected interest. The second step is the claim that the absence of justifying conditions is part of the wrongful act. Thus, victim consent or title serves to make the act not wrongful, and does so regardless of whether the accused is aware of them. But although these examples illustrate Robinson's approach, they do not establish his desired conclusion, namely, that we can always tell whether a legally protected interest has been invaded without any inquiries into what the accused might have thought. Some justifications have these feature, but others do not. Nor does Robinson's argument show that all justifications justify acts because they have no impact on the victim's interest. Not all justifications reflect the absence of harm done, or waiver on the part of the victim.

No argument from the general structure of the criminal law could establish that justifications must apply independently of the accused's beliefs about the circumstances, or that all justifications show that no harm was done. At the same time, no argument from the general structure of the criminal law could show that there must be justifications that are only available if the accused is aware of them. The only

[73] Robinson, "A Theory of Justification: Societal Harm as a Prerequisite for Criminal Liability," 23 *U.C.L.A. Law Review* 166 (1975).

way to settle these questions is by examining particular justifications.[74] Most of this chapter has sought to do just that.

Robinson's account rests on the idea that justifications render otherwise illegal behavior harmless. Thus, in the case of both consent and self-defense, the acts of the consenting person or aggressor serve as a sort of waiver or forfeiture of some other right. Having acted in the appropriate way, those who would have been victims render the acts of others legally harmless. Yet if we focus on the underlying idea of waiver, it is difficult to see just what is being waived. One does not have a right not to be visited or be free of sexual intercourse that is somehow waived by consent. Instead, consent enables cooperative activities. Consent serves to justify acts that would otherwise be wrongful because the would-be victim's security interest is intact, and his liberty interest enhanced, if he consents to some interaction. Each person has a right to be free of various nonconsensual interactions with others, but that is derivative of the importance of consent, not an explanation of it.

Self-defense is different. Aggression does not enable anything; others can act to prevent aggression. The interests of the person injured through the legitimate use of force are unquestionably set back. The use of force is nonetheless justified because it is used by someone who is protecting his or her rights, or the rights of others. One has a right to be free of unlawful force, that is, to be free of force that is not justified by its role in protecting the rights of others. That right is not waived by unlawful activity; it is limited by the importance of enforceable rights.

Self-defense is thus importantly like the state's normal monopoly on the legitimate use of force to which it marks an exception. State officials are only allowed to use force on appropriate grounds. Arrests cannot be made on hunches, nor homes or businesses searched out of curiosity. Nor can illegal arrests or searches be redeemed by their consequences. In cases in which the state is not available to protect someone, citizens may take the law into their own hands, and act to

---

[74] In *R. v. Dadson* (1850) 3 Car. & Kir. 148, 4 Cox C.C. 358 (C.C.R.), a police constable shot a fleeing thief. The thief turned out to have been convicted twice before; as a result, his crime was a felony. According to law, the use of force in arresting a felon was justified. Dadson himself was not aware of the prior convictions, and was not allowed to defend himself by appealing to them. Dadson's mistake is a peculiar one (not unlike the mistake made by the person who mistakes a child under the legal age limit for a child over it) in that the justifying circumstances of which he was not aware was an artifact of a statute.

protect rights. And like the exercise of force by the state, such force cannot be redeemed by its consequences.

Because defensive force is only justified as a way of protecting rights, it only justifies force when the person using it is aware of the justifying circumstances. As a result, the fact that one person was out to kill another does not render the attempt to murder him impossible. By contrast, victim consent renders an attempted assault impossible because one person cannot unilaterally violate another's right to refuse consent: If I consent, you cannot violate my right to consent. Although consent is a public act that gets its importance from its role in enabling cooperation, it is an act that is done by one person. As a result, doing something without victim consent is legally impossible in certain cases. In the same way, stealing my own umbrella is impossible because the umbrella has the wrong legal status.

Chapter 7

Recklessness and Attempts

In this chapter, I explore two further respects in which chance plays an important role in the criminal law. The first of these concerns recklessness: Those who recklessly expose others to the risk of serious injury commit serious crimes if those risks ripen, but are at most guilty of other, usually distinct, crimes if they do not. The second concerns the role of chance in the modern law of attempts: Attempted crimes are punished much less severely than completed ones. The second issue has attracted a good deal of scholarly attention, because, according to a prominent view, successful and failed attempts differ only through the arbitrary role of chance. Attempts will be the main focus of the chapter, but in the midst of discussing them, I will turn to recklessness, for one of the key issues in the law of attempts is the requirement of intention for attempt liability, even if the corresponding completed crime can be committed recklessly. The relation between attempts and recklessness is also brought out by another feature of the law of attempts, namely, the boundary between mere preparation and attempt. Once these issues are clarified, the rationale for the decreased punishment given to failed attempts becomes clear. Attempts merit less severe punishment because they rest on a different basis of criminality than do completed crimes.

All three features of the law of attempts are controversial. I recognize that some may take my ability to explain them as a sort of *reductio ad absurdum* of the ideas to which I appeal. Many suppose those features should be absent from the law. Here, at last, common sense appears to be on my side. As I note in what follows, one prominent, if dismissive, explanation of the reduced punishments for attempts is that lawmakers have feared that if attempts and completed crimes received the same punishment, juries would acquit unsuccessful attempters. On this view, a compromise with common sense is required to avoid jury nullification.

I will argue, though, that the law's emphasis on harm is justified on the soundest theory of criminal wrongdoing. The supposed problem of attempt liability arises because of a conception of wrongdoing that is of a piece with the subjectivism that would reject reasonableness tests for consent and the use of defensive force. I criticized subjectivism at length in the last chapter; I revisit it here because attempt liability reveals the significance of the act requirement for criminal liability. Ordinary legal understandings suppose that the wrongdoer's thoughts are necessary to criminal liability, but not sufficient. If (some) subjectivists are right, bad thoughts and completed crimes are at bottom morally, though not evidentially indistinguishable. The subjectivist view that responsibility is monadic creates the impression that attempters and successful criminals differ only by their luck, and additional puzzles about the signficance of the distinction between preparation and attempt.

7.1   THE PUZZLE

Many commentators have suggested that the distinction between attempts and completed crimes reflect unsavory features of social attitudes toward crime. Hart describes them as confusing punishment with compensation, Schulhofer as a form of resentment at odds with the criminal law's emphasis on moral culpability.[1] Ashworth suggests that the law's approach reflects confused public sentiments, which no rational approach to punishment can incorporate. Glanville Williams puts the point most forcefully when he writes that "The only theory of punishment that explains the present law is a crude retaliation theory, where the degree of punishment is linked rather to the amount of damage done than to the intention of the actor."[2]

The supposed irrationality of the law of attempts has led to many proposals for reform. For example, the American Law Institute's *Model Penal Code* makes no distinction between attempts and completed crimes. The rationale is that sentencing is supposed to reflect the degree of antisocial behavior, which is the same, regardless of chance

---

[1]   H. L. A. Hart, "Intention and Punishment," in his *Punishment and Responsibility* (Oxford: Oxford University Press, 1968), p. 131. Stephen Schulhofer, "Attempt" in *The Encyclopaedia of Crime and Justice* edited by Sanford H. Kadish (New York: The Free Press, 1983).

[2]   Glanville Williams, *Criminal Law – The General Part* (London: Stevens, 1961), s. 49, 2:136. See also *Textbook of the Criminal Law,* 2d ed. (London: Stevens, 1984), p. 405.

result.[3] Although many of its provisions have been widely adopted, most of the states that adopted the attempt provision in the 1960s have since gone back to the traditional approach. And although many jurisdictions make some exceptions – in Canada, attempted murder and murder have been treated alike since capital punishment was abolished; in New York, difficulties of proof in the "war on drugs" has led to attempted trafficking and successful trafficking being treated alike[4] – the overall trend persists.

The puzzle about reduced punishment for attempts seems most pressing when we look at it in isolation from the settled practice regarding attempts. The puzzle gets its edge from what I will call the additive assumption, according to which a completed crime is the sum of an attempt and favorable circumstances (or unfavorable ones, depending on whose perspective is taken). On the additive assumption, attempts and completed crimes differ only by chance. If we are to treat like cases alike, attempters and successful criminals do not differ in any way that is relevant to responsibility. But the additive assumption is at odds with the practice it means to criticize. The additive assumption presumes that the primary focus of the criminal law is to forbid attempts, and that it enhances punishments for those attempts that cause harm. In fact, the criminal law's primary focus is on completed crimes. In most jurisdictions, serious crimes can be committed knowingly or recklessly, but those crimes can only be attempted intentionally. As a result, a serious crime can be committed without being attempted. Now it may be that the appropriate response is to restore the additive assumption, either by allowing such crimes to be attempted recklessly, or by requiring intention for all serious crimes. Were either of those steps taken, the law would conform to the additive approach, and the puzzle about punishment could arise neatly.

Completed crimes are widely thought to be more *serious* than attempts; the question for a theory of punishment is to explain why a more severe punishment is appropriate. Many commentators have remarked on the analogy between reduced punishment for attempts

---

[3] *Model Penal Code,* section 5.05 (1). The rationale can be found in *Model Penal Code and Commentaries* 490 (1985). The commentary allows that the use of severe sentences may be "economized" by reducing punishments for unconsummated crimes, although it does not explain why a practice is acceptable that is, according to its rationale, unrelated to culpability.

[4] Presumably the drug attempt provision also serves to allow undercover officers to intervene sooner in transactions.

and the way in which compensatory damages in tort are measured by the plaintiff's loss. Most of those remarks have been critical, and some critics have suggested that the law's treatment of attempts rests on a confusion between compensation and punishment. Although there are obvious disanalogies between tort liability and attempt liability – there is no tort liability unless there is an injury, whereas criminal attempts receive some punishment even when they are harmless – comparing them is illuminating. Those who attempt crimes are only culpable for the injuries that would have occurred had their attempts succeeded; those who are reckless are only culpable for harm within the risk of their recklessness.[5] Moreover, even the apparent disanalogy is interesting. There is an important sense in which punishment for criminal attempts appears anomalous from the point of view of general principles of criminality. Punishment for attempts does not directly serve to protect freedom or to vindicate the rights of victims. Both the rights and freedom of victims are intact after a failed attempt.

On the approach I will defend, the settled practice makes sense. A completed crime is not an attempt plus favorable circumstances. Instead, a completed crime is intentional or reckless imposition of a wrongful risk plus harm within the risk. That is why many serious crimes can be committed recklessly.[6] Risk provides the basis of culpability for intentional crimes as well as for reckless ones, because, as the existence of failed attempts shows, even intentional crimes sometimes fail. A focus on wrongful risk creation leads us directly to two new questions: Why require intention to attempt crimes that can be committed recklessly? Why punish attempts at all?

The answers to both questions follow directly from general structural features of the criminal law. Those features require that attempts be criminalized, but they form a separate class of crime from completed crimes. Those same features explain the distinction between attempts and mere preparation. If that line is drawn properly, the

---

5   The point in the text is somewhat overstated; many jurisdictions have strongly objective standards, so that someone may be liable for murder simply because death ensues in the course of a felony. For example, in a recent North Carolina case, a drunk driver was convicted of first-degree murder and sentenced to life in prison as a result of a collision (*New York Times*, May 8, 1997), p. A.2.
6   Negligence short of recklessness is not sufficient for serious crimes, except in cases where someone has an affirmative duty of diligence. Absent the disregard of such a duty, merely failing to consider the interests of others does not involve the substitution of private rationality for public reasonableness.

commonsense claim that completed crimes are more serious than attempts can be redeemed.[7]

7.2 SOME FAILED ATTEMPTS

Both retributivists and deterrence theorists have offered heroic accounts of why established legal practice makes sense. Bentham supposed that the aim of punishment is to deter, but that suffering in pursuit of that goal should be minimized. As a result, he thought that some lenient punishments could be mixed with more severe ones without undermining the overall deterrent effects. Attempt liability provides an opportunity for such mixing because wrongdoers considering crimes will not know in advance into which category they will fall. Beccaria bruited the idea that reduced penalties of attempts might encourage less committed criminals to act on their second thoughts while they still have time.[8] Others have suggested that reduced liability for attempts prevents those who have failed at their first try from trying again, since they have something to lose.

More recently, David Lewis has argued that wrongdoers alike in subjective guilt might legitimately be treated differently if we think of punishment in terms of a penal lottery. The severity of punishment for a given crime would be defined in terms of a chance of punishment, where the punishment inflicted is equal to the expected value of punishment from the lottery. The lottery ties the probability of punishment to the likelihood of a particular attempter's success. The rationale for doing so might be explained in terms of deterrence; those contemplating crimes need a high enough chance of punishment in order to be deterred. Some economies in punishment costs can be realized if severe punishments are withheld, as long as they are not distributed according to too predictable a pattern. In order to achieve such economies, we can measure the likelihood of success in some coarse-grained way, and structure a lottery accordingly. Alternatively,

---

[7] I put aside the wrong of a sense of insecurity that would follow from even a failed attempt. That sense of insecurity is a real harm – those whose homes are almost burglarized are rightly uneasy, and those who escape attempts on their lives even more so. I leave out those harms for two reasons. First, they are less serious than the harms of completed crimes, so any account of their place in punishment requires a prior account of why the degree of harm should fix the level of punishment. Second, the sense of insecurity created is not always proportional to the seriousness of the crime attempted.

[8] Beccaria, *On Crimes and Punishments,* translated by Richard Davies (Cambridge: Cambridge University Press, 1995), p. 96.

we could be more creative in our use of randomizing devices, and structure the lottery in the most fine-grained way possible, by tying the likelihood of punishment to the likelihood of success. The likelihood of success is difficult to measure prospectively, but retrospectively measuring it is a simple matter. The likelihood of punishment can be tied to the actual success, which is a reflection of the likelihood of success. Once the rationale from the probabilities is so calculated, though, the lotteries drop out of the picture, for we can use their sure-thing equivalents: Any attempt at a crime is exactly as likely to succeed as it is to be assigned the more serious punishment, so the severity of the punishment can be tied to the success of the attempt.[9] Lewis offers his account as an explanation of existing practice, though he concedes it may also be a *reductio* of attempt liability. The account fits the phenomena, but casts them in a strikingly unattractive light. Since the actual causal upshots of the attempts are only a proxy for the lottery, some other randomizing device would be acceptable by the same reasoning.

Although each of these solutions shows considerable ingenuity, each concedes that the law's settled practice is fundamentally unfair, and go on to render it less objectionable by showing it to be otherwise than it seems. None seems to take seriously the intuitive idea that consequences *should* make a difference. At most, the prominence of that idea in the public consciousness is treated as a given around which the law must work. Instead of taking that idea at face value, each of the proposals we've canvassed offers an account of how consequences can be *allowed* to make a difference, either as evidential or as a device for economizing on the use of severe punishments. All display features of what Amartya Sen and Bernard Williams have called "government house" moral reasoning.[10] Each supposes that popular sentiments that assume attempts differ from completed crimes are confused. As a result, policies are selected because they conform to the sentiments, even though their real rationale lies elsewhere. Glanville Williams suggests that those who complete crimes are more likely to feel remorse than those who attempt them, and that the law should accommodate those feelings.[11] Hart and Honoré make the

---

[9]   David Lewis, "The Punishment that Leaves Something to Chance," 18 *Philosophy and Public Affairs* 53 (1989).

[10] Amartya Sen and Bernard Williams, "Introduction," in their *Utilitarianism and Beyond* (Cambridge: Cambridge University Press, 1982), p. 16.

[11] Glanville Williams, *Textbook of Criminal Law*, 2d ed. (London: Stevens, 1983), p. 483.

point in terms of the responses of others to crime. They suggest that reduced liability for attempts is a response to jury nullification, and can be defended on deterrence grounds because it will lead to more attempters being punished.[12] Yet if attempt liability really is as irrational as Hart and Honoré suggest – especially if its irrationality amounts to injustice – an acceptable deterrence theory cannot accommodate it. In other cases, deterrence theorists would presumably bridle at the thought of playing into prejudices that are irrational and unjust. In the American South, blacks who kill whites are four times more likely to be executed than are whites who kill blacks.[13] Plainly this is irrational and unjust. Few would think of defending the practice on the grounds that juries would probably otherwise acquit whites who have killed blacks. If lesser punishment for attempts really is arbitrary and unjust, it cannot be rendered acceptable by higher conviction rates. Schulhofer makes the comparison explicit: "[I]f the element of harm is no more relevant to punishment than the color of the defendant's skin, penalties imposed on the basis of harm would be as discriminatory in principle as those imposed according to the racial prejudices of the jury."[14] Just as patterns of state treatment that reflect such arbitrary and immutable characteristics as race or gender are objectionable, so too are patterns that reflect the role of mere chance. Both might be thought to single out people for hard treatment based on factors beyond their control.

7.3 HARM

I think there are sound reasons for treating attempt liability in the way the law has, and that those reasons reflect the importance of consequences. Just as I sought to show that tort liability is more than a facade by revealing the structure standing behind it, so I now seek to show that attempt liability is not a facade for other social policies, but rather expresses the deep structure of the criminal law: That structure makes results important. It also makes those results matter in relation to risks.

---

[12] H. L. A. Hart and Tony Honoré, *Causation in the Law*, 2d ed. (Oxford: Oxford University Press, 1985), p. 396.

[13] See David C. Baldus et al., *Equal Justice and the Death Penalty* (Boston: Northeastern University Press, 1989). An earlier version of Baldus's study was deemed irrelevant to the death penalty in *McCleskey v. Kemp*, 107 S. Ct. 176 (1987).

[14] Schulhofer, "Harm and Punishment: A Critique of the Emphasis on the Results of Conduct in the Criminal Law," 122 *University of Pennsylvania Law Review* 1497, 1523 (1974).

The basic feature of crime is the substitution of private rationality for public reasonableness, and the proper measure of punishment is the seriousness of the wrong. Consequences are relevant to culpability because they enter into the seriousness of the wrong. That seriousness is measured by the denial of the victim's rights, rather than by the actual harm. The thief who is arrested with the loot, like the kidnapper whose captive escapes, has successfully violated the autonomy of his victim even if he fails by his own lights. Their crimes are more serious than failed attempts, even if they fail to do substantial harm.

7.3.1   Is Chance Always Arbitrary?

The criminal law's treatment of attempts needs to be taken at face value. Before turning to my own positive account, I offer a few observations meant to erode the idea that chance is always arbitrary. My point in making them is to call into question the view that the supposed worries about the role of chance in criminal liability are worries about *chance* at all.

The intuition that causation is arbitrary is probably at its strongest when the state is involved, because the role of luck in determining treatment at the hands of the state is readily equated with the arbitrary use of state power. As I've argued in earlier chapters, though, the mere presence of chance does not render an outcome arbitrary; instead, whether chance is arbitrary depends on how it comes to play the role that it does.

Chance enters into the administration of justice in a variety of unobjectionable ways. Consider (genuinely) random police patrols. The likelihood of arrest of criminals in the process of committing crimes depends on the presence or absence of the police, which is, we may suppose, a matter of chance. Yet none who are apprehended as a result of random patrols have any grounds to complain just because others who committed similar crimes escaped because of luck. Any such complaint would be out of place for two reasons. First, those who are arrested while committing crimes had a straightforward way of avoiding arrest, namely, by not committing those crimes. It is through their own deeds that they made chance relevant to their arrest.[15] As a result, no member of the class of wrongdoers has any complaints

---

[15]   Victims of crimes may also receive different treatment from the state as a result of random patrols. Such differences are to be regretted, but if they are the result of random patrols, it is hard to see how any injustice is involved.

with respect to their treatment relative to others in that class. Imagine the complaint of the successful criminal who is later arrested: "[I]t is just a matter of bad luck that I was not caught in the act, as a result of which I would have been convicted only of an attempt." This complaint seems no less perverse than "Others have gotten away with crimes like this, so it is just my bad luck that I was caught at all." Second, given the purposes of police patrols, there is nothing arbitrary about random patrols. Random patrols increase the element of surprise, and make it more difficult for criminals to plan. Indeed, if anything, random patterns seem to make police patrols more, rather than less, fair. It is when patterns of enforcement are nonrandom that complaints of arbitrary use of police powers have the most force. If (as is apparently too often the case) patterns of patrols and arrests reflect differential protection and stereotyping, those who are arrested may have grounds for complaint, as may those victims of crimes that go unprotected. Thus, the person whose chance of apprehension is much higher because of police racism does have grounds for complaint. The grounds for his complaint is not that his arrest was random, though, but precisely that it was nonrandom in a morally troubling way. The state must play fair with its citizens, but to show that attempt liability is unfair, more needs to be shown than that it depends on chance.

It might be objected that this analogy is misleading. The role of chance in police patrols is unavoidable. They are expensive and, beyond a certain level, intrusive. So randomization may be the fairest method of allocating a given level of police activity. Punishment, by contrast, is deliberate, and so the role of chance may be thought to be more objectionable. No arguments of economy apply, because the total amount of incarceration could be fixed by punishing attempters more and successful criminals less.

The objection misunderstands the point of the example. Random police patrols are not an injustice with which we compromise for the sake of other values. They are no injustice at all. The practice of random patrols leads to a situation in which two people who are alike in their intentions and acts are treated differently as a result of factors they could not control. Those who are apprehended cannot complain that they have been treated unjustly, because they exposed themselves to the risk through their own wrongdoing. Were police patrols constant – were the policeman of Chapter 5 always at every elbow – presumably wrongdoers would not have broken the law at all. Having knowingly played the up side of random patrols in the hope of not getting caught, they cannot complain of injustice when chance deals them a bad hand. Nor can they complain of arbitrary treatment.[16] Even if allowing the state's treatment of its citizens to depend on chance is not objectionable in and of itself, more needs to be shown in order to claim that those who complete crimes *deserve* more punishment than those who merely attempt them. Nobody would suppose that apprehended criminals deserve greater punishment than those who escape detection. I will now show why guilt is tied to results.

7.4   VINDICATING RIGHTS

Kant argued that the point of coercive institutions is not to reward virtue and punish wickedness, but to create a space within which virtue is possible. Kant's view helps to make sense of many of the broad structural features of legal systems. Negligent injuries must be repaired so that one person's carelessness does not limit another's freedom. Intentional injuries must both be repaired and denounced, so that nobody's freedom is denied. If we think about crimes in this way, there is no way to eliminate the effects of chance, because what happens is so crucial to the extent of the freedom of others. Bad thoughts do not interfere with the freedom of others. Bad deeds do.[17]

---

[16]   It might be objected that the risk of arrest is not fully analogous with the element of chance in the completion of crimes. If the result of random patrols were that all criminals were apprehended, and so treated alike, the effects of chance would be eliminated. Yet if the effects of chance were eliminated for attempters and successful criminals, our practice would look very different. This objection rests on a simple confusion: The only way random patrols could be uniformly effective is if, by chance, they worked out that way. All those who attempted crimes could also earn similar treatment as a result of chance, because all might succeed, or fail. In either case, chance is not eliminated. Rather, all are treated alike because of chance.

[17]   It is surprising that Kant's views are so frequently invoked in support of the claim that results are irrelevant to morality. Perhaps this is true from the perspective of the quality of an agent's will or character. In the *Grounding for the Metaphysics of Morals*, translated by James W. Ellington (Indianapolis: Hackett, 1993), p. 1, Kant says that only a good will is good in itself. Yet Kant gives considerably more weight to consequences when he looks at praise and blame. He argues in various places that those who do wrong are responsible for the full consequences of their wrongful deeds, including unforeseeable ones, and that those who do more than duty demands are praiseworthy when good results accrue, even if they could not have been foreseen. Thus, the person who fails to repay a debt may be culpable for the creditor's subsequent losses, whereas the person who makes a gratuitous gift may be praiseworthy for the recipient's success. Yet the donor bears no responsibility for the recipient's failures, and the debtor gains no credit for the creditor's successes, even if the financial shortfall was a spur to ingenuity. Most notoriously, the person who lies in the

Put differently, if a crime is completed, there is a wrong to right; if an attempt fails, there is no wrong to right.

On this understanding of the nature of criminal wrongdoing, the puzzling case is the attempter, who does not manage to injure anyone. Why punish those who intend to injure others but fail? This is a specifically modern question; before the seventeenth century, attempts were not systematically punished at common law.[18] To see *why* such punishment is appropriate, we must understand *when* it is appropriate. The law imposes two requirements. First, the attempter must do more than merely prepare for the crime. Second, the attempt must be intentional, not merely reckless. Those who take sufficient steps toward a crime substitute private rationality for public standards of reasonableness. Hence, punishment is appropriate, even though nobody is wronged. Those who are reckless do not take a sufficient step to attempt the crimes they might have committed.

7.4.1 Hegel's Stone, Again

In Chapter 3, I noted Hegel's approving quotation of the proverb "The stone belongs to the devil when it leaves the hand that threw it."[19] We saw its implications for tort in Chapter 3. Suitably articulated, it is equally applicable to the criminal law.

Those who knowingly expose others to wrongful risks are subject to Hegel's stone. The risks they create are theirs, and the consequences of the risk taking are theirs. Consider some examples. *X* means to beat his victim within an inch of his life, but the beating goes an extra inch, because *X* gets carried away, misjudges his own strength, or because his victim is in poor health. His malice is sufficient for murder. A terrorist calls in a warning that a bomb will explode in an hour, knowing full well that experts will try to defuse it, though perhaps wishing they wouldn't. If the bomb explodes as planned, killing the sap-

---

attempt to save another's life is to be blamed if the would-be murderer kills the wrong person. See "On a supposed Right to Lie because of Philanthropic Concerns," in *Grounding*, p. 63. Thus, the intuition does not have the Kantian provenance sometimes claimed for it.

18 James Fitzjames Stephen, *A History of the Criminal Law of England* (New York: Burt Franklin, 1973; reprint of 1883 ed.), pp. 2:223–4. General liability for attempt was introduced by Star Chamber, but adopted by other courts after its abolition. Stephen suggests that earlier courts typically found unsuccessful attempters guilty of other crimes.

19 G. W. F. Hegel, *Elements of the Philosophy of Right*, translated by H. B. Nisbet (Cambridge: Cambridge University Press, 1991), para. 119A, p. 148.

per, the terrorist commits murder.[20] A woman set fire to the home of the fiancé of her former lover in the hope of scaring her out of town. The fiancé and her son escaped unharmed, but her two daughters were killed.[21] A kidnapper ties up his victim on a narrow ledge with a wire noose around her neck. The victim slips and dies.[22]

In each of these examples, the accused meant to commit one crime, and in so doing, committed another, more serious one. Although each may claim that they did not mean to kill, any such claim will ring hollow. In each case, death was a readily foreseeable, indeed foreseen, albeit not certain, consequence of the wrongful act. In each case, the risk of death was a sufficient reason not to perform the act. The beater and the bomber both consider the chance of death, and act in the face of it. The arsonist actually hopes her intended victim will fear for her life, though she does not want anyone to die, especially not her former lover. And the kidnapper wants his victim to live, but not to escape.

It seems natural to say that each of the beater, the bomber, the arsonist, and the kidnapper killed their victims. It seems to misdescribe the situation to say what the subjectivist would have us say, namely, that they performed various deeds, and people died. In each case, the connection is closer than that. In each case, it is natural and obvious to say that they killed, because the risk of death was in some sense part of what gave point to their actions. As a result, they cannot disown that risk when it comes to fruition.

Each of these cases involves causing death, and in each case, the risk of death is a prominent enough feature of the act that most criminal codes would classify them as murder, on grounds of "implied malice."[23] Those who seek to injure others just short of death commit murder if they kill. Murder is nonetheless somewhat unrepresentative, because recklessness often does not suffice. For example, few cases of causing death by reckless driving are appropriately classified as murder. Still, responsibility through recklessness regularly arises in crimes less serious than murder: To return to Hegel's example, the person who recklessly throws a stone near a window commits no

---

[20] Antony Duff, *Intention, Agency, and Criminal Liability* (Oxford: Blackwell, 1990), p. 81.

[21] *R. v. Hyam* (1973) [1974] Q.B. 99 (C.A.) Aff'd sub nom *Hyam v. D.P.P.* (1974) [1975] A.C. 55 (H.L.).

[22] *Nielson* [1976], *The Times* (London), June 15–16, 18, 23–6, 29; July 1, 6–7, 10, 15–17, 20–1. Cited in Duff, *Intention, Agency, and Criminal Liability*, p. 176.

[23] See the discussion in Antony Duff, *Criminal Attempts* (Oxford: Oxford University Press, 1996), p. 363. See also the *Canadian Criminal Code*, s. 229., and *Model Penal Code*, s. 210.2(1)b.

crime, but commits criminal damage if the window is broken, and battery if someone is injured.

7.5 SOME FAMILIAR FEATURES OF ACTION

In the introduction, I promised to rely on only a few familiar and uncontroversial features of human action. Those features were implicit in my account of tort liability, but probably need to be made explicit here. It is a commonplace feature of human action that the way in which an act is characterized always depends in part on the purposes for which we are characterizing it. We can include more or less by way of consequences, depending on what we are trying to understand, explain, or evaluate. This is, I take it, a completely uncontroversial feature of action, one which competing philosophical theories of action seek to explain. Whether, for example, my flipping the switch and the light disturbing your nap are one act or two need not concern us here; the important point is that both are things that I have done. Philosophers and lawyers have offered various criteria for distinguishing acts from other events.[24] For criminal responsibility, though, we need very little by way of action theory, for the kinds of things that are candidates for punishment are almost always uncontroversially acts.[25] Whatever the general criteria for distinguishing acts from other things that happen, the arsonist, the assailant, the thief, the mugger, and the murderer all pass all of them. Whether my act is described as flipping the switch or waking you from your nap depends in part on what happens – if you continue to sleep uninterrupted, I have merely flipped the switch. But the apt description also depends on why we are interested in the act. If we want to know what woke you up, my flipping of the switch is part of the explanation. If we want to know how I knew the power failure was over, my flipping of the switch enters in another way. Joel Feinberg has called this the "accordion effect" – we can pull out the accordion, including as

---

[24] Such questions include, for example, whether actions are identical with bodily movements, whether some actions, such as raising one's arm, are the basic constituents of all action. As I suggested in Chapter 1, these metaphysical issues need not be resolved in order to think about responsibility in tort and criminal law.

[25] The one exception, most developed in Canadian law, is the defense of noninsane automatism. Automatism is typically thought to preclude liability because the accused does not act in the relevant sense. See Dennis Klimchuk, "Involuntariness, Agency, and the Criminal Law," unpublished Ph.D. diss., University of Toronto, 1995.

parts of an action what we might for other purposes think of as consequences of an action, or push it in, depending on what is of interest in the action.[26] Pulling out the accordion is not just a matter of extending the spatial or temporal consequences of a deed. The accordion can be pulled in a variety of different directions, and at least as important as how far we pull it out is the direction in which we pull it.

The important question for legal theory concerns the appropriate description of the action for purposes of punishment. The fact that the agent acted intentionally qualifies something to be described as an action. But that alone does not tell us how to describe it. Although we frequently give priority to the actor's own description of an act, we need not. Thus, I may come to acknowledge that I must have been the one who ruined your nap by flipping the switch, even though I meant to do no such thing. As long as I meant to do *something*, in doing that thing, I can manage to do any number of other things. Which things I have done depends both on what happens and on why we are asking.

The way in which actions admit of multiple descriptions is the converse of the play in the notion of causation that we saw in Chapter 2. Like varying causal explanations of a single event, varying descriptions of a single action need not be incompatible. We saw in Chapter 2 that the appropriate description of who did what always depends on looking at the interaction from the appropriate point of view. Although the point of view selects from among the competing descriptions, not just anything will do as a causal claim. The indeterminacy of causal explanations is not irresolvable, and does not mean that causal explanations are simply made up. Rather, it is a reflection of the fact that "A caused B," like "A did B" is a matter of giving priority to one particular factor.

In Chapters 2 and 3, we saw that tort law handles the seemingly endless proliferation of causal explanations by looking at questions of who did what in terms of an underlying conception of equality. That idea of equality shapes the reasonable person standard; those who behave reasonably do not count as acting at all for purposes of negligence law. Moreover, negligence law also takes no interest in those who behave negligently without injuring others. In Chapter 6, we found that same idea of equality – that the law must protect people

---

[26]   Joel Feinberg, "Action and Responsibility," in his *Doing and Deserving: Essays on the Theory of Responsibility* (Princeton: Princeton University Press, 1970), p. 134.

equally from each other – at the heart of the criminal law. In place of a metaphysical theory of action, the law imports a political conception of equality to figure out who did what.

For purposes of assessing punishment, the idea of equality lets us choose between the endless proliferation of action descriptions in the same way. Just as the point of view of equality provided a standpoint for determining what counted as a reasonable fear, so it provides one to determine the appropriate description of an act. The action includes the kinds of consequences that make it wrongful, consequences within the risk to which the criminal's intention adverts. If he is reckless with respect to the risk of property damage, and property is damaged by his reckless act, he has done it. If he is reckless with respect to the risk of death, and somebody dies, he has killed that person. Likewise if either of those consequences are intended, what the criminal has done depends on what happens. In each case, those wrongful consequences get their significance from the fact that the criminal chose to risk them, and the choice to risk them gets *its* significance from its relation to the consequences. When we conceive of persons as bearers of rights, we characterize their interactions in terms of the invasions of those rights.[27] As a result, actions that invade rights are characterized in terms of their consequences for rights.

Talk of points of view and conceptions of the person here involves nothing mysterious. To say that responsibility shows up only from a particular point of view is not to say that it is spurious, or merely conventional. It is rather to say that significant features are only apparent in abstraction from other features that might be interesting for other purposes. There is no point in asking whether someone is really responsible for a consequence, except from the point of view of some particular normative inquiry such as the criminal law. We might conclude that someone is not responsible for legal purposes, yet she might rightly feel terrible about what she did, when judging her action from some other point of view. Conversely, someone might rationalize his behavior so that he sees himself as innocent when the law judges him to be guilty. A gangster might conceive of his action in terms of fidelity to his crime family, rather than the rights of his victims. The criminal law need not answer to the preferred descrip-

---

[27] The same point might be put another way: The primary duties imposed by the criminal law are (qualified) duties of noninjury. That is, they are duties not to intentionally, knowingly, or recklessly injure others in particular ways. They are not duties not to intend to injure others.

tions of action of those it judges, any more than it needs to answer to some metaphysically defined criteria. Its aim is to enforce norms of justice, and to do so it must protect people equally from each other. That requires that it conceive of persons as responsible and equal bearers of rights.

Because our interest in criminal acts is a matter of their impact on the rights of others, what happens to the rights of others determines the appropriate characterization of an action. The more substantial the rights violation, the more substantial the punishment. Both those who attempt crimes and those who are reckless choose specific risks. They are neither passive victims nor do they open themselves to utterly arbitrary forces. Instead, their liability is given by the risks with respect to which they act unreasonably. That is why those who are reckless can be culpable for foreseen but unintended consequences. In both intentional and reckless wrongdoing, though, the culpability of the criminal is limited to the dangers that make the conduct wrongful.[28] Because the wrongfulness of the conduct is nonaccidentally related to its results, the appropriate response to the conduct depends on those results. Just as the light coming on is part of the same act as flicking the switch, so the victim's death is part of the reckless act of sitting someone on a narrow ledge with a wire rope around her neck. If the victim dies, we conclude that she was murdered because her death was the result of someone recklessly risking her life.

At the same time, because our interest in crimes is in the substitution of private rationality for public reasonableness, a risk must be adverted to in order for it to enter into the appropriate description of an action. Those who are merely negligent take risks with the security of others, but they do not take account of and disregard the rights of those they injure, and so they do not choose to put those rights in jeopardy.[29] Both intentional and reckless wrongdoing are sufficient

---

[28]   This is presumably why felony murder is such a difficult case. The person who uses a firearm in the commission of a felony may not intend that anyone die, but violent death is plainly within the wrongful risk imposed by threatening others with weapons. Yet it is equally plainly not within the wrongful risk imposed by the commissions of many other felonies. More fine-grained statutes would certainly help in this regard.

[29]   Crimes of criminal negligence may seem to inculpate people who in no way consider the rights of others. The situation is more complicated, though. Most cases involve parents or unlicensed physicians with affirmative duties of care. Doctors who put small children on diets without protein or calories have a duty to know what they are doing, as do parents who withhold medical treatment or perform dangerous exorcisms. They are culpable for their deeds even if they were acting on the basis of honest beliefs because they had a duty to find out.

levels of awareness. The intentional killer adverts to the risk, for he intends to realize it. The reckless killer adverts to it and proceeds despite awareness of it. Both consider the rights of their victims, and act in the face of them. The intentional killer cannot go on to disown the victim's death, because it is the intended consequence of his action. From the point of view of punishment, the reckless killer cannot disown the death either, because he considered the risk and acted anyway. Both killers might come to regret the deaths, wishing things had worked out differently, or even to regret their deeds, wishing they had not even started on their courses of action. Regret or remorse may or may not be relevant to sentencing or parole; I take no stand on that question here. But it is not relevant to attribution.

The possibility of severe punishments for crimes committed through recklessness may strike some as overly harsh. Subjectivists are likely to treat recklessness as less serious than intentional wrongdoing, and object, for example, to characterizing (let alone punishing) reckless murderers as severely as intentional ones, or reckless stone throwers as severely as intentional ones. Perhaps there are moral considerations for judging any evil done out of the intention to do evil as somehow worse than the same evil done merely out of indifference.[30] If there are such grounds, though, their relevance to criminal culpability is not obvious. (On the moral question, my own view is that there is no uniform grading that always makes reckless wrongs less serious than the corresponding intentional wrongs. In the case of killing, intentionally taking life seems worse than recklessly risking it, until we attend to the various other ways in which both intentional and reckless killers can differ among themselves. When it comes to injuring persons and damaging property, the moral quality of recklessness is even more apparent.)

For purposes of punishment, though, the ranking of wrongs in terms of their seriousness is somewhat clearer. Punishment serves to denounce the wrongful substitution of private rationality for public reasonableness. That substitution depends on the knowing wrongful

---

[30] There is a large literature on the "doctrine of double effect" that purports to draw a morally significant distinction between harms that are intended and those that are merely foreseen. That doctrine claims that foreseen evils can be justified if they arise as side effects of the intentional pursuit of moral goods, but not otherwise. Yet even the most ardent defenders of the principle would not want to claim that harms foreseen in pursuit of *evil* ends are acceptable. Thus, whatever we make of "double effect," it cannot distinguish intention from recklessness for purposes of the criminal law.

imposition of risk, on injuries that ensue from the decision to disregard the rights of others. The person who recklessly injures another really does injure them.[31] Thus, he commits a serious crime.

If a completed crime is not an attempt plus propitious circumstances, we face a new question: Why punish attempts at all? To answer that question, we need an account of what counts as an attempt.

7.6   PREPARATION AND ATTEMPT

Bad thoughts are not sufficient for an attempt. Nor are bad acts, if they are merely preparatory. Instead, a criminal act is required. It is often a nice question whether an act crosses the line between preparation and attempt. Consider some examples. James was apprehended while looking through the glove compartment of a car, in the hope of finding the keys so that he might steal it.[32] Has he attempted to steal the car or only prepared to do so? Croatian nationalists planning to bomb a building assembled all the necessary equipment and proceeded to the scene of the intended bombing. Their plan ran into difficulty because they were unable to find a parking place to carry out their plans.[33] Did they attempt a bombing or only prepare for it? Staples[34] rented office space above a bank, and drilled some holes in the floor above the vault. He then lost either his lease or his nerve, and did not completely cut through to the vault. In each of these cases, the accused has plainly gone a good distance toward committing a crime, yet may seem to fall short of attempting. The common law traditionally required that the accused complete the "last act" required to commit the crime, after which ordinary causal processes would take over. The *Model Penal Code* requires only a substantial step toward the commission of the crime, and would convict in all three cases. If we judge attempt liability through the lens of either deterrence or subjective guilt, the *Model Penal Code* approach may seem plausible. Having taken a substantial step toward committing a crime, one may be able to control some subsequent steps – whether or not one continues drilling or looking for a parking space, for example. But although subsequent

---

[31] It is remarkably difficult to assess whether a criminal code has a single consistent way of grading intention, knowledge, and recklessness for all crimes, and the idea that it should is difficult to defend. See Douglas N. Husak, "The Sequential Principle of Relative Culpability," 1 *Legal Theory* 493 (1995).

[32] *R. v. James* (1970) [1971] 1 O.R. 661 (C.A.).

[33] *United States v. Ivic,* 700 F.2d 51 (2d Cir. 1983).

[34] *People v. Staples,* 85 Cal. Rptr. 589 (1970).

steps may remain within one's control, the substantial step is itself both something that could be deterred and sufficient to reveal criminal intent.

If we think of crime in terms of the idea of the reasonable, rather than as evidential of bad character, a different line can be drawn between preparation and attempt. The reasonableness test goes as follows: Whether someone is attempting to commit a crime will depend on whether a reasonable person would take them to be. The test may seem to simply restate the problem, but it does not. The point of the test is that something only counts as an attempt if the act is identifiable as attempting a particular crime *apart from* the accused's intentions. An act that a reasonable person would so construe is not sufficient for attempt liability; intention is also required. But intention alone cannot convert an outwardly innocent act into an attempt.

In *The King v. Barker,*[35] Salmond, J., laid out the classic version of this test. After noting that to be convicted of attempting a crime, one must do more than prepare but less than complete it, Salmond invoked the Latin maxim *res ipsa loquitur* – to constitute an attempt, an act must be one that speaks for itself in revealing a criminal intent. He illustrates with an example: "to buy a box of matches with intent to use them in burning a haystack is not an attempt to commit arson, for it is in itself and in its appearance an innocent act, there being many other reasons than arson for buying matches. . . . But he who takes matches to a haystack and there lights one of them, and blows it out on finding that he is observed, has done an act which speaks for itself and he is guilty of criminal attempt accordingly. . . ." Only if the act speaks for itself is further evidence of the wrongdoer's thoughts relevant. In *Stonehouse,*[36] Lord Diplock formulated the equivalent test as the requirement that the offender "must have crossed his Rubicon and burned his boats."

Salmond's emphasis on appearances suggests that he is appealing to a principle we found in our discussion of self-defense, namely, the right to act on appearances. As we saw, defensive force may be used when a reasonable person would suppose himself to be in danger with no nonviolent alternatives open to him. Where a reasonable person would so suppose himself to be in danger, the person who poses the threat should reasonably recognize the threat posed. Where a reasonable person would not perceive a threat, the putative attacker's

[35] *The King v. Barker* [1924] N.Z.L.R. 865.
[36] *D.P.P. v. Stonehouse* [1978] A.C. 55 at 68.

acts are, for legal purposes, innocent. The right to act within appearances is correlative to the right to act on them.

The same point applies to the state's right to punish. The rights of citizens with respect to each other are the basis for state intervention, whether police action or punishment. An act can only be punished if it is wrongful, but to be wrongful, it must be a wrongful *act*, that is, one that the state would be warranted in preventing. The appropriateness of intervention is not a sufficient condition for the use of force, but it is a necessary one. The state may only use force in response to an act a reasonable person would take to put rights in jeopardy.[37] That requirement expresses a requirement of publicity, that is, a requirement that citizens be able to know the legal consequences of their acts. As long as they act within the standards of reasonable behavior, they can avoid legal sanction. As a result, those who act innocently are entitled to be taken to be acting innocently, even if their thoughts are guilty. They are also entitled to be taken to be acting innocently with respect to one crime even if they are committing another. Even if Staples has wrongfully damaged property, he has not yet attempted robbery. The right to act within appearances limits the rights of others to intervene. The same right limits the right of the state to punish suspicious actions.[38] Put differently, planning a crime is not a crime.[39]

The parallel between the unequivocality test and self-defense does not rest on the idea that self-defense is a type of private punishment or on the idea that punishment is a form of self-defense.[40] The point is rather that both punishment and self-defense involve the use of force, and the legitimate use of force is always limited by the freedom to act in ways that others might suspect. As long as agents stay within

---

[37]   In this sense, the act requirement in the criminal law is of a piece with the foreseeability requirement in tort law. Each expresses an ideal of publicity, according to which people must be able to know what they can do without fear of legal sanction.

[38]   I leave to one side the question of whether the right of the police to intervene in cases of suspicious behavior is itself limited by the same reasonableness tests. I limit myself to the utterly conventional observation that although increased police powers to stop and search people would perhaps reduce crime, they might also infringe liberty in an unacceptable way.

[39]   Conspiracy is an exception to this claim. Perhaps that is why so many critics have found conspiracy laws too open-ended.

[40]   For accounts that suppose punishment to be ultimately defensive, see Warren Quinn, "The Right to Threaten and the Right to Punish," in his *Morality and Action* (Cambridge: Cambridge University Press, 1993), pp. 52–100; and Daniel M. Farrell, "The Justification of General Deterrence," 94 *Philosophical Review* 367 at 370 (1985).

reasonable bounds, neither individuals nor the state may act on mere suspicions. Only once an act is unequivocal, that is, only once it has no other plausible noncriminal trajectory, does it become criminal. The risk of attempt going unpunished is different from the risk posed by mistakes about the danger someone poses; the point of the parallel is that the zone of free action is set by the reasonable expectations and reasonable beliefs about others.

The requirement that an act speak for itself may sometimes lead to results at odds with the right to act on appearances to which Salmond's principle gives voice. Antony Duff objects to Salmond's principle on the grounds that it would acquit of attempted arson the person who threatened to burn a haystack, and approached it with matches and with a pipe in his mouth, since his act would be equivocal.[41] Although we would not want to convict any smoker who approached a haystack of attempted arson, Duff's intuition is that we should convict the person who intends to burn the haystack, even when he is able to make his act ambiguous. Indeed, Duff's worry seems to be with the possibility that Salmond's test would give an advantage to those able to disguise the true nature of their acts. Yet the sense in which an act must speak for itself is not that the accused dictates the preferred description of the act, so that the would-be arsonist can insist that he be redescribed as a smoker. If we understand the unequivocality test in terms of what a reasonable person would take the accused to be doing, no such problems arise. Just as the right to use defensive force is not undermined by the fact that the attacker against whom the force was used meant to disguise himself as to avoid detection, so too the question of whether something counts as an attempt depends on what a reasonable person would take the act to be, rather than on how the attacker hoped others might construe his act. Although past threats and altercations do not by themselves license the use of defensive force, they may entitle someone to conclude that an attack is in progress when the attacker's act might be construed innocently by someone less familiar with the attacker's behavior.[42] The same point applies to Duff's smoker, and to other, parallel cases. Sorrell and Bondett were found trying to enter Aunt Lucy's Fried Chicken shop, wearing balaclavas in July. The shop had

---

[41] Duff, *Criminal Attempts*, p. 51.
[42] This is a familiar scenario in cases in which women who have been in abusive relationships use force against their batterers. I discuss this issue in "Self Defense and Equal Protection," 57 *University of Pittsburgh Law Review* 685 (1996).

closed early, so the doors were locked. Both men had weapons, but had not drawn them, having been frustrated by the circumstances. Have they attempted robbery?[43] Outside evidence of earlier preparatory steps resolves any ambiguity about their intent. Those steps may have been carried out in secret, but that alone need not run afoul of the publicity condition. The point of the publicity condition is that it must be possible to interpret the act as wrongful without looking to the intentions of the accused. Duff's construal of the test makes it look to just those thoughts, for it allows the accused's intention to render equivocal an otherwise unequivocal act.

Salmond defended the unequivocality requirement on the grounds that imposing culpability any sooner would prevent those who might reconsider from doing so.[44] It is important to distinguish this claim from a superficially similar one about deterrence, discussed earlier, according to which premature culpability would leave wrongdoers with nothing to lose. As I suggested, such an argument depends on the dubious assumption that the likelihood of detection at various stages of a criminal enterprise is constant. In ordinary circumstances, the likelihood of detection also increases as the crime progresses. The point of waiting for a *locus poenitentiae* is rather that the act remains innocent as long as it is merely preparatory. One can repent of evil purposes before they become wrongful deeds. Once the deeds are wrongful, though, the repentance comes too late. Both the poisoner who seeks to kill by repeated doses and the person who sets a time bomb that can still be defused have opportunity to abandon their projects. Repentance comes too late for them to escape culpability, though, for each has already done a wrongful act.[45]

The unequivocality test is thus substantive rather than evidential. It does not show that the agent really has a firm intention, where firmness of intention is something distinct from a wrongful act. Instead, it shows that a potentially wrongful act has been performed. Only once an act is unequivocal is there occasion for any inquiry into the apparent attempter's state of mind. That is, the unequivocality test is an expression of the act requirement for criminal culpability. It thus contrasts with other tests, such as the *Model Penal Code*'s "substantial-step" criterion, which takes certain actions to provide evidence of criminal intent. The substantial-step requirement may actually be

---

[43]   *R. v. Sorrell* (1978) 41. C.C.C. (2d) 9 (Ont. C.A.).
[44]   *The King v. Barker* at 875.
[45]   *R. v. White* [1910] 2 K.B. 124 (C.C.A.).

easier to apply in practice. Its major difficulty is theoretical rather than practical, because any merely evidential test raises questions about why an act is required at all. If the point is to punish bad thoughts, or even danger to others, other evidence might do equally well. The unequivocality test, by contrast, does not stand in a problematic relation to some underlying feature which makes acts criminal. It is constitutive of criminality.

The unequivocality test may be difficult for judges or juries to apply in particular cases. Like other legal tests of reasonableness, its application turns in part on questions about the importance of specific interests in liberty and security, as well as on various questions of detail about the accused's acts. These difficulties do not, however, make the test impracticable, any more than reasonableness tests elsewhere in the law are impracticable. The details of implementation are real, but need not concern us here; the central conceptual point is that publicly wrongful behavior is a necessary condition of crime, including attempted crime. As a necessary condition of criminality, it must be established independently of the question of the accused's thoughts.

7.7 MANIFEST CRIMINALITY

The unequivocality test serves to draw a line between innocent and guilty acts. With this rationale for the unequivocality test in hand, we can now see why attempts should be criminalized. If an act is guilty, it needs to be denounced. So it must be punished. In the vocabulary of Chapter 5, an unequivocal act manifests the substitution of private rationality for public reasonableness. Having so acted, one has done wrong. Those who plan crimes but do not act are free of criminal culpability, whereas those who act on their plans are culpable. Although subjectivists had difficulty explaining that requirement, an account of criminality that focuses on acts does not. Until a sufficiently substantial step has been taken, there is no criminal act, and until there is a criminal act, there is no wrong, however nasty the person's thoughts may be.

Far from being the basis of all culpability, then, culpability for attempts is derivative, and required by the more general structural features of the criminal law. Once there is an unequivocal act, private rationality has been substituted for public reasonableness, so a crime has been committed. Attempts are thus an example of what George

240

Fletcher has called "manifest criminality."[46] The criminality is manifest because the wrongdoer acts in pursuit of private ends despite the public standards of reasonable behavior. Attempters fit this category. The attempter acts so as to violate the autonomy of others. As a result, the attempt is made criminal by the general structural features of the criminal law. Because it is criminal, it must be denounced, and to be denounced, it must be punished. A criminal attempt meets all the criteria for punishment: The wrongdoer acts to deny the rights of others, and that wrongful act must be denounced. Its seriousness is tied to the seriousness of the intended wrong, but that wrong does not occur. Instead, another, different wrong does.[47]

Attempts are not the only category of criminality without harm. The other prominent one is accessories after the fact. Generally, accessories before the fact of a crime – the person who supplies the burglar with tools, say – are punishable as principals. Accessories after the fact – those who, as Blackstone put it, "receive, relieve, comfort or assist" – receive reduced punishment.[48] The reasons are not hard to find. Like failed attempters, accessories after the fact do no harm. Yet their actions satisfy the definitional elements of criminality: They seek their private ends in the face of public standards of reasonableness. Yet they do not simply commit minor regulatory offenses, or even serious ones. Instead, the wrongfulness of what they do is tied to the wrongdoing of those they aid. Just as the culpability of failed attempters is proportional to the crimes they attempt, so the seriousness of accessories after the fact of crimes is proportional to the crimes of those they comfort or assist.

---

[46] George Fletcher, *Rethinking Criminal Law* (Boston: Little, Brown, 1978), pp. 115 ff.
[47] Resolving the puzzle about punishing attempts may seem to leave us with another puzzle. If a completed crime is not the sum of an attempt and propitious circumstances, why not punish successful criminals for both the attempt and successful crime? Although not all jurisdictions merge the attempt and the completed crime into a single offense, multiple convictions for attempt and completed crime are barred. In England, they are not merged. In Canada, conviction for an attempt is a bar to conviction for the completed crime (*Canadian Criminal Code*, s. 661(2). The *Model Penal Code* also bars multiple convictions (s. 5.05). Whereas successful criminals can be charged with attempts, they cannot be punished for both. This is puzzling if we suppose that attempts are a different species of crime. But the puzzle is spurious. Completed crimes are wrongful because the consequences are part of the act. Since there is only one act, there is only one crime.
[48] In the *Canadian Criminal Code*, accessories after the fact and failed attempts are covered under the same section (s. 463).

Both failed attempts and accessories after the fact are criminal because they involve the substitution of private rationality for public reasonableness. At the same time, the criminal law aims to protect freedom against intentional invasions. Both failed attempts and accessories after the fact act in the face of public standards, but they do not invade the freedom of others. They commit crimes, but do so by default. Some punishment is required: Because they manifestly violated fair terms of interaction, society must authoritatively distance itself from them. Because they do not invade freedom, though, there is no wrong to right, and so the normal basis for punishment is absent.

On the account of punishment I defended in Chapter 5, punishment can only denounce if it would deter an ordinary person from committing the same crime. Since deterrence operates prospectively, it would seem to apply *only* to attempts, and leave no room to distinguish attempts from completed crimes. Because attempt liability is derivative, though, punishment for attempts needs to be scaled to the punishment of completed crimes on which they are parasitic. Just as accessories after the fact appropriately receive reduced but scaled punishments, so too should failed attempts. As unequivocally criminal acts, they must be punished; because they do not infringe the freedom of their intended victims, they are less serious. The standard practice of punishing attempts at a fixed fraction of the punishment for the comparable completed crime gives expression to the idea of ordinal ranking, as does the grading of punishments more generally.

7.8   RECKLESSNESS, AGAIN

The relation between the unequivocality test and the idea of public standards of reasonableness on the one hand and the act requirement on the other enables us to see why recklessness is sufficient for completed crimes. As we saw, some crimes such as aggravated arson and murder can be committed either intentionally or recklessly. Yet attempting those same crimes requires intent. The terrorist who blows up a building has murdered those he kills even if he didn't mean to kill; yet if nobody is killed, he has not attempted murder. The assassin who misses her target *has* attempted murder, even if her shot is usually less lethal than her comrade's bomb. And if the arsonist's victims had escaped, she would only have committed arson, not attempted murder. Why the difference? Both the terrorist and the arsonist have committed other crimes, and serious ones at that. But they

242

do not attempt the crimes that, had things worked out differently, they would have completed.[49]

These distinctions follow directly from the unequivocality test. Those who intend to commit crimes and take unequivocal steps toward them attempt those crimes. Both the arsonist and the terrorist have done something seriously wrong, but neither has taken a substantial step toward the crime of murder. This distinction may seem scholastic: What could be a more unequivocal step toward killing than detonating a bomb? It is important, though, to keep track of which wrongs the bomber has committed. In relation to murder, the bombing is equivocal.[50] The bomber has done no wrong in relation to human life. If death ensues, though, the bombing becomes unequivocal with respect to death. What did the bomber do? He killed three bystanders. Circumstances sometimes resolve the ambiguity in what would have been an equivocal act. As a result, the act comes to speak for itself. On the other hand, the arsonist and bomber who injure nobody are guilty of destroying property, but do not injure the liberty or security interests of those whose lives they endanger (or would have endangered). Unlike the person who intends to murder, the lives of their victims are not implicated in their deeds unless those

[49]   At the same time, other crimes can be attempted recklessly. The person who attempts sexual intercourse but is reckless with regard to consent has attempted rape. The person who uses defensive force on the basis of an unreasonable belief about the danger posed by his supposed attacker attempts murder. Although recklessness with respect to consequences does not suffice for an attempt, recklessness with respect to circumstances does.
      Michael Moore has questioned the distinction between circumstances and consequences on the grounds that all acts require agents to move their bodies in ways that bring about results. The same analysis is supposed to apply to attempts: Attempting a crime requires that the "actor cause a proximity to success"; *Act and Crime* (Oxford: Oxford University Press, 1993), p. 223. I must admit that I do not know what it means to cause such a thing. The distinction between consequences and circumstances is relevant here is between elements that make something be a particular type of act, such as a killing, and those that make conduct wrongful, such as the absence of justifying circumstances. Even if they cause proximity, wrongdoers do not cause the absence of justifying circumstances.

[50]   Antony Duff has made a similar point in arguing that intentional wrongdoing is "internally related" to its wrongful object. As a result, those who mean to do wrong are related to the wrong even if they fail, since their actions get their significance from their wrongful intent. Those who are only reckless with respect to some wrong are only related to that wrong if it eventuates. Thus, they have not attempted the wrong in question, since their acts do not get their significance from the wrong. Were the terrorist's plot to be foiled, he would have attempted bombing, but not murder. But because the death was within the risk, it becomes part of the act. See Duff, *Criminal Attempts*, pp. 363 ff.

lives are actually lost. More generally, those who are reckless typically act within the protected zone of appearance, at least with regard to the risk with respect to which they are reckless. As a result, their creation of risk does not itself need to be denounced.[51]

The person who kills recklessly has taken the life of another in pursuit of his private ends. Because he was aware of the risk, he cannot disown that description. In the same way, the person who attempts murder and succeeds cannot disown the description; his act also speaks for itself. In the case of the unsuccessful attempter, the act was not ambiguous, so there is no ambiguity that we need to wait for the world to resolve. The reckless person whose risk does not ripen performs an act that is equivocal, so no murder is attempted. We need to investigate the wrongdoer's thoughts to know he was reckless with regard to the possibility of death. But unless someone dies, because the act of bombing is itself equivocal, we need not ask about his intentions with regard to that risk.

The difference between recklessness and intention for purposes of punishment shows one important difference between the right to act on appearance in self-defense and the right to act within appearances when being judged for purposes of punishment. The right to act on appearances in self-defense allows the use of force to prevent reckless as well as intentional acts. Force can be used against the arsonist or terrorist who endanger life *because* they endanger life, even though they may have no such intention. The right to stop them follows from the urgency of the situation. Nobody needs to wait and see what will happen before using force. Although their acts are equivocal, they are sufficiently dangerous that others need not passively bear the risks they pose. Once those risks have ripened, and life is no longer in danger, the issue is one of the appropriate punitive response. Only an unequivocal appearance of intent requires such a response.

The same rationale applies to recklessness with regard to the use of defensive force. The person who uses force in circumstances in which the danger does not warrant it has attempted murder. Here too the risk of mistake is part of the structure of criminal wrongdoing, not a further consequence with respect to which there are dangers. In Duff's vocabulary, that wrongful feature is related to their act even if

---

[51] These considerations do not rule out various statutory crimes of reckless endangerment. Most jurisdictions have misdemeanors of this sort, especially in relation to specific activities, such as driving. Such crimes are not tied to a completed offense of which they are lesser versions.

it is not completed. Thus, the *Morgan* defendants treated their victim's consent as irrelevant to their pursuit of their aim, and attempted to carry through their aim in spite of the likelihood that they were mistaken. Had their attempt failed, it would still have been an attempt.

7.9 CONCLUSION

Criminal law differs from tort in three distinctive ways. First, in order to qualify as a crime, the risk of wrongful injury must be chosen, not merely taken. Second, criminals are punished. Third, the state is charged with punishment and appears as a party to a criminal proceeding. These differences have led some to conclude that punishment must be based exclusively on factors that a person can control. We have seen three versions of this view in the last three chapters. Fletcher's account of excuses supposes that excusing conditions should be individualized, so that a wrongdoer should be excused if he succumbed to circumstances, quite apart from whether an ordinary person would have done the same. The subjectivist account of mistakes supposes that all mistaken beliefs should excuse, including unreasonable mistakes about consent, provided that they are sincere. And the broadly subjectivist account of attempt liability supposes that attempts and the corresponding completed crime should be treated alike. If we look at wrongdoers only in terms of their thoughts, distinguishing among those who succumb to circumstances on the basis of the circumstances seems arbitrary. So too does distinguishing among different people who make mistakes, and between those who succeed and those who fail in their criminal purposes.

Nonetheless, we have seen reasons for rejecting each of the views that emphasize control. In different ways, each supposes that the criminal law is at least sometimes driven by concerns unrelated to equality. Fletcher's account of excuses supposes that compassion animates our readiness to excuse; the subjectivist accounts of mistakes and attempt liability differ in important ways, and sometimes have different proponents, but are alike in supposing that punishment is meant to address a problem in the criminal's thoughts. Control matters, but equality requires that it not be the entire story. For whether someone controlled something is a monadic feature of that person, whereas equality is relational.

245

Chapter 8

Beyond Corrective and Retributive Justice? Marx and Pashukanis on the "Narrow Horizons of Bourgeois Right"

The previous seven chapters have sought to show that individual responsibility and social equality are not opposed. Both tort law and criminal justice can be understood as expressions of a particular understanding of equality. The law serves to protect people equally from each other, and can do so only if the minimal normative conditions of responsible agency are satisfied. The underlying conception of responsibility is political rather than moral, inasmuch as it looks to external relations between people rather than the quality of either their character or their wills. It is also political because it is concerned with the legitimate basis for coercion.

This chapter considers issues of responsibility from the perspective of what offers itself as a more thoroughgoing conception of equality. A world of individual responsibility is a world in which people have ends of their own, and may or may not take any interest in each other. The law's failure to protect ultrasensitive plaintiffs provides an illustration of this; the absence of a legal duty to rescue provides another. The ways in which a regime of individual responsibility does not require caring relations between people has led some to reject it as an ideal. The egalitarian who rejects ideas of responsibility shares the view held by the libertarian of Chapter 2, according to which equality and responsibility are incompatible, but unlike the libertarian, chooses to discard responsibility in the face of this perceived conflict.

There are, broadly speaking, three kinds of "left-wing" critiques of legal ideas of responsibility. One is the claim that ideas of reasonableness and objectivity are nothing more then a facade behind which those with power decide cases on whatever grounds appeal to them. On this view, judgments about reasonableness involve so many considerations that might be given such different weight, that they might lead to any result whatsoever. Sometimes this point is put in terms of the inevitable indeterminacy of the language in which legal standards are formulated and judgments rendered,[1] other times in terms of an account of how decisions are reached. One aim of the last seven chapters has been to show that the ideas of reasonableness and objectivity are more than a facade, by revealing the structure that stands behind them. Showing how competing considerations enter into that structure in a determinate way reveals a unified underlying conception of equality and responsibility. To be sure, it's a structure only. That is, the structure of fair terms of cooperation that standards of reasonable behavior serve to protect can be used to protect (or fail to protect) a variety of interests. The substantive questions about which interests in liberty and security are most important is not answered by the idea of the reasonable alone.

A second type of critique acknowledges that fundamental ideas of equality and responsibility form a coherent whole, but maintains that its material preconditions are not satisfied. That argument can take either of two forms: Understood piecemeal, it might underwrite specific defenses on specific occasions. For example, one understanding of the criminal defense of entrapment appeals to the idea that the state must play fair with its citizens if it is to claim the right to punish them. Insofar as a state has what courts call "unclean hands" in a particular crime, it cannot ask a court to dispense justice on its behalf. As a leading Canadian entrapment case puts it, the point of entrapment is "not that the accused is entitled to an acquittal, but that the prosecution is not entitled to a conviction."[2] Again, the same strategy might be applied in cases in which a person who the state has failed to protect in the past uses defensive force unreasonably.[3] The same general considerations lie behind some arguments in favor of a more representative judiciary, and greater access to legal services. Such arguments, which I will not examine here, seek to ensure that legal systems live up to their own aspirations, but do not question the justice of those aspirations.

Alternatively, the same style of argument might take a much more

---

[1]   See, for example, Mark Tushnet, "Following the Rules Laid Down: A Critique of Interpretivism and Neutral Principles," 96 *Harvard Law Review* 781 (1983). Invoking Wittgenstein's remarks about rules, Tushnet maintains that all rules are shot through with indeterminacy. If everything is shot through with such indeterminacy, though, law faces no special problems.

[2]   *Mack v. R.* [1988] 2. S.C.R. 903.

[3]   I examine these issues in "Self-defense and Equal Protection," 57 *University of Pittsburgh Law Review* 605, 706 (1996).

general form: Unless resources and opportunities are fairly and equally distributed, the results of "voluntary" interactions will reflect unfair starting points rather than responsible agency. This latter claim is worth taking seriously, and I will explore it in the next chapter.

The third, and most profound, type of criticism looks at responsibility from what purports to be a more thoroughgoing conception of equality. That conception acknowledges the internal coherence of the legal concept of responsibility, but goes on to argue that it is debased. The idea that people should bear the costs of their choices only makes as much sense as the idea that people should bear responsibility for their own mistakes. Some reject that idea. For Marx and those writing in his tradition, the idea that particular people are responsible for their actions is an expression of human estrangement. Individual responsibility is particularly suspect because it expresses the alienation of people from each other, and the unwillingness to share common burdens. For Marx, the path to true freedom lies beyond the model of individual responsibility that focuses on the costs of activities.

In this chapter, I look to what is probably the most sophisticated articulation of the Marxist critique of individual responsibility, Soviet jurist Evgeny Pashukanis's analysis of the legal form.[4] Some contemporary critics of responsibility equate it with egoism, and in the end, have little to suggest other than that people should imagine alternative worlds in which people treat each other better.[5] Pashukanis, however, begins his analysis with a sophisticated grasp of the legal form. He thus avoids the temptation to see law as nothing more than politics carried on by other means; at the same time, he avoids undue reverence for the order implicit in it. Pashukanis's argument shares important features with the voluntarist idea of responsibility that we encountered in earlier chapters. Pashukanis's central claim is that freedom and equality are merely formal, and that the very idea of responsibility is an expression of people's estrangement from each other and lack of real control over their lives. In its place, Pashukanis advocates a world of equality without any ideas of responsibility, a world in which all misfortunes, indeed all disappointments, are held in common. In the concluding section of this chapter, I explore the

---

[4] Evgeny Pashukanis, *Law and Marxism: A General Theory*, translated by Barbara Einhorn (London, Ink Links, 1978).
[5] Joseph William Singer, "The Player and the Cards: Nihilism and Legal Theory," 94 *Yale Law Journal* 1 (1984); Mark Kelman, *A Guide to Critical Legal Studies* (Cambridge, MA: Harvard University Press, 1987).

limits of that ideal, and consider whether (and when) the sort of control that Pashukanis advocates is a coherent ideal.

8.1 PASHUKANIS ON THE LEGAL FORM

Pashukanis's account of legality is both conceptual and historical. He maintains that a certain kind of conflict is the logical premise of the legal form. His conceptual account of law begins with the idea that the idea of a responsible agent – what he calls "the legal subject," is specific to a particular way of organizing society. He takes private law as his starting point, arguing that public law is best viewed as a degenerate sort of hybrid, superimposing the legal form on nonlegal relationships. Sometimes this takes the form of spurious modeling of social interactions as contractual and consensual. Other times it appears as the regulation of public affairs through a characteristically legal ordering of rights. Pashukanis insists that it is only with a more general understanding of legality and the nature of legal rights that we can understand the ways in which public affairs can come to take a legal form.

Pashukanis's conception of legality centers around the protection of a particular conception of freedom, the freedom of property owners meeting in the market: "The category of the subject serves precisely as the most general expression of this freedom."[6] Pashukanis argues that the very concepts of a legal subject and that of legal freedom are inseparable, and that the distinction between the subject and "mere" things is central to the legal form. Subjects are capable of putting their wills into objects, and, having done so, are owners, who must regulate their affairs in light of the fact that other persons have put their wills into other things. Mere things, by contrast, get their juridical significance from being owned by legal subjects.

The core idea of legality is that property is consolidated as something more than possession when it takes the form of a right that "follows the object wherever chance may take it."[7] This feature is crucial for Pashukanis; the law can ask of any object, "Who owns it?" This makes it possible to treat everything in legal terms, because it creates an exhaustive dichotomy between persons and things. One can always ask, "Who caused what changes to which things owned by whom?" As a result, both conflicts and their appropriate resolution can be represented in a particular way.

---

[6] Pashukanis, *Law and Marxism*, p. 110.
[7] Ibid., p. 115.

The development of the idea of legal personality brings with it the development of the idea of specifically legal *authority*. Legal authority is marked by impartiality. In this, the authority of a judge differs from that of a lord or manager, inasmuch as legal authority is supposed to have no interests in relation to the interests of the disputing parties before it. Instead, its interest is entirely juridical. By contrast, consider the authority of a teacher over a student, a manager over an employee, a master over a slave, or a lord over a serf. These cases differ in important ways, yet they all share an abstract structure: The authority is exercised in pursuit of a particular goal, and the subordinate defers to the superior's judgment about how best to achieve it. Sometimes the goal is specific to the person exercising the authority, as in the case of masters and slaves. Other times it is one that the person over whom the authority is exercised can be expected to share in some broad sense, as is the case (we hope) in teacher/student relationships. What all of these examples share is the way in which authority flows from the relation between person and purpose. In this sense, one party can unilaterally set the conditions of interaction.

Legal and technical authority are abstract classifications, which may turn out to subsist together in various ways. For example, the rise of employment law has meant that employer/employee relations are increasingly legalized; the more general triumph of the legal form has led to its influence in teacher/student and parent/child relations. The same influences sometimes flow in the opposite direction. For example, technical authority often makes its way into the criminal law, particularly when public safety is held out as a reason for limited procedural protections of defendants, as well as in various forms of preventative detention. Technical authority also shows up in those areas of private law that have been most influenced by economic analysis. Where the Learned Hand test of tort liability is understood in terms of maximizing overall wealth, both parties are required to act in light of a goal that neither might accept.

With the impartiality of legal authority comes an idea of formal equality; to be impartial between two parties, the court must treat them as alike. With that equality comes the need to treat like cases alike, and with that, the need for an abstract specification of the respects in which they are alike. Pashukanis expresses the underlying ideal of equality as "a single principle, according to which neither of two people exchanging in a market can regulate the exchange relation unilaterally; rather this requires a third party who personifies the reciprocal guarantees which the owners of commodities mutually agree to as proprietors, and hence promulgates the regulations governing transactions between commodity owners."[8]

Pashukanis's most striking claim, though, is that the idea of impartiality carries with it a specific form of individual responsibility. The basic idea should be familiar by now: Questions of responsibility are always questions about who did what, and whose problem various things are. Assigning responsibility requires not just a prior assignment of rights, but, more significantly, requires that that prior assignment take the form of an assignment of *ownership*.

That ownership is prerequisite to, for example, the making of enforceable contracts seems uncontroversial. Pashukanis makes the more ambitious claim that the same idea of ownership is central to the idea of responsibility more generally. We can see how this would be so. Consider the issues of responsibility for accidents that occupied us for the first several chapters. We saw there that it is possible to understand both the fault system and limited pockets of strict liability in terms of the ownership of risks. To own a risk is to be able to trade it in various ways, though risks of injury are owned as liabilities rather than assets. As long as I exercise appropriate care, the accidental outcomes of my activities belong to those who they befall, because I was not making any forced transfers of risks to them. If I fail to exercise appropriate care, the risks that ensue are mine. Again, dangerous work will command a premium because risks are the sort of things that can be traded.

Pashukanis hopes to extend the same account to the criminal law. Historically, criminal law begins to supplant revenge when the ideas of compensation and finality are introduced. The idea of compensation is always a commodity-bound idea, because it is the idea of an equivalent. The criminal law pits the state against the wrongdoer, but the injured party signifies "the context of the criminal action taking place. The abstraction of injured public interest is based on the perfectly real figure of the injured party."[9] Individual liability reflects the radical individualism of law; in antiquity, the wrongs of the father were visited upon the children; in the Middle Ages, the entire community was responsible for unsolved crimes. Although elements of a therapeutic approach are present in modern law, Pashukanis notes that they sit uneasily with ideas like that of the punishment fitting the crime. "If punishment is a matter of settling accounts, the notion of responsibility is indispensable . . . the concept of liability would be

---

[8] Ibid., p. 149.   [9] Ibid., p. 177.

quite superfluous in a situation where punishment had lost the character of an equivalent."[10]

Pashukanis's account is worth taking seriously for two reasons. First, it is an account of a society for which impartial adjudication is the organizing principle. Although earlier societies had institutions of impartial adjudication, Pashukanis's account applies with its greatest force to liberal societies that take that principle to its full extreme. Second, Pashukanis's claims about the relation among impartiality, scarcity, and the making up of losses have something to them.

8.2 FETISHISM

Unlike Lon Fuller, who drew a parallel distinction between legal and managerial authority,[11] Pashukanis does not regard the law's underlying ideals of formal equality and individual responsibility as evidence that the law expresses an independently appealing morality. Instead, he regards them as symptoms of estrangement. The lawyer appears on the scene when people have opposed interests, and recognize that opposition. For Pashukanis as for Marx, all class societies turn on the opposition of interests; the distinctive feature of capitalism is that the opposition of interests is mediated through voluntary agreements. In some social formations, such as slavery and feudalism, the relations of power and dependence are direct and personal: A particular slave is owned by a particular master, a particular serf owes service or produce to a particular lord. Slave and serf thus stand in relations of personal dependence. Workers in a capitalist society, by contrast, appear to be free contractors. Marx maintains nonetheless that they are involved in relations of dependence. In capitalism, however, the dependence is impersonal. Marx sometimes puts this point in terms of the idea that workers are externally related to their own activity, because each must sell whatever he or she has to sell at the going market rate. As a result, people must adapt themselves not to the needs of others, but rather to the profitability of the market as a whole. The situation of workers in capitalist society thus contrasts in important ways with the situation of a medieval serf. Marx was no

---

[10] Ibid., p. 179.
[11] Lon L. Fuller, *The Morality of Law* (New Haven: Yale University Press, 1969), pp. 33–44. Fuller discusses Pashukanis's book in "Pashukanis and Vyshinski: A Study in the Development of Marxian Legal Theory," 47 *Michigan Law Review* 1157 (1949).

admirer of agrarian societies; he praised capitalism for rescuing considerable numbers from "the idiocy of rural life"; he elsewhere compares French peasants unfavorably with potatoes in a sack. At the same time, the serf's relation to his own activity was direct, inasmuch as the serf produced in order to feed himself and his family, and consumed that product directly. The worker in capitalism, by contrast, stands in a mediated relation to his own activity, because the purposes and conditions of that activity are given by the market as a whole. The result is what Marx calls "impersonal dependence." Each worker is free of relationships of personal dependence, since he or she is not tied to any particular capitalist or task, but is instead free to sell his or her labor power to whoever might be willing to buy it. Nonetheless, each is dependent on the profitability of the market as a whole, and vulnerable to fluctuations within that market.[12]

Pashukanis takes Marx's idea of impersonal dependence and carries it one step further. Because market exchange takes place between responsible and independent agents, impersonal dependence takes the form of personal independence. Despite that form, life conditions remain outside any particular person's control. The relation between what someone does and their subsequent advantages and opportunities reflects the aggregate tastes and resources of those who might buy whatever that person produces, and the comparative opportunities for earning a return by capitalists.

For Pashukanis, the legal form is simply the inversion of this impersonal dependence. The legal form makes the proprietor central, supposing the commodity to be at his mercy, thus inverting the fetishism of commodities whereby the agent is in fact at the mercy of the market. In the market, people have no more significance than objects, since how they fare depends on the willingness of others to buy what they have on offer. Law represents the situation as just the reverse, creating the appearance that objects receive their significance from people. The ideas of agency and mastery are for Pashukanis thus illusory, because the choices for which agents are responsible are themselves shaped by the market. Despite presenting itself as a regime of individual responsibility and control, a legal order makes people's lives depend on the choices of others. While protecting people against

---

[12] Karl Marx, *Capital*, Volume 1 translated by Ben Fowkes (New York: Vintage Books, 1977), pp. 163–77. I. I. Rubin, Pashukanis's contemporary, explains fetishism in roughly these terms in *Essays on Marx's Theory of Value* (Detroit: Black and Red, 1972), pp. 1–60.

each other, it also renders them totally dependent, because the choices available to each person are set by the choices of others.

8.3 BEYOND THE NARROW HORIZON?

Pashukanis's critique of law expresses the hope of getting beyond what Marx, in *The Critique of the Gotha Program* called, "the narrow horizon of bourgeois right."[13] For both Marx and Pashukanis, the solution beyond both bourgeois life and individual responsibility is a domain of individual freedom in which "the free development of each is the precondition of the free development of all." Where Kant maintains that law makes freedom possible, Marx claims that law itself reflects circumstance of scarcity in which true freedom is not possible.

Still, the thesis that law will wither away admits of several distinct interpretations. On one, it is only the coerciveness of law that is an artifact of estrangement. On this view, familiar in the work of some members of the school of Critical Legal Studies, law reflects the difficulty that people have in getting along and working out their disputes amicably. Critical legal scholars sometimes suggest that more imagination, or more democracy, is the appropriate antidote to law. Lenin sometimes writes in a similar vein, when he suggests that habit might replace law in communist society.[14] Provided people have the right habits, no coercion of adults would be necessary, even if various forms of treatment occasionally would be. From a different direction, Robert Ellickson has praised the close knit community of Shasta County, California, where disputes are regularly resolved through informal norms without recourse to either impartial arbitration or coercive enforcement.[15] Olufemi Taiwo defends a similar version of the withering-away thesis, arguing that the readiness of disputing parties to resort to law is a sign that things are going badly in their interaction. As Taiwo puts it, neighbors who sue each other are neighbors in name only.[16] Each of these exemplifies an idea of reciprocity without coercion, but none comes close to the idea put forward by Marx and Pashukanis. Each accepts what Pashukanis char-

13 Karl Marx, *"Critique of the Gotha Programme,"* in Karl Marx and Friedrich Engels, *Selected Works* (New York: International, 1969), p. 3:19.
14 V. I. Lenin, *State and Revolution* (Peking: Foreign Languages Press, 1976), pp. 108–9.
15 Robert C. Ellickson, *Order Without Law: How Neighbors Settle Disputes* (Cambridge, MA: Harvard University Press, 1991).
16 Olufemi Taiwo, *Legal Naturalism* (Ithaca, NY: Cornell University Press, 1996).

acterizes as the essence of legalism, and wishes only to achieve it without enforcement. Ellickson's farmers and ranchers, for example, get along well in part because they are roughly equal in power, and share a sense of what is fair in their interactions. But that is just to say they adopt the legal solution without legal procedures. Theirs is still a regime of individual responsibility in which neither party can unilaterally set the terms of an interaction. Taiwo's neighbors go to court precisely when their interaction ceases to be neighborly, when they cannot agree as to the fair, that is, impartial, solution. And Lenin's model of habit as an alternative to law can be read as a description of a world in which all behave reasonably in the legal sense, so that recourse to coercion is never necessary. That is just to say that on each of these models of the withering away of law, people behave responsibly and so no issues of responsibility ever need to be decided by coercive institutions.

Pashukanis's version of the withering-away thesis is more interesting because it is more ambitious. He imagines a world in which people do not order their relationships in light of the law's understanding of fairness and equality, a world in which the idea of individual responsibility has no place. For Pashukanis, the only way to abolish legality is to abolish conflicting purposes.

The end of the idea of the legal person need not be the end of the idea of individuality. The idea of the free development of each as the condition of the free development of all is an idea of radical individuality, in which all live their own lives together in peace. It is also an idea of a world in which there is unlimited room for nonconformity in action. It is, at the same time, a world of perfect community, because in such a world, all misfortunes are thought of as common losses.

If we appreciate the force of Pashukanis's argument, and suppose that individual responsibility is deeply linked to a particular way of organizing scarcity, we are left with the question of its significance in a world still, and probably permanently, facing material scarcity. Pashukanis, writing in the early years of the Soviet Union, held it out as an example of a world in which individual responsibility could be overcome and perfect community realized. Pashukanis spoke to the individual "dissolving" in the community, and finding "his greatest joy" in the service of others.[17] On this reading of the abolition of

---

[17]   Whether he believed it or said so only for the benefit of the censor, I leave to others to decide; his claim that law, including Soviet law, is ultimately "bourgeois" led to his eventual disappearance.

legality, the founding idea that neither of two parties to a dispute could unilaterally set the terms of interaction would give way either because there would be no distinctive parties to disputes or because such individuals as there were did not have conflicting interests. Should each find his or her interests entirely exhausted in the interests of others, there would be no disputes to resolve.

Pashukanis's claim is not that people would never disagree about anything. Doubtless Pashukanis had considerable optimism about the degree to which all conflicts could be overcome, and human energies devoted to more fruitful ends.[18] Still, the claim that people would take great joy in serving others is not just an expression of unbounded optimism. It is rather the more specific claim that such disagreements as might survive would not take the form of legal disputes. Instead, they might be resolved in any number of other ways. What those alternative modes of conflict resolution would presumably share is their focus on the future, rather than on who had done what.

To understand how this is possible, consider the plight of Captain Vere in Melville's novella *Billy Budd*.[19] A sailor strikes a superior officer who has severely provoked him; the officer dies from a blow almost anyone would have survived. Vere, who was the only witness to the incident, decides that he has no choice but to execute the sailor, who he believes to be morally innocent. Although the story is often discussed as an example of the conflict between law and morality, Vere's way of framing the situation illustrates the ways in which issues of responsibility can cloud a person's responses to conflict. Vere concedes that executing Budd might lead the other sailors to mutiny. So too might mitigating the sentence. His conclusion is that if Budd is hanged and there is a mutiny, it will not be his responsibility, but if Budd is released, he will be responsible for a mutiny if one results. There is something at once familiar and striking about Vere's need to see possible loss and conflict not in terms of its overall costs, but in terms of whose responsibility it might be. In the same way, Pashukanis wants to question the idea that conflict more generally must be analyzed in terms of responsibility. Just as Captain Vere might have looked to the likelihood of mutiny rather than whose fault it might

---

[18] Trotsky, writing at roughly the same time, suggested that the average person would be as good a poet as Goethe. See Leon Trotsky, *Literature and Revolution* (New York: Russell and Russell, 1957), p. 201.

[19] Herman Melville, *Billy Budd* (New York: New American Library, 1961).

be, so more accommodating communist citizens might look to making good losses rather than assigning them to responsible persons.

Like Marx, Pashukanis was not keen to offer blueprints. Still, certain broad outlines of his view of a future nonlegal system are not difficult to fill in. The core idea is that legality gives shape to conflicts where there need not be any. Legality and commodity production create conflict insofar as problems that arise need to be assigned to people. If one person injured another, legality requires an impartial and authoritative finding of responsibility. That in turn requires both processes for fact finding and substantial doctrinal development. In Pashukanis's nonlegal world, the concern would be with repairing the injury, not with who was responsible for it. As a result, there would be no conflict in need of impartial resolution. If a car and a bicycle collide, the injured cyclist would still need medical treatment, and both car and bicycle might need repair. But no issues about whose fault it was would need to arise if those losses were made good socially. Again, if property were socially held, there could be few disputes about boundary crossings. People might still disagree about personal possessions, but such disagreements could presumably be resolved through the informal means as are ordinarily used for such things now. Such matters do not require impartial adjudication or fact finding, and ordinarily when people appeal to them – when neighbors sue each other, for example – it is a sign that things have gone very badly in their interactions. Except for goods with special sentimental value, almost anything could be replaced without costs. Thus, there would be no need to assess fault, because the idea of a problem or cost makes no sense.

Without scarcity, something close to perfect community is possible precisely because in the absence of scarcity, it makes no sense to ask whose problem various things were. Provided that there were unlimited resources to make up any losses or injuries, and to compensate for any standing misfortunes, there would not only be no point to asking where various misfortunes should lie; there would be no sense to be made of the question. Responsibility for losses is only an issue when it makes a difference where they lie. For goods that are not scarce, there is no possibility of asking where losses of them properly lie because in some sense there is no such thing as a loss. Of course, there are some things that are necessarily scarce, especially the time in a person's life. That one person can waste another's time is surely an inevitable feature of any society, quite apart from the scarcity of other things. Yet such losses cannot be compensated anyway. In a world without material scarcity, more ordinary losses could not be compensated for the converse reason: The idea of transferring something that is in unlimited supply from one person to another makes no sense. As a result, the idea of individual holdings makes no sense either.

Pashukanis imagines that the demise of the idea of individual responsibility would also lead to the demise of the idea of punishment. Not only does he suppose that abundance would drastically reduce the incentives to crime. He also supposes that responses to crime under such circumstances would be therapeutic rather than punitive. The argument here seems to be that the idea of a protected interest in autonomy is tied up with the more general idea of exchangeable interests. Perhaps the point is that the very idea of reasonableness and fair terms of cooperation would vanish were scarcity to be overcome. In the absence of scarcity, presumably there would be no need to moderate one's claims in terms of the interests of others. Without conflicts, there can be no intentional denial of the interest of others. Although the people in such a world would presumably have exclusive control over minor personal possessions, one person's possessions would be of no interest to others, since they would be readily replaceable. In the absence of scarcity, the apparent rationality of injuring others would presumably also disappear. The only crimes that would still be possible in such a world would be done solely out of spite or malice. If we can conceive of such a world at all, perhaps it is a world in which punishment would make no sense. Punishment is addressed to the crime's putative rationality. Yet all crimes would be irrational in a world without scarcity, and so without advantage.

Some crimes might nonetheless survive in a world beyond scarcity. Such crimes may merit public response; Pashukanis's claim is that punishment is not the appropriate form for that response. Instead, the residual response to wrongdoing in such a society would be of a piece with the treatments of unwelcome behavior by technical forms of authority. Think of the way an officer disciplines a soldier, a teacher a student, or a supervisor an employee. Various forms of sanctions are available in each of these examples, yet none of them need involve the application of a standard that is impartial between parties. Instead, the standard is summarily applied – the teacher deducts marks for the late paper, the soldier is ordered to do forty push-ups, the employee has his pay docked. Like laws that forbid certain felons from practicing certain professions, all of these are expressions of managerial authority, and have nothing to do with vindicating the rights of victims, or even with denouncing deeds as unreasonable. In each case, there may be legitimate concerns abut abuse of power, and various tribunals and forms of review may be appropriate. But even such seemingly hybrid forms of authority are not about impartiality but about protecting process. Again, although there is plenty of reason to worry about the content of the rules being enforced in each of these examples, those rules bear no special relation to fair terms of social cooperation.

Needless to say, it is very difficult to conceive of what such a world would be like. The absence of pressing scarcity is easy enough to imagine, and some proportion of the world's population now lives under such favorable conditions. Yet those who live beyond pressing scarcity are deeply attached to their legal rights. Moderate scarcity remains a condition of justice. The total absence of material scarcity is much more difficult to fathom. If scarcity is measured in terms of people's wants, a world without scarcity would be a world of different wants than today. An endless supply of various luxury goods – business class seats on transatlantic flights, or hand-knotted Persian rugs, or antique chairs – is out of the question. A world in which nobody valued private possession of such goods might be one in which scarcity of goods could be overcome. Indeed, that is perhaps why cultural criticism in the Marxist tradition has often focused on the ways in which bourgeois society has bred acquisitive and competitive consumers. The conflicts born of such personality types presumably could be overcome if they are a reflection of social conditions.

Perhaps this is not really Marx's or Pashukanis's ideal. Perhaps instead they hope only for the abolition of the pressing sort of scarcity that makes markets necessary. They might claim, with some plausibility, that the further scarcity of luxury goods is itself a product of market societies, rather than the cause of them. Whether this is true is largely an empirical question. Perhaps such desires would wither in a socialist society. Even if they did, there would still be plenty of room for conflict. Yet law would not be a solution to conflict created by the scarcity of irreplaceable and nonexchangeable goods. Whatever might be done to redress injuries to such goods, the legal remedy of damages would not be available, because the damages could only be provided in terms of things that were not themselves scarce.

8.4 SCARCITY AND PERFECT COMMUNITY

Suppose instead that Marx and Pashukanis advocate the abolition of responsibility in a world in which scarcity is largely, but not entirely, overcome. On this reading, they offer an alternative to individual responsibility appropriate to a world in which people must moderate their claims in light of the legitimate interests of others. In such a world, all misfortunes would be held in common, and no distinction would be made between what someone did and what merely happens. A world in which all ordinary losses can be held in common in this way may be easier to conceive, if not to reach, for those who lived in such a world might never want for the sorts of goods whose loss legal systems allocate. A world in which activity, rather than possession, became life's prime want for most people, in which the most widely desired activities did not themselves face constraints of material scarcity, might be one in which responsibility could wither in a way that enhanced human freedom. Yet if people have to moderate claims central to their lives in light of the interests of others, the picture changes.

Marx never explicitly put the idea of perfect community in a world of scarcity as an ideal, but there are passages in which Pashukanis appears to do just that. To see why the ideal is not appealing, consider that the world of perfect community is in important ways the mirror image of Hobbes's conception of the "state of nature." In the Hobbesian state of nature, all misfortunes lie where they fall. If one person is able to transfer a cost to someone else, whether through force or in any other way, it lies where it now falls. That is, in the Hobbesian state of nature, not only mere misfortunes lie where they fall; so too do misfortunes one person creates for another, whether willfully or carelessly. The world of perfect community is the mirror image of the state of nature because here too, costs that people create for themselves or each other, whether willfully or carelessly, are held in common. Absent any idea of individual responsibility – of particular things being the problem of someone in particular – there is no room for a distinction between misfortunes and various forms of mischief. All are alike, because all lead to losses that must somehow be made up.

Where the idea of individual responsibility demarcated boundaries between persons by treating some interests as legitimate and others as not, a world of perfect community must treat all interests as alike. As such, it would reproduce the very fetishism that worried Marx, as relations of impersonal dependence would remain. A world of perfect community, like a world organized solely around a model of love between parents and children, would forgive all in a way that made all equally vulnerable. Each person's security would be fully subject to all of the choices of others.

Put slightly differently, a world of perfect community under conditions of scarcity would be subject to a familiar objection to direct versions of utilitarianism. That objection focuses on the fact that utilitarianism is a doctrine of negative responsibility – one is responsible for everything one can do anything about. Each person is required to make such sacrifices as are required to benefit others, regardless of how the unsatisfied desires came about. The distinction between what someone does and what merely happens is effaced because there is only one undifferentiated duty. Rawls sums up these problems with the claim that utilitarianism ignores the distinctness of persons.[20] More sophisticated versions of utilitarianism may or may not be able to overcome these problems. The problem with a world in which all misfortunes are held in common is of interest not because of the embarrassment it may cause utilitarians, but because it is unable to solve the problem of fetishism that Pashukanis identified. Indeed, utilitarians have a better hope of addressing these worries, because they can at least assert that better overall consequences are achieved by setting up a framework within which people pursue their own ends.[21] In a world of scarcity, Pashukanis's approach requires that each person adapt his or her activities to all of the shifting choices of others. Rather than asking each person to take responsibility for his or her own choices, each is expected instead to take responsibility for all of the choices of others, whether or not those others moderate their choices in any way. Thus, Pashukanis's concern that freedom is illusory cannot be overcome by holding all misfortunes in common, because giving up on the idea of individual responsibility leaves every person's life at the mercy of everyone else's choices.

The problems faced by Pashukanis are not specific to his particular view of perfect community. In fact, similar problems arise for views that suppose that justice requires some particular set of holdings, as opposed to some structure within which holdings depend on the results of individual choices.[22] If equality of result is construed as a goal

[20]   John Rawls, *A Theory of Justice* (Cambridge, MA: Harvard University Press, 1971), pp. 27, 187.

[21]   See, for example, L. W. Sumner, *The Moral Foundations of Rights* (Oxford: Clarendon Press, 1987).

[22]   For a recent example, see G. A. Cohen, "Where the Action Is: On the Site of Distributive Justice," 26 *Philosophy and Public Affairs* 3 (1997). Cohen argues that a just society requires people to moderate their behavior in light of its overall effects on the equality of distribution. For Cohen, the demands of justice apply to uncoerced choices as well as to the basis of coercion. Uncoerced choices have at least as great an impact on the well-being of others as do the

that all must have, it does conflict with liberty, if not at the institutional level of the basic structure of society, then within the set of normative demands faced by each individual.

At the beginning of this chapter, I suggested that the criticism of the idea of individual responsibility at the heart of Pashukanis's argument bore an important affinity to the voluntarist view of responsibility we have encountered in earlier chapters. Pashukanis's rejection of responsibility as an expression of impersonal dependence turns on the ways in a person's life in a society mediated by legal relations appears to depend on that person's choices, but is actually subject to the choices of others. Where the voluntarist positions of earlier chapters focused on the arbitrariness of natural causation, Pashukanis focuses on the arbitrary effects of other people's choices when human interactions are mediated by legal categories. People are required to bear the costs of their choices, but those costs are set largely by the choices of others. We have seen in earlier chapters that the voluntarist urge cannot be fully accommodated within legal institutions if those institutions are to treat people as equals. In this chapter, I have argued that the voluntarist urge cannot be accommodated by the abolition of legal institutions either. The idea of a world in which how each person's life goes depends only on things he or she can control is a chimera. The only way to get close to such a world is to give up on the idea of unlimited control, and in its place articulate an ideal of freedom as mutual respect. The idea that Pashukanis sought to reject, that one person cannot unilaterally set the terms of interaction, protects freedom in a world of scarcity.

8.5 CONCLUSION

Despite these difficulties for Pashukanis's account of perfect community, there is surely something to his concern with the ways in which formal freedom may leave people entirely at the mercy of, and hold them responsible for, the results of vast impersonal forces. But the solution is not to efface the distinction between what people do

coercively enforced rules of public order. Thus, uncoerced choices are crucial expressions of each person's concern for others. By making concern for others the mark of a just society, Cohen abandons the idea of people respecting each other's freedom. Thus, it rests not on an idea of reciprocity, but of love of the other. Although I feel somewhat churlish in rejecting the love of others as a moral ideal, I think I am on firmer ground in rejecting it as an organizing basis for society.

and what merely happens, and hold all misfortunes in common. Nonetheless, holding some in common is appropriate. It is the task of an account of distributive justice to show which ones properly are so held, and articulate a principled way of distinguishing between mischief and misfortune. Accident law and criminal law provide ways of drawing that distinction in some contexts; distributive justice does so with respect to the background conditions under which people make choices. It is to that topic that we now must turn.

Chapter 9

Reciprocity and Responsibility in Distributive Justice

Most of this book has examined the ways in which the effects of wrongful acts must be undone in order to uphold fair terms of interaction. Tort law is concerned with undoing wrongful losses; the criminal law is concerned with vindicating fair terms of interaction. This concluding chapter examines the ways in which the same conception of justice applies to the other ways in which luck can shape a person's prospects. Sometimes, a person's life is shaped in advance by standing misfortunes of ability and situation. Other times they are shaped by risks a person ought to have recognized. Most often they lie somewhere in between, and are shaped by unanticipated consequences of prospectively sensible choices. If holdings are to be justified by the ways in which they came about, at least some of the time, the background effects of luck must also be controlled.

The relationship between distributive justice and responsibility is important for two reasons, one conceptual, the other political. Conceptually, the idea of a fair division of risks requires an account of the background risks that are largely independent of interaction. If terms of interaction are to be fair, some of those risks should not be borne by anyone in particular. Instead, they should be held in common, by the community as a whole. Otherwise, the effects of those risks will unfairly infect subsequent holdings.

It is possible in principle to deploy some of the apparatus of the earlier chapters without holding any sort of misfortunes in common. The conception of the person that legal practice works with is a conception tied to an idea of reciprocity. Although it is not a metaphysical conception of the person, it can be applied without considering background misfortunes. Indeed, in the common law's formative period, the ideas of responsibility that I have articulated were employed without any thought about distributive justice. So employing a reciprocity-based account of responsibility in isolation is possible.

But if it is possible to deploy that apparatus without looking to background questions, doing so would lack normative interest. A conception of responsibility that focuses on reciprocity is connected to the idea of fair terms of interaction that are meant to make their outcomes legitimate. As a result, we cannot abstract away from questions about fair starting points if we are to take seriously the idea that people should be made to bear the costs of their choices.[1]

The topic of background misfortunes gets its political importance from a familiar feature of political debates. Conservative critics of equality often argue that liberals who favor redistribution thereby give up on the idea of individual responsibility. Many egalitarians give in to the conservative charge too readily. Recent discussions of the relation between equality and responsibility provide a case in point. A central aim of those discussions has been to draw a line between cases in which the effects of luck are arbitrary, and cases where they are not. Unfortunately, those discussions have typically tied responsibility to control. We have seen the difficulties faced by variants of this view in tort law and in the punishment of criminal attempts. The problems here are parallel. To indemnify one person against the effects of luck on his or her life prospects is to shift that luck onto others, who could not control it either. As a result, friends of equality need an account of when it is fair to shift the effects of luck.[2] If we care about individual responsibility, equality of condition is not an attractive ideal.

In this chapter, I will follow the same approach as in earlier ones, arguing that responsibility is to be understood in terms of reciprocity and fair terms of interaction. Justice requires treating like cases alike; the idea of fair terms of interaction sets out the ways in which persons should be thought of as alike. I will also appeal once again to the idea that one person may not unilaterally set the terms of their interactions with others. In the case of tort law, that idea led to the

---

[1]   Matters would be different if some of the metaphysical notions of responsibility we considered in earlier chapters had stood up to scrutiny. For example, Weinrib's account of corrective justice in terms of the capacity for choice, Perry's account of moral responsibility as the basis of tort liability, and Hegel's account of the will's implicit commitments each seek to provide a normative grounding for legal practices in terms of facts about human capacities. Had they succeeded, each of those accounts might ignore more general questions about fair terms of interaction. Because the accounts fail on their own terms, questions about fair terms of interaction cannot be put aside.

[2]   Because the case of distributive justice is parallel to the cases we have already examined, I worry that some readers may find this discussion repetitive. Indeed, I almost hope some will; if they do, I will have established the parallel between corrective and distributive justice.

rejection of a subjective standard of liability in favor of a standard of reasonable care, set in terms of important interests in both liberty and security that all can be supposed to share. In the criminal law, the same idea explained the distinction between mistakes of fact and mistakes of law, and a reasonableness requirement in assessing beliefs about consent or the need for defensive force. In the case of distributive justice, that same idea translates into the requirement that the line between the choices for which a person may be held responsible, and circumstances for which he may not, is set objectively, rather than by any specific features of that person's understanding of their choice.

My account of distributive justice also follows my more general account of responsibility by incorporating the two features that were central to my accounts of the fault system and the criminal law's idea of the reasonable person. First of all, it depends on substantive views about the importance of various specific interests in both liberty and security. Second, it employs the strategy of balancing those interests against one another by weighing them within the representative reasonable person, rather than across persons. This approach makes sense of the ways in which particular interests matter, without inappropriately attaching weight to such matters as the expense of either safety precautions or compensation in any particular cases. As a result, the idea of the reasonable person provides an attractive account of equality: People are treated as equals when each is allowed a like liberty and security in light of the interests of others.

9.1   HOLDING MISFORTUNES IN COMMON

Questions of distributive justice concern the distribution of things for which people are not responsible. Those questions are prior to any questions about how *particular* holdings came about, because unless background conditions are fair, the fact that people made particular choices is not sufficient to justify any conclusions about the resulting burdens and benefits. We have seen many instances of this general point: The fact that one person could have avoided injuring another is not a basis for liability unless that person ought to have; the fact that someone knowingly used force against another is not grounds for culpability if that force was proportional and defensive.

I will approach the question of distributive justice by considering which misfortunes should be held in common: Those misfortunes that preclude a person having meaningful choices about his or her life – such misfortunes as physical disabilities, illness, or extreme poverty –

need to be held in common if people are to properly be held responsible for their choices.

We saw in Chapter 2 that anything at all can be represented as taking a risk, since various things might have been done to avoid any particular risk. Moreover, virtually any unwelcome outcome is the result of multiple factors. This opened up the problem of too much responsibility. We saw that the solution to that problem is to make attributions of responsibility turn on considerations of reasonableness, understood in terms of reciprocity. The role of reasonableness tests in tort law is to ensure that the risks of injury associated with ordinary interactions were fairly divided; in the criminal law, the same idea of reasonableness leads to a fair division of the risk of mistakes about justifying circumstances. In each case, reasonableness tests set public limits to the extent to which people must moderate their activities in light of the interests of others. In each case, to put all of the risk on those who might act unduly burdens their liberty; to put all of the risks on those who might be injured unduly burdens their security. The solution is to divide those risks, based on some understanding of the interests in both liberty and security that all can be expected to share.

The same conception of reasonableness is needed to determine the costs for which a person can be held responsible. If all risks were borne by those who acted, liberty would be too limited. If all risks were held in common, each person's security would be totally subject to the actions of others. The solution is, as always, to divide the risks based on some understanding of the interests that all can be expected to share. The relevant interests in the case of distributive justice are of a piece with interests in liberty and security: Each person has an interest in having the way his or her life goes depend on what he or she thinks important, as well as an interest in having how that life goes not depend on the choices of others. Reasonable terms of cooperation treat persons as equals by giving each the wherewithal to choose his or her own ends, while protecting each from the excessive burdens that the choices of others might create.

A reasonable balance between these two interests leads to a limit to the costs people can impose on each other, but also a limit on the costs people can be required to bear. Although people have a responsibility to moderate their activities in light of their fair shares, they do not need to do everything in their power to avoid imposing costs on others. Every action involves a variety of risks, in the sense that it changes the probability of a variety of outcomes. Treating some action as taking some particular risk does not require treating it as risking all of its consequences. The person who takes the risks involved in trying to live the life of an artist need not thereby also be thought of as taking the risk of starvation. The latter risk can be treated differently because of its obviously disastrous consequences. It can be so treated even though the artist could perhaps have taken further precautions to prevent it.

The underlying principle is that the fact that someone could have avoided some outcome does not mean that its risks cannot be held in common. The point is not that people (nor even all adults) should be made to bear all costs they could, in principle, have avoided. Nor is it that people should be made to bear only the costs that they chose. Instead, they should bear only such costs as it is reasonable that they bear in light of the interests of others.

9.1.1 Practical Reason Approaches

I will develop my account of distributive justice by contrasting it with an alternative family of views, which I'll call "the practical reason view." This family of views seeks a formal account of which misfortunes should be held in common, that is, an account that looks to the formal features of individual choices, rather than their content. I will argue that a formal account is not possible. As was the case in torts and for reasonableness tests in the criminal law, we cannot determine the scope of individual responsibility except by asking questions about the importance of various interests. In distributive justice, the practical reason view supposes that a person's responsibility ought to be limited to the chances that he chose to take. The notion of choice here has been cashed out in a variety of ways. For example, Ronald Dworkin advocates holding people responsible only for the choices that issue from preferences with which they identify. G. A. Cohen and Richard Arneson advocate holding people responsible for only those choices that are made with full awareness of their consequences. John Roemer supposes people should only be held responsible for their choices if those choices are ones that others, similarly situated, would have avoided. Each of these develops a familiar position from recent debates about free will and moral responsibility. As a result, they all look to questions about the nature of the choice some person faced. One account looks to the person's higher-order attitudes toward his choices, and holds him responsible for the choices with which he identifies; others look to whether the agent was aware of the consequences, or whether others would have done the same.

The difficulty I will point to in all of these approaches is that they make the agent's practical reason the basis of ascriptions of responsibility. Although often relevant to questions of blame, the ways in which a person thinks about a choice he or she is making is not necessarily relevant to the questions of whether he or she should be made to bear the costs of that choice. All of the practical reason approaches collapse the question of whether someone has *taken* a particular risk to that of whether that person has *chosen* that risk. The idea of taking a risk is related to the idea that the risk is that person's problem. We saw in Chapter 2 that not everything that creates a risk to others counts as taking that risk. And we saw in Chapter 3 that someone may take a risk, say, by driving carelessly, or using solvents near an open flame, without giving that risk any thought whatsoever. If we suppose that he should have thought of it, we might plausibly say that he *took* a risk, but not, I think, that he chose it. As a result, such a person might be required to bear the costs of the injuries that resulted, even though he didn't mean to cause them at all, and even if he would have avoided them if he'd given the matter any thought at all. The distinction between risks that are taken and those that are chosen is, as we saw in Chapter 5, constitutive of the difference between crimes and torts. It is, however, the wrong place to look for an account of distributive justice. Choosing a risk is neither necessary nor sufficient for taking a risk.

If we are asking in the abstract whether someone is responsible for some outcome, the character of the reasoning processes leading to some choice is perhaps an appropriate place to start. But if our concern is with another familiar question of responsibility, namely, whether someone can rightly be asked to bear a certain cost, matters are different. The hardest questions about responsibility arise when people weren't thinking. That is why the main focus of this book has been on accidents, emergencies, and mistakes. Each involves problems that will not go away, and will not cease to be serious problems, even though nobody wanted them to happen. Approaches that look only to the options a person faced fail to take seriously those questions, because they leave out questions of how else those costs might be borne. Whenever we relieve one person of the cost of something because he or she didn't identify with the choice, or didn't think about it, or wished it wouldn't happen, someone else ends up bearing the cost, typically someone else who didn't want, or couldn't control the result either. The idea that a person's life should depend only on the things he can control may make sense in the case of a particular individual if others are ready to devote their lives and resources to covering that person's losses. But it cannot be made sense of in the case of a plurality of persons living together on terms of mutual respect.

Now it might be thought that in treating distributive justice as parallel to tort liability, I am overlooking two important differences. First, Aristotle famously distinguished between distributive and corrective justice, noting that they employ different conceptions of equality. Corrective justice seeks to restore the equality of the parties when one injures another, whereas distributive justice seeks to treat people as equals by making distributive shares proportional to some factor. On this understanding, an egalitarian view of distributive justice must be committed to distributing resources equally, rather than taking any sort of interest in responsibility. Corrective justice takes an interest only in responsibility, and none in source of the holdings that it seeks to restore.[3]

The Aristotelian contrast is too sharp, however. Aristotle's conception of distributive justice is tied to an ideal of entitlement in proportion to virtue, and his view of corrective justice looks at particular interactions in abstraction from the more general virtues of the parties involved. For Aristotle, corrective and distributive justice differ because of the irrelevance of virtue to the former; we can take an interest in both insofar as we take an interest in both virtue and particular interactions.[4] On the view I have defended in this book, by contrast, corrective justice is important because of a general picture of how fair terms of interaction justify their results. Provided that starting points are fair and tortious wrongs are righted, a set of holdings is legitimate if it is the result of uncoerced interaction. Thus, the normative force of corrective justice is not purely corrective in Aristotle's sense. Instead, fair terms of interaction determine which changes in holdings are wrongful losses in need of correction. Conversely, distributive justice takes an interest in fair starting points, but takes that interest precisely because they are starting points of interaction. They have

---

[3] Aristotle, *Nichomachean Ethics*, V.ii, translated by Martin Ostwald (Indianapolis: Bobbs-Merrill, 1962); Ernest Weinrib, *The Idea of Private Law* (Cambridge, MA: Harvard University Press, 1995).

[4] Aquinas draws the same distinction, because he shares Aristotle's view of the state as a kind of organism, rather than as a means of protecting fair terms of interaction. It is interesting to note that Aquinas's view of self-defense supposes that the use of lethal force against an aggressor can be excused, but not justified, because the taking of life is a wrong against the body politic. See Michael Thompson, "Aquinas, Locke, and Self-Defense," 57 *University of Pittsburgh Law Review* 677 (1996).

no independent interest. Indeed, if we think of the cases of distributive justice that most readily fit Aristotle's model – dividing up a cake into equal slices, say – people are free to do as they will with their pieces. Once they have been divided fairly, the fact that some might give away, consume, or destroy their pieces of cake is of no importance. Aristotle offers an account of what, in Chapter 2, I referred to as patterned distribution. Questions about who should bear which costs only come up in the context of an historical account; as such, they are not distributive in Aristotle's narrow sense.

The second apparent difference flows from the fact that when misfortunes are held in common, the costs for which people are not responsible are spread rather than directly borne by some other particular person. As a result, any loss that is indemnified by a larger group adds a trivial burden to each person. But the significance of that difference is limited. For the same reasons that having adequate material resources is a precondition of freedom, being asked to bear even a share of some cost is a limitation on freedom. More importantly, though, an acceptable account of responsibility must have an idea of reciprocity at its core, and so must place systematic limits on the ways in which people are relieved of responsibility. Consider an example that combines corrective and distributive considerations. Suppose a society has socialized health care, and that the health care system does not have rights of subrogation that allow it to recover costs from tort-feasors. If one person carelessly injures another, the costs of the injury will be absorbed by the society as a whole. But the fact that the health insurance system insures that the injured party need not worry about his health does not mean that the injurer's carelessness is morally trivial. It is not only unfair to the injured person to have failed to look out for her injuries. It is also unfair to others who end up bearing the cost of carelessness.

There is, nonetheless, an important contrast that both putative differences draw on. When someone lacks the capacity for choice as a result of some natural misfortune, there may well be no other, particular, person who is the appropriate bearer of the costs of enabling that person to regain the capacity. In arguing that those costs must sometimes be held in common, I am not claiming that others are somehow to blame for such misfortunes. Instead, the point is that a person's choices are only normatively significant if he or she has the capacity to choose and is in a position to exercise that capacity in a meaningful way. The capacity to choose that is of interest to responsibility is neither a metaphysical property that is discovered, nor an abstract capacity that is somehow imputed to all conscious or self-conscious beings. Instead, we hold persons responsible within a system of fair terms of interaction. If someone lacks the wherewithal to make meaningful choices, those terms of interaction are not fair, and the results of those interactions are suspect on grounds of justice.

9.2 PROTECTING THE CAPACITY FOR RESPONSIBLE AGENCY

In Chapter 4, I described the capacity for foresight in terms of Rawls's idea of a range property, that is, a property that people might have to varying degrees. I suggested there that fairness to others requires that a person be held responsible as long as he or she has the requisite capacities to the minimal degree required to moderate his or her activities in light of the claims of others. I now want to return to that idea, and to Rawls, to explain why the idea that people should bear the costs of their choices imposes certain requirements on economic distribution. The basic idea is simple: In order for a person to be responsible for the costs his choices impose on others, he must have the capacity to make choices. That capacity, in turn, requires that he also have the opportunity to make such choices. If someone's opportunities are severely limited, say, by poverty or ill health, it is unfair to hold him responsible for the costs of his choices.

The idea that people should bear the costs of their choices requires an account of how the capacity for responsible agency will be protected. On its own, though, it does not provide such an account. Questions about what is required for responsible agency, like questions about which risks are reasonable, are substantive. Although the capacity for choice can perhaps be described abstractly, questions about whether that capacity is exercised in a significant way cannot be answered abstractly. In answering them, we have no choice but to look at what is required for a choice to be significant. That such questions are substantive does not mean that they are always difficult or controversial; for example, having enough to eat and the intellectual wherewithal to understand the options one faces are clearly relevant. Other things, such as health, mobility, and security from various catastrophes, are also plausible among the preconditions for normatively significant choice. At the same time, how much of these things are needed will depend in part on the kinds of things that it is important that people be able to choose. If a life of monkish self-denial was thought to be the only valuable sort of life, the enabling conditions for choosing that life would be simpler. Because other sorts of lives are plausibly thought of as valuable, the wherewithal to lead a self-directing life is more complex.

9.2.1   Primary Goods

John Rawls introduces what he calls "primary goods" as the basis for fair distributive shares. Rawls describes them as things people can reasonably be expected to want as much of as possible, and any inequalities in their distribution must be justified. Although Rawls sometimes describes primary goods as "all-purpose means" for various conceptions of the good, the role for which I hope to employ them (and Rawls himself sometimes does) is slightly different.[5] Like the fault system, primary goods provide an objective standard for treating people as equals. A public measure of important interests makes interpersonal judgments of fairness possible, and lets us distinguish between those misfortunes that lie where they fall, and those that are to be thought of as belonging to everyone.

Rawls employs the idea of primary goods together with the idea of representative persons. Although Rawls himself makes the point in terms of a hypothetical contract, the basic idea does not depend on the contract metaphor. Instead, the basic idea is the same one as I employed in explaining the standard of care in tort law: Rather than trying to weigh one person's liberty against another's security, we weigh particular interests in liberty and security against one another within the reasonable person. Thus, people are treated as equals, because they are allowed a like liberty, but also protected equally from each other. The same strategy applied dividing the risks of mistake in cases of self-defense and consent. It also applies here: Primary goods are things in which all persons can be supposed to take an interest. They take that interest because those goods are prerequisite to their ability to pursue whatever ends they have. Just as the extent of acceptable risk creation was made to depend on protecting important interests in both liberty and security, so a focus on primary goods gives priority to protecting the capacities for exercising important liberties. It also demarcates risks that are taken from those that merely arise, by determining which risks are always to be held in common.

---

5   John Rawls, *A Theory of Justice* (Cambridge, MA: Harvard University Press, 1971), p. 90. "Social Unity and Primary Goods," in *Utilitarianism and Beyond*, edited by Amartya Sen and Bernard Williams (Cambridge: Cambridge University Press, 1982), pp. 159–85.

An index of primary goods is objective in two distinct senses. First, it is objective in its *content,* that is, in its specification of the things in which distributive justice takes an interest. Like the fault standard, an index of primary goods cannot adapt itself to individual idiosyncrasies. Some people might have different values, thinking that certain unusual abilities or resources are essential to any decent life, and object to the choice to pool risks other than those on their own preferred list. After all, they are being asked to give other things up for benefits they do not actually want. But the person who wants other goods does not have a claim in justice against others any more than does the person who would rather risk being injured in return for being less careful, or the person who would gladly give up liberty in order to be protected against exposure to behavior that he finds offensive. Nor does the person who is unhappy with his or her share, nor the person who finds that liberty makes life more difficult. None of these people has a claim in justice because each effectively asks that their own view be allowed to fix what does and doesn't count as a cost of their activities to others, or of other's activities to them.

Once primary goods are equally distributed, the particular risks a person takes, either by squandering his share of resources, or exposing others to injury, are that person's risks to bear. Periodic redistribution will no doubt be needed to ensure that people continue to have the wherewithal to take responsibility for their choices. That redistribution need not bear any systematic relation to the pattern of past choices. Its point is to ensure that the aggregate effect of those choices does not undermine the capacity for responsible agency.

An index of primary goods is also objective in a second way, in that the ease or difficulty with which someone lives up to a standard of fairness is irrelevant to assessments of responsibility. People are expected to moderate their claims in light of the legitimate interests of others. As such, they must take responsibility for their choices. Like all duties resting on the protected interests of others, some people will have an easier time meeting them than others. In the normal range of cases – excluding cases of total incapacity to choose, brought on by childhood, or, in a very different way, mental illness – the difficulties a person might have in moderating his activities in particular cases are irrelevant to questions of responsibility.[6] Thus, the fact that some-

---

[6] This point needs to be distinguished from another. As Amartya Sen has pointed out, what counts as having enough of various things necessary to make choices

one's tastes are expensive to satisfy does not give him a claim on a special subsidy, even though he may need to work harder in order to live a life he thinks of as worthwhile.

Primary goods provide the background against which talk about taking responsibility for one's choices gets its normative interest. Those who lack a fair share of primary goods would have grounds for complaint were they made to bear the costs of the compromised choices they made. It is unfair to make people confined to wheelchairs pay the costs of making buildings accessible. But it is not unfair to hold those who have adequate resources and opportunities responsible for their choices even if they themselves experience those choices as compromised. It is not unfair to leave gourmets with a difficult choice between foregoing exquisite food and foregoing something else.[7] The latter, unlike the former, are in a position to decide what matters to them in light of the possibilities open to them.

Which things count as primary goods? Those that are necessary to the ability to plan one's own life, and to moderate one's activities in light of the claims of others. Health, wealth, and mobility are obvious examples. What is important in distributing these things is above all that everyone have enough, because those who do not have enough cannot rightly be held responsible for the compromised choices they make. If a misfortune is held in common, it is so held not because otherwise shares would diverge, but rather because it prevents the person it befalls from living a self-directing life. Thus, education is also obviously an important primary good, as is the possession of some level of marketable skills. Some of these things can only be distributed equally if they are to be distributed to all, such as the social bases of self-respect. Others are best distributed through institutional mechanisms, such as the tax system.

will vary with such factors as metabolism and geography, as well as with economic and cultural infrastructure. See Amartya Sen, "Justice: Means vs. Freedoms,"19 *Philosophy and Public Affairs* 111 (1990). Such considerations are themselves objective in the sense with which I am concerned, and they contrast with the disappointments someone might have because he was guaranteed things that were not especially important to his own conception of the good life.

The sorts of factors Sen identifies are obviously important to the *measurement* of shares of primary goods. I put the issue of measurement aside here. As important as these considerations are in practice, they revolve around the implementation of the same basic idea of enabling people to make important choices.

[7] I think this is even true in cases in which an obsession with fine dining arises as a result of a stroke. See Marilynn Larkin, "Eating Passion Unleashed by Brain Lesions," *Lancet* 1997; 349 (9065): 1607 (May 31, 1997).

9.2.2   Needs

The theory of distributive justice is not simply the theory of need.[8] But the idea of holding some misfortunes in common has a great deal to learn from accounts of needs: The distinction between one person's disappointments and the misfortunes of which others must take account is best understood in terms of the importance of particular interests.[9] An acceptable theory of distributive justice will attach greater priority to some interests than to others. Suppose that you have a serious, but treatable illness. There are strong moral reasons for others to help you find the resources to pay for the medical treatment you require. The arguments in favor of socialized medicine are familiar and compelling, whatever the administrative complications of their application. Suppose, though, that you would prefer to suffer through your illness, but see Mount Kilimanjaro before illness claims you. You might even point out that the trip to Kenya is less expensive than the medical treatment you require. Nonetheless, we do not hesitate to treat your desire for the trip as simply your desire, which has no substantial moral claim on us.[10] Your claim based on need cannot be

---

[8]   Compelling accounts of the role of needs in distributive justice can be found in two papers by David Copp, "Reason and Needs," in *Value, Welfare and Morality*, edited by R. G. Frey and C. W. Morris (Cambridge: Cambridge University Press, 1993), pp. 112–37; and "Equality, Justice and the Basic Needs," in *Necessary Goods*, edited by Gillian Brock (Totowa, N.J.: Roman and Allanhelld, forthcoming). For more general reflections on the moral significance of needs, see T. M. Scanlon, "Preference and Urgency," 82 *Journal of Philosophy* 655 (1975).

[9]   This emphasis on particular goods might be thought to be at odds with liberalism's commitment to neutrality. To abandon neutrality in this way is not to give up on liberalism, though, any more than the tort law's readiness to protect some security interests but not others need not be thought of as giving up on liberalism. In the case of tort law, persons are not regarded as simply pursuing their several aims, each with an interest in his or her own welfare, nor as all pursuing some shared or common conception of the good. Instead, all are presumed to have interests in liberty and in security, and all are presumed to be capable of moderating their activities in light of others' interests in both liberty and security. Because interests in both liberty and security are important to people who desire their own plans of life, tort law is neutral on many questions about the good life. But it is neutral in the way in which Switzerland purports to be neutral, that is, unwilling to take sides in particular disputes. It is not neutral in the way in which an old joke claimed the former Czechoslovakia was so neutral that it didn't even intervene in its own internal affairs. Such neutrality is enough to respond to the pragmatic worries that are frequently said to underwrite liberal neutrality. Broad agreement on protecting the basic conditions of agency prerequisite to holding people responsible need not elude a society in which people disagree about what matters most in life.

[10]   This is not only a feature of political morality. If we are your children, we might

276

traded, even for something less expensive. To characterize a claim as one of need is to characterize its significance for a person's ability to live his or her own life. Illness is not bad because it falls randomly or is outside a person's control, but rather because it typically jeopardizes a person's ability to live the life they choose.

A primary good such as health is not tradeable because a person's claim to it is not based on how well or badly that person's life is going from his own point of view. Instead, it is based on the importance of those goods for a person's ability to plan his own life. As a result, fair distributive shares are not fungible resources. In this respect, a person's claim to primary goods plays the same role in the political morality of responsibility as the right to vote does in the political morality of democracy. The right to vote is an important part of democratic citizenship. Different people attach varying importance to it, and it doesn't matter at all to some. Those people would find their welfare enhanced if they could sell their votes to others who valued them more highly. But votes are not tradeable in this way because they are not a resource for enhancing welfare. In the same way, one's claim on socialized health care is not tradeable because it is not simply a resource for welfare enhancement. Because some measure of health is a prerequisite to control over one's own life, its claim on our attention is different in kind.

In-kind transfers, such as public provision of health care, are the exception, rather than the rule, in the provision of primary goods. Nonetheless, they illustrate how primary goods are important because they protect autonomy, rather than as means to be used autonomously. The example of in-kind transfers also reminds us that the purpose of primary goods is not to compensate for disadvantages in the way in which tort damages do, or to equalize relative position by making up one sort of loss in terms of some other benefit. Instead, their purpose is to enable the capacity for choice. These differences are important, because those who behave irresponsibly and find themselves with nothing are entitled to have their autonomy protected, but have no claim to use the resources needed to do so as they see fit.

Other primary goods, especially income, get their value from the fact that they can be exchanged. At the same time, even though money is exchangeable, the primary good of freedom from poverty is not.

willingly forego our inheritance to extend your life, but legitimately resent the fact that you leave us nothing in order to make a final journey before you make your final journey.

The freedom of choice that money can bring[11] is important to a society of responsible agents. Those who face limited choices because of poverty require aid for the same reason that those who suffer from ill health do.[12] Failure to provide either with the means to be self-directing would infect all of their subsequent choices.

9.3 BRUTE LUCK AND OPTION LUCK

Some of Rawls's critics have objected that the primary goods approach leads us to ignore the role of choice in determining the size of each person's share of primary goods.[13] Those who are badly off because lazy or wasteful have less of a claim on our aid than those who are badly off through no fault of their own. If someone gambles in the hope of reaping a substantial gain, he has no business asking others to reimburse his losses. Yet if things become bad enough for such a person, a focus on protecting the capacity for agency would require that others do just that.

Because of this putative difficulty with Rawls's approach, a number of writers have sought to draw a different sort of distinction between those things that should be held in common and those that are a matter of individual responsibility. According to this line of thought, a cost should be held in common just in case nobody is responsible for it. If lazy and wasteful people are badly off because of choices they have made, they have no claim on us; if people with disabilities are badly off through no choice of their own, they are entitled to indemnification. Commonsense examples make this picture plausible. Perhaps trapped miners, or children who fall down wells, are entitled to rescue at public expense. But wilderness adventurers and ice fishermen who get themselves into dangerous situations should pay for their own rescues.

Ronald Dworkin was the first to criticize Rawls on this score.[14] His attempt to distinguish between costs that should be internalized and those that should not repays close attention.

---

[11] G. A. Cohen, *Self-Ownership, Freedom, and Equality* (Cambridge: Cambridge University Press, 1995), pp. 59–60.

[12] From the point of view of justice, in-kind transfers to the poor are probably more appropriate. In practice, the potentially humiliating effects of such a policy might make it inappropriate.

[13] See, for example, Will Kymlicka, *Contemporary Political Philosophy: An Introduction* (Oxford: Oxford University Press, 1990), p. 75.

[14] Ronald Dworkin, "What Is Equality? Part II: Equality of Resources," 10 *Philosophy and Public Affairs* 283 (1981).

Dworkin's account appeals to "a certain view of the distinction between a person and his circumstances, and assigns his tastes and ambitions to his person, and his physical and mental powers to his circumstances."[15] In order for interactions to be fair, people must be held responsible for some things, but exempted from responsibility for the circumstances in which they find themselves. The general approach is attractive on two grounds. It frees people from the arbitrary effects of fortune, by making up losses they could not avoid. At the same time, by requiring people to bear costs for which they are responsible, it frees others from the need to bear them. As Will Kymlicka sums up the point, "It is unjust if people are disadvantaged by inequalities in their circumstances, but it is equally unjust for me to demand that someone else pay for the costs of my choices."[16]

The distinction between choices and circumstances is related to the economic idea of opportunity costs. In conditions of scarcity, a person with fixed resources must forego some things in order to have others; thus, any choice has costs in terms of other opportunities foregone. Opportunity costs are important in defining costs across persons, for they make it possible to define prices. Dworkin emphasizes the important role of markets in defining equality of resources. When markets function efficiently, prices reflect the degree to which people value various goods that are for sale. If something is scarce and many people want it, it is appropriate that its price should be high. That higher price reflects the costs to others – what they must forego to have the good in question – of any particular individual's choices.[17] Again, if I produce something others want, those who consume it will consume less of other things. The advantage I gain from selling those things is the result of the resources created or freed up by the opportunities I have created. Should I decide to do something self-indulgent, it is appropriate that I should have to forego other things I might otherwise have been able to do. It is also appropriate that the costs of my decision lie with me. No other person or larger group has a responsibility to provide me with resources to carry out my plans simply because they are my plans. The costs are mine because they result from

---

[15] Ibid., p. 302.
[16] Kymlicka, *Contemporary Political Philosophy*, p. 75.
[17] It does not, however, reflect aggregation in any objectionable sense. One person is not deprived of some thing because many other people want the same sort of thing; instead, each faces a problem of choice in which he or she must decide what to compromise, given the desires of others. Prices make the idea of moderating one's claims determinate.

my choices. Of course, in making any such decision, I take a chance: If things work out for me, great; if not it is simply my own bad luck – bad option luck.

In order for the idea of opportunity costs to reflect an interpretation of equality, the distinction between choices and circumstances must be in place. Costs will not reflect my choices or their opportunity costs to others fully unless the effects of brute luck are somehow canceled. If people are to bear the costs of their choices, the irrelevant effects of circumstances must be eliminated. If someone begins with a larger bundle of goods, that person's preferences get extra weight in the market. That extra weight means that his ability to outbid others for scarce resources (and the prices each must pay) reflects initial good fortune rather than the costs of his or her choices. Likewise, the person who starts off poor or handicapped will, through no choice of her own, have to meet needs that others do not have, and as a result have fewer resources with which to bid for the things she wants. Dworkin explains the idea of opportunity costs in light of a distinction between what he calls "brute luck" and "option luck." Brute luck is luck that lies outside anyone's responsibility; as a result, it is to be held in common. By contrast, option luck, the luck to which people expose themselves, is the responsibility of those who expose themselves to it, and so not to be held in common. Once brute luck is controlled, those who gamble and win are entitled to the results of their choices; those who gamble and lose are left with the results of theirs. Generally speaking, if the effects of brute luck are left in place, the costs of my choices will reflect its contingencies rather than my choices. Dworkin's root idea is that if my fortune in life is to reflect my choices and not my circumstances, the effects of those circumstances must be canceled. There are two ways in which that might be done. One is to change the circumstances – to make sure that no person's circumstances reflect arbitrary fortune. This can be done with respect to certain circumstances – vaccines eradicate the effects of serious childhood diseases, for example. The other is to cancel their effects. In either case, equality demands that the costs of so doing be held in common. If they are held in common, then the results of voluntary interactions will be to leave everyone with fair shares, as measured by their opportunity costs to others.

Absent some way of removing either the existence or the effects of brute luck, though, the costs of choices cannot be defined in a morally significant way. If the idea that someone should bear the costs of their choices is to be anything but the idea that people are stuck bearing whatever costs they happen to bear, some costs must be treated as separable from a person's choices. Those costs created by the arbitrary reign of fortune – genetically induced illness or disability, for example – fit tidily into this category. But so does much else. Agency and ownership are only related in the appropriate context, so no concerns about violations of agency that might arise in a different context can even come up.

The required distinction between choices and circumstances can be drawn in a number of ways. The second strand of Dworkin's argument seeks to fill out one such idea. In the rest of this section, I examine, and reject, both Dworkin's and another prominent account. Although they differ in important ways, they share a single difficulty. Dworkin's invocation of opportunity costs expresses an attractive idea of reciprocity. The intuitive idea is that people should bear the costs they create because it would be unfair to impose them on *others*. Conversely, it would unfairly advantage others if people were made to bear the costs of their circumstances. At the root of the standard ways of drawing the distinction between choices and circumstances is another idea, though, an idea of individual practical reason. The two ideas line up in certain kinds of cases. It is unfair to ask hardworking ants to subsidize lazy grasshoppers. Moreover, the grasshopper is to be faulted if it demands extra resources despite recognizing this unfairness. The grasshopper seems to be cynically exploiting the idea of need in order to get more for itself. But the unfairness of the demand is the same, even if the grasshopper's bad judgment is blameless.

In criticizing Dworkin's approach, I should make it clear that I mean only to criticize one part of it, and not another. My objection is to Dworkin's rationale for drawing the line between choices and circumstances in terms of each person's conception of his own responsibility. Dworkin's fully developed account appeals to hypothetical insurance markets, the net effect of which is to introduce progressive taxation in order to protect people against poverty and unemployment in something very much like the ways Rawls's account would. Dworkin gets his insurance results by introducing attractive assumptions about ignorance of the risks one faces, and the effects of circumstances on certain foolish choices not to insure that people might in fact have made. As I understand those assumptions, they serve to reintroduce the feature that I suggested makes Rawls's account attractive, namely, its objectivity. The overall effect of Dworkin's ideal insurance markets is to erase the effects of his preferred way of drawing the distinction between choices and circumstances. In its place, we get the plausible conclusion that people would protect themselves against what they prospectively regard as disastrous outcomes, namely, those things that would destroy or severely compromise their capacity to live their own lives as they see fit. Rather than protecting the particular things they hold most dear, they protect their ability to function, so that should disaster strike, they do not lose the ability to decide their own priorities.

Where the fault system divides risks in a way that aims to treat persons as equals, ideal insurance pools them. It does so in abstraction from particular choices, and also from particular experiences of choice. "From the inside," we neither identify with, nor regard ourselves as having chosen, what we would have chosen if we knew more. In order to apply the ideal insurance approach, we need to construct representative persons, and have two possible ways of doing so. First, we might appeal to statistical evidence about what people actually insure against. Second, we might appeal to a normative model of the important interests that people ought to protect. I suspect that the two approaches wouldn't differ too much in application. The important point, though, is that they both come apart from people's experience of choice from the inside. Given that they diverge from that experience, the normative model of ideal choice has the advantage of making clear why social institutions would take an interest in something that is not experienced from the inside. So understood, though, Dworkin's insurance model employs the same fundamental approach as Rawls's veil of ignorance.

9.3.1 Choices and Circumstances: Dworkin's Cut

Dworkin himself draws the line between choices and circumstances in terms of identification. Those who willingly undertake risks are responsible for those risks; those who willingly cultivate expensive tastes or identify with the expensive tastes with which they find themselves are also responsible for their tastes. The line between expensive tastes and expensive needs depends on the agent's own attitude to the desire in question. If someone has what he sadly regards as an uncontrollable craving for champagne and caviar, it becomes part of his circumstances, and he is not responsible for it. If someone else identifies with his need for expensive medicine, he is responsible for the costs of the medication.[18] Dworkin's rationale for drawing the distinction in this way is that it is the way in which people draw the distinction in assessing the success of their own lives. The understanding of responsibility appropriate to political life should be the same as the one in light of which people understand their responsibility for their own choices "from the inside."[19] Although Dworkin does not put the point in quite this way, I think that the intuitive appeal of this approach flows from a more general understanding of the idea that the exercise of state power should not be arbitrary. Holding people responsible for the things for which they hold themselves responsible does not open up a gap between how people conceive of themselves and how they are treated by the state. If people are held responsible for those things for which they already acknowledge responsibility, none will have any reason to complain of arbitrary treatment. At the same time, each will regard his successes and failures as his own doing, because they will not depend on anything on which he himself does not think it should.

Dworkin's account has been criticized because it makes the costs that one's choices impose on others depend in part on one's own conception of those costs.[20] The problem is not the practical one of difficulty in ascertaining individual views about responsibility; any institutional mechanism that seeks to be sensitive to individual responsibility will rely on imperfect measures in order to do so. Nor is the problem that the extent of responsibility will be idiosyncratic and variable. The underlying point is more important than either of these: An acceptable account of responsibility rests on the idea that people

---

[18]   There may be some hard questions about how any set of institutions could keep track of the factors that Dworkin's theory requires. In addition, there is a danger that any such institutions would themselves have an important role in shaping the desires with which people identify. From one direction, this problem appears because people tend to genuinely identify with things that work out well and (perfectly understandably) to distance themselves from their failures. From another, the temptations to distance oneself from expensive tastes would be considerable. The satisfactions of an unwanted craving might be substantial, enough even to outweigh the emotional costs of being unable to shed it. Still, I put those question to one side here.

[19]   Ronald Dworkin, "Justice, Insurance, Luck," paper presented to the NYU Program for the study of Law, Philosophy, and Social Theory, September 5, 1996.

[20]   G. A. Cohen, "On the Currency of Egalitarian Justice," 99 *Ethics* 906 (July 1989); John Roemer, "Equality and Responsibility," 20 *Boston Review* 1 (April/May 1995).

should moderate their claims based on the interests of others. It is not up to me to decide which of the interests of others are grounds for moderating my claims or up to others to dictate to me when I must give way to their interests. Of course, the person who identifies with some preference and not others does not mean to decide about the protected interests of others. Such a person is concerned only with what gives meaning to his or her own life. The trouble is, the extent of the protected interests of others ends up depending on those choices. The fact that I refuse to take responsibility for some loss because I didn't identify with the preference that leads me to choose it cannot, by itself, entitle me to indemnification. To allow one person's tastes to determine when others must indemnify her would place an unreasonable burden on others.[21] People frequently act on preferences with which they do not fully identify. When they do, the costs of the choices arising out of such preferences do not thereby disappear. They still must be borne by someone.

The entire appeal of a market-based account of equality was that the notion of opportunity costs appeared to provide a way of measuring the costs of each person's choices to *others*. That idea seems to be lost. In particular cases, the requirement that people bear the costs to others of their choices may overlap with the requirement that people only be held responsible for choices with which they identify. They are conceptually distinct, though, for at bottom, they represent fundamentally different conceptions of responsibility. Dworkin's account requires only that people moderate their claims insofar as they identify with them. As such, the idea that one should moderate one's claims because of others is a distinct and conflicting principle.

9.3.2 Choices and Circumstances: Control

The problem with the identification account is that it makes the line between choices and circumstances itself too nearly a matter of choice. As a result, it appears to make the extent of a person's responsibility depend in part on factors for which that person is responsible. It might be thought that the source of the problem is that what a person identifies with is within his or her control, and that responsibil-

---

[21] How *large* the burden would be is a separate question. That depends on various details about the parties involved. The burden is unreasonable regardless of its size, for it is the result of one person's choices setting the limits of the freedom of others.

ity should depend on control. The control view looks like it is also tied to our first-person experience of responsibility, since "I can't help it" expresses a familiar first-person response to illegitimate attributions of responsibility.

If responsibility and control are linked, it might be thought, the problem cannot arise. I now want to argue that this is no solution at all, because the problem with the identification account was not that it was voluntary, but that its determination of the scope of a person's responsibility was resolved by looking only to facts about that person. As a result, a version of the same problem bedevils all accounts that emphasize the chooser's own practical reason. I'll illustrate this point by looking at accounts of responsibility that suppose that a person should only be held responsible for things that are within his or her control.

The idea of control is notoriously slippery. To begin with, there is an important distinction between the things a person could not control and the things that person did not control. Comparatively few things fall into the former category, whereas almost everything falls into the latter. Depending on how far back we are prepared to look, there is usually something a person could have done to avoid acquiring a taste they now have.[22]

The ambiguities in the notion of control are compounded by the fact that many of the examples in the literature on distributive justice involve people who unwittingly developed a taste for champagne, or plover's eggs, or classical music, and find themselves unable to abandon it. Cohen contrasts cases in which someone could not have helped forming some taste and could not now unlearn it with those in which the person could have forestalled, or could now unlearn that taste.[23] I have to admit that I do not fully understand what it is to have tastes that fall into the former category.[24] Regardless of how they are

---

[22]   Cohen writes, "we should therefore compensate only for those welfare deficits that are not in some way traceable to the individual's choices"; "On the Currency of Egalitarian Justice," p. 923. The difficulty comes in interpreting the words "in some way."

[23]   Ibid., p. 923.

[24]   Eric Rakowski points out that many of the examples in the literature involve people who can only live what they regard as an adequate life if they consume some particular expensive thing. Almost nobody stands in that sort of relation to their conception of the good. This is especially true in cases where the conception of the good involves consumption. A typical connoisseur wants to consume as high quality a product as possible, not to consume only the finest imaginable. See Eric Rakowski, *Equal Justice* (Oxford: Oxford University Press, 1991), pp. 57–8.

acquired, tastes are almost never experienced as something that cannot be unlearned no matter what else is at stake. The familiar English "policeman at the elbow" test for compulsion in the criminal law is a reminder of this fact. Although it may be difficult to resist various desires, most people are almost never incapable of resisting them. Some smokers may really be unable to quit, but a taste for champagne or plover's eggs isn't ordinarily experienced in anything like that way. Instead, they are experienced as one desire among others.[25] Those who need to compromise their favorite tastes, or deepest convictions about how they should live their lives, may be unhappy, perhaps desperately so. But that is a different issue from any questions about control. Most of what people do, including most things that are done under the pressure of circumstances, are things that a person could control.[26] And most of the time, even difficult situations reflect earlier decisions. As we saw in Chapter 2, Pascal was right to point out that most unhappiness could be avoided if people would just learn to stay in their rooms.[27]

The latter category is easier to understand, but its significance is unclear. People sometimes set out to develop particular tastes, teaching themselves to appreciate opera, or fine wines. Such cases typically involve training oneself to appreciate something one already judges to be valuable – the opera lover is drawn to something about opera, and decides to learn more about it. Even in cases where people develop tastes in the attempt to appear tasteful, they do so because of

---

[25] Roemer offers the hypothetical example of a person who, as a result of hypnosis, vomits if fed anything other than filet mignon. I agree that such a person might be entitled to special consideration. I doubt that such bizarre cases show us anything interesting about the role of control, however. I think such a person is best thought of as having a somewhat expensive need for an unusual medicine. As such, the person would be entitled to special consideration even if his condition was self-inflicted, and perhaps even if it was the predictable result of a high-protein diet. See my exchange with Roemer, 20 *Boston Review* 12, 15 (April/May 1995).

[26] In Chapter 5, we saw Kant's invocation of Cicero's example of two shipwrecked sailors struggling over a plank. Kant characterized the sailor who expelled the other as culpable but not punishable, noting that he was beyond the deterrent reach of the law. Yet even in such dire circumstances, the claim that he lacked control doesn't shed much light on the episode, for it treats his response as the equivalent of going berserk. If he was acting cooly and calmly, he still would have been beyond the law's deterrent reach. Had he been committed to an ethic of self-sacrifice, he would have done otherwise. He was compelled by circumstances to do what he thought most sensible in those circumstances.

[27] This point should be familiar from the discussion of Pascal and Coase in Chapter 2.

valuing being (or being thought) a certain sort of person. But the initial inchoate recognition of value is not itself something chosen, so we might wonder why, if the emphasis is on control, someone would be held responsible for it.

9.3.2.1 Responsibility and Excuses. The obvious response to the worry that control is indeterminate is to explicate a notion of control in terms of some independently specifiable factor. Richard Arneson and G. A. Cohen have offered one approach to this task, and John Roemer another. Arneson and Cohen focus on the relation between informed choice and responsibility.[28] Roemer focuses instead on whether similarly situated people would have succumbed to the same temptations.[29]

Arneson's and Cohen's appeal to informed choice gets its moral appeal from the readiness with which people are absolved of blame when they make mistakes. Although Arneson and Cohen differ in important ways,[30] the strand that connects their views is a focus on the ways in which someone came to take an interest in the goods or activities from which they derive welfare or advantage. For both Cohen and Arneson, we assess a person's desire or need for some good or activity by looking at how that person came to take an interest in it. If that interest developed due to ignorance or lack of foresight, then the pursuit of it should be subsidized. By contrast, if someone chose to develop the interest, fully aware of its costs, he must bear those costs himself.[31] Cohen contrasts the example of someone who requires resources to make an expensive pilgrimage that is deeply important to him with another who wants to make the same pilgrimage

---

[28] Richard Arneson, "Equality and Equality of Opportunity for Welfare," 55 *Philosophical Studies* 77 (1989); and "Liberalism, Distributive Subjectivism, and Equal Opportunity for Welfare," 19 *Philosophy and Public Affairs* 159 (1990). Cohen, "On the Currency of Egalitarian Justice," p. 99, *Ethics* 906 (July 1989).

[29] John Roemer, "A Pragmatic Theory of Responsibility for the Egalitarian Planner," in his *Egalitarian Perspectives* (Cambridge: Cambridge University Press, 1994), pp. 179–98.

[30] Arneson thinks access to welfare should be equalized, but Cohen supposes that access to something broader, which he calls advantage, should be. For Arneson, welfare is defined in terms of the perspective of the person whose welfare it is, but for Cohen, it is defined at least in part objectively, in order to determine what counts as an advantage.

[31] Full information enters Arneson's view in another way as well: Arneson's concern is with the satisfaction of the preferences a person would endorse if fully informed. For criticism of the idea of informed preference, see my "Preference," in *Value, Welfare, and Morality*, edited by R. G. Frey and C. W. Morris (Cambridge: Cambridge University Press, 1993), pp. 93–111.

because it is expensive, and argues that the former has a claim on our aid, but the latter does not.[32]

Roemer's account gets its moral appeal from another familiar thought – "there but for fortune go you or I," the idea that we lack moral standing to criticize people who are no worse than ourselves. Even those who are unusually heroic have no business holding others to the standards that most would fail to meet.[33] Applied to concrete cases, Roemer argues that if someone makes choices typical of those in their socioeconomic type, we may treat them as expressions of circumstances, not choices. In Roemer's favored example, the factory worker who smokes may be indemnified for his loss of health on the grounds that the majority of similarly situated factory workers do the same.[34] A wealthy lawyer who smokes would not be indemnified because other wealthy lawyers do not take up smoking, and so her habit is not considered a product of her circumstances.[35] Roemer offers his account as a pragmatic test for control, but I take it that the root idea is that he supposes it is an operational measure of some *independent* fact about the agents making the choices.

I mention both approaches here because they illustrate an important misconception about the role of individual responsibility in questions of distributive justice. Despite their differences, Arneson, Cohen, and Roemer all seek to explicate responsibility in terms of factors that are germane to blame[36] but not to questions of who should bear

---

[32] Cohen, "On the Currency of Egalitarian Justice," p. 938.

[33] Roemer also argues that the question of whether ordinary Germans are responsible for their complicity in the Holocaust depends on whether their behavior was statistically ordinary. See Roemer, "A Pragmatic Theory of Responsibility," p. 193. If it was, then they are not responsible, no matter how atrocious their behavior, because we have reason to believe that their acts are the product of their circumstances. Roemer concedes that we might blame or punish such people on exemplary grounds, but insists that neither blame nor punishment is deserved. I should perhaps say that I don't find Roemer's account very convincing as an account of blame either. I put those worries aside here because it is at least recognizable as an account of blame.

[34] Roemer offers this example in both "A Pragmatic Theory of Responsibility" and "Equality and Responsibility."

[35] Roemer's approach does somewhat better as a partial principle for rationing scarce medical resources than as a general account of responsibility. Organ transplant waiting lists, for example, might give priority to those whose illnesses are not the result of statistically unusual risk taking. Perhaps blameworthiness is one consideration. Even here, however, the account does not seem to capture the morally relevant dimension of blame.

[36] Cohen explicitly denies concern with criticism, noting that whether a person develops an expensive taste is his business, but it is nobody else's business

which costs. Each tries to explicate control in terms of the risks a person chose, not the risks they took. That is why their accounts all center around familiar excusing conditions. Both law and morality recognize a wide variety of excusing conditions, but they are all rooted in the familiar idea that someone "couldn't help it." The things a person couldn't help cluster primarily around two basic types: "I didn't realize" and "Anyone would have done the same."[37] The Arneson/Cohen account takes up the first strand; Roemer's account takes up the second. Of course, both accounts are put forward as ways of defining just entitlements. Yet their focus on familiar ways in which responsibility can be avoided leads them astray.

Excuses are important to questions of responsibility, but a striking feature of legal excuses – one which they share with moral excuses – is that the very factors that excuse a person's action from blame or punishment serve also to make that person liable for losses that result. As we saw in Chapters 4 and 5, if I take your raincoat, believing it to be my own, I escape punishment because I act under color of right, and, provided my mistake was not itself culpable, I escape blame also. (As J. L. Austin points out, inadvertence may excuse my stepping on your toe, but not on your baby.)[38] If I break into your cabin to save myself from a storm, I escape punishment, and perhaps also blame, because anyone would have done the same. But in each case, the very thing that entitles me to use your goods also means that I must replace them in the condition in which I took them. Both morally and legally, mistake and necessity make my use of your goods the equivalent of a gratuitous loan of them. As with gratuitous loans, so with excuses: The goods must be returned in the condition in which they were taken. So, although mistake and the fact that anyone would have done the same relieve one of blame for one's choices, they do not relieve one of the costs of those choices.

The same point applies to injuries where there is no suggestion of a crime; if I carelessly injure you, I'm liable, even if I honestly misestimated, or didn't even advert to, the risks my actions create. An excusing condition model is appropriate in criminal law but not in tort

---

to pick up the tab; "On the Currency of Egalitarian Justice," p. 923. The rest of Cohen's argument focuses on considerations that are relevant to blame, however.

[37]   Other excuses appeal to general incapacity, such as childhood or mental illness.

[38]   J. L. Austin, "A Plea for Excuses," in *The Philosophy of Action*, edited by A. R. White (Oxford: Oxford University Press, 1968), pp. 19–43.

because the costs in tort law are already sunk.[39] Any excuse that is granted to one person leaves the costs with others. By contrast, in the criminal law, if the accused is excused, nobody else ends up going to jail instead. Put slightly differently, liability in tort is relational; excuses from punishment are monadic. Although I have offered my own account of legal excuses in Chapter 5, this point can be made on any of a number of accounts of excuses. On all such accounts, someone may be excused from blame or punishment but nonetheless liable for the consequences of his deeds.

On this understanding, excusing conditions do not serve to relieve people of responsibility entirely. Instead, excuses make certain kinds of responses to responsibility inappropriate, absolving of blame (morally) or relieving of punishment (legally). Those who are excused have failed to do what they ought to have done. The question remains of what should become of the consequences of that failure. For example, if I make a mistake, I may well be excused. But it is still *my* mistake, and I can legitimately be asked to bear its costs. The absence of excusing conditions in tort (and any corresponding moral duty of repair) does not reflect liability without responsibility, but rather the distinction between liability and blame.

Holding someone responsible for the costs of their choices is neither an expression of disapproval nor a form of hard treatment meted out for some further purpose. Instead, it is a matter of fairness across persons. If distributive institutions are to bring the arbitrariness of misfortune under the discipline of justice, they must avoid inquiring into individual blameworthiness.

The general point might be put this way. Excusing conditions are parasitic on independently defined duties, and must be if failure to live up to those duties is to be excused. In cases of distributive justice, the duties require that each person moderate his or her claims in light of the legitimate claims of others. Both Arneson and Cohen in their way, and Roemer in his, go wrong in supposing that what we owe each other can be fixed by factors that are at most relevant to excusing conditions. Excusing conditions apply a standard of individualized concern, rather than public justice. Because they focus on whether or not risks are chosen rather than on whether or not risks are taken, they lose contact with the idea that people should take ac-

---

[39] Insofar as tort law includes anything that might be called excuses, they involve incapacities, such as childhood and mental illness. There are no tort excuses that function only on some particular occasion.

count of the interests of others. Both conceptions of choosing risks look to the chooser's relation to the risk, but not to the chooser's relations to others. As we've seen in earlier chapters, whether someone is accountable for taking a risk can only be determined in relation to the protected interests of others. In general,[40] whether someone can be held accountable for choosing a risk depends on inquiries only about that person.

The root of these difficulties is the attempt to understand responsibility in terms of practical reasoning. That may well be the best way to approach the philosophical problem of free will,[41] and perhaps even the question of excusing conditions in the criminal law. But it fails to make contact with questions about who bears which costs, because most of the time, issues about costs come up where nobody chose the risk – accidents, mistakes, and emergencies are the law's hard cases. Insofar as distributive justice is concerned with how costs ought to be borne, it faces the same hard cases.[42]

9.4   THE REASONABLE PERSON, AGAIN

The solution to the problems faced by the practical reason view is the same as the solution to the problems faced by the libertarian in Chapter 2: The introduction of a reasonable person standard. In tort, the idea of a reasonable person serves to divide risks fairly, so that the results of luck are not morally arbitrary. Reasonableness tests in distributive justice serve to draw a distinction between arbitrary fortune and nonarbitrary fortune, but do so without mapping that distinction onto a distinction between what a person can and cannot control.

The idea of the reasonable person is just the idea that the boundaries

---

[40]   The exception to this generalization is that people who fail to consider the rights of others – those who make, broadly speaking, mistakes of law – are culpable.

[41]   Thus, Dworkin's identification test bears important affinities to Harry Frankfurt's influential view of free will. See the latter's "Freedom of the Will and the Concept of a Person," in his *The Importance of What we Care About: Philosophical Essays* (Cambridge: Cambridge University Press, 1988), pp. 11–25. Charles Taylor has criticized Frankfurt's account for failing to explain why higher-order desires are so obviously important. See Taylor, "Responsibility for Self," in *The Identities of Persons*, edited by Amélie Oksenberg Rorty (Berkeley: University of California Press, 1976), pp. 281–300. In the same way, Dworkin's account does not explain the features of the interests that people would protect.

[42]   The problem is structurally analogous to the one libertarians face in dealing with risks: Undoing the results of force or fraud is easy, because the forcer or fraud is obviously blameworthy. The hard part is deciding who should bear costs when nobody meant to do anything wrong.

of responsibility are set by whether making individuals bear the costs of particular choices places an undue burden on them. Those costs still lie somewhere. The question of where they lie is not answered by looking to how difficult it was for the particular person, but by looking to the costs, in terms of important interests, in facing that choice. The person who is faced with a difficult choice is not relieved of responsibility because he or she lacked control – whatever that means – but rather because the choice is too much to ask of a person.

Rather than looking for an account of control that shows us whether someone really was in control of her choice, we do better to look at why we take an interest in control at all. Questions about control gain their interest against the background of views about the reasonableness of the other options a person faces. As I've suggested, almost everything can be represented as within a person's control. Any taste or commitment could be compromised if circumstances were dire enough, and anyone could face up to almost any circumstances no matter how dire, provided their commitment to doing so were strong enough. It is often inappropriate to require people to make such difficult choices. That is not because they cannot make them, or will be unhappy with the results, but because the burdens of choice in such cases are unreasonable. Conversely, it is unfair to others to make them bear the costs of a choice just because someone would find it difficult to bear. It is unfair because it requires people to adapt themselves to the efforts of others. Equality requires that people take responsibility for their choices, and so it requires that nobody face greater burdens than anyone else. But the appropriate measurement of those burdens is in terms of important interests in liberty and security, not in terms of any one person's efforts or tastes.

The introduction of reasonableness tests is more than a minor correction to practical reason views of responsibility. In fact, it undoes their main point, because it makes the line between choice and circumstance normative, not only in the sense that we draw it on the basis of normative arguments, but because the requisite concept of choice is given by a normative conception of equality, rather than by a metaphysical conception of choice or practical reason. As a result, the distinction between choices and circumstances may be different from any particular person's first-person conception of how that distinction applies in his or her own life. People may be held legally responsible for things for which they themselves are unwilling to take responsibility, or relieved of responsibility for things for which they hold themselves responsible.

Questions of responsibility turn on the interests of others; as I put it in Chapter 1, they are relational, rather than monadic. This isn't to say that ascriptions of responsibility are institutional, in the sense that they are the creatures of contingent political arrangements. It is to say that they are normative. If we think of responsibility in this normative way, we also have no need for devices such as Dworkin's ideal insurance markets. Rather than speculating about what people would have actually done in very different circumstances, we can proceed directly to questions about how much it is reasonable to ask of a person.

What about the pair of examples that gave the practical reason account its appeal? The first concerned the person who gambled and lost so badly that his capacity to live a self-directing life in the future is compromised. A focus on guaranteeing the conditions of agency ignores the fact that his desperate condition is self-imposed. The person who gambles and loses is entitled to the protection of some sort of safety net, even if his choices work out badly. Because his claim is based on need, he is entitled to a second chance. (And, if it should come to that, a third, fourth, and nth chance.) Had he gambled and won, a just society would have taxed away part of his winnings, and part of that tax would have gone to a fund to protect his agency against foreseeable disasters. Some might still worry that such a policy would reward those who cynically manipulate any safety net, allowing them to take risks that they shouldn't, knowing that they will not have to bear the costs. Like the media images of welfare queens that it feeds, this concern is almost certainly exaggerated. Moreover, taxes on gambling might include a portion for insurance against economic disasters, spreading them among those who take such risks.[43]

The second example involved the difference between someone who injures himself while on a wilderness adventure and the person who suffers from a disability through no fault of her own. I conceded that the latter has more of a claim on our aid than the former does; I now want to explain that intuition without appealing to the idea of practical reason in any of its guises. The priority that attaches to the needs of persons suffering from a disability has more to do with the fact that they didn't have a fair chance at a decent life, whereas the adventurer had a chance, however badly things worked out. Those who have a fair chance and take risks properly bear their costs, regardless of how they thought about them.

---

[43] I am assuming, of course, that this is legal gambling. Criminal activity is another matter.

Because of the nature of the risks taken by adventurers, it may be appropriate to set up some mechanism, such as mandatory insurance to make sure people only engage in activities if they are in a position to internalize the costs. Although such a requirement may make some activities too expensive for some, the added cost of such insurance is unlikely to be prohibitive, given the already high costs of such activities. Also, lack of access because of limited income is no more important here than in other places. The fact that some are unable to afford to do some of the things they would like to is not itself a pressing social problem, although it may be indicative of poverty, which is one.

Not all of the costs of foolish choices can be covered in advance. Yet some claim of health survives even in the face of foolish choices. In this, health is similar to certain aspects of safety, in that one's past bad behavior does not constitute a waiver of one's rights. Consider the ways in which drivers are expected to slow down for pedestrians. Some of those pedestrians might be unusually slow, and of that group, some might be slow because they have injured themselves, foolishly or even intentionally. It seems fair to make drivers slow down for those pedestrians, even though they could have avoided the burden to the drivers. We do not suppose that pedestrians who are slow because of their past choices get what they deserve when they are run down, for we do not suppose that in taking (or even choosing) some risks they forego all other protections.

9.5 UNDUE BURDENS AND PRIMARY GOODS, AGAIN

This brings us back to primary goods. Whether or not the burdens of choice are too great depends on the circumstances in which a choice was faced. Those circumstances are assessed in terms of that person's share of primary goods. If poverty, disease, lack of education, or lack of opportunity or marketable skills make particular choices burdensome, a person cannot be asked to bear its costs, because the choice itself is more than it is reasonable to ask a person to bear. Where primary goods have been taken care of properly, the choices a person makes are his to bear. Dworkin was right to focus on "the distinction between a person and his circumstances," and to assign "tastes and ambitions to his person, and his physical and mental powers to his circumstances."[44] But tastes and ambitions are not identified from the point of view of that person's reasoning processes. The distinction be-

[44] Dworkin, "What Is Equality?" p. 302.

294

tween things that are mine and those that are to be held in common is *not* a distinction we experience from the inside, any more than the criminal law's distinction between fact and law is so experienced. Instead, they are identified as those things that are best left up to a person, the things for which each of us must take responsibility.

9.6 CONCLUDING REMARKS

In this chapter and the ones that have preceded it, I have developed an account of responsibility that has the ideas of reciprocity and reasonableness at its core. That account understands the boundaries of responsibility in terms of fair terms of interaction, and specifies fair terms of interaction in terms of the device of a representative reasonable person. The idea of reasonableness carries a lot of weight in the entire account, for it provides the basis of my explanation of the four areas in which the effects of luck seem ineliminable: Accidents, mistakes, emergencies, and failed attempts. It also provides an explanation of why some sorts of bad luck must be held in common if the entire apparatus of responsibility is to be normatively compelling.

The idea of reasonableness is not enough, on its own, to determine the particular interests in liberty and security that the law must protect. Nor does it, taken alone, tell us how much weight to give to particular interests in liberty or security. The answers to those questions are often very easy, but sometimes more difficult. Even where their application is fraught with controversy, though, the ideas of reasonableness and reciprocity explored here serve to focus those disagreements on questions of equality. By allowing costs to be measured across persons, without allowing them to be aggregated across persons, the idea of the reasonable person articulates a powerful ideal of justice as equal respect and equal freedom.

Index

Index

compensation
  commensurability 157–8
  damages 3, 6, 20, 33, 47–9, 53–4,
    58, 75, 102, 117, 120–1, 148,
    259
  extent of injury 58, 78, 89–90,
    101
  pure economic loss 95 n1
  unusual type of injury 43, 64,
    89–90
consent
  as tort defense 190, 208
  compared with self-defense 22,
    190, 202, 212, 214–7
  contrast with self-defense as a
    defense 214–17
  contrast with victim death as a
    defense 208
  in boxing 212–3
  legal significance of 208
  mistakes about 11, 22, 173, 177,
    201–8, 209–14
  publicity of acts of (non)consent
    206–8, 211
  rationale in terms of protecting
    cooperative activities
    202–8, 211–3, 216
  rationale in terms of taking re-
    sponsibility 34, 203
  rights vs. welfare 205–6
  role of liberty and security inter-
    ests in defining 202, 204,
    213, 216
  surgery 203–4, 213
  theoretical and practical
    standpoints in assessing
    207–8
conservative view of responsibility 1, 265
conspiracy 237 n39
contract 61, 79, 83, 249, 251
control 72 n41, 98
  limited role in distributive jus-
    tice 269, 285
  problems of definition 285

relation to objective standards
  84–6
  see also voluntarism
contributory negligence see comparative negligence
conversion
  and theft 150
  forced purchase as remedy for
    150
Copp, David 276 n8
corrective justice
  basis of damages 20
  duty of care 49, 94, 111
  remoteness 49, 67, 89
  standard of care 48–9, 51–2, 57,
    59, 63 n20, 64, 71–2 n41, 74,
    174, 201, 273
crime
  defined as substitution of ra-
    tionality for reasonableness
    10, 134, 141, 144, 152, 155,
    161, 168, 228, 240–2
  punishment as response to 134,
    156, 161–2, 174, 220
  see also attempt, arson,
    assault, consent, excuses,
    murder, rape, self-defense,
    theft
crimes mala prohibita 156
crimes mala in se 148, 157, 183–4
crimes and torts
  contrast in attempt liability 220–1
  contrast in mental element 138
  contrast in role of excusing con-
    ditions 138, 289
  different responses to 6
  parallels between in conception
    of causation and rights pro-
    tected 138
  treating rights as tradeable
    148–9, 153–4, 182
culpability 18, 133–5, 148 n25, 173,
  176, 178, 181, 188, 191 n30,
  205, 211 n68, 215, 219, 221,
  225, 233, 240–1, 266

particular liberty interests important 43, 49, 55–7
Locke, John 2, 13, 34 n11, 45
luck
  brute vs. option in distributive justice 278–91
  relation to control 33, 73, 85–7, 265
  supposed arbitrariness of 3, 73–5, 80–4, 225–7, 290
  see also emergencies, mistakes, attempts

manifest criminality
  accessories after the fact 241–2
  attempts 240–2
Marx, Karl 22, 248, 252–4, 257, 259–60
McHale v. Watson 106 n20
mens rea 133, 175–7
metaphysics 15, 232
misfortune 26
  holding in common 44, 65, 92, 248, 255, 260–1, 263–72, 275–6
  standing 257, 264
  see also luck
mistakes
  comparison with necessity 121
  intention and 178–9, 210
  in tort 190
  of fact in criminal law 22, 108–9, 179–82, 183–8, 200, 211
  of identity 173, 200–01
  of law in criminal law 16, 22, 108–9, 179–82, 183–8
  relation to foreseeability and intervening causes 108–17
  subjectivist account of 173–7, 179–82, 245
monadic properties
  distinguished from relational 103, 245, 290, 293
  problems as account of reciprocity 187

morality, political 5, 12–15, 18, 109
murder
  attempted 220, 242–5
  consent not a defense to 157, 203
  reckless commission of 229, 234, 244
  provocation as a defense to 170
  self-defense 191, 214, 217

Nagel, Thomas 73
necessity
  as a bar to punishment 164–7, 169
  compared with mistake 120–3
  contrasted with "lesser evils" 166
  does not undermine tort liability 119–20, 169
  limits on availability of defense 167–9
  ordinary person standard 68, 166–7
needs
  and distributive shares 276–8, 293
  and tradability 276–7
  relation of to capacity for choice 277–8
negligence
  contributory 110, 111, 113, 124
  disproportion test for 62–3
  Learned Hand test for 58–61, 63, 67
  not a mental state 74
  risk ownership explanation of 53–8, 65–72, 123
  standard of care 21, 48, 90
nonfeasance and misfeasance
  as problem for Perry's account 104n16
  basis of difference 64, 91–2
  contrasted with act/omission distinction 91
  duty to rescue 64, 91–2
  easy rescues 92